THE CAMBRIDGE COMPANION TO THE AUSTRALIAN NOVEL

The Cambridge Companion to the Australian Novel provides a clear, lively, and accessible account of the novel in Australia. The chapters of this book survey significant issues and developments in the Australian novel, offer historical and conceptual frameworks, and demonstrate what reading an Australian novel looks like in practice. The book begins with novels by literary visitors to Australia and concludes with those by refugees. In between, the reader encounters the Australian novel in its splendid contradictoriness, from nineteenth-century settler fiction by women writers through to literary images of the Anthropocene, from sexuality in the novels of Patrick White to Waanyi writer Alexis Wright's call for a sovereign First Nations literature. This book is an invitation to students, instructors, and researchers alike to expand and broaden their knowledge of the complex histories and crucial present of the Australian novel.

Nicholas Birns teaches at New York University. He is author of *The Hyperlocal in Eighteenth- and Nineteenth-Century Literary Space* (2019) and *Contemporary Australian Literature: A World Not Yet Dead* (2015), among other books. He edited the US-based journal of Australian literature *Antipodes* from 2001 to 2018. He has published in journals such as *Angelaki, Exemplaria, Partial Answers, Victorian Studies,* and *The Journal of New Zealand Literature,* and has reviewed for *Modernism/modernity, The New York Times Book Review,* and *MLQ.*

Louis Klee is a Junior Research Fellow at Clare College, Cambridge. He received the Association for the Study of Australian Literature (ASAL)'s A. D. Hope Prize and the *Australian Book Review*'s Peter Porter Prize. He also holds a Juncture Fellowship at the *Sydney Review of Books.*

T0384771

THE CAMBRIDGE COMPANION TO
THE AUSTRALIAN NOVEL

EDITED BY

NICHOLAS BIRNS
New York University

LOUIS KLEE
University of Cambridge

Shaftesbury Road, Cambridge CB2 8EA, United Kingdom

One Liberty Plaza, 20th Floor, New York, NY 10006, USA

477 Williamstown Road, Port Melbourne, VIC 3207, Australia

314–321, 3rd Floor, Plot 3, Splendor Forum, Jasola District Centre,
New Delhi – 110025, India

103 Penang Road, #05–06/07, Visioncrest Commercial, Singapore 238467

Cambridge University Press is part of Cambridge University Press & Assessment,
a department of the University of Cambridge.

We share the University's mission to contribute to society through the pursuit of
education, learning and research at the highest international levels of excellence.

www.cambridge.org
Information on this title: www.cambridge.org/9781316514481

DOI: 10.1017/9781009083409

© Cambridge University Press & Assessment 2023

First published 2023

A catalogue record for this publication is available from the British Library.

Library of Congress Cataloging-in-Publication Data
NAMES: Birns, Nicholas, editor. | Klee, Louis, editor.
TITLE: The Cambridge companion to the Australian novel /
[edited by] Nicholas Birns, Louis Klee.
DESCRIPTION: Cambridge ; New York, NY : Cambridge University Press, 2022. |
Includes bibliographical references and index.
IDENTIFIERS: LCCN 2022031329 | ISBN 9781316514481 (hardback) |
ISBN 9781009083409 (ebook)
SUBJECTS: LCSH: Australian fiction – History and criticism.
CLASSIFICATION: LCC PR9612.2 .C36 2022 | DDC 823–dcundefined
LC record available at https://lccn.loc.gov/2022031329

ISBN 978-1-316-51448-1 Hardback
ISBN 978-1-009-08758-2 Paperback

CONTENTS

Contents

Contents

CONTRIBUTORS

KEYVAN ALLAHYARI is Postdoctoral Fellow in the English Department at the University of Tübingen. He is the author of *Making Global Literature: Peter Carey and the Economy of Literary Celebrity* (Palgrave, 2022). He is currently writing his second book, on the militarization of border regimes and contemporary world literature. He completed his PhD at the University of Melbourne in 2019.

EVELYN ARALUEN is a Goorie/Koorie poet, editor, and lecturer at Deakin University. Her debut poetry collection *Dropbear* was released in 2021 by the University of Queensland Press. She is the co-editor of *Overland Literary Magazine*.

NICHOLAS BIRNS teaches at New York University. He is author of *The Hyperlocal in Eighteenth- and Nineteenth-Century Literary Space* (Lexington, 2019) and *Contemporary Australian Literature: A World Not Yet Dead* (University of Sydney Press, 2015), among other books. He edited the US-based journal of Australian literature *Antipodes* from 2001 to 2018. He has published in journals such as *Angelaki, Exemplaria, Partial Answers, Victorian Studies,* and *The Journal of New Zealand Literature,* and has reviewed for *Modernism/modernity, The New York Times Book Review,* and *MLQ*.

LACHLAN BROWN is a Senior Lecturer in English at Charles Sturt University, Wagga Wagga. Lachlan's literary studies research includes explorations of the poetry of Kevin Hart, Australian poetry and the sacred, and transnational Australian short fiction. He is the author of two books of poetry, *Limited Cities* (2012) and *Lunar Inheritance* (2021).

MICHELLE CAHILL was born in Kenya and has lived in the UK. Her short story collection *Letter to Pessoa* won the NSW Premier's Literary Award for New Writing. *Daisy and Woolf* was published by Hachette in 2022. Her awards include a fellowship at Hawthornden Castle, the Arts Queensland

Val Vallis Award, and the Red Room Australian Poetry Fellowship. She was a Creative Writing Fellow at Kingston Writing School and at UNC Charlotte.

BRENDAN CASEY is a writer and researcher living in Naarm (Melbourne), and Scholarly Editor at *Cordite Poetry Review*. He is currently completing a PhD at the University of Melbourne.

DECLAN FRY, born on Wongatha country in Kalgoorlie, has written for the *Guardian*, *Griffith Review*, *Overland*, the *Australian Book Review*, *Westerly*, and elsewhere. He holds a degree in literature from the University of Western Australia and a Juris Doctor in law from the University of Melbourne. For his *Meanjin* essay, "Justice for Elijah or a Spiritual Dialogue with Ziggy Ramo, Dancing" he received the 2021 Peter Blazey Fellowship and he has been shortlisted for the Judith Wright Poetry Prize.

PAUL GILES is Professor of English at the Institute for Humanities and Social Sciences of Australian Catholic University, Melbourne. He is also currently serving as President of the International Association of University Professors of English. He has published extensively on transnational American literature, and the focus of his recent research is representations of temporality in an antipodean context. His latest books are *American World Literature: An Introduction* (Blackwell, 2019), *Backgazing: Reverse Time in Modernist Culture* (Oxford University Press, 2019), and *The Planetary Clock: Antipodean Time and Spherical Postmodern Fictions* (Oxford University Press, 2021).

MICHAEL R. GRIFFITHS is Senior Lecturer in English Literature at the University of Wollongong. The author of *The Distribution of Settlement: Appropriation and Refusal in Australian Literature and Culture* (University of Western Australia Press, 2018), his essays have appeared in *Textual Practice*, *Settler Colonial Studies*, *Discourse*, *Postcolonial Studies*, the *Australian Humanities Review*, and in many other journals and publications. Griffiths edited the book *Biopolitics and Memory in Postcolonial Literature and Culture* (Ashgate, 2016). He also co-edited with Bruno Cornellier a special issue of *Settler Colonial Studies* entitled "Globalizing Unsettlement," and with Tanja Dreher and Timothy Laurie the book *Unsettled Voices: Beyond Free Speech in the Late Liberal Era* (Routledge, 2021).

LESLEY HAWKES is Associate Professor and Academic Lead of Research Training in the School of Communication, Creative Industries Faculty, Queensland University of Technology, Brisbane, Australia. Her specialist areas of research are how Australian places of belonging are created, and the connections and relationships between modes of transport (specifically railways) and Australian imaginative spaces.

TONY HUGHES D'AETH is the Chair of Australian Literature at the University of Western Australia. His books include *Like Nothing on this Earth: A Literary History of the Wheatbelt* (University of Western Australia Press 2017), which won the Walter McRae Russell Prize for Australian literary scholarship, and *Paper Nation: The Story of the Picturesque Atlas of Australasia* (Melbourne University Press, 2001), which won the Ernest Scott and W. K. Hancock prizes for Australian history. In 2019, he convened the annual Association for the Studies of Australian Literature (ASAL) Conference in Perth. He is also the Director of the Westerly Centre, which publishes *Westerly Magazine,* a literary journal founded in 1956.

CHEN HONG is Professor of Australian Culture at East China Normal University (ECNU) in Shanghai, China, where he directs the Australian Studies Centre. He received his PhD in 2006 with a dissertation on sexuality and Patrick White's fiction and is the Chinese translator of David Marr's biography of White.

LOUIS KLEE is a Junior Research Fellow at Clare College, Cambridge. He has been awarded the Association for the Study of Australian Literature (ASAL)'s A. D. Hope Prize and the *Australian Book Review*'s Peter Porter Prize. He also holds a Juncture Fellowship at the *Sydney Review of Books.*

JEANINE LEANE is a Wiradjuri writer, poet, and academic from southwest New South Wales. Her poetry and short stories have been published in *Hecate: An Interdisciplinary Journal of Women's Liberation, The Journal for the Association European Studies of Australia,* the *Australian Poetry Journal, Antipodes, Overland,* and the *Australian Book Review.* Jeanine has published widely in the area of Aboriginal literature, writing otherness and creative nonfiction. She teaches creative writing and Aboriginal literature at the University of Melbourne. Jeanine edited *Guwayu – For All Times*, a collection of First Nations Poetry published in 2020 by Magabala Books.

FIONA MORRISON is an Associate Professor in English at University of New South Wales (UNSW) Australia. Her most recent publication is *Christina Stead and the Matter of America* (Sydney University Press, 2019), and she is currently working on the transnational career of Henry Handel Richardson.

LYNDA NG is an Honorary Associate with the School of Languages and Cultures at the University of Sydney, and also an Adjunct Fellow with the Writing and Society Research Centre at Western Sydney University. She is the editor of *Indigenous Transnationalism: Alexis Wright's Carpentaria* (Giramondo Publishing, 2018) and, in addition to her work on Indigenous literatures, she has published on migrant writing, interimperialism, eco-criticism, and neoliberalism.

MARK PICCINI is Lecturer in the School of Communication at the Queensland University of Technology. He completed his PhD in 2016 at Queensland University of Technology in the field of cultural studies, focusing on narrative strategies of resistance to stereotyping and global cultural complexities. His specialist areas of interest include Australian literature, representations of violence in the Global South, and psychoanalytic cultural theory.

BRIGID ROONEY has taught Australian literature at the University of Sydney. She has published widely on twentieth-century and contemporary Australian literature and co-edited scholarly collections on such topics as Christina Stead and Australian literature as world literature. Her books include *Literary Activists: Writer-Intellectuals and Australian Public Life* (University of Queensland Press, 2009) and *Suburban Space, the Novel and Australian Modernity* (Anthem Press, 2018).

JOSEPH STEINBERG is a doctoral candidate at the University of Cambridge. His articles and reviews have been published in the *Journal of the Association for the Study of Australian Literature*, the *Australian Humanities Review*, *The Cambridge Quarterly*, and *Australian Literary Studies*. In 2023, he will begin a three-year Forrest Fellowship at the University of Western Australia.

EMMETT STINSON is a Lecturer in Literary Cultures at the University of Tasmania. He is the author of *Satirizing Modernism* (Bloomsbury Publishing, 2017) and *Known Unknowns* (Affirm Press, 2010). He was a Chief Investigator on the Australia Research Council Discovery Project, "New Tastemakers and Australia's Post-Digital Literary Culture."

ACKNOWLEDGMENTS

It has been an immense pleasure working with the team at Cambridge University Press. Thank you to Ray Ryan for believing in this project from the outset. Thank you to Edgar Mendez, Natasha Burton, and Ranjith Kumar for their expert help and tireless support, and to Charles Phillips for copyediting. We are immensely thankful for their work. This book came together during the period of Australian megafires of 2019–2020 and the COVID-19 pandemic. We are immensely grateful for the dedication of our contributors through this difficult period. The cover image is detail from Judy Watson's *asylum seeker vessel (kuujbu narrunguja)*, 2019, exhausted indigo, acrylic, canvas, cotton, graphite on canvas, 201.2 × 164.5 cm. Image courtesy the artist and Milani Gallery, Brisbane. Thank you to Judy for allowing us to use her incredible artwork, and thank you to Georgia Boe at the Milani Gallery for generously facilitating this. We are very grateful to Joseph Steinberg for his meticulous work on the Chronology and Further Reading list for this volume. Thank you to Jeanine Leane, Shino Konishi, and Sean Ulm for advising him on the chronology. We are also grateful for the comments of our anonymous reviewers, which shaped the direction of this book.

CHRONOLOGY

COMPILED BY JOSEPH STEINBERG

This chronology does not attempt to offer an exhaustive list of dates, texts, and events in Australian literary history. It aims to provide an introductory timeline for scholars and students, informed by the works cited by this volume's contributors. My hope is that the chronology might alert the reader to surprising or unexpected synchronicities. The reader will note that it includes several nonfiction prose works, such as First Nations autobiographical and testimonial narratives, that have been important to the development of the novel in Australia. It omits collections and anthologies of poetry, other than verse novels, on the grounds that a chronology of these works will be available in *The Cambridge Companion to Australian Poetry*, and does not include films (with the exception of noting firsts in Indigenous filmmaking in Australia), plays, or artworks. Finally, it is worth noting that the form of a chronology itself is problematic in the context of Australian history because it risks playing into settler colonial myths about Australia's "historylessness." I present this heuristic in the conviction that such problems will be somewhat ameliorated, or at least made evident, when read alongside the chapters of this volume. For advice, critiques, and suggestions, I would like to thank Jeanine Leane, Shino Konishi, and Sean Ulm.

65,000 BCE	Archaeological evidence from Madjedbebe [Arnhem Land] in what is now the Northern Territory confirms the presence of Indigenous peoples on the Australian continent from at least this date.
40,000	Earliest currently existing evidence of the presence of Indigenous peoples in lutruwita [Tasmania]. Extinction of megafauna due to environmental change.
30,000	Earliest dated instances of Indigenous rock art. Sea levels drop as the last ice age begins, creating a continuous landmass that stretched between

the landmasses now known as Papua New Guinea, Australia, and lutruwita.

20,000   Gwion Gwion rock art paintings in the Kimberley establish that boomerangs were used from at least this date.

14,000   The gradual thawing of ice causes sea levels to rise, separating lutruwita from the mainland.

1488 CE   Bartolomeu Dias, a Portuguese navigator, rounds the Cape of Good Hope, thus commencing the period of European navigation in the southern hemisphere and search for *Terra Australis*, the fabled "great south land" hypothesized by early European maps.

1605   Pedro Fernandes de Queirós leaves Peru with the aim of claiming the "great south land" for Spain.

1606, Feb.–Mar.   Willem Janszoon, captain of the Dutch East India Company ship the *Duyfken*, begins to map the Australian continent. Conflict with the Wik people; only the death of some nine crew members is reported.

1606, May   Queirós arrives in what is now Vanuatu; believing it to be a part of the southern continent, he names it *Austrialia del Espiritu Santo*.

1616, Oct. 25   Dutch navigator Dirk Hartog lands on an island that now bears his name, off the western coast.

1629   Dutch vessel *Batavia* is shipwrecked at the Abrolhos Islands off Australia's western coast. Initially, 200 survive. A brutal series of rapes, mutinies, and murders ensue: three months later, only seventy survivors remain. Two mutineers, abandoned as punishment, could possibly be considered Australia's first European settlers.

1697   *A New Voyage Round the World* by William Dampier, the first Englishman to explore parts of the Australian coastline.

1700   The trepang industry, including trade between the Makassar people from Sulawesi (now Indonesia) and Aboriginal people in what is now the Kimberley and Arnhem Land can be traced to at least this time, although there is evidence of earlier Makassan visits.

1703   *A Voyage to New Holland in the Year 1699* by William Dampier.

1719	Daniel Defoe, *Robinson Crusoe*.
1770, Aug. 22	Lieutenant James Cook, captain of HMB *Endeavour*, claims land for the British Crown, renaming it New South Wales.
1788, Jan. 26	Captain Arthur Phillip, commander of the First Fleet, begins the British invasion of Australia, establishing a convict settlement at Sydney Cove, Port Jackson. The lands occupied were never ceded by their traditional owners, the Eora.
1792–1802	Bidjigal Dharug warrior Pemulwuy leads resistance against the incursion of white settlers onto his people's lands.
1789	Watkin Tench, *A Narrative of the Expedition to Botany Bay*. Beginning of the first smallpox epidemic.
1794	First acknowledged massacre of Indigenous people by white settlers takes place on Dharug land, at Hawkesbury River in New South Wales.
1801–1803	British explorer Matthew Flinders circumnavigates the continent and names it Australia.
1803	First European settlement is established in Van Deimen's Land, on muwinina land, near nipaluna [Hobart].
1804, Mar. 4	Castle Hill Rebellion. Irish convicts attempt to overthrow British rule in New South Wales; an estimated thirty-nine die.
1815, May 7	Governor Lachlan Macquarie establishes the first inland European settlement at Bathurst, prompting a decade of armed conflict as the Wiradjuri people, led by the warrior Windradyne, resist the theft of their lands.
1824	Moreton Bay Penal Settlement is established on Turrubal and Jagera lands in what is now known as Brisbane, Queensland. Governor Thomas Brisbane declares martial law, enabling settler militia to take up arms against the Wiradjuri people.
1829	Captain James Stirling establishes the Swan River Colony on Whadjuk Noongar land in Western Australia. Henry Savery, *The Hermit in Van Diemen's Land*.

1830	Lieutenant-Governor George Arthur orders thousands of able-bodied settlers to form a human chain known as the "Black Line," in an attempt to capture the remaining palawa people in lutruwita.
1830–1831	Henry Savery, *Quintus Servinton*.
1833	Peak of convict transportation to Australia – approximately 7,000 in a single year.
1836	South Australia, established on Kaurna Country, is declared a colony of free settlers.
1838	Anna Maria Bunn, *The Guardian*.
1840	End of transportation of convicts to New South Wales.
1845	Thomas McCombie, *Arabin*.
1847	The first indentured laborers from the South Pacific islands are brought to work on Queensland's cotton and sugar plantations.
	Alexander Harris, *Settlers and Convicts*.
1848	New South Wales establishes a native police force, consisting primarily of Indigenous troopers under the command of Europeans.
1849	Alexander Harris, *The Emigrant Family*.
1850	First convicts sent to Western Australia.
	The University of Sydney is established.
1851	Colony of Victoria gains independence from New South Wales.
	"Black Thursday" bushfires devastate Victoria.
	Gold is discovered in New South Wales and Victoria.
1852	Godfrey Mundy, *Our Antipodes*.
1853	Melbourne University is established.
1854	Miners from the Victorian town of Ballarat, frustrated with the colonial government's administration of the goldfields, swear allegiance to the Southern Cross flag at Bakery Hill and build a stockade at the nearby Eureka diggings, where they are attacked by government troops.
	Catherine Helen Spence, *Clara Morison*.
	W. A. Cawthorne, *The Kangaroo Islanders*.
1856	Van Diemen's Land is renamed Tasmania.
	Stonemasons strike in Melbourne, inaugurating the eight-hour day movement.
	Catherine Helen Spence, *Tender and True*.

1857	Louisa Atkinson, *Gertrude the Emigrant*.
1859	Queensland becomes a separate colony.
	Establishment of Australia's first stock exchange.
	Rabbits are introduced into Australia.
	Oliné Keese [Caroline Leakey], *The Broad Arrow*.
	Henry Kingsley, *The Recollections of Geoffry Hamlyn*.
	Louisa Atkinson, *Cowanda, the Veteran's Grant*.
1860	Mary Theresa Vidal, *Bengala; or Some Time Ago*.
1861	Two hundred and fifty Chinese miners are injured in racist riots at Lambing Flat goldfields, New South Wales.
	Louisa Atkinson, *Debatable Ground, or, The Carlillawarra Claimants* [serialized by *Sydney Mail*].
1863	Northern Territory is annexed by South Australia.
1864	Louisa Atkinson, *Myra* [serialized by *Sydney Mail*].
1865	First issue of *Australian Journal* (1865–1962).
	Catherine Helen Spence, *Mr. Hogarth's Will*.
1867	Beginning of the gold rush in Queensland.
	Thomas McCombie, *Frank Henly*.
1868	End of convict transportation to Australia.
	Catherine Helen Spence, *The Author's Daughter*.
1869	The Aboriginal Protection Act is established in Victoria, the first state to do this.
1871	The Australian Natives Association is formed.
	Louisa Atkinson, *Tom Hellcar's Children* [serialized by *Sydney Mail*].
	Iota [Mary Meredith], *Kooroona*.
1872	The Education Act 1872 makes a free secular education compulsory for children in Victoria.
	Louisa Atkinson, *Tressa's Resolve* [serialized by *Sydney Mail*].
	Donald Cameron, *The Mysteries and Miseries of Scripopolis*.
1874	Marcus Clarke, *His Natural Life* [serialized in *Australian Journal* as *For the Term of His Natural Life*, 1872–1874].
	Anthony Trollope, *Harry Heathcote of Gangoil*.
1875	Ada Cambridge, *Up the Murray* [serialized in the *Australasian*].
1879	Anthony Trollope, *John Caldigate*.

1880	Following a heroic last stand at Glenrowan, Victoria, Ned Kelly is captured and hanged in Melbourne.
	The *Bulletin* is established.
	Rosa Praed, *An Australian Heroine*.
1881	Rosa Praed, *Policy and Passion*.
	Marcus Clarke, *The Mystery of Major Molineux*.
1882	Ada Cambridge, *A Mere Chance* [first serialized in 1880].
1883	Frances Ellen Talbot, *Philberta*.
1884	Catherine Helen Spence, *An Agnostic's Progress from the Known to the Unknown*.
1886	Fergus Hume, *The Mystery of a Hansom Cab*.
1887	Ada Cambridge, "The Perversity of Human Nature."
1888	*The Dawn: A Journal for Australian Women* (1888–1905).
	Rolf Boldrewood [Thomas Alexander Browne], *Robbery Under Arms* [first serialized by *Sydney Mail* in 1882–1883].
1889	Jessie Cathrine Couvrier, *Uncle Piper of Piper's Hill*.
	Ernest Giles, *Australia Twice Traversed*.
	Catherine Helen Spence, *A Week in the Future*.
	Ada Cambridge, *A Woman's Friendship* [serialized in the *Age*].
1890	The University of Tasmania is established.
	Ada Cambridge, *A Marked Man*.
	Catherine Martin, *An Australian Girl*.
1891	The Great Shearers' Strike takes place in central Queensland.
	Ada Cambridge, *The Three Miss Kings*.
1892	Gold found in Western Australia.
	The Manifesto of the Queensland Labor Party is read out under the Tree of Knowledge at Barcaldine, Queensland.
	William Lane, *The Workingman's Paradise*.
	Ada Cambridge, *Not All in Vain*.
1893	Depression, exacerbated by drought.
	Alfred Bernie Bell, *The Pioneers*.
	Wulla Merrii [John Cameron], *The Fire Stick*.
	W. I. Thrower, *Younâh!: A Tasmanian Aboriginal*.

1894	Ethel Turner, *Seven Little Australians*.
	Louis Becke, *By Reef and Palm*.
	Alfred Bernie Bell, *Oscar*.
	Alfred Bernie Bell, *Australian Camp Fire Tales*.
	Henry Lawson, *Short Stories in Prose and Verse*.
1895	Ada Cambridge, *Fidelis*.
1896	First film made in Australia.
	Louis Becke, *Ebbing by Tide*.
1897	The Aboriginals Protection and Restriction of the Sale of Opium Act is established in Queensland.
1898	David Carnegie, *Spinifex and Sand*.
	Ada Cambridge, *Materfamilias*.
1900	Edmund Barton is sworn in as Australia's first prime minister.
	Ada Cambridge, *Path and Goal*.
1901	Establishment of the Commonwealth of Australia, first federal election.
	The Immigration Restriction Act and Pacific Island Labourers Act enshrines the White Australia Policy in law.
	Miles Franklin, *My Brilliant Career*.
1902	The Commonwealth Franchise Act grants women the right to vote in federal elections. This did not include First Nations women (or men), who were not granted the right to vote until 1962.
	Barbara Baynton, *Bush Studies*.
1903	Alfred Deakin succeeds Barton as prime minister.
	Joseph Furphy, *Such is Life*.
1905	The Aborigines Act is established in Western Australia.
1908	Establishment of the Commonwealth Literary Fund.
	Jeannie Gunn, *We of the Never Never*.
	Henry Handel Richardson, *Maurice Guest*.
1909	The Aborigines Protection Act is established in New South Wales.
	The University of Queensland is established.
1910	The Labor Party, led by Andrew Fisher, wins the federal election for the first time.
	Henry Handel Richardson, *The Getting of Wisdom*.
1911	The Aborigines Act is established in South Australia.
	The University of Western Australia is established.

1914, July 28 – 1918, Nov. 11	World War I.
1914	Ada Cambridge, *The Making of Rachel Rowe*.
1915	Allied landing at Gallipoli in Turkey on 25 April, later commemorated as Anzac Day.
	Amendments to the Aborigines Protection Act 1909 grant the New South Wales Aborigines Protection Board the power to remove Indigenous children from their families.
1916	The Eight Hours Act is passed in Victoria.
1917	Capel Boake [Doris Boake Kerr], *Painted Clay*.
1919	Australia joins the League of Nations.
1922	Havelock Ellis, *Kanga Creek*.
1923	D. H. Lawrence, *Kangaroo*.
	Capel Boake [Doris Boake Kerr], *The Romany Mark*.
1924	The Australian Aboriginal Progressive Association is formed.
1925	Chester Cobb, *Mr Moffatt*.
1926	Katharine Susannah Prichard, *Working Bullocks*.
	Chester Cobb, *Days of Disillusion*.
1929	Katharine Susannah Prichard, *Coonardoo*.
1930	David Unaipon, *Myths and Legends of the Australian Aboriginals*; W. Ramsay Smith was falsely attributed as the author.
	Norman Lindsay, *Redheap*.
	Vance Palmer, *The Passage*.
	Theresa Clements, *From Old Maloga: The Memoirs of an Aboriginal Woman*.
	Henry Handel Richardson, *The Fortunes of Richard Mahony*.
1931	The Statute of Westminster effectively grants self-rule to British dominions.
	Ion Idriess, *Lasseter's Last Ride*.
1932	Opening of the Sydney Harbour Bridge, 19 Mar.
	Height of the Great Depression, with an unemployment rate of 32 percent.
	Establishment of the Australian Broadcasting Commission (ABC); becomes Corporation in 1983.

1933	Establishment of the Commonwealth Grants Commission.
1934	The Australian government attempts, unsuccessfully, to exclude Egon Kisch from visiting Australia.
	Eleanor Dark, *Prelude to Christopher.*
	Christina Stead, *Seven Poor Men of Sydney.*
1935	The University of Western Australia Press is established.
	Kylie Tennant, *Tiburon.*
	Godfrey Blunden, *No More Reality.*
1936	lutruwita's thylacine becomes extinct.
	Dymphna Cusack, *Jungfrau.*
	Kenneth Mackenzie, *The Young Desire It.*
	Jean Devanny, *Sugar Heaven.*
	Capel Boake [Doris Boake Kerr], *The Dark Thread.*
1937	The Aborigines Progressive Association is formed in New South Wales.
	Katharine Susannah Prichard, *Intimate Strangers.*
1938	The Australian Aborigines' League (AAL) and the Aboriginal Progressive Association (APA) observe a Day of Mourning and Protest on Jan. 26, a counter-observance to celebrations of the 150-year anniversary of the First Fleet landing.
	Xavier Herbert, *Capricornia.*
1939	*Southerly,* the official journal of the English Association, is founded in Sydney.
	"Black Friday" bushfires in Victoria cause seventy-one deaths.
	Patrick White, *Happy Valley.*
1939 Sept. 1 –1945, Sept. 2	World War II.
1940	*Meanjin Papers* founded by C. B. Christesen in Brisbane; later, after moving to Melbourne, its title is abbreviated to *Meanjin.*
	Christina Stead, *The Man Who Loved Children.*
1941, Dec. 7	Japanese bombing of the Pearl Harbor Naval Base in Honolulu, Hawaii, provokes the US into entering World War II.
	Eleanor Dark, *The Timeless Land.*
	Kylie Tennant, *The Battlers.*

1942	Eve Langley, *The Pea-Pickers*.
1943	James McAuley and Harold Stewart submit poems under a pseudonym, Ern Malley, to the modernist literary journal *Angry Penguins*, beginning a hoax that would come to be known as "the Ern Malley Affair."
	Kylie Tennant, *Ride on Stranger*.
1944	Christina Stead, *For Love Alone*.
	The First Realist Writers' Group is founded in Melbourne.
1945	Arthur Calwell is appointed Australia's first minister for immigration in July; over the next two decades, 2 million immigrants arrive in Australia, primarily from southern and eastern Europe.
	Australia is a founding member of the United Nations.
	Pinchas Goldhar's work appears in *Southern Stories*.
1946	Martin Boyd, *Lucinda Brayford*.
	Christina Stead, *Letty Fox: Her Luck*.
	Capel Boake [Doris Boake Kerr], *The Twig is Bent*.
	Bill Onus makes a short documentary, becoming possibly the first Aboriginal filmmaker.
1947	M. Barnard Eldershaw, *Tomorrow and Tomorrow and Tomorrow*.
	Herz Bergner, *Zwishn Himl un Waser* [translated into English as *Between Sky & Sea*].
1948	The Nationality and Citizenship Act 1948 creates the status of an Australian citizen.
	The University of Queensland Press is established.
	Patrick White, *The Aunt's Story*.
	Christina Stead, *A Little Tea, A Little Chat*.
	Eleanor Dark, *Storm of Time*.
1949	Liberals are elected to government. Robert Menzies becomes prime minister.
	Charmian Clift and George Johnston, *High Valley*.
1950	Frank Hardy, *Power Without Glory*.
	Nevil Shute, *A Town Like Alice*.
1951	Australia and Aotearoa [New Zealand] sign the ANZUS defense treaty.
	Dymphna Cusack and Florence James, *Come in Spinner*.
	Martin Boyd, *The Cardboard Crown*.
	Dal Stivens, *Jimmy Brockett*.
1952	Judah Waten, *Alien Son*.

	Ronald Morgan, *Reminiscences of the Aboriginal Station at Cummeragunga and its Aboriginal People.*
1953	Eleanor Dark, *No Barrier.*
	Alekos Doukas, Στην Πάλη, Στα Νειάτα [*To Struggle, To Youth*].
1954	Stephen Murray-Smith founds *Overland*, a journal of progressive politics and culture.
	Vladimir Petrov, a KGB officer posted in Canberra, defects to Australia.
	David Unaipon, *My Life Story.*
1955	Canberra University College offers the first year-long university course in Australian Literature.
	Patrick White, *The Tree of Man.*
	D'Arcy Niland, *The Shiralee.*
1956	*Westerly* is founded at the University of Western Australia.
	Quadrant is founded in Sydney by Richard Krygier.
	Kylie Tennant, *The Honey Flow.*
1957	Patrick White becomes the first recipient of the Miles Franklin Award, for *Voss.*
1958	Elizabeth Harrower, *The Long Prospect.*
	Randolph Stow, *To the Islands.*
	Dal Stivens, *The Wide Arch.*
	Hall Porter, *A Handful of Pennies.*
1959	Dorothy Hewett, *Bobbin Up.*
1960	The National Library of Australia is established.
	The Adelaide Festival of the Arts is held for the first time.
	Charmian Clift, *Walk to the Paradise Gardens.*
1961	Patrick White, *Riders in the Chariot.*
	Hal Porter, *The Titled Cross.*
1962	Gerald Alfred Wilkes is appointed to the first chair in Australian Literature, at the University of Sydney.
	The Australian Writers' Guild is established.
	Thea Astley, *The Well Dressed Explorer.*
	Hal Porter, *A Bachelor's Children.*
1963	Establishment of the Australian Society of Authors.
	Laurie Hergehnan founds the journal *Australian Literary Studies* at the University of Tasmania.
	Hal Porter, *The Watcher on the Cast-Iron Balcony.*
	Randolph Stow, *Tourmaline.*
	Jessica Anderson, *An Ordinary Lunacy.*

	Sumner Locke Elliott, *Careful, He Might Hear You.*
	Alekos Doukas, Κάτω από ξένους ουρανούς [*Under Foreign Skies*].
1964	The editors of the satirical *Oz* magazine (1963–1969) are prosecuted for obscenity.
	George Johnston, *My Brother Jack.*
	Charmian Clift, *Honour's Mimic.*
1965	Australian troops are dispatched to Vietnam.
	Australia's Freedom Ride protest takes place, led by Charles Perkins.
	Mudrooroo Narogin [Colin Johnson], *Wild Cat Falling.*
	Thea Astley, *The Slow Natives.*
	Hal Porter, *The Cats of Venice.*
	Randolph Stow, *The Merry-Go-Round in the Sea.*
1966	Decimal currency is introduced.
	Elizabeth Harrower, *The Watch Tower.*
	Patrick White, *The Solid Mandala.*
1967	A referendum to amend the constitution to include Aboriginal and Torres Strait Islander people on the census is held. Almost 91 percent of the electorate vote Yes.
	Thomas Keneally, *Bring Larks and Heroes.*
1968	Prime Minister John Gorton establishes the Australia Council for the Arts.
	Joan Lindsay, *Picnic at Hanging Rock.*
	Thomas Keneally, *Three Cheers for the Paraclete.*
	Dal Stivens, *Three Persons Make a Tiger.*
1969	The Conciliation and Arbitration Commission accepts the principle that women should receive equal pay for equal work.
	The Institute for Aboriginal Development Incorporated (IAD) is established.
1970	Macquarie University becomes the first Australian university to offer classes in creative writing.
	Dal Stivens, *A Horse of Air.*
	Patrick White, *The Vivisector.*
1971	Luritja artist Harold Thomas designs the Australian Aboriginal flag.
	Neville Bonner becomes the first Aboriginal member of Federal Parliament.

Jack Davis and Barrie Ovenden found the magazine *Identity*.

David Ireland, *The Unknown Industrial Prisoner*.

Frank Hardy, *Outcasts of Foolgarah*.

1972   Gough Whitlam wins the federal election, becoming the first Labor prime minister in twenty-three years. Agrees to establish diplomatic relations with the People's Republic of China.

The Aboriginal Tent Embassy is first established outside Parliament House.

Thea Astley, *The Acolyte*.

Thomas Keneally, *The Chant of Jimmie Blacksmith*.

Frank Moorhouse, *The Americans, Baby*.

1973   Patrick White is awarded the Nobel Prize in Literature.

Formal end of the White Australia Policy's migration restrictions for non-Europeans.

Patrick White, *The Eye of the Storm*.

Barbara Hanrahan, *The Scent of Eucalyptus*.

1974   The Western Australian Institute of Technology offers a major in creative writing.

Thea Astley, *A Kindness Cup*.

Peter Carey, *The Fat Man in History and Other Stories*.

Hal Porter, *Fredo Fuss Love Life*.

Ronald McKie, *The Mango Tree*.

1975   Whitlam's Labor government is dismissed by Governor-General Sir John Kerr.

The Racial Discrimination Act is passed.

McPhee Gribble Publishers is established.

Xavier Herbert, *Poor Fellow My Country*.

David Malouf, *Johnno*.

Charlie Perkins, *A Bastard Like Me*.

Jessica Anderson, *The Commandant*.

Elizabeth Riley [Kerryn Higgs], *All That False Instruction*.

Antigone Kefala, *The First Journey*.

Frank Hardy, *But the Dead Are Many*.

1976   Fremantle Arts Centre Press is established.

Robert Drewe, *The Savage Crows*.

Patrick White, *A Fringe of Leaves*.

Helen Hodgman, *Blue Skies*.
David Ireland, *The Glass Canoe*.
Elizabeth Jolley, *Five Acre Virgin and Other Stories*.

1977   Association for the Study of Australian Literature is established, its inaugural conference at Monash University convened the following year by Mary Lord.

Helen Garner, *Monkey Grip*.
Amy Witting, *The Visit*.
Margaret Tucker, *If Everybody Cared*.
Jimmie Barker, *The Two Worlds of Jimmie Barker*.

1978   The Association for the Study of Australian Literature is founded at Monash University.

The Sydney Gay and Lesbian Mardi Gras is established.

The *Australian Book Review* is revived.
Jessica Anderson, *Tirra Lirra by the River*.
Michel Butor, *Courrier des Antipodes* [*Letters from the Antipodes*].
Christopher Koch, *The Year of Living Dangerously*.
David Malouf, *An Imaginary Life*.
Morris Lurie, *Flying Home*.

1979   *Island* magazine founded in lutruwita.

Randolph Stow, *Visitants*.
Patrick White, *The Twyborn Affair*.
David Ireland, *A Woman of the Future*.

1980   Murray Bail, *Homesickness*.

Barbara Hanrahan, *The Frangipani Gardens*.
Shirley Hazzard, *The Transit of Venus*.
Robert Bropho, *Fringedweller*.

1981   *Scripsi* is founded at the University of Melbourne by Michael Heyward and Peter Craven.

David Foster, *Moonlite*.
Rosa Cappiello, *Paese fortunato* [later translated into English as *Oh Lucky Country* in 1984].
Patrick White, *Flaws in the Glass*.
Peter Carey, *Bliss*.
David Malouf, *Child's Play*.
Albert Facey, *A Fortunate Life*.
Archie Weller, *Day of the Dog*.
Shirley Perry Smith, *Mum Shirl*.

Angelo Loukakis, *For the Patriarch.*

Frank Hardy, *Who Shot George Kirkland?*

1982   Thomas Keneally wins the Booker Prize for *Schindler's Ark.*

Olga Masters, *The Home Girls.*

Tim Winton, *An Open Swimmer.*

Gerald Murnane, *The Plains.*

1983   The first National Conference of Aboriginal Writers is held at Murdoch University.

Bob Hawke's Labor government wins the federal election.

Elizabeth Jolley, *Miss Peabody's Inheritance.*

Mudrooroo Narogin [Colin Johnson], *Doctor Wooreddy's Prescription for Enduring the Ending of the World.*

Brian Castro, *Birds of Passage.*

1984   Kimberley Aboriginal Law and Culture Centre (KALACC) is established.

Helen Garner, *The Children's Bach.*

Tim Winton, *Shallows.*

Ida West, *Pride Against Prejudice.*

Olga Masters, *Loving Daughters.*

Antigone Kefala, *The Island.*

1985   Hawke's Labor government returns the title deeds for the Uluru-Kata National Park to the Anangu people.

Establishment of the Victorian Premier's Literary Awards.

The University of Wollongong becomes the first Australian university to offer a doctorate of creative arts in creative writing.

Peter Carey, *Illywhacker.*

Kate Grenville, *Lilian's Story.*

Gerald Murnane, *Landscape with Landscape.*

Helen Garner, *Postcards from Surfers.*

1986   The American Association of Australian Literary Studies is established in New York; *Antipodes*, the Association's journal, is first published the following year.

Elizabeth Jolley, *The Well.*

Christina Stead, *I'm Dying Laughing.*

Lesbia Harford, *The Invaluable Mystery* [written c.1921].

Glenyse Ward, *Wandering Girl.*
Patrick White, *Memoirs of the Many in One.*

1987   The Royal Commission into Aboriginal Deaths in Custody is established by Hawke's Labor government.
Sally Morgan, *My Place.*
Eric Willmot, *Pemulwuy.*
Thea Astley, *It's Raining in Mango.*
Glenda Adams, *Dancing on Coral.*

1988   Bicentennial celebrations. Survival/Invasion Day protests in Sydney.
Gough Whitlam launches the AustLit database.
Peter Carey wins the Booker Prize for *Oscar and Lucinda.*
Ruby Langford Ginibi, *Don't Take Your Love to Town.*
Gerald Murnane, *Inland.*
Kate Grenville, *Joan Makes History.*
Bruce Pascoe, *Fox.*
Archie Weller, *Land of the Golden Clouds.*
Tim Winton, *In the Winter Dark.*

1989   Fall of the Berlin Wall.
The Australian Institute of Aboriginal and Torres Strait Islander Studies is established.
Mary Fallon, *Working Hot.*
Elizabeth Jolley, *My Father's Moon.*
Georges Perec, *53 jours* [*53 Days*].
Amy Witting, *I for Isobel.*
Jessica Anderson, *Taking Shelter.*
Jill Ker Conway, *The Road from Coorain.*
Nicholas Jose, *Avenue of Eternal Peace.*

1990   The Aboriginal and Torres Strait Islander Commission (ATSIC) is established.
Paperbark, an important anthology of Australian Aboriginal writing, is published.
Magabala Books becomes the first independent Indigenous press.
Thea Astley, *Reaching Tin River.*
David Malouf, *The Great World.*
Beverley Farmer, *A Body of Water.*
Elizabeth Jolley, *Cabin Fever.*
Sam Watson, *The Kadaitcha Sung.*

1991   The Council for Aboriginal Reconciliation is established.

Tim Winton, *Cloudstreet*.

Mudrooroo Narogin [Colin Johnson], *Master of the Ghost Dreaming*.

Doris Pilkington Garimara, *Caprice*.

Yasmine Gooneratne, *A Change of Skies*.

Glenyse Ward, *Unna You Fullas*.

Brian Castro, *Double-Wolf*.

Gillian Mears, *The Mint Lawn*.

1992   A landmark decision by the High Court of Australia in the case of *Mabo* v. *Queensland (No. 2)* acknowledges the traditional rights of the Meriam people to Mer (Murray Island), and in doing so gives legal recognition to native title and renders the doctrine of *terra nullius* a legal fiction. Legislation the following year enables some traditional owners to seek native title.

Labor prime minister Paul Keating's Redfern address publicly acknowledges the dispossession of Aboriginal and Torres Strait Islanders.

Formation of the Australian Greens.

Brian Castro, *After China*.

Philip McLaren, *Sweet Water – Stolen Land*.

Beth Yahp, *The Crocodile Fury*.

Helen Garner, *Cosmo Cosmolino*.

Andrew McGahan, *Praise*.

Alex Miller, *The Ancestor Game*.

1993   The Native Title Act is passed.

Alex Miller, *The Ancestor Game*.

David Malouf, *Remembering Babylon*.

Frank Moorhouse, *Grand Days*.

Madeleine St John, *The Women in Black*.

Kim Scott, *True Country*.

Elizabeth Jolley, *The George's Wife*.

Fiona McGregor, *Au Pair*.

1994   Text Publishing is founded.

Rodney Hall, *The Yandilli Trilogy*.

John Muk Muk Burke, *Bridge of Triangles*.

Dorothy Porter, *The Monkey's Mask*.

Amy Witting, *A Change in the Lighting*.

Jessica Anderson, *One for the Wattle Birds.*
Richard Flanagan, *Death of a River Guide.*

1995   Giramondo Publishing is founded.
Helen Demidenko [Helen Dale], *The Hand that Signed the Paper.*
Justine Ettler, *The River Ophelia.*
Gilliam Mears, *The Grass Sister.*

1996   John Howard is elected prime minister.
HEAT magazine is published by Giramondo and the University of Western Sydney.
The first conference of the Australian Association of Writing Programs is held.
Wik Peoples v. *Queensland* decision establishes that native title can coexist with pastoral leases by private landowners.
Robert Drewe, *The Drowner.*
Yasmine Gooneratne, *The Pleasures of Conquest.*
David Malouf, *The Conversations at Curlow Creek.*
David Foster, *The Glade within the Grove.*
Robert Dessaix, *Night Letters.*
Rodney Hall, *The Island in the Mind.*
Thea Astley, *The Multiple Effects of Rainshadow.*

1997   The Bringing them Home report is tabled in parliament, raising public awareness of the systemic removal of Indigenous children from their families. Liberal prime minister John Howard refuses to apologize.
Peter Carey, *Jack Maggs.*
Richard Flanagan, *The Sound of One Hand Clapping.*
Melissa Lucashenko, *Steam Pigs.*
Alexis Wright, *Plains of Promise.*
Anthony Macris, *Capital: Volume One.*
Delia Falconer, *The Service of Clouds.*
Arlene J. Chai, *The Last Time I Saw Mother.*
George Alexander, *Mortal Divide: The Autobiography of Yiorgos Alexandroglou.*

1998   Murray Bail, *Eucalyptus.*
Les Murray, *Fredy Neptune.*
Amy Witting *Maria's War.*
Elliot Perlman, *Three Dollars.*
Marion May Campbell, *Not Being Miriam.*
Eva Sallis, *Hiam.*

1999	The proposal that Australia should become a republic is put to a referendum and defeated. Kim Scott, *Benang*. Melissa Lucashenko, *Hard Yards*. Thea Astley, *Drylands*. Kate Grenville, *The Idea of Perfection*. Amy Witting, *Isobel on the Way to the Corner Shop*. Fiona Capp, *Last of the Sane Days*. Drusilla Modjeska, *Stravinsky's Lunch*. Julia Leigh, *The Hunter*. Marion May Campbell, *Prowler*. Michelle de Kretser, *The Rose Grower*. Brian Castro, *Drift*.
2000	Sydney Olympic Games. Peter Carey, *True History of the Kelly Gang*. Wins the Booker Prize the following year. Frank Moorhouse, *Dark Palace*.
2001	Australian troops board the Norwegian freighter MV *Tampa* off Christmas Island. The vessel was attempting to bring asylum seekers to Australia, and the incident sparks procedural offshore detainment policies. Richard Flanagan, *Gould's Book of Fish*. Tim Winton, *Dirt Music*. Amy Witting, *After Cynthia*. Robert Dessaix, *Corfu*. Vivienne Cleven, *Bitin' Back*. Alex Miller, *Journey to the Stone Country*. Joan London, *Gilgamesh*. Venero Armanno, *The Volcano*.
2002	The *Journal of the Association for the Study of Australian Literature* is founded. Bruce Pascoe, *Bloke*. Geraldine Brooks, *Year of Wonders*. Vivienne Cleven, *Her Sister's Eye*. Fiona McGregor, *Chemical Palace*. Gail Jones, *Black Mirror*. Fabienne Bayet-Charlton, *Finding Ullagundahi Island*.
2003	J. M. Coetzee is awarded the Nobel Prize in Literature. J. M. Coetzee, *Elizabeth Costello*. Shirley Hazzard, *The Great Fire*.

Antigone Kefala, *Summer Visit.*
Tara June Winch, *Swallow the Air.*
Eva Sallis, *Mahjar.*
Elliott Perlman, *Seven Types of Ambiguity.*
2004 Larissa Behrendt, *Home.*
Wayne Macauley, *Blueprints for a Barbed-Wire Canoe.*
Gail Jones, *Sixty Lights.*
Haruki Murakami, シドニー! [*Sydney!*].
Andrew McGahan, *The White Earth.*
Craig Silvey, *Rhubarb.*
Charlotte Wood, *The Submerged Cathedral.*
2005 Cronulla race riots in Sydney.
J. M. Coetzee, *Slow Man.*
Kate Grenville, *The Secret River.*
Brian Castro, *The Garden Book.*
Terri Janke, *Butterfly Song.*
Hazel Brown and Kim Scott, *Kayang & Me.*
Merlinda Bobis, *Banana Heart Summer.*
Nicholas Jose, *Original Face.*
2006 Alexis Wright, *Carpentaria.*
Tony Birch, *Shadowboxing.*
Gail Jones, *Dreams of Speaking.*
2007 The Little Children Are Sacred report is published.
The Northern Territory Emergency Response Act is passed, leading to federal intervention in the Northern Territory and suspension of the Racial Discrimination Act.
J. M. Coetzee, *Diary of a Bad Year.*
Adib Khan, *Spiral Road.*
Wayne Macauley, *Caravan Story.*
Antoni Jach, *Napoleon's Double.*
Gail Jones, *Sorry.*
2008 Global financial crisis.
Kevin Rudd makes a formal apology to First Nations Australians for the Stolen Generations, the policies that led to the forced removal of First Nations children from their families.
Establishment of the Prime Minister's Literary Award.
Nam Le, *The Boat.*
Richard Flanagan, *Wanting.*

Tim Winton, *Breath*.
Helen Garner, *The Spare Room*.
Christos Tsiolkas, *The Slap*.
Merlinda Bobis, *The Solemn Lantern Maker*.
Joan London, *Good Parents*.
Steve Toltz, *A Fraction of the Whole*.

2009   Black Saturday bushfires in Victoria result in 173 deaths.
Australia signs the United Nations Declaration of the Rights of Indigenous People.
J. M. Coetzee, *Summertime*.
David Malouf, *Ransom*.
Tom Cho, *Look Who's Morphing*.
Tony Birch, *Father's Day*.
Marie Munkara, *Every Secret Thing*.

2010   Julia Gillard defeats Kevin Rudd in a leadership challenge, becoming Australia's first female prime minister.
Kim Scott, *That Deadman Dance*.
Ouyang Yu, *The English Class*.
Fiona McGregor, *Indelible Ink*.
David Musgrave, *Glissando*.

2011   Tony Birch, *Blood*.
Kate Grenville, *Sarah Thornhill*.
Gillian Mears, *Foal's Bread*.
Ouyang Yu, *Loose*.
Merlinda Bobis, *Fish-hair Woman*.
Arlene J. Chai, *Eating Fire and Drinking Water*.
Jeanine Leane, *Purple Threads*.
Wayne Macauley, *The Cook*.
Gail Jones, *Five Bells*.
Charlotte Wood, *Animal People*.

2012   Michelle de Kretser, *Questions of Travel*.
Patrick White, *The Hanging Garden* [published posthumously].
Anthony Macris, *Great Western Highway*.
Carrie Tiffany, *Mateship with Birds*.
Ali Cobby Eckermann, *Ruby Moonlight*.

2013   Establishment of the Stella Prize, for writing by women in any genre.
Richard Flanagan, *The Narrow Road to the Deep North*. Wins the Booker Prize the following year.

J. M. Coetzee, *The Childhood of Jesus*.
Alexis Wright, *The Swan Book*.
Melissa Lucashenko, *Mullumbimby*.
Hannah Kent, *Burial Rites*.

2014   Joan London, *The Golden Age*.
Ellen van Neerven, *Heat and Light*.
Omar Musa, Here *Come the Dogs*.
Tony Birch, *The Promise*.
Marie Munkara, *A Most Peculiar Act*.
Sofie Laguna, *The Eye of the Sheep*.
Alice Pung, *Laurinda*.
Michael Mohammed Ahmad, *The Tribe*.
Ouyang Yu, *Diary of a Naked Official*.
Sonya Hartnett, *Golden Boys*.
Wayne Macauley, *Demons*.
Jared Thomas, *Calypso Summer*.

2015   Anita Heiss, *Tiddas*.
Gail Jones, *A Guide to Berlin*.
Jen Craig, *Panthers and the Museum of Fire*.
Maxine Beneba Clarke, *Foreign Soil*.
Lucy Treloar, *Salt Creek*.
Tony Birch, *Ghost River*.
Pemulwuy Weeatunga [John M. Wenitong], *The Fethafoot Chronicles*.
Charlotte Wood, *The Natural Way of Things*.
Mireille Juchau, *The World Without Us*.
Steve Toltz, *Quicksand*.

2016   Tara June Winch, *After the Carnage*.
J. M. Coetzee, *The Schooldays of Jesus*.
Jack Cox, *Dodge Rose*.
Michelle Cahill, *Letter to Pessoa*.
Julie Koh, *Portable Curiosities*.

2017   The *Uluru Statement from the Heart* is offered, but its recommendations are rejected by Liberal prime minister Malcolm Turnbull.
Peter Carey, *A Long Way From Home*.
Gerald Murnane, *Border Districts*.
Kim Scott, *Taboo*.
Josephine Wilson, *Extinctions*.
Melanie Cheng, *Australia Day*.
Claire G. Coleman, *Terra Nullius*.

	Tony Birch, *Common People*.
	Paul Collis, *Dancing Home*.
	Anita Heiss, *Barbed Wire and Cherry Blossoms*.
	Beth Yahp, *The Red Pearl and Other Stories*.
	Shaun Prescott, *The Town*.
	Elizabeth Tan, *Rubik*.
	Alexis Wright, *Tracker*.
2018	Gail Jones, *The Death of Noah Glass*.
	Melissa Lucashenko, *Too Much Lip*.
	Michael Mohammed Ahmad, *The Lebs*.
	Jennifer Mills, *Dyschronia*.
2019	J. M. Coetzee, *The Death of Jesus*.
	Claire G. Coleman, *The Old Lie*.
	Leah Purcell, *The Drover's Wife*.
	Gus Henderson, *The Wounded Sinner*.
	Tony Birch, *The White Girl*.
	Carly Cappielli, *Listurbia*.
	Robbie Arnott, *Flames*.
	Elizabeth Bryer, *From Here On, Monsters*.
June 2019 – May 2020	"Black Summer" bushfires devastate Australia.
2020	COVID-19 global pandemic.
	Nardi Simpson, *Song of the Crocodile*.
	Karen Wyld, *Where the Fruit Falls*.
	Tony Birch, *The White Girl*.
	Mirandi Riwoe, *Stone Sky Gold Mountain*.
	Gail Jones, *Our Shadows*.
	Rawah Arja, *The F Team*.
	Aravind Adiga, *Amnesty*.
	Vivian Pham, *The Coconut Children*.
	Amanda Lohrey, *The Labyrinth*.
	Richard Flanagan, *The Living Sea of Waking Dreams*.
	Elizabeth Tan, *Smart Ovens for Lonely People*.
2021	Anita Heiss, *Bila Yarrudhanggalangdhuray*.
	Tony Birch, *Dark as Last Night*.
	Adam Thompson, *Born into This*.
	Larissa Behrendt, *After Story*.
	Michael Winkler, *Grimmish*.
	Emily Bitto, *Wild Abandon*.
	Michelle de Kretser, *Scary Monsters*.

2022   Anthony Albanese's Labor Government is elected. Committing to the *Uluru Statement*, he promises to initiate a referendum on whether to constitutionally enshrine a First Nations voice to parliament.
Jessica Au, *Cold Enough for Snow*.
Alexis Wright, *Praiseworthy*.
Jennifer Down, *Bodies of Light*.
Geraldine Brooks, *Horse*.
Michelle Cahill, *Daisy and Woolf*.
Yumna Kassab, *Australiana*.
Luke Carman, *An Ordinary Ecstasy*.
Shaun Prescott, *Bon and Lesley*.

LOUIS KLEE AND NICHOLAS BIRNS

Introduction

Preoccupations of the Australian Novel

When asked how to write a novel, Michael Mohammed Ahmad once paused to explain how *not* to write one: forget, he counseled, "the story of the writer as the person who sits under a tree and writes the great Australian nothing."[1] Ahmad's image plays on the words of Patrick White (1912–1990). In a brief 1958 essay "The Prodigal Son," White declares:

> In all directions stretched the Great Australian Emptiness, in which the mind is the least of all possessions, in which the rich man is the important man, in which the schoolmaster and the journalist rule what intellectual roost there is, in which beautiful youths and girls stare at life through blind blue eyes, in which human teeth fall like autumn leaves, the buttocks of cars grow hourly glassier, food means cake and steak, muscles prevail, and the march of material ugliness does not raise a quiver from the average nerves.[2]

Often read as a critique of white Australia's philistinism, mediocracy, ugliness, and materialism, White's vision has had a surprisingly enduring appeal. There are also good reasons to question it, not least because, as Stan Grant puts it: "the great Australian emptiness. Yes, terra nullius. That is the song of Australia. It's [*sic*] foundation story. It is what Australians celebrate each January 26."[3] But Ahmad evokes White's image with different intentions. In interviews, he seeks to bury the exalted vision of the Australian novelist surveying the abyss in the hope of returning to the patient labor of crafting a sentence. "[E]very experience," as he puts it, "every interaction, every thought, every breath, influences how I will write my next sentence. Even this one. And that one ..."[4] Yet Ahmad's sentences themselves – those that make up his novels such as *The Tribe* (2014) and *The Lebs* (2018) – share more with White than his remarks might suggest. Pitching himself against the Australian mainstream and its white settlers' canon (one that would include White himself!), Ahmad's writing thrives on flouting expectations, speaking "my version of the truth regardless of the consequences," or perhaps just "exaggerating [...] because I get off on scaring the White folks [reading this]."⁵ A novel like *The Lebs* revels in the Australian void, as though, to follow Brigid Rooney, "the void is what provokes the hunger for narration."⁶ Paradoxically, then, Ahmad's opposition to a tradition may be what locates him in it. He could be speaking for White, too, when he proclaims: "For me, un-Australian-ness constitutes Australian-ness."⁷

This *Companion* considers the Australian novel in its splendid contradictoriness. It begins with novels by literary visitors to Australia and concludes with those by refugees. In between, we encounter many kinds of Australian novels, from the nineteenth-century fictions of Oliné Keese, Catherine Helen Spence, and Ada Cambridge through to literary attempts to imagine the climate crisis, Christos Tsiolkas and David Malouf's queering of mateship, and Waanyi novelist Alexis Wright's call for a sovereign Indigenous literature. The chapters of this book are as diverse in perspective as the topics they approach. They are written in no single style and proceed from no one standpoint. *The Cambridge Companion to the Australian Novel* embraces this multiplicity of approaches, but it also makes no claims to exhaustiveness. It would be impossible for one volume to encompass the Australian novel in all its dimensions. We concur with Rooney when she notes: "The field today is so heterogeneous as to resist any simple narrative of national progress."⁸ Indeed, many of the chapters of this book challenge the national frame of the volume itself. Sometimes they are animated by a recognition that nations arise out of transnational forces – by a sense of what Anna Clark calls the "transnationalism of national history."⁹ Far from seeking to assemble an overview or a comprehensive history, this *Companion* aims to introduce the reader to significant and newly forming areas of research, to offer new readings of Australian novels, and to give a sense of some enduring and emerging directions in the field. Each of this book's nineteen chapters invites the reader to expand and broaden their knowledge of the complex histories and crucial present of the novel in Australia.

In this spirit, this introduction offers a tentative outline of some "preoccupations" of the Australian novel, drawing inspiration and sampling from the chapters of this volume. In the first section, we revisit debates over the historical development of the novel in Australia and its place within world literature. Riffing on the opening of Judith Wright's *Preoccupations in Australian Poetry* (1966), we consider how the novel is intimately bound up with histories of colonialism that preceded and shaped the invasion and occupation of Australia. We then introduce First Nations novels and finally turn to contemporary fiction that reflects on cosmopolitanism, multiculturalism, transnationalism, and forced displacement. Our analysis here turns on a reading of two significant contemporary novels: Alexis Wright's *Carpentaria* (2006) and Michelle de Kretser's *Questions of Travel* (2012).

Ultimately, this introduction strives to contextualize the myriad approaches to the novel found in the chapters of this *Companion*.

The Novel as Preoccupation

What is an Australian novel? If we leave aside the tautological and dreary – that it is, say, a novel written by an Australian or one that bears some relation to Australia's national space – the question has a surprising tenacity and can give rise to interesting trains of thought. Despite the seismic shifts in Australian society in the last few decades (shifts that have, for instance, made the Australian population even larger and more culturally diverse), we concur with Martin Harrison's claim that "the subtle, deep questions of what is meant by a literature [...] in Australia have not gone away."[10]

Most immediately notable is the fact that, though the novel rose to cultural predominance relatively recently, this literary form predates the country now known as Australia. There were, to paraphrase Roberto Schwarz, novels in Australia before there were novelists and, like many things in the settler colony, they were imported.[11] The vast majority of overviews of the Australian novel, however, start not with imports but with exports. They begin by noting that the first (and the first, by convention at least, is Henry Savery's *Quintus Servinton*, published in Hobart in 1830–1831) Australian novels were written for a European readership and were often picaresque, full of daring exploits and exotic wonders, and populated with recognizably Australian social types such as bushrangers, squatters, settlers, convicts, and swagmen.[12] One of the best-known novels of this period, Henry Kingsley's *The Recollections of Geoffry Hamlyn* (1859), stirred divided opinions among later writers, with Marcus Clarke declaring it "the best Australian novel that has been, and probably will be written" and Tom Collins, the "offensively Australian" narrator of Joseph Furphy's in *Such is Life* (1901), insisting, by contrast, that it is an "exceedingly trashy and misleading novel," filled with "insufferable twaddle."[13] In the context of settler fiction, divided assessments of literary merit are particularly loaded. Later Australian writers, such as Miles Franklin (1879–1954), often turned to earlier Australian fiction with a "polemically nationalist agenda," eager to find allegories of national emergence in the formation of a distinct and accomplished Australian novel. The irony, as Paul Giles observes in his chapter in this book, is that we cannot fully understand nineteenth-century novels in Australia from within a nationalist framework. For Giles, it is only by reading "in comparative rather than nationalistic terms" and challenging "circumscribed academic fiefdoms" that scholars can hope to make sense of the rich and still underappreciated field of nineteenth-century Australian fiction.

Giles' claims here resonate with recent scholarship on settler colonial literatures, which has not only embraced comparativist perspectives but also sought to shift and expand the terms of comparison. One particularly noteworthy and ambitious approach is that of Sarah Comyn and Porscha Fermanis, who propose a hemispheric, southern-centered framework that would take the British-controlled settler colonies of what is now Australia, Aotearoa New Zealand, and South Africa as a single "southern archive" or "interregion" of literary analysis.[14] Comyn and Fermanis argue that a "wider southern regionalism" would help bring to light the often neglected and marginalized "horizontal south-south identities, exchanges, and connections," while also highlighting "racialized spectres of violence, labour exploitation, carcerality, and otherness that mark out the distinctive character of the interconnected southern settler colonies."[15] The theoretical advantage of this approach lies in its synthesis of a south-centric particularism with a broader transnational methodology. On the practical level, it invites us to consider novels like Olive Schreiner's *The Story of an African Farm* (1883) alongside equivalent novels from Australia to Aotearoa New Zealand.

While there is undoubtedly something distinctive to southern literatures, Australian novels have also been shaped by broader, global patterns. Australia shares a kinship with other peripheral and semi-peripheral countries in the capitalist world system, where the novel frequently emerged not, in Franco Moretti's influential formulation, from an "autonomous development but as a compromise between a western formal influence (usually French and English) and local materials."[16] As in countries such as Brazil, Egypt, and Mexico, the novel has often been successful in Australia when it has affirmed this formal problem as a source of vitality and strength, and sought the truth of the Australian situation in feelings of fraudulence, anxiety, guilt, maladaptation, and ineptitude. Many of these feelings were memorably crystallized as the "cultural cringe" by A. A. Phillips, who suggested that "colonialism has a pervasive psychological effect, setting up a relationship as intimate and uneasy as that between an adolescent and his parents," while noting that the only cure known to him lay in "the art of being unself-consciously ourselves."[17] While today the malaise outlined by Phillips is just as likely to be cited in critical disavowals as affirmed, his "cure" has a certain persistence (though, arguably, it takes a *self-conscious* rather than unself-conscious form). One striking example is a proposal made by J. M. Coetzee in a seminar on "*Literaturas del Sur*" ["Literatures of the South"] at the Universidad Nacional de San Martín in Buenos Aires in 2015. He urges southern writers to "ignore the gaze of the north" and "begin to see the South through Southern eyes."[18] By "the South," Coetzee means not the Global South, which he dismisses as "a concept merely, an abstraction invented by social scientists," but a "real," hemispheric south, where countries share not only similar environments and histories of settler colonialism, but where, more elusively, "the winds blow in a certain way and the leaves fall in a certain way and the sun beats down in a certain way that is instantly recognisable from one part of the South to another."[19]

Coetzee's assertion of an imaginative connection between southern literatures pointedly unlinked to the dominant publishing centers of London and New York also resonates with Ivor Indyk's notion of the "provincial imagination." The provincial imagination, in Indyk's words, is "a distinctive kind of literary aesthetic" evident in Australian writers who draw their imaginative strength from the fact that they "live at some distance from the metropolitan centers of political and cultural power."[20] Indyk has identified the provincial imagination with the revalorization of "shyness, awkwardness, self-consciousness, obsession" and the "capacity of wonder," which he locates in everything from the declaration of sovereignty in the vast fictions of Alexis Wright, the encyclopedic ambitions of Murray Bail, the fascination with wonder in Delia Falconer, the baroque aspects of Patrick White, the digressive and associative prose of Gerald Murnane, and the playful self-dramatization of failure in the novels of Brian Castro.[21] To insist upon the distinctly provincial character of the Australian novel typifies one response to the question: Is Australian literature world literature?[22] In "Proust in Caloudra" (2014), Philip Mead considers this question, noting the answers offered by influential frameworks, from the ecocritical to the postcolonial. Perhaps Australian literature is world literature *because* it remains an unnetworked, idiosyncratic literary "micro-climate" where "the prevailing winds of postcolonial and world literature often sweep past."[23] All the same, Mead thinks the "short answer is: get real."[24]

To think the Australian novel on its terms and champion its marginal status as a source of strength is a familiar enough strategy in peripheral literatures. Yet there is also an Australian intricacy to it – one that arises from First Nations priority and survivance. It is impossible to understand the novel in Australia while proceeding as if, in Yiman and Bidjara scholar Marcia Langton's words, "none of the brutality, murder and land clearances occurred."[25] And while the very notion of "settler colonialism" highlights a structure in which colonizers seek to "eliminate" and "replace" First Nations peoples – a structure that has been borne out through the frontier wars, policies of forced cultural assimilation, and waves of military intervention – it is important to remember how, as Yamatji scholar Crystal McKinnon stresses, "Indigenous people have survived despite an often relentless onslaught from invading colonial forces" through "multiple forms of resistance."[26]

This ongoing history of dispossession and resistance permeates the Australian novel at all levels, shaping not simply its explicit thematic pre-occupations but also its form. Even novels that seem on the surface to have little to say about these histories can be read rewardingly for their silences, avoidances, and elisions. The novelist Luke Carman alludes to this when, rehearsing a theory he mischievously borrows from a fearsome, though unnamed, Australian literary critic, he observes that the dominant styles of non-Indigenous Australian literature – on the one hand, a "restrained, mini-malist aesthetic exhibited by writers like Helen Garner, or Antigone Kefala" and, on the other, a "Baroque, ornate, ecstatistician's approach demonstrated most evidently in Patrick White" – ultimately stem from the "deterritorialised loss at the heart of Australia's colonial culture."[27] In a similar (though less mischievous) vein, several chapters in this *Companion* explore the ways in which the histories of colonialism shape how critics read Australian novels. Michael Griffiths' chapter for this volume analyses the "construction, trans-lation, and dissemination of Aboriginal culture to white readers through the medium of the Australian novel," while Evelyn Araluen's chapter critiques the idea of the *Mabo* "turn" in the Australian novel, emphasizing instead continuities in both settler colonial ideology and First Nations response.

This situation appears even more complex when we consider that the novel form is itself bound up with colonization. This is the other meaning we intend by "pre-occupation": the novel made possible a kind of imaginative occupa-tion before Captain James Cook marked the annexation of the east coast of Australia with a flag and three cannon shots at "Possession Island" in August 1770 and before the First Fleet landed at Botany Bay in January 1788. To insist on the novel's place in colonization is not to reduce colonialism to something cultural or metaphorical, but to underline how literary forms can anticipate and even shape the material processes of empire. For the novel was not simply pivotal to the development of "imperial attitudes, references, and experiences," as Edward W. Said contends in *Culture and Imperialism* (1993); it is "*the* aesthetic object whose connection to the expanding societies of Britain and France is particularly interesting to study."[28]

Said here turns to the archetypical realist novel in English, *Robinson Crusoe* (1719), which famously depicts a shipwrecked Englishman indus-triously transforming an island into his own dominion.[29] While it is the case that narrative prose fiction stretches back thousands of years and has diverse origins across the globe from China to ancient Mesopotamia, the emergence of what we now recognize as the realist novel in late seventeenth- and early eighteenth-century England was fundamentally tied to the rise of the bourgeoisie and unthinkable without the vertiginously vast networks of connection that coalesced through capitalism and empire.[30] "Of all the major literary forms," as Said's argument goes, "the novel is the most recent, its emergence the most datable, its occurrence the most Western, its normative pattern of social authority the most structured; imperialism and the novel fortified each other to such a degree that it is impossible [...] to read one without in some way dealing with the other."[31] One of the texts underpinning Said's account here is Ian Watt's important study *The Rise of the Novel* (1957), which links the form's distinctive way of representing reality – its fidelity in reporting "particular individuals having particular experiences at particular times and at particular places" – to the rise of bourgeois individualism.[32] For Watt, *Robinson Crusoe* is "very appropriately used by many economic theorists as their illustration of *homo economicus*," since Crusoe's "original sin" is really "the dynamic tendency of capitalism itself, whose aim is never merely to maintain the *status quo*, but to transform it incessantly. Leaving home, improving on the lot one was born to, is a vital feature of the individualist pattern of life."[33] It is hardly a coincidence that Australia's colonists were also fond of Crusoe stories. The prototype of the realist novel in English thus becomes a prototype for the settler colony of Australia: *Robinson Crusoe* is referenced everywhere from the writing of the pioneer John Batman and the First Fleet surgeon George Worgan through to the explorer Matthew Flinders' wish, on his deathbed in 1814, that someone dispatch him the latest edition of this book he had long admired.[34] "Thanks to this book," as Alan Atkinson has it, "the European settlement in Australia was to live in the common imagination long before it was a given a name and a real dwelling place," and long afterward, as Karen Downing argues, in the "restlessness" of settler masculinity in the Australian colonies.[35] At the risk of anachronism, these histories invite us to hear another meaning in Crusoe's resonant phrase: "As I imagin'd it, so it was."[36]

When the twentieth-century poet Judith Wright set out the opening theses of *Preoccupations in Australian Poetry*, she was carried by a similar intuition. In characterizing the "double aspect of inner Australia," as she called it, or the "two strands of feeling" in Australian writing, she curiously, but for our purposes strikingly, drew her examples not from the subject matter of her book, poetry, but from the novel. *Preoccupations in Australian Poetry* makes its argument through reference to Australia's canonical novelists: Marcus Clarke, Joseph Furphy, Henry Lawson, D. H. Lawrence (whose *Kangaroo* she considers to "strike further home into the central relationship of white Australian and his country, perhaps, than any written by the native-born"), Eve Langley, Christina Stead, Eleanor Dark, Martin Boyd, Patrick White, and Henry Handel Richardson ("our two greatest novelists," as she describes the latter two).[37] The fact is not lost on Wright that her examples are all, like Wright herself, white settler writers – Australia's "white invaders" in her words – who at best, in a form ill-fitted to the realities of a country taken by force, "ironise form through strong political purpose."[38]

For Wright, these preoccupations emerge in two valences. On the one hand, there is a conservative, exilic, and often nostalgic consciousness in novelists like Richardson and Boyd. In their fiction, Australia appears as a kind of prison, or else as a strange, hostile, uninhabitable landscape in which all European forms are misplaced, clumsy, and second-hand. The only way this exilic consciousness can overcome its restlessness and acquire a sense of reconciliation and homecoming is, Wright argues, through death and literal interment in the longed-for country – an extreme and metaphysical variety of what Eve Tuck and K. Wayne Yang describe as "trying to make the settler indigenous to the land he occupies."[39] And so an unprecedented description of the natural world concludes Richardson's trilogy *The Fortunes of Richard Mahony* (1930), as the narrative opens out on to a view of the sea and the sky in which the "rich and kindly earth of his adopted country absorbed his perishable body, as the country itself had never contrived to make its own, his wayward, vagrant spirit," while Judd, the murderer and betrayer in White's *Voss* (1957), explains: "You see, if you live and suffer long enough in a place, you do not leave it altogether. Your spirit is still there."[40]

In writers such as Furphy and Lawson, by contrast, Wright discerns a countertradition that takes this same alienation as a boon. Here Australia is not a prison: It is a paradise of potential.[41] According to Wright, Australia offers the settler a great opportunity to repudiate the injustices and inequalities of the so-called "old world", to shake off inherited cultural forms, and forge new notions of liberty, equality, and independence – even extravagance, dandyism, and largesse. Yet Wright also warns that the egalitarian, homosocial notion of "mateship" in this utopian strand can end up becoming inseparable from self-serving nationalist myths, and thus feed into the same cultural cringe of exilic consciousness. She concludes that the two traditions of settler writing are intertwined in a self-perpetuating dynamic:

> [T]he true function of an art and a culture is to interpret us to ourselves, and to relate us to the country and the society in which we live. So the new Australian (and all of us, to some extent, are new Australians) has in truth died a little. This is what our "literature of exile" recognises in us, and here it has the real importance of true literature. For if we reject outright the literature of nostalgia, we fail to understand something important about ourselves, and will not be able to set about making Australia into our real spiritual home. In the same way, if we accept it too wholeheartedly, and take too seriously the notion that ours is a transplanted community, we deny the second aspect of our situation as Australians – the opportunity that is given us to make our loss into a gain,

to turn Australia into a reality, to become something new in the world; to be not, as Hope puts it, "second-hand Europeans" timidly pullulating on alien shores, but a people who have seized the chance to make a new kind of consciousness out of our conditions.[42]

This may hardly be recognizable as a description of the Australian novel today. Indeed, Wright herself came to think that this dilemma could not be resolved in literary terms alone, but required activism and political struggle.[43] Yet we revisit Wright's 1966 discussion because these "preoccupations" do resurface, in various forms, in the chapters of this *Companion*. In fact, we would argue that it is important to emphasize the continued pertinence of the tension Wright identifies, given how repetition shapes Australian literary history.

One of the reasons that Wright spoke of "preoccupations," rather than, say, a tradition is because she recognized that discussions of Australian art and culture appear to start all over again every couple of decades – an "endlessly repeated moment of contemporary overthrow" that is itself a kind of literary equivalent to the settler sense of "historylessness" in Australia.[44] In part, this cycle stems from Australia's peripheral place within world literature. To again echo Roberto Schwarz, each generation of novelists feels the need not only to acquire and adapt the latest aesthetic innovations from abroad and reshape them to their immediate environment but also – and this is often secondary, if it occurs at all – to master the past literature of their own country. The consequence is that there is little meaningful aesthetic continuity across generations of Australian novelists (even if much exciting scholarship has been devoted to unearthing underappreciated connections between Australian writers). Often Australian novelists simply acquire some know-how from their predecessors, some tricks of the trade, in the vein that Tim Winton describes with gentle irony in his piece "Remembering Elizabeth Jolley" (2007). The only influence that Winton owns up to from his experience of being taught by Jolley in creative writing at the Western Australian Institute of Technology (now Curtin University) is a practical one. "Writing – the act itself – remains a personal mystery"; it is untransferable, but "the student of writing often learns despite what they're being taught."[45] What they learn, he claims, is the "public and procedural aspect of the writing life": the "peculiar suite of skills, which have nothing to do with art"; pragmatic strategies that can help the writer to get their writing published and "survive honourably."[46] An aesthetic argument between Australian novels carried out across generations is a rarer thing. In this light, we may picture past settler writers as the poet Chris Wallace-Crabbe does: a line of "solemn effigies, staring back towards us, but without so much as a sidelong glance at one another."[47] Because there is no "significant imaginative connection" between them, Wallace-Crabbe argues that the "Australian literary tradition [does] not flow as a stream," as fluvial metaphors of literary influence would suggest.[48] It stands "as a succession of waterholes," a discontinuous series of oases that recalls the nineteenth-century poet Charles Harpur's image of "[t]he sylvan eyelash always of remote / Australian waters."[49] These waters wink at each other, forming a negative tradition of accidental repetition and uncanny echo.[50] Such discontinuities among settler writers may also account for the periodic alarmism seen, for instance, in Geordie Williamson's *The Burning Library* (2012). Taking his guiding image from Walter Benjamin's idea of classics as slow-burning fuses, *The Burning Library* seeks to resurrect the reputations of past novelists such as Dal Stivens, Jessica Anderson, and Amy Witting, in the hope of reviving what he calls the "lost back-story of our literature."[51]

A Sovereign Literature

Though pivoting no less on questions of continuity and discontinuity, a different set of preoccupations emerge in First Nations novels. First Nations novels, which are central to five of the chapters of this *Companion*, represent some of the most significant writing in Australia today. Like Indigenous writing broadly, First Nations novels are often "caught in the gaze," as Araluen puts it, "of too little too much."[52] They are at once revolutionary in their reconfiguration of the novel form *and* deeply rooted in living traditions of storytelling that have been embodied in the communal, aesthetic event of words performed, spoken, and sung – in "one hundred thousand years of dreams," as Alexis Wright puts it in *Carpentaria*.[53] This forces us to modify the question posed at the outset of this introduction. How can we conceive of the novel in Australia, given not simply that the novel form predates the settler colony, but that First Nations storytelling existed long before the idea of a *Terra Australis* occurred to Europeans as a cartographical conjecture to balance the northern hemisphere's landmass on maps? The paradox in this question is only an apparent one. "The form has changed," as Araluen writes, "as have we, but the songlines still hum in the soil while we read and write upon it."[54]

One complexity of First Nations novels in Australia arises from the fact that many Indigenous writers have been compelled to consciously forge their own lines of continuity to ancient cultural traditions in the wake of violent dispossession and forced cultural assimilation. For one thing, "[m]ost Aboriginal writers," as Jeanine Leane puts it in her chapter for this book, "speak English either first and/or equally alongside their first languages," and yet "[m]any of us, like me, have to go back as adults to First Language programs to learn the language/s that should have been our birth right." In the process, First Nations writers have reckoned with the novel as a literary form tied to the legacies of colonialism. For instance, First Nations novels often resist superficial dichotomies between politics and form. As Lynda Ng argues in her chapter for this volume: "the act of writing has always possessed a political dimension for Aboriginal people which is impossible to separate from the literature itself." Indeed, many First Nations novelists have found that it is only by subjecting the novel form to radical and subversive innovations that they can convey what Leane calls Aboriginal storytelling's "vastness of voice."[55] It may take a novel on "a grand scale," because "our country," as Wright has it in *Carpentaria*, "is a very big story."[56]

Scholars today credit Monica Clare's posthumously published *Karobran* (1978) as the first Indigenous novel in Australia, but it is important to contextualize this "first" within a rich field of First Nations writing beyond the novel, as well as to recognize, with Peter Minter and Belinda Wheeler, that the "virtual absence" of First Nations novels before the 1970s "correlates with the oppressions of colonization."[57] When First Nations writers did eventually turn to the novel form, they built on earlier achievements in poetry and life writing. This is something foregrounded, for instance, by Oodgeroo Noonuccal. She published an important prose collection, *Stradbroke Dreamtime*, in 1972, but long maintained that poetry, rather than the novel, would be "the breakthrough" for Indigenous storytelling, given the concentrated attention it pays to the effects of voice.[58] Like poetry, autobiographical prose narratives have been crucial to the development of the First Nations novel. Important aspects of contemporary Indigenous novels – what Minter and Wheeler call preoccupations – are anticipated by earlier works such as Theresa Clement's *From Old Maloga* (1930) and David Unaipon's *My Life Story* (1954).[59] For Minter and Wheeler, these preoccupations include representations of the Stolen Generations, challenges to the legal fiction of *terra nullius*, and depictions of urban disenfranchisement, all of which come together in an original "synthesis of dialogic orality and the autobiographical voice."[60]

Early poetic and autobiographical writing laid the foundations for a burst of Indigenous creativity in the lead-up to the bicentenary in 1988 that has continued through to the present moment. We are now, as Gomeroi writer Alison Whittaker declares, "in the midst of a renaissance in First Nations literature [...] a golden age."[61] Part of the vitality of the contemporary First Nations novel can be traced to the productive tension of reasserting continuity with oral art and storytelling in the written form of the novel. This is captivatingly evident in the case of Alexis Wright's *Carpentaria*. In its efforts to encompass the rhythms, voice, temporality, scope, and "pattern of the great ancient sagas that define the laws, customs and values of our culture," *Carpentaria* has reinvented the novel in ways that are unique in the history of the form.[62] Wright's originality is even more evident if we recall a thesis of Walter Benjamin, first set out in his 1930 essay "The Crisis of the Novel," that the novel "differs from all other types of prose – folktales, legends, proverbs, comical stories – in that it neither comes from nor feeds into the oral tradition. This distinguishes it above all from storytelling."[63] Part of the achievement of *Carpentaria* consists in how it turns a form supposedly defined, as Benjamin thought, by communication in solitude and the consumption of strangers' fates into a means for the transmission of experience situated within a community of listeners.

This is apparent in Wright's use of "a story-telling narrative voice," as she calls it, which is rhythmically punctuated by exclamations like "But listen!," "Well!," "So!," "My! My!," "Real!," "You better believe it."[64] But more than that, *Carpentaria* depicts the working of oral history, from the interminable monologues of Mozzie Fishman "taken from his epistle without end" to the "library chock-a-block full of stories of the old country [...] the good information, intelligence, etiquette of the what to do, how to behave for knowing how to live like a proper human being" that Norm Phantom keeps stored in his head.[65] In fact, Wright also reveals the white settlers of the Gulf country town Desperance to have their own "folktale of ancient times [...] stored in treasure chests in [their] minds."[66] But because they only attach value to written archival documents, like the town's "Book of Books," the settlers of Desperance remain "'illiterate' orally."[67] Unable to appreciate the power of their own storytelling, they are controlled by impoverished forms of orality like rumor and hearsay, which feeds into their profound lack of self-understanding, as well as collective acts of hysteria, scapegoating, and injustice.

There is an even more radical way, however, that *Carpentaria* transforms the novel form through its use of storytelling. "Wright envisages the novel," Ng argues, "not as a capstone to oral techniques, but rather as an extension of an oral literature capable of positing an Aboriginal-inflected modernity." In "On Writing *Carpentaria*" (2007), Wright recalls that her two principal concerns were "firstly, how to understand the idea of Indigenous people living with the stories of all the times of this country, and secondly, how to write from this perspective."[68] She aimed to achieve this not simply by writing in a way that replicated "the storytelling voices of ordinary Aboriginal people whom I have heard all of my life," writing "a novel as though some old Aboriginal person was telling a story," but also by playing with the novel's mode of address. "I felt I was telling a contemporary story about ourselves to the ancestors," she affirms.[69]

Significantly, the preposition is *to* – *Carpentaria* turns the novel's isolated address to an unknown reader into an open-ended intimacy and trust between the storyteller and a whole potential community that is living and dead, past, present, and future. Indeed, Wright aims to portray through the novel "the

world of Indigenous Australia as being in constant opposition between different spaces of time."[70] In an insight she has developed from the Mexican novelist Carlos Fuentes, she declares that "all times are important, and no time has
ever been resolved."[71] Fuentes outlines this "fabulous totality and instantaneity
of true Mexican time" in a passage from *A New Time for Mexico* (1994):

> In Mexico, all times are living, all pasts are present. [...] The coexistence [...]
> of multiple historical levels is but the external sign of a deep subconscious
> decision made by the country and its people: all times must be maintained,
> all times must be kept alive. Why? Because no Mexican time has yet fulfilled
> itself. We are a horizon of latent, promising or frustrated, never fully achieved
> potentialities. A country of suspended times.[72]

Carpentaria strives to capture a similarly recursive temporal layering familiar to Indigenous orality. Though the novel form is often famed for its infinite
adaptability, it is not nearly capacious enough for the kind of stories that
Will Phantom witnesses in *Carpentaria*: "[s]tories that know no boundaries,"
"epics of speculation."[73] In a series of recent speeches laying out a literary
notion of self-governance, Wright has drawn attention to the "sovereignty
of the imagination" – "boundless as it is borderless and bountiful" – which
is the novelistic counterpart to political calls for Indigenous sovereignty.[74]
The result is a distinctive cosmopolitanism rooted in Indigenous experience
and storytelling. Wright's fiction thus gestures, in its most hopeful aspect, to
a new model for world literature in which political sovereignty is inseparable from the boundary-defying power of the novelistic imagination.

Questions of Travel

Despite the ceaselessly traveling, border-crossing imagination on show in
Carpentaria, Wright also notes that her vast novel will be ill-suited "to a
tourist reader."[75] In a similar vein, Leane's chapter in this book distinguishes
modes of engagement with First Nations novels. While the "invader" is
appropriative and the "tourist" superficial, the "visitor" enters a novel "bearing mind it is *not their space*," that the stories here are not "the same as the
one they left." This brings us to a final preoccupation of the Australian novel:
insistent questions of displacement, restlessness, exile, migrancy, transnationalism, tourism, and travel. Many chapters in this *Companion* respond directly
to this cluster of concerns. Brendan Casey's chapter investigates novels by
literary visitors to Australia; Fiona Morrison analyses Christina Stead's oceanic transnationalism and involvement in leftist internationalism; and Keyvan
Allahyari interrogates the viability of the idea of an "Australian" refugee novel.
Michelle Cahill uses ficto-criticism to question reductive tropes, silencing,
belonging, and cultural safety for culturally and linguistically diverse writers

(CALD), and other minorities.[76] From the robust groundwork of her writing and editing contributions to Australian literature, she critiques the framework of cosmopolitanism through a reading of short fictions. Together, these chapters give a very different meaning to the exilic strand in the Australian novel identified by Judith Wright. Even in the case of Judah Waten's *Alien Son* (1952), often cited as the first "migrant fiction" in Australia, the truth is much more complex. Were we to attend to the milieu of Yiddish-speaking writers around Waten, such as Herz Bergner and Pinchas Goldhar, what we would find is not so much an Australian multiculturalism *avant la lettre* as a body of writing that understood itself in transnational terms even before these novelists set foot in Australia.[77] It is also worth noting, especially given the relative absence of class in discussions of Australian literature today compared to the twentieth century, that for Waten, a committed communist, the "prevailing discourses [...] were not those of ethnicity or nation," but rather "the internationalism of the avant-garde [and] of the proletariat."[78]

Many of these aspects of contemporary transnationalism are elegantly brought together and thematized by recent Australian novels. Chief among these is Michelle de Kretser's 2012 novel *Questions of Travel*, an expansive novel on the philosophy and politics of travel that sets up this counterpoint in its opening pages:

> On that day in 1779 when Captain Cook died in Kealakekua Bay, an Italian apothecary arrived in Gallee on a ship registered in Rotterdam to the Dutch East India Company. One of these men was already famous and the other would die in obscurity, but each had his part in a great global enterprise that ran on greed, curiosity and the human reluctance to stay still.[79]

The novel juxtaposes two lives: that of a Singhalese man, Ravi, who lives through the Sri Lankan Civil War (1983–2009) and emigrates to Australia after the murder of his wife and child, and an Anglo-Australian woman, Laura, who is the embodiment of allophilia (a "late-twentieth-century global person. Geography was beside the point").[80] After roaming and living abroad, Laura becomes a travel writer and works for a tourist guidebook company in Sydney. The lives of both share some tangential connection to the author's own as a Sri Lankan Burgher of mixed Singhalese and Dutch descent, who emigrated to Australia at fourteen after changes to language education policy in Sri Lanka, and who worked for a decade for the well-known Australian guidebook publisher Lonely Planet.[81] One of de Kretser's frustrations with the ideology of Lonely Planet is put directly into the mouth of Laura:

> "Have you noticed, the only word you never hear around this place is 'tourism'? Because tourism's about dollars, no argument. But 'travel' lets you pretend. Travel has an aura. It allows us to believe that publishing guidebooks is,

you know, a good thing. We can tell ourselves that what we do contributes to global harmony, international understanding, you know the stuff I mean. It's understood without being spelled out."[82]

While Laura's point is lost on her bemused co-worker Robin, the reader, who has simultaneously been following the story of Ravi, is intensely cognizant of the disparities between those who can travel and those who cannot, and the reasons why. The lives of both Ravi and Laura are directly shaped by epochal shifts in the internet and global mobility. Yet both remain unconvinced by the blustering narratives of globalization that herald greater connectedness. Ravi builds an archive of the "abandoned websites," gaps in the meshwork of interconnectivity that elicit a "melancholy charm" in the way that they "resisted tourism" and the "beguiling, hypermodern façade of the web," while Laura finds the moments that matter most in travel are "intractable" and cannot be "moulded into the shapely narratives" of the cliché-ridden, commodified travel writing that de Kretser satirizes.[83] Like Ravi, Laura keeps a folder "on her laptop of material she couldn't sell" or fit into formulas such as *"checked out hipster bars," "explored the Beijing art scene,"* or *"This is where worlds collide."*[84]

The novel's fundamental statement on the untranslatability of experience is delivered, however, through its narrative form. *Questions of Travel* not only invites comparisons between the two very different lives and experiences of mobility, but implicitly generates a readerly anticipation that Ravi and Laura will be brought together in some meaningful way. When they finally meet, de Kretser defies this expectation in a sly denouement. In the middle of a paragraph more than halfway through the novel, we learn that "Laura recognised the new web guy, Ravi" out in Ramsey Travel's company car park.[85] Made to narrativize his life to make a convincing asylum claim, Ravi realizes that much of his memory contains "details of the wrong kind, details that proved nothing."[86] In a similar way, *Questions of Travel* puts two lives in counterpoint that remain illegible to one another. Ravi and Laura see each other "as a tourist looks" on a landscape – with a momentary wistfulness "while picking up a bag with a sense of onward motion."[87]

De Kretser's novel powerfully poses questions of travel that have only intensified in the last decade. As Allahyari notes in his chapter in this book, today "more than one percent of the world's population is forcibly deracinated." One among these millions is the writer Behrouz Boochani, a Kurdish Iranian refugee who was incarcerated by the Australian government in Manus Island from 2013 to 2019. Allahyari reads Boochani's *No Friend but the Mountains* (2018) as a novel that "resists the demands of nation-building that the Australian literary field has carried around since its inception." *No Friend but the Mountains* is not always considered a novel, let alone an

"Australian" one, but for Boochani it was the novel form itself that con-ferred meaning on his experience. Speaking via video link from Manus, when he had won a major literary award in Australia, Boochani declared: "When I arrived in Manus, I created another image for myself. I imagined myself a novelist in a remote prison. Sometimes I would work half naked beside the prison fences and imagine a novelist locked up right there, in that place. This image was awe inspiring."[88] Allahyari argues that the refugee novel has a unique epistemological status for understanding Australia: With increased state secrecy and newly draconian laws, he suggests that "most of what we know of the cruelty of Australian processing centers are from the detention 'literature'." But more than this epistemological value, refugee novels may have a subtle impact on politics and governance. Marooning, to return to the outset of this introduction, may be the originary scene of the realist novel, and yet this link between refugees and *Robinson Crusoe* could be read as more than a coincidence. In *Human Rights, Inc.* (2009), Joseph Slaughter argues that the drafters of the Universal Declaration of Human Rights turned to *Robinson Crusoe* as "an enabling fiction" for the concept of human rights.[89] One can only speculate that things might have been different if they were reading *No Friend but the Mountains* instead.

The Chapters

This *Companion* is divided into three sections: Contexts, Authorships, and Futures. The first section sets out several historical and critical frameworks for reading Australian novels. This volume places particular emphasis on the modern and contemporary Australian novel with the anticipation that further historical coverage will be provided by David Carter's *The Cambridge History of the Australian Novel*. It opens with Jeanine Leane's "Presencing: Writing in the Decolonial Space," which critiques past settler strategies of reading First Nations novels and proposes "a more culturally grounded framework [...] that could be applied to all forms of Aboriginal literary production." The theme of the literary visitor that concludes Leane's essay is then taken up by Brendan Casey in "Literary Visitors and the Australian Novel." Casey con-structs a "heterogenous anti-canon of visitor-novels" that ranges from Henry Savery's *Quintus Servinton* (1830–1831) and D. H. Lawrence's *Kangaroo* (1923) to George Perec's *53 jours* [*53 Days*] (1989) and Haruki Murakami's 2004 diary work シドニー! [*Sydney!*]. Paul Giles' "Settler Colonial Fictions: Between Nationalism and Universalism" sets out to consider the emergence of settler colonial novels in the nineteenth century, arguing that "antipodean perspectives" are always already situated within a "global framework." In "White Writing, Indigenous Australia, and the Chronotopes of the Settler

Novel," Michael Griffiths examines representations of Indigenous characters and temporality in novels by Marcus Clarke, Rolf Boldrewood, Eleanor Dark, Xavier Herbert, and Katharine Susannah Prichard. Evelyn Araluen's "*Mabo*, Mob, and the Novel" critiques settler framings of the *Mabo* decision. In "Publishing the Australian Novel," Emmett Stinson gives a detailed sociological analysis of the Australian publishing field, demonstrating how significant literary editors such as Beatrice Davis and small publishers such as Giramondo have shaped the reception of the Australian novel.

The second section looks at a small selection of individual writers from the modern and contemporary periods. While we have foregrounded writers who have had a major impact on how Australian literature is viewed worldwide, it will be obvious that we have not had space to allocate a chapter to all significant Australian novelists (for example, we lack a full chapter on Henry Handel Richardson). While this book does place a greater emphasis on, for instance, First Nations writing, queer sexuality, and transnationalism than previous reference books, the chapters in this section are not seeking to assemble a revisionary canon. Rather, they aim to demonstrate what reading an Australian novel looks like in practice and model close reading and analysis. This section opens with Fiona Morrison's "'Rich and Strange': Christina Stead and the Transnational Novel," which examines Stead's expatriate career in terms of the tropes of oceanic mobility. In "Sexuality in Patrick White's Fiction," Chen Hong traces White's complex representations of homosexuality, heterosexuality, and bisexuality across his oeuvre. Louis Klee's "Constellational Form in Gerald Murnane" focuses on the associative style of Murnane's fiction. In "Helen Garner's House of Fiction," Brigid Rooney examines the shared, communal households of *Monkey Grip* (1977), the decaying Sweetpea Mansions of *Cosmo Cosmolino* (1992), and the dynamics of hospitality in *The Spare Room* (2008). Lynda Ng's "Alexis Wright's Novel Activism" considers Wright's trajectory as a writer from *Grog War* (1997) to *The Swan Book* (2013), arguing that her body of work "puts forward a remarkably consistent and cohesive literary vision that is at once Aboriginal and Australian, modern and ancient, local and yet outward-looking." Joseph Steinberg's "Kim Scott and the Doctoral Novel" situates Scott's 2010 novel *That Deadman Dance* against the institutional background of the university creative writing degree.

The final section of this *Companion* examines several important developments in the Australian novel, among them Anthropocene fiction, refugee novels, the verse novel in Australia, Indigenous transnationalism, and cosmopolitanism. In "The Contemporary Western Sydney Novel," Lachlan Brown analyses the emergence of a new generation of novelists seeking to represent the suburbs of Sydney's west. Declan Fry's

"First Nations Transnationalism" explores cross-cultural exchange in First Nations writing, drawing on writers such as Ellen van Neerven, Alexis Wright, Evelyn Araluen, and Billy-Ray Belcourt. Michelle Cahill's "Beyond Cosmopolitanism: Small Dangerous Fragments" examines short fiction by Tom Cho, Nicholas Jose, Melanie Cheng, Michelle Wright, and Elizabeth Tan, and includes a critical reflection on her acclaimed metafictions in *Letter to Pessoa*. In "Craft and Truth: The Australian Verse Novel," Nicholas Birns discusses the unusual prominence of the verse novel in Australia. In "Queering Mateship," Lesley Hawkes and Mark Piccini explore how the lyrical yearning of David Malouf and the visceral realism of Christos Tsiolkas act as queer subversions of dominant and conventional forms of Australian masculinity. In "Australian Fiction in the Anthropocene," Tony Hughes-D'Aeth asks how the Anthropocene changes "the way that writers write and readers read in Australia." Finally, in "What is the (Australian) Refugee Novel?", Keyvan Allahyari explores the "awkward" category of the refugee novel in the Australian context, considering writing by Behrouz Boochani, Nam Le, Michelle de Kretser, and Felicity Castagna. Together these chapters seek to introduce a new generation of students and researchers to significant developments in the Australian novel.

Notes

We wish to thank Brigid Rooney and Joseph Steinberg for advice on this essay. Any mistakes are our own.

1 Michael Mohammed Ahmad, "Interview with Astrid Edwards," The Garret: *Writers on Writing*, June 24, 2021: https://thegarretpodcast.com/at-home-with-michael-mohammed-ahmad/.
2 Patrick White, "The Prodigal Son," in *Patrick White Speaks* (London: Penguin, 1992), pp. 13–17 (p. 15).
3 Stan Grant, "On Australia Day, is There a Song of our Divided Nation?," *ABC News*, January 25, 2020: www.abc.net.au/news/2020-01-26/on-australia-day-2020-is-there-a-song-of-our-nation/11892290. January 26 is the date that the First Fleet landed, now observed as Invasion Day/Survival Day or Australia Day.
4 Michael Mohammed Ahmad, "Interview with Simon Clark," *The Au Review*, March 13, 2018: www.theaureview.com/books/interview-michael-mohammed-ahmad-on-his-new-novel-the-lebs-and-the-inspiration-behind-it/.
5 Michael Mohammed Ahmad, "Lebs and Punchbowl Prison," *Sydney Review of Books*, November 29, 2016: https://sydneyreviewofbooks.com/essay/lebs-and-punchbowl-prison/.
6 Brigid Rooney, *Suburban Space, the Novel and Australian Modernity* (London: Anthem Press, 2018), p. 65.
7 Ahmad, "Interview with Simon Clark." The term "un-Australian" was popularized by Prime Minister John Howard in the 1990s. See also *Macquarie Dictionary*, s. v. "un-Australian".

8 Brigid Rooney, "The Novel in Australia from the 1950s," in *The Oxford History of the Novel in English: Volume 12: The Novel in Australia, Canada, New Zealand, and the South Pacific Since 1950*, eds. Coral Ann Howells, Paul Sharrad, and Gerry Turcotte (Oxford: Oxford University Press, 2017), pp. 81–96 (p. 81).

9 Anna Clark, *Making Australian History* (Melbourne: Vintage, 2022), p. 9. See also Christopher Bayly in Bayly et al., "AHR Conversation: On Transnational History," *The American Historical Review*, 111:5 (2006): 1440–1464 (p. 1449).

10 Martin Harrison, *Who Wants to Create Australia?* (Sydney: Halstead Press, 2004), p. 14. See also Rooney, "The Novel."

11 Roberto Schwarz, "The Importing of the Novel to Brazil and its Contradictions in the Work of Alencar," in *Misplaced Ideas: Essays on Brazilian Culture*, ed. John Gledson (London and New York: Verso, 1992), pp. 41–77 (p. 41).

12 See, Ken Gelder and Rachael Weaver, *Colonial Australian Fiction: Character Types, Social Formations and the Colonial Economy* (Sydney: Sydney University Press, 2017), p. 31ff.

13 Marcus Clarke as cited in Gelder and Weaver, *Colonial Australian Fiction*, p. 40; Joseph Furphy, *Such is Life: Being Certain Extracts from the Diary of Tom Collins* (Penrith: The Discovery Press, 1968), p. 205. The phrase "offensively Australian" is from an 1897 letter from Joseph Furphy to the editor of the Sydney *Bulletin*, Jules François Archibald, as cited in John Barnes, "Introduction," in *Such is Life*, n.p.

14 Sarah Comyn and Porscha Fermanis, "Rethinking Nineteenth-Century Literary Culture: British Worlds, Southern Latitudes, and Hemispheric Methods," *The Journal of Commonwealth Literature* (2021): pp. 1–18 (p. 3).

15 Comyn and Fermanis, "Rethinking Nineteenth-Century Literary Culture," p. 8.

16 Franco Moretti, "Conjectures on World Literature," in *Distant Reading* (London and New York: Verso, 2013), pp. 43–62 (p. 50). Cf. John Docker, *Australian Cultural Elites: Intellectual Traditions in Sydney and Melbourne* (Sydney: Angus & Robertson, 1974).

17 A. A. Phillips, "Australian Literature," in *Taking Stock: Aspects of Mid-Century Life in Australia*, ed. W. V. Aughterson (Melbourne: Cheshire, 1953), pp. 79–96 (p. 81); A. A. Phillips, "The Cultural Cringe," *Meanjin* 9.4 (1950), pp. 299–302 (p. 302).

18 J. M. Coetzee, as cited in Derek Attridge, "The South According to Coetzee," *Public Books* 25 August 2019: www.publicbooks.org/the-south-according-to-coetzee/. See also Raewyn Connell, *Southern Theory: The Global Dynamics of Knowledge in Social Science* (Cambridge: Polity Press, 2007).

19 Coetzee in Attridge, "The South According to Coetzee." See also Elleke Boehmer, "The South in the World," in *Worlding the South: Nineteenth-Century Literary Culture and the Southern Settler Colonies*, eds. Sarah Comyn and Porscha Fermanis (Manchester: Manchester University Press, 2021), pp. 378–391 (pp. 380–381).

20 Ivor Indyk, "Publishing from the Provinces," *Sydney Review of Books*, February 18, 2020: https://sydneyreviewofbooks.com/essay/publishing-from-the-provinces.

21 See, for instance, Ivor Indyk, "The Provincial Imagination," *Music & Literature: An Arts Magazine* 3 (2013): pp. 45–56 and Indyk's other essays.

22 This question is the subtitle of a significant volume: Robert Dixon and Brigid Rooney's *Scenes of Reading: Is Australian Literature a World Literature?* (North Melbourne: Australian Scholarly Publishing, 2013).

23 Ben Etherington, "Unsettled Poetics: Contemporary Australian and South African Poetry," *Wasafiri* 31.2 (2016): pp. 1–4 (p. 1).

24 Philip Mead, "Proust at Caloudra," *JASAL: Journal of the Association for the Study of Australian Literature* 14:5 (2014): pp. 1–14 (p. 1).

25 Marcia Langton, *"Well, I Heard It on the Radio and I Saw It on the Television ..."* (Sydney: Australian Film Commission, 1993), p. 46. See Giles's chapter.

26 Crystal McKinnon, "Indigenous Music as a Space of Resistance," in *Making Settler Colonial Space: Perspectives on Race, Place and Identity*, eds. Tracey Banivanua Mar and Penelope Edmonds (London: Palgrave Macmillan, 2010), pp. 255–272 (p. 256). The literature on settler colonialism often takes Patrick Wolfe's discussion of the "elimination of the native" as foundational. For discussion of Wolfe's work and his legacy in the Australian context, see Shino Konishi, "First Nations Scholars, Settler Colonial Studies, and Indigenous History," *Australian Historical Studies* 50.3 (2019): pp. 285–304.

27 Luke Carman, "To the Eye Untrained," in *Gerald Murnane: Another World in This One*, ed. Anthony Uhlmann (Sydney: Sydney University Press, 2020), pp. 13–28 (p. 21).

28 Edward W. Said, *Culture and Imperialism* (London: Vintage Books, 1994), p. xii.

29 Said, *Culture and Imperialism*, pp. xii–xiii.

30 See Alexander Beercroft, "Rises of the Novel, Ancient and Modern," in *The Cambridge Companion to the Novel*, ed. Eric Bulson (Cambridge: Cambridge University Press, 2018), pp. 43–56.

31 Said, *Culture and Imperialism*, p. 84.

32 Ian Watt, *The Rise of the Novel: Studies in Defoe, Richardson and Fielding* (Berkeley: University of California Press, 1957), p. 31.

33 Watt, *The Rise of the Novel*, pp. 63–65.

34 Karen Downing, *Restless Men: Masculinity and Robinson Crusoe, 1788–1840* (London: Palgrave Macmillan, 2014), pp. 1ff.

35 Alan Atkinson, *Europeans in Australia: A History. Volume 1 – The Beginning* (Melbourne: Oxford University Press, 1997), p. 41. See also Suvendrini Perera, *Australia and the Insular Imagination: Beaches, Borders, Boats, and Bodies* (New York: Palgrave Macmillan, 2009), p. 25.

36 Daniel Defoe, *Robinson Crusoe*, ed. Thomas Keymer (Oxford: Oxford University Press, 2007), p. 45.

37 Judith Wright, "Introduction: Australia's Double Aspect," in *Preoccupations in Australian Poetry* (Melbourne: Oxford University Press, 1965), pp. xvi–xvii.

38 Wright, "Introduction," p. xii; John Kinsella, "Introduction," in *A Human Pattern: Selected Poetry* (Manchester: Carcanet Press, 2010), p. xxii.

39 Eve Tuck and K. Wayne Yang, "Decolonization is Not a Metaphor," *Decolonization: Indigeneity, Education & Society* 1.1 (2012): pp. 1–40 (p. 8).

40 Wright, "Introduction," pp. xv–xvi.

41 On this slippage between prison and paradise, see Elizabeth McMahon, *Islands, Identity and the Literary Imagination* (London: Anthem Press, 2016), p. 194.

42 Wright, "Introduction," p. xviii.

43 On Wright's activism and its relation to her writing, see Brigid Rooney, *Literary Activists: Writer-Intellectuals and Australian Public Life* (St Lucia: University of Queensland Press, 2009).

44 Harrison, *Who Wants to Create Australia?*, p. 71; Jeanine Leane, "Historyless People," in *Long History, Deep Time: Deepening Histories of Place*, ed. Ann McGrath

and Mary Anne Jebb (Canberra: Australian National University Press, 2015), pp. 151–162 (p. 161). We are again transposing Roberto Schwarz' arguments about Brazil to the Australian context. The claim from Schwarz we are paraphrasing is: "In Brazil intellectual life seems to start from scratch with each generation. The hankering for the advanced countries' latest products nearly always has as its reverse side a lack of interest in the work of the previous generation of Brazilian writers, and results in a lack of intellectual continuity." See Roberto Schwarz, "Misplaced Ideas," in *Misplaced Ideas: Essays on Brazilian Culture*, ed. John Gledson (London and New York: Verson, 1992), pp. 1–18 (p. 2).

45 Tim Winton, "Remembering Elizabeth Jolley," *Westerly* 52 (2007): pp. 27–34 (p. 29).

46 Winton, "Remembering Elizabeth Jolley," p. 32.

47 Chris Wallace-Crabbe, "The Solitary Shapers," in *Essays on Australian Literature and Society* (Sydney: Angus & Robertson, 1974), pp. 3–11 (p. 3).

48 Wallace-Crabbe, "The Solitary Shapers," p. 3.

49 Wallace-Crabbe, "The Solitary Shapers," p. 3; Charles Harpur, "The Creek of Four Graves," in *The Poetical Works of Charles Harpur*, ed. Elizabeth Perkins (Sydney: 1984), pp. 161–162 (p. 161).

50 See Paul Kane, *Australian Poetry: Negativity and Romanticism* (Cambridge: Cambridge University Press, 1996).

51 Geordie Williamson, *The Burning Library: Our Great Novelists Lost and Found* (Melbourne: Text Publishing, 2012), pp. 8, 14.

52 Evelyn Araluen, "Too Little, Too Much," *Meanjin* 6 July 2020: <https://meanjin .com.au/blog/too-little-too-much>.

53 Alexis Wright, *Carpentaria* (Sydney: Giramondo, 2006), p. 436. Our claim here echoes and draws upon an argument in Ivor Indyk, "Assimilation or Appropriation: Uses of European Literary Forms in Black Australian Writing," *Australian Literary Studies* 15.4 (1992): pp. 249–260 (p. 249).

54 Araluen, "Too Little, Too Much."

55 Jeanine Leane, "The Vastness of Voice," in *Indigenous Transnationalism: Alexis Wright's Carpentaria*, ed. Lynda Ng (Sydney: Giramondo, 2018), pp. 211–214.

56 Wright, *Carpentaria*, p. 411.

57 Peter Minter and Belinda Wheeler, "The Indigenous Australian Novel," in *The Oxford History of the Novel in English*, pp. 285–299 (p. 285).

58 Kath Walker, "Interview," *Meanjin* 36.4 (1977), pp. 428–441 (p. 428). See also Penny van Toorn, *Writing Never Arrives Naked: Early Aboriginal Cultures of Writing in Australia* (Canberra: Aboriginal Studies Press, 2006), p. 3.

59 Minter and Wheeler, "The Indigenous Australian Novel," p. 284.

60 Minter and Wheeler, "The Indigenous Australian Novel," pp. 284–285.

61 Alison Whittaker, "White Critics Don't Know How to Deal with the Golden Age of Indigenous Stories," the *Guardian*, March 15, 2019: www.theguardian.com/ australia-news/2019/mar/15/nakkiah-lui-indigenous-literature-white-criticism.

62 Alexis Wright, "*On Writing Carpentaria*," in *Indigenous Transnationalism: Alexis Wright's Carpentaria*, ed. Lynda Ng (Sydney: Giramondo, 2018), pp. 217–232 (p. 218).

63 Walter Benjamin, *The Storyteller Essays*, ed. Samuel Titan, trans. Tess Lewis (New York: New York Review Books, 2019), p. 9. See Ng's chapter in this volume for more on this comparison to Benjamin.

64 Alexis Wright, "Gulf Music," *The Australian*, June, 9, 2007: www.theaustralian
.news.com.au/story/0,20867,21853571-5001986,00.html; Wright, *Carpentaria*,
pp. 72, 56, 96, 108, 498, 50.

65 Wright, *Carpentaria*, pp. 146, 246.

66 Wright, *Carpentaria*, p. 50.

67 Wright, *Carpentaria*, p. 84; Geoff Rodoreda, "Orality and Narrative Invention
in Alexis Wright's Carpentaria," *JASAL: Journal of the Association for the
Study of Australian Literature* 16.2 (2016): pp. 1–13 (p. 5).

68 Wright, "On Writing *Carpentaria*," p. 218.

69 Alexis Wright, "A Self-Governing Literature," *Meanjin* (2020): https://meanjin.com.au/
essays/a-self-governing-literature/. See also Wright, "On Writing *Carpentaria*," p. 223.

70 Wright, "On Writing *Carpentaria*," p. 221.

71 Wright, "A Self-Governing Literature." See also Alexis Wright, "Politics of Writing," *Southerly* 62.2 (2002): pp. 10–20 (p. 20); Alexis Wright, "The Ancient Library
and a Self-Governing Literature," *Sydney Review of Books*, January 28, 2019:
https://sydneyreviewofbooks.com/essay/the-ancient-library-and-a-self-governing-
literature; Wright, "On Writing *Carpentaria*," p. 220.

72 Carlos Fuentes, *A New Time for Mexico*, trans. Marina Gutman Castañeda and
Carlos Fuentes (New York: Farrar, Straus and Giroux, 1996), pp. 22, 16.

73 Wright, *Carpentaria*, p. 386.

74 Wright, "A Self-Governing Literature."

75 Wright, "On Writing *Carpentaria*," p. 225.

76 See "What is CALD writing?", *Mascara Literary Review* www.mascarareview
.com/research.

77 For more detail, see Louis Klee, "A Forest Without Trees," *The Sydney Review
of Books*, August 24, 2018: https://sydneyreviewofbooks.com/essay/pinchas-
goldhar-collected-stories-herz-bergner.

78 David Carter, *A Career in Writing: Judah Waten and the Cultural Politics of a
Literary Career* (Canberra: Association for the Study of Australian Literature,
1997), p. 53. See also Tim Winton, "The C Word: Some Thoughts about Class
in Australia," *The Monthly* December 2013 to February 2014: www.themonthly
.com.au/issue/2013/december/1385816400/tim-winton/c-word#mtr.

79 Michelle de Kretser, *Questions of Travel* (Sydney: Allen & Unwin, 2014), p. 17.

80 De Kretser, *Questions of Travel*, p. 184.

81 Michelle de Kretser, "Tourists, Travellers, Refugees: An Interview with Michelle
De Kretser," *Journal of Postcolonial Studies* 52.5 (2016): pp. 572–580 (p. 573).

82 De Kretser, *Questions of Travel*, p. 314.

83 De Kretser, *Questions of Travel*, pp. 321–322, 186.

84 De Kretser, *Questions of Travel*, p. 184.

85 De Kretser, *Questions of Travel*, p. 396.

86 De Kretser, *Questions of Travel*, p. 250.

87 De Kretser, *Questions of Travel*, p. 216.

88 Behrouz Boochani, "Literary Prize Acceptance Speech – Full Transcript,"
the *Guardian*, February 1, 2019: www.theguardian.com/world/2019/feb/01/
behrouz-boochani-on-literary-prize-words-still-have-the-power-to-challenge-
inhumane-systems.

89 Joseph Slaughter, *Human Rights, Inc.* (New York: Fordham University Press,
2007), p. 48.

PART I

Contexts

I

JEANINE LEANE

Presencing

Writing in the Decolonial Space

Despite the slow trickle of Aboriginal-published literature that began to appear from the mid-sixties onwards with the appearance of Oodgeroo Noonuccal's poetry in 1964, First Nations writing did not really arrive on the Australian literary landscape until the aftermath of the 1988 bicentenary of invasion. Since then, settler critics' attempts to read this body of work have been largely filtered through existing paradigms of Western literary analysis. By contrast, this chapter offers a more culturally grounded framework for reading Aboriginal writing in post-invasion Australia.

As late as 1957, the settler critic Frederick Macartney produced an essay entitled "Literature and the Aborigines" in which he claimed that Aboriginal people were incapable of producing literature because "Aborigines [*sic*] blur the distinction between self and external objects."[1] Macartney's absurd argument met with no resistance from the white literary establishment. In the twenty-first century, while the surface of Australian literary critique appears to have shifted, a deeper investigation of white critical and scholarly reception of, and engagement with, First Nations literature reveals that Macartney's words still resonate with contemporary attitudes, if concealed by more euphemistic and contemporary turns of phrase.

Aboriginal people have written since the invasion. Since the 1790s, Aboriginal peoples have used writing in English as a tool of resistance. Nonfiction – in the form of pamphlets, posters, letters, and magazines – was published by Aboriginal activists and community members throughout the nineteenth and twentieth centuries. For example, Pearl Gibbs, David Unaipon, Jack Patten, and Fred Maynard all produced political activist pamphlets from the late nineteenth century onwards. However, this discussion focuses on the production of more conventional forms of writing - such as fiction and poetry by First Nations authors as it has appeared in print since the 1960s. Although the focus of this volume is, necessarily, the novel form, I wish to draw on the first published collection of Aboriginal poetry – generally regarded as the first work of literature published in English by an Aboriginal author. I wish to do so to elicit this moment as the beginning of the ongoing legacy of the limitations of white-settler critical engagement with First Nations writing. I wish to draw on the responses to the early poetry of Oodgeroo to clarify this problem. From there, I will go on to offer a more expansive way of reading that could be applied to all forms of Aboriginal literary production. The intention is to provide a more expansive framework through which to read and critique novels and long-form prose by First Nations authors. A key objective is to retheorize the space "between" reader and text, to encompass a wider view of the discursive space in which both text and reader "are produced" in contested knowledge terrains that interface in the same space of the nation simultaneously. A further aim is to elicit the intergenerational accretions of settler responses to First Nations writings that form a framework of perception against which Aboriginal writers are still struggling to receive honest critical engagement.

The first Aboriginal poetry collection to appear in print was *We Are Going* by the late Oodgeroo Noonuccal (*aka* Kath Walker) in 1964. Early critiques are largely negative and reveal more about white-settlers' expectations of, and attitudes towards, Aboriginal Peoples at the time than they do about Oodgeroo's creative production as a new form of poetics. It is worth considering some of these early reviewers and critics, as their works offer an important benchmark from which we can reflect on the present in relation to 1964 – the present and the past being interconnected rather than disconnected spaces. In her foreword to *Aborigines Now* (1964), a collection of thirteen anthropological essays, Marie Reay noted the publication of *We Are Going* and commented:

> Kath Walker, an aboriginal poet [*sic*], has shown considerable promise in a volume of verse that is mainly propagandist for her people, but I see a real danger that she and others may find recognition before their grasp of the craftsmanship of writing gives them the literary stature to justify it. I would not like to see their work acclaimed just because it is written by aborigines [*sic*] and not because of any intrinsic merit it may have: the prospect calls to mind a circus in which fleas and elephants are applauded because they perform actions that are commonplace in humans.[2]

An anonymous review, published in the *Australian Book Review* in 1964, claimed of Oodgeroo's poetry:

> This is bad verse [...] jingles, clichés, laborious rhymes all piled up, plus the incessant, unvarying thud of a single message [...]. This may be useful propagandist writing [...]. It may well be the most powerful social-protest material so far produced in the struggle for aboriginal [*sic*] advancement [...]. But this has nothing to do with poetry.[3]

Underneath the negative, chauvinistic approach to Oodgeroo's work is a clear "staking out" of territorial boundaries by settler critics, demarcating "poetry" and "merit" as nominally unpolitical, white, "neutral" space. Martin Heidegger noted that a border or boundary is signified not by where something ends, but where something else begins: its "presencing" [*anwesen* and *das Anwesen*].⁴ Evident here is the role of the limit, and the limitations of what *is* and *isn't* Western literature, according to Western academics. What may not be evident, though, is how constraining reviews and attitudes such as those above continue to be for white critics, reviewers, and scholars engaging with our writings. Settler poetry criticism, as evidenced by the two reviews above, sets up a clear boundary between what *is* and *isn't* poetry. Aboriginal poetry – the first literary work by an Aboriginal writer as such – is placed outside of this limit. Early settler reviewers saw this as a dismissal, a failing in Aboriginal writing to "fit" and/or conform to a set of literary guidelines, values, and protocols harking back to Macartney's claim. Notwithstanding, however, this hostility from the settler elite, Oodgeroo's works were selling very well to the public despite the hostility from the settler elite.

This chapter repositions these intended criticisms as signifiers of the limits of the Western literary imagination. The criticisms signify the failure of this imagination to grasp that its previous borders no longer contain or control what can be imagined with the imposed colonial paradigms of the English language, or that which is written by First Nations writers using the introduced colonial language through molding, repurposing, and, in some cases, disregarding the conventions imposed by the English language, and what is defined as literature in Australia by Aboriginal writers. This "beyond the limits" capacity of Aboriginal writing is what has thwarted Western engagement with, and nuanced rigorous critique of, our works since the 1990s, and continues to do so in the present moment.

A 2020 review of a recent collection of First Nations poetry and essays demonstrates this, and provides a stark reminder of how little, if at all, Western engagement and critique of our work has shifted. *Fire Front: First Nations Poetry and Power Today* (2020), edited by Gomeroi poet and legal scholar Alison Whittaker, was patronizingly reviewed by settler poet and critic, Geoff Page. Writing in *The Canberra Times*, Page claimed:

> Inevitably, most of the poetry is "political," just as Oodgeroo Noonuccal's was back in 1964 when, as Kath Walker, she first published *We Are Going*. Back then she described her poetry, unapologetically, as "sloganistic, civil-rightish, plain and simple." [...] Strangely, however, the overall levels of artistry displayed [in *Fire Front*] tend to be below the technical accomplishment seen so clearly in the work of Aboriginal actors such as Aaron Pedersen,

Leah Purcell and Deborah Mailman, or Aboriginal film makers such as Rachel Perkins, Ivan Sen and Warwick Thornton. For those who love poetry, it's sad to wonder why this should be so.[5]

Beyond the striking and worrying resonance between this critique and the older responses to First Nations writing cited above, what is apparent in the closing lines of Page's review is the persisting view that the benchmark of success or failure for Aboriginal writing is whether or not it satisfies a Western audience. This is the gap this chapter addresses – the gap between the writing and the critique. In this chapter, too, I seek to push and hopefully widen the horizon of Western literary analysis in its engagement with First Nations literature.

Frameworks of Reading and Interpretation

In 1987, settler academic Vijay Mishra drew on Edward W. Said's work to develop the term "Aboriginalism," which describes the literary establishment's "reduction of a culture to a dominant discourse" that "overpowers the pluralities of Aboriginal voices."[6] In the aftermath of Mishra's exposure of the ongoing academic and social discourse of Aboriginalism, settler academics such as Bob Hodge, Bain Attwood, and Stephen Muecke, for example, have examined historical and contemporary expressions of Aboriginalism in various contexts including education, film, literature, anthropology, archaeology, media, and theatre. But like previous academic lenses that have been used to "read," "interpret," and "place" First Nations peoples in the settler discourse of the colonial project (such as primitivism, protest, romanticism), these practices were later critiqued by those who first applied them. The assumption here was that such practices, now that they have been critiqued at the academic table are "done and dusted" and can now be "put on the shelf." Thus, the paradigm of Aboriginalism was subsequently disregarded in favor of new lenses of placement and "interpretation," such as postcolonialism. Literary faddism among Western academics in most cases obscures the text in favor of the "new" predetermined theory applied to it.

As a First Nations "subject" who has been read through these lenses, it is apparent that they do not disappear, but are merely subsumed into the new lens. Ironically, this is not a new experience for First Nations writers. Instead, it is a new name for an old practice with an extra tier added. The old lenses are subsumed into the new one and repackaged with a different label. Yet when deconstructed, it is apparent that the accretions of previous settler frameworks remain the building blocks or scaffolds of the new naming. For example, Aboriginalism is co-opted into the postcolonial frame of literary analysis. This has the effect of reclassifying the engagement with First Nations texts under a new name, while still applying a reductionist deficit analysis and the same constraining binaries. Chickasaw literary scholar Chadwick Allen has summarized the Western binary approach to reading First Nations literature as a tendency to reduce discussions to "poetry" or "story" vs. "protest," "literature" vs. "propaganda," and/or "techniques" vs. "themes."[7] And to Allen's list I would like to add the continuing and constraining "urban" vs. "traditional" binary. These binaries have been and still are in many cases the central rubric of critical assessment and formal scholarship. The centrality of the binary has only intensified since 1964, as evidenced by more recent reviews of *Fire Front*.

The Postcolonial Myth in Settler Literary Analysis

It is crucial to critique the application of the terms "postcolonial" or "post-colonialism" for settler colonies such as Australia, Aotearoa New Zealand, or Turtle Island Canada, and the United States. Colonialism is an ongoing structure – a continuing process in such nations, not a single event after which the colonial power left.[8] Under a different name postcolonialism *is* Aboriginalism that is applied by settler academics across First Nations Countries invaded by the British Empire. Settlers' continual application of a postcolonial framework to our writings is not only oblivious to the ongoing benefits of colonialism for settler readers and critics living on stolen land. It also recolonizes our writings by placing them within settler understandings of changes *in* and *to* the external appearance of the ongoing colonial structure, which a settler majority can preemptively celebrate as progress.

For example, the colonial governments of the late twentieth and early twenty-first centuries *may* demonstrate a greater awareness and recognition of the rights of First Nations peoples than previous colonial governments and, therefore, from a settler perspective, colonialism has "shifted." The fact that First Nations peoples are more visible in the media – in music, in journalism, in visual and performing arts, in academia and literature, and so on – may be interpreted by a settler audience as a postcolonial development. However, this is not postcolonialism, but the resistance and presencing of First Nations peoples through our creative literary works in a *continuing* colonial structure. For Aboriginal writers, this is an act of resistance regardless of the literary mode used to express that resistance. The very act of refusing invisibility through creative expression is itself stepping out of the colonial subject positions deployed to silence Aboriginal voices and stories.

Presencing – the Ever-Now

I am using Heidegger's term "presencing" as a way of referencing the present continuous to describe something that *is* happening in a continuum. Grammatically, the present continuous verb tense can be used to describe both events that are happening in the *present* – right now, while you are talking about them – or in the foreseeable future, something that may or will happen later on. The term has a connectedness that, as a reading framework, could open a space for a more expansive, nuanced, and rigorous reading and reviewing/critiquing of First Nations work. In a settler colony, presencing describes acts of cultural production, in this case literature, that form part of a continuing decolonial force within a broader colonial structure. Decolonial is not post-colonial. Decolonial writing entails a continued eliciting and critique of the shifting exterior of colonialism through policies, practices, and discourses that attempt to mask and obscure the deeper unchanging origin of stolen lands and the ongoing benefits through dispossession.

Driftpile Cree First Nations scholar Billy-Ray Belcourt refers to settler engagements with our writings and the continuing practice of naming our works within a settler framework as a process of "fatal naming rituals."[9] Belcourt notes that: "In narratives that hinge on proving our humanness, Indigenous people sit stilled in the role of the described. As described, our words are pit against us."[10] Here Belcourt aptly and eloquently captures the current state of settler literary analysis of and engagements with First Nations writings as a type of cognitive cannibalization of our creative productions. He goes on to say that:

> We are all caught up in the Singularity of coloniality. But, each book, each poem, each story, is against the trauma of description, those ways of reading and listening that make vampires out of people, possessed by an insatiable hunger for a racialized simplicity that makes us into objects of study to be fed through the poorly oiled machine of analysis.[11]

Writing against the trauma of description – the tyranny of labels assigned to our works by a foreign academy – means continuing to *presence ourselves* through our creative works *and* through our own frameworks of culturally inclusive and expansive critique. Belcourt emphasizes the significance of what I refer to as presencing in different words in the powerful conclusion to his essay: "All of my writing is against the poverty of simplicity. All of my writing is against the trauma of description. There is only here here, only land here."[12] Presencing means the recognition that First Nations works are happening in the same "now" as the settler reader. The writer and the reader are in the same moment in time, but *this moment in time* is interpreted from different cultural standpoints and perspectives. First Nations writers and settler readers share the same temporal interface and interpret it from different sociocultural perspectives.

Torres Strait Islander academic Martin Nakata has suggested that:

> What is needed is consideration of a different conceptualisation of the cross-cultural space, not as a clash of opposites and differences but as a layered and very complex entanglement of concepts, theories and sets of meanings of a knowledge system.[13]

It is important for settler readers to carefully consider how they are part of the decolonial project to address the lies and omissions that continue to shape Australian history. As we have seen, the insistence of contemporary settler critics on patronizing and reductive interpretive lenses does not demonstrate a willingness to come to terms with this reality. To reflect back on the earlier reviews of Oodgeroo's work in comparison to the words of First Nations critics such as Nakata and Belcourt is to elicit the stark contrast between the strength and nuance of scholars and critics at the interface and the largely stagnant and static trajectory of white-settlers' engagement with First Nations and other minority literatures.

The Present Moment

Alison Whittaker describes the current crisis in a 2019 article published in the *Guardian* entitled "White Critics Don't Know How to Deal with the Golden Age of Indigenous Stories." Whittaker is worth quoting at length here:

> Blak literature is in a golden age. Our white audiences, who are majorities in both literary industry and buying power, are deep in an unseen crisis of how to deal with it. It's taboo for us to acknowledge this crisis; instead Blak writers are expected to meekly show gratitude for the small white gestures that get us onto the page or stage where we belong. [...] That devaluation is maybe most visible in how those voices are critically engaged with, prevalent across a whole gamut of white reviews – positive and negative – that evade dealing with the text before them. Many responses to Indigenous literature obligingly call it "important", as if that was a useful assessment rather than an empty flattery.[14]

As Whittaker pointed out, more recent analysis of Aboriginal writing focuses on dilemmas and constraints *for* Aboriginal writers. For example, as First Nations writers giving representation to our world, shaped through a different knowledge tradition and a particular historical/colonial experience, but constricted in the telling by the English language and its literary styles and conventions. Or as writers whose representations from Aboriginal standpoints are sites for judging the validity, credibility, and truth of Aboriginal identity and experience according to Western framings of what it means to be Aboriginal. Interestingly, the constraints of the settler cultural standpoint and the limited Enlightenment literary language that goes with it are rarely, if ever, questioned as a limitation

The authenticity of an "Aboriginality" grounded in centuries of anthropological discourse, alongside settler-perceived "difficulties of Aboriginal writers expressing ourselves in English," are together two of the most pernicious and limiting assumptions of the deficit discourse that settler readers, reviewers, and critics still bring to our literature. The irony and the tragedy of this is that it is *only* settler readers and critics who obsess over this deficit framework of authentic Aboriginality. The greater irony is that settlers themselves cannot agree on what is authentic for us. Meanwhile these futile debates distract from the actual writing we continue to produce in the present. It is also worth noting that the binaries that preoccupy much of the settler discourse around Aboriginal writing are also incapable of registering the fact that many Aboriginal writers deliberately invoke settler forms and traditions to disrupt and unsettle them, a practice of critique that is opaque to the deficit model's obsession with authenticity and language-loss.

Thus, the binaries I describe as an inherent part of settler criticism are also incapable of registering the fact that many Aboriginal writers (Alexis Wright, Kim Scott, Melissa Lucashenko, and Evelyn Araluen, to name just a few) deliberately invoke settler forms and traditions to disrupt, unsettle, and critique our colonizers. And here we are not taking the masters' tools and using them to dismantle their house. Audre Lorde aptly pointed out that the masters' tools will never dismantle their houses.[15] This is an example of First Nations writers wielding the masters' tools that have been forced upon us and using them just as effectively as our invaders to build our own safe houses of criticism and literary theory. The settler may enter but remember to leave your shoes at the door and be guided by the rules of those who own the houses. Likewise, the "concern" with which settler critics often lament the fact of Aboriginal literature being written in English: While none among us will deny that English is the language of the invaders that was forced upon Aboriginal peoples, that lament is ours to feel and to articulate – not yours. *You*, settler readers, are invited to engage with the works that we have very competently and very originally written in English. While a settler readership is "lamenting" that we no longer speak our first languages, it ignores the critique and the challenge our writing in English delivers in the *ever-now* and the *here-here* – temporalities that implicate the settler reading audience with an ongoing role as dispossessors in the colonial project.

The reality is that in the twentieth and twenty-first century, most Aboriginal writers speak English either first and/or equally alongside their first languages. Many of us, like me, have to go back as adults to First

Language programs to learn the language/s that should have been our birthright. While we never deny the injustice of this, this miscarriage of justice does not impact our ability to speak the colonizer's language. We are not incompetent English speakers, many if not most of us who are writers *do not* struggle to articulate ourselves in English. The recent spate of Miles Franklin-winning First Nations authors (Tara June Winch, Melissa Lucashenko, Alexis Wright, and Kim Scott) evidence this. Couched in the language of concern and lament, debates over our authenticity and our use of English move the focus of analysis away from a meaningful engagement with the literature we produce. Yet if the world of Aboriginal literature cannot transport settler readers across these historical, cultural, and (in some cases) imagined divides into the less familiar (for the settler reader) and thus far uncontemplated worlds of our experiences within the cultural interface that settlers and First Nations peoples now share, then how will the First Nations' position come to be represented outside the Western gaze? This is the space we find ourselves in, the crisis Whittaker describes.

How Do You Read in Someone Else's Cultural Space?

Quandamooka scholar Aileen Moreton-Robinson pointed out that the very act of writing by an Aboriginal person is a sovereign act.[16] Our literature operates as a decolonial act: speaking within the context of a colonial situation that has sought to erase and eliminate us constitutes by its very nature a decolonial force. Decolonial writing and decolonial critique are not only the work of Aboriginal writers, scholars, and activists. Exposing ongoing colonial forces through decolonial critique is ideally the responsibility of settlers, too – at least those with a commitment to the ongoing process of reconciliation and the addressing of social justice agendas. And, most importantly, for the purposes of reading and reviewing, decolonial does not mean *grounded in polar difference or divided by unbridgeable binaries*. The decolonial space must be an interface between First Nations writers and settler readers and critics.

Nakata posited the cultural interface visually. For example, the spaces in which daily life is enacted, such as homes, schools, universities, and workplaces, which intersect with theoretical and conceptual spaces, like mindmaps and/or emotional and intellectual ways of knowing and understanding the world. For the purposes of settler literary engagement with First Nations writings, let us consider a First Nations-authored text as a physical/visual animate space intersected by, and interpreted through, settler colonial emotional and intellectual ways of knowing and understanding. The disconnect that Whittaker and Belcourt identify now becomes clearer. The problem becomes *how* the space of the text is entered into. Or, in other words, to use a visual analogy, settler colonial readers have a literary suitcase permanently packed in the mind that allows them to sojourn comfortably within the space of another Anglo-Euro authored text. When it comes to a First Nations work, however, settler readers have packed the wrong suitcase. They've brought a tightly packed bag of northern-hemisphere attire to the southern hemisphere, more specifically to Australia, the largest landmass in the southern hemisphere, where the climate, topography, history of place, First People of place, philosophies of self and ownership are completely different. First Nations peoples, on the other hand, have, for quite some time now, had to pack a different suitcase. A suitcase that will enable us to exist in two spaces simultaneously. We have been aware for quite some time now of how to survive and thrive in a settler space that is not necessarily to our liking, but is the only space we have available under the colonial structure. Settlers, though, are mostly not accustomed to moving between two spaces, and are largely unaware of how *they are influenced and effected by our presence in the same space.*

Conclusion: Where Do We Go from Here?

To be a First Nations person in Australia (and other settler colonies) today is to live and write within the space of entanglement. We inherit the literatures and the stories of our ancestors that existed and continue to exist within the colonial structure. But we also make new stories of our experiences, concerns, her/histories, and aspirations in the cultural interface that is inhabited by both First Nations and settler peoples. Our literature is part of our agency in the entangled space of the interface. Maintaining agency within this space and making and keeping this as a decolonial space is key to achieving and maintaining sovereignty of the mind. To be entangled is to recognize that the flow of agency moves both ways. We alter our tools as our tools alter us.

The decolonial space is the reversal of the colonial space. Settler readers need to enter as an outsider – leave your Western literary toolkit at the door. Some of it may be useful, but do not assume it. In my teaching of creative writing alongside teaching First Nations literature to a mainly settler demographic, I make use of the following writing analogies when critiquing the ongoing and pernicious practice, central to white privilege, of writing otherness from the outside. For example, producing novels and similar creative works that seek to describe and, in some cases, speak from and for First Nations' (and other minority) perspectives. In using these analogies, I am borrowing from African American scholar and teacher Nisi Shawl. Shawl describes three types of writing positions that she has identified from which outsiders attempt to write "otherness."[17] I have adapted and critiqued these to my own classroom practice as both reading and writing positions.

The first of these, as described by Shawl, are people who write from the position of an *invader*. Invaders come uninvited; they steal, appropriate, take what they want, dispossess, and do not acknowledge their thefts. In Australian literature, the invader readers can be seen in the works of the Jindyworobaks of the 1930s and 1940s, who appropriated Aboriginal language/s and stories to sell "uniquely Australian" poetry and prose and develop a body of critique around such works. Or novelists such as Katharine Susannah Prichard and Patrick White, who appropriated an Aboriginal story or characters and language to tell a white story. It would be a mistake to think that settler readers no longer deploy invader reading positions.

The second is the *tourist*. Tourists are expected to pay their way – and, for the most part, they do. But tourists spell pain, too, because they are not invited and frequently pop in and out of a situation/scene/or place with no or at best very superficial knowledge of that place or situation. Tourists are voyeuristic and frequently form impressions and opinions of places and/or peoples based on their limited outside position as one who is just passing through. Their perspective is informed by the values of their outsider status. Tourists take souvenirs to prove that they have been somewhere, albeit briefly and without engaging with the locals and the locales beyond the resort. They leave a lot of rubbish and refuse for locals to clean up. Tourists present false and shallow representations of the place they have just visited to the rest of the world. Tourists have no sense of reciprocity. It is all just take, take, take. A typical tourist critic is one who is eager to consume the latest Aboriginal book and write about it through Western theoretical lenses, once more performing settler entitlement to the containment of Aboriginal expression. This kind of critic expects a constant supply of Aboriginal works for their consumption because they see it as "educative" or at the very least "the right thing to do," yet the level of engagement they offer does not extend beyond their standard Western literary toolkit.

The third writing position is that of the *visitor*. A visitor is invited into a space/place situation. A visitor (ideally) will come respectfully into another's space, bearing in mind that it is *not their space*. A visitor will (ideally) understands that the protocols, practices, values, expectations, and stories in the place to which you are invited will not necessarily be the same as the one they left. And, visitors will ideally ask for some advice in advance about what to pack in their suitcases before they arrive and enter someone else's space.

With my own variations, I use Shawl's critiques of writing positions in my teachings of First Nations literatures. Some settler reviews and critiques like those of Macartney and the early engagements with Oodgeroo's works are written from the judgmental, dismissive, and dispossessive perspective redolent of the invader. Most settler critique in the late twentieth- and early twenty-first century is written from the tourist perspective. What this means for the settler reviewer/scholar is that your theorizations of our works are not unexpected. But you come with a lot of (in most cases too many) assumptions and you are not necessarily invited. Also, you don't ask what you need to pack in your cognitive suitcase. You just arrive with one already packed. And, for the most part, you don't ask if the representation/critique you make and present to the world *is* truly representative, or if it is just reconsuming and repackaging to your own liking. The reading position that should inform settler engagements with our work should be that of the visitor, or the invited guest, as I like to tell my students. This involves doing and committing to the following: Don't come with lots of questions. Come to listen. Leave your questions at the door. Begin every Indigenous text with the premise that this is a statement of Aboriginality now. Not how authentic is it? Or do I recognize it? Ask: How does this First Nations story implicate me (not how is it about me/or what is this about outside of me)? How am I, as a settler, implicated? What responsibilities do I have as a reader of this text? How do you, the settlers, engage with this work as a piece of literature while simultaneously engaging with this writing as a critique of Australian society that *you* are also part of? In answering, the first and foremost responsibility of settler readers is to listen and resist the temptation to speak. *This is cultural protocol.* You earn the right to speak and do not speak until you have listened.

To take the point above into the field of critique and literary analysis means resisting the temptation to write first. My experience of Western academics is that they are very eager to write about First Nations works and, in doing so, to pull out one of the Western theorists in their tightly packed cognitive suitcase and apply them. But applying *only* Western theorists to First Nations works only has the effect of recolonizing our writings. Colonizers occupy space and decolonizers yield it. I also hear it said among settler circles that they are "advocating" for First Nations works through and by writing about it. But, as Palyku author and legal scholar Ambelin Kwaymullina points out in their groundbreaking charter towards decolonization, *Living on Stolen Land* (2020), any ethical advocate seeks to make themselves "redundant."[18] Furthermore, as a settler writer, you are not advocating for First Nations writing by recolonizing it with Western theories. If you are only applying Western theorists to Aboriginal Australian writing, then your scholarship is lazy at best, and reductionist at worst. As Alison Whittaker points out:

> It feels like a moment where we are angry and ready enough to address how white Australian review culture maligns Indigenous work by only superficially engaging with it. It feels like a moment where we are ready to sustain our own review culture. We have centuries of white engagement with Indigenous story as evidence for the need to change; we also have our own critics, who show us what's possible when whiteness loses its frame of evaluative authority over a work.[19]

In the twenty-first century, there are no excuses for settler academics not engaging with the works of First Nations theorists both at home and abroad. First Nations scholars such as Aileen Moreton-Robinson, Martin Nakata, Alison Whittaker, Larissa Behrendt, Ambelin Kwaymullina, and Jennifer Kemarre Martiniello in Australia, in addition to First Nations scholars in North America such as Eve Tuck, Chadwick Allen, Daniel Heath Justice, and Leanne Betasamosake Simpson, provide a wealth of sociocultural commentary and critique that can be fruitfully combined with First Nations literature. It is the works of these and other First Nations scholars to which settler academics should be referring first if they are serious and earnest about taking responsibility for yielding their own space to make way for a shared decolonial space.

The Aboriginal text is not an inanimate object to be studied from outside, from which information is to be gleaned. It is an animate textual space that speaks to readers and implicates and locates readers in the interactive "now" of the First Nations writer. Contemporary Aboriginal long-form prose is a site of deliberate engagement with and resistance to the tropes and binaries that settler Australian writing continues to use in engaging with First Nations writers and our experiences. In concluding, I ask: What would a literary landscape that truly recognizes and acknowledges Aboriginal literary excellence look like? In answering, I would like to return to the invited guest model. Any movement towards a recognition of the complexity, nuance, and agency of contemporary First Nations writings must be led by First Nations scholars, reviewers, and critics who can model more culturally appropriate language and frameworks to raise the benchmark of existing literary critique. It also requires an acknowledgment that settler understandings of Aboriginality, based on a long trajectory of literary and historical misrepresentation, need to be unlearned and permanently packed away. Settlers need to approach our works with an empty cognitive suitcase and wait to be told what to bring into someone else's space. In this case, come as an invited guest into the textual realm of First Nations writing as literary presencing and be prepared to yield the colonial space that you are so accustomed to occupying to make way for decolonial critique, spearheaded by First Nations writers, thinkers, reviewers, and critics.

Notes

1 Frederick Thomas Macartney, *Australian Literary Essays* (Sydney: Angus & Robertson, 1957), p. 117.
2 Marie Reay (ed.), *Aborigines Now: New Perspectives in the Study of Aboriginal Communities* (Sydney: Angus & Robertson, 1964), p. xiv.

3 [untitled review of *We Are Going*], *Australian Book Review* (1964), p. 143.

4 See Richard Capobianco, "Presencing (*Anwesen*)," in *The Cambridge Heidegger Lexicon*, ed. Mark A. Wrathall (Cambridge: Cambridge University Press, 2021), pp. 603–605.

5 Geoff Page, "*Fire Front* Is an Ambitious Collection of First Nations Poetry," *The Canberra Times*, August 1, 2020: www.canberratimes.com.au/story/6851767/poetry-and-power-leap-off-the-page.

6 Vijay Mishra, "Aboriginal Representations in Australian Texts," *Continuum: Journal of Media & Cultural Studies* 2.1 (1987): pp. 165–188 (p. 165).

7 Chadwick Allen, "Dreaming in the Present Progressive: Kath Walker Across, Beyond, and Through an Indigenous 1964," *JASAL: Journal of the Association for the Study of Australia Literature* 17.1 (2017): pp. 1–16 (p. 7).

8 See J. Kēhaulani Kauanui, "'A Structure, Not an Event': Settler Colonialism and Enduring Indigeneity," *Lateral* 5.1 (2016): https://doi.org/10.25158/L5.1.7.

9 Billy-Ray Belcourt, "Fatal Naming Rituals," *Hazlitt*, July 19, 2018: https://hazlitt.net/feature/fatal-naming-rituals.

10 Belcourt, "Fatal Naming Rituals."

11 Belcourt, "Fatal Naming Rituals."

12 Belcourt, "Fatal Naming Rituals."

13 Martin Nakata, "Australian Indigenous Studies: A Question of Discipline," *The Australian Journal of Anthropology* 17.3 (2006): pp. 265–275 (p. 272).

14 Alison Whittaker, "White Critics Don't Know How to Deal with the Golden Age of Indigenous Stories," the *Guardian*, March 15, 2019: www.theguardian.com/australia-news/2019/mar/15/nakkiah-lui-indigenous-literature-white-criticism.

15 Audre Lorde, "The Master's Tools Will Never Dismantle the Master's House," in *Sister Outsider: Essays and Speeches* (Berkeley: Crossing Press, 2007; 1984), pp. 110–113.

16 See Aileen Moreton-Robinson, "Introduction," in *Sovereign Studies: Indigenous Sovereignty Matters*, ed, by Aileen Moreton-Robinson (Crows Nest: Allen & Unwin, 2007), pp. 1–11.

17 Nisi Shawl, "Appropriate Cultural Appropriation," *Writing the Other*, August 20, 2016: https://writingtheother.com/appropriate-cultural-appropriation.

18 Ambelin Kwaymullina, "Thoughts of Being an Ally of Indigenous Writers," *Justine Larbalestier* November 14, 2016: https://justinelarbalestier.com/blog/2016/11/14/guest-post-ambelin-kwaymullina-thoughts-on-being-an-ally-of-indigenous-writers. See also Ambelin Kwaymullina, *Living on Stolen Land* (Broome: Magabala Books, 2020).

19 Whittaker, "White Critics Don't Know How to Deal."

2

BRENDAN CASEY

Literary Visitors and the Australian Novel

A remarkable feature of settler Australian literature is that its founding poet, Barron Field, who published the hagiographically titled *First Fruits of Australian Poetry* in 1819, was in fact not a settler but a visitor. Born in London in 1786, Field arrived as the reluctant first judge of the Supreme Court of New South Wales in 1817, before uprooting again in 1828, when he was offered a posting as the Deputy Advocate Fiscal in Ceylon.[1] An equal transnational itineracy characterizes the life of Australia's first novelist, Henry Savery. Savery's fictionalized autobiography, *Quintus Servinton: A Tale Founded upon Incidents of Real Occurrence* (first published in three anonymous volumes, 1830–1831), dramatizes the misfortunes of an Englishman leading up to his penal transportation to Botany Bay, "bereft of home, of character, of property, of almost everything, desirable in life."[2] Savery's novel imagines a happy ending for its protagonist, recounting his return to a comfortable cottage in the Devonshire hills, where he retires with his ever-faithful wife. But the arc of the author's own life tended toward tragedy, not triumph: His wife left him in frustration in 1829, and, after being granted a provisional pardon in 1838, he was convicted once again of forgery two years later and died in Port Arthur, Tasmania, in 1842.

Savery's hapless personal trajectory has made him a difficult figure for Australian literary scholarship to parse, and he seldom receives more than a fleeting mention in histories of the Australian novel. This is not because he was dissatisfied with life in the antipodes; generations of later settler writers would describe equal feelings of alienation and unbelonging: Marcus Clarke's quintessentially gothic description of the "weird melancholy" of the Australian bush or the tragic journey into the unknown narrated in Patrick White's *Voss* (1957) being particularly potent examples.[3] However, as a British-born convict, unwillingly transported halfway around the world, Savery never fully identified with his Australian exile. His fiction trespasses on what has traditionally been considered the main business of a national literature: to learn to see a place clearly, to describe it in an original manner, appropriate to the new prospects it affords. England, rather than Australia, is Savery's main focus; an antipodean setting appears only in the third and final section of the novel, the colony's social life and natural landscape never explored with any realism, attention, or detail. Calling *Quintus Servinton* "infuriating" for the lack of insight it provides into the "*real* conditions of convict life in Australia in the 1820s," Brian Elliott writes that the "novel is, obligatory, but not very enjoyable, reading."[4]

Given this, it is possible to ask if Savery, our first novelist, can properly be considered an Australian writer? Is he better classified as a British novelist who was, by mistake and misfortune, compelled to write about Australia? To how many writers of Australia's colonial period might this description apply? What marks a novelist as Australian? These questions troubled the librarian and scholar E. Morris Miller when, in the late 1930s, he set about establishing Australian literature as an academic discipline. "[C]riticism cannot accomplish its purpose without the aid of bibliography," he wrote in an introduction to the two volume *Australian Literature from its Beginnings to 1935* (1940), the first attempt at a comprehensive definition and record of the field.[5] In compiling a chronology of Australia's novelists, poets, playwrights, and essayists, Miller's bibliography was intended as an assertion of cultural independence; his objective was to legitimize local literature, to emphasize its separateness from the foreign British canon; and to achieve this, he argued, boundaries needed to be enforced. In constructing the terms of this "scholarly apparatus," he was particularly uncertain how to treat writer-visitors, those authors "who have merely paid flying visits to Australia as tourists or globe trotters, and who, after returning to their homes, have ventured to write about Australia and its peoples."[6] His solution was to create a special appendix, titled "Non-Australian Authors of Novels Associated with Australia," in which to quarantine liminal figures who disturbed the mainstream of the settler canon.[7] Some transnational writers could not be exhumed without disturbing the foundations of the tradition Miller sought to establish – both Savery and Field make it into the bibliography proper – but other more influential, arguably more significant, writers are segregated to the appendix: Anthony Trollope, for instance, who wrote an enormously popular two-volume travelogue after visiting the antipodes in 1871–1872, and two Australian-set novels, *Harry Heathcote of Gangoil* (1874) and *John Caldigate* (1879).

Revisiting these foundational questions in the introduction to *Australian Literature: Postcolonialism, Racism, Transnationalism* (2007), Graham Huggan ponderously suggests that it is "reasonable to expect that an Australian passport should be the minimum requirement for eligibility as an Australian writer."[8] Citizenship, as a minimum condition for membership of the canon, was not available to Savery, who wrote prior to Federation in 1901. But, significantly, the arrival of European colonizers in Australia in 1788 coincides with the advent of modern ideas of nationality, which, as Benedict Anderson argues, emerged in the wake of the French Revolution and Enlightenment debates about what it meant to owe allegiance to a particular sovereign or a certain territory.[9] And, prior to the birth of Australia as a nation-state, local distinctions between the "native-born" and the "new chum," the settled local and the unassimilated new arrival, were already a significant ideological feature of settler life.[10] Even today, nationality and residency are regularly affirmed as standard benchmarks by historians of Australian literature, if not at the explicit level of methodology, then in a more tacit approval, evidenced by the authors included in a scholar's canon. Australian literature, to quote poet-critic Andrew Taylor, is defined "always and inexorably, in terms of what it is not."[11] Penal transportation, migration, dual citizenship, and, most acutely, transnational visitation threaten an identity crisis at the limits of settler Australian literature. "Within these limits we have Australian writing," Taylor continues; "[b]eyond them we have something else."[12]

Much like the Dewey Decimal System of a library, scholarship preferences writers who can be neatly classified as one thing or another: either Australian *or* British, either the purview of Australian studies *or* the responsibility of a different discipline, but never the two simultaneously. These strict boundaries have been troubled by postcolonial studies and the renaissance of First Nations literature in Australia. The settler canon of "Australian literature" has imagined that it can accommodate the writing of Indigenous authors, at least since First Nations people were granted citizenship in 1967. However, before the voices of the colonized shook the nationalist canon, non-Australian visitors who wrote Australian novels exposed the constitutive cracks in the settler canon's foundations.

D. H. Lawrence's *Kangaroo* (1923), composed in a flurry of literary inspiration during the author's brief visit in 1922, is a seminal Australian novel by an international visitor. It provides a compelling illustration of the troubling liminality of the novels produced by writer-visitors. Lawrence was in Australia for just over one hundred days, splitting his time (albeit not evenly) between Fremantle, Perth, Adelaide, Melbourne, Sydney, and the small township of Thirroul on the New South Wales coast. "The critical reception of a novel about Australia by [...] a brilliant English sojourner" could be seen as a literary coup, but, as Brigid Rooney writes, academic and nonacademic responses to the novel have "been ambivalent."[13] "Until the 1950s," recalls sociologist Peter Beilharz, "university courses in Australian literature began with *Kangaroo*," but this curriculum today seems a relic of "colonial attitudes and perhaps especially of the cultural cringe."[14] For Katherine Susannah Prichard, who belatedly reviewed the novel in 1950,

"[*Kangaroo*] is a reflection of Lawrence in Australia, [and has] little reality where the people of our country, their struggles, aspirations and achievements are concerned."[15] The poet A. D. Hope shared Prichard's incredulity; in 1974, he wrote that Lawrence had devalued Australia as if the "continent itself has dominated and reduced the population, drawn it back into the fern age," while portraying settler Australians as "really sub-human."[16] It is a description which, ironically, might be applied to Hope's own poem "Australia" (1955): "[Australia's] five cities," he scathingly writes, "like five teeming sores / Each drains her: a vast parasite robber-state / Where second-hand Europeans pullulate / Timidly on the edge of alien shores."[17] Hope believed that he had earned the right to pass judgment on his home; Lawrence, the tourist, had not.[18]

To explain the smoldering hostility *Kangaroo* has triggered in some Australian readers, Beilharz turns to A. A. Phillips' influential essay "The Cultural Cringe," first published in the same 1950 issue of *Meanjin* as Prichard's negative review. The essay describes an awkward self-consciousness endemic to Australia as a provincial culture: "The Cringe mainly appears in an inability to escape needless comparisons," writes Phillips, identifying an almost embarrassed uncertainty, a lack of faith in one's own creative and critical faculties. "The Australian reader," he concludes, "hedges and hesitates," always conscious of the watchful eye of an imagined imperial auditor, "asking himself, 'Yes, but what would a cultivated Englishman think of this?'"[19]

Cringe, as a society-wide inferiority complex in which local achievements are measured and found wanting against the cultural products of the metropole, is captured in a memorable anecdote about J. I. M. Stewart, professor of English at the University of Adelaide from 1935–1945. Here, Geoffrey Dutton recounts Stewart's comments at the inaugural Commonwealth Literary Fund Lecture in 1940:

> Stewart took his place in the lecture theatre and said in his high voice: "I am most grateful to the C. L. F. for providing the funds to give this lecture on Australian Literature, but unfortunately they have neglected to provide any literature – I will lecture therefore on *Kangaroo* by D.H. Lawrence.[20]

As Dutton stresses, Stewart's words were meant as a self-deprecating joke (he was, in fact, a supporter of Australian art and culture, and his joke was met by laughter from his audience). But the story has since come to represent a kind of primal scene or original trauma for several Australian critics: "This insult to our literary pride was hardly Lawrence's fault," writes Susan Lever, "but it contributed to the residual hostility to his novel."[21] "When Professor Stewart reduced Australian literature to a single book by a foreign author," writes editor Michael Heyward, "he had available to him *The Fortunes of Richard Mahony, Such is Life, My Brilliant Career*, the stories of Lawson and Barbara Baynton."[22] In 2012, Heyward turned the anecdote into a rallying cry when launching Text Australian Classics, a series republishing under-recognized or forgotten books by Australian authors: "The Text Classics series is designed to unearth some of the lost marvels of our literature," Heyward wrote. "Stewart had the excuse of being an Englishman marooned in what he understood to be a colony of the mind. What's our excuse?"[23]

*

Lawrence, however, was alive to these foundational concerns, and a significant subplot of *Kangaroo* deals with the question of national literary culture. The novel recounts the experiences of Richard Lovat Somers, a poet, essayist, and recent arrival in Australia, who has fled old, decaying Europe, ravaged in the wake of World War II, to seek inspiration in the New World. While visiting Sydney, Somers attends meetings of a clandestine army of Diggers, a quasi-fascist paramilitary organization of returned servicemen led by Ben "Kangaroo" Cooley. Cooley, an avowed nationalist, understands the contribution writers make to a state's civic culture, and tries to recruit Somers to his cause: "I hope you are going to write something for us," he says; "Australia is waiting for her Homer – or her Theocritus."[24] This qualification, as Peter Conrad has noted, is significant, "because the founding of a literature requires you to get the genres in the proper order."[25] As Conrad identifies, Lawrence is alluding to the Virgilian *cursus* or progression, in which pastoral (symbolized here by Theocritus), must come before the Georgic and the Epic (Homer), not only in the apprenticeship of a poet, but in the development of a nation.

This is the historiographic narrative that Andrew Taylor ascribes to his reading of Australian literature: "Beginning as a process of submission yet imitation, then giving way to a rebellion leading finally through self-discovery to independence, it is clearly akin to the development of a child through adolescence to adulthood."[26] Ken Goodwin puts it more succinctly when he writes: "Writing in Australia obviously began as a literature metaphorically in chains, the shackles of British expectation of what a colony and its writing should be."[27] The idea of the settler nation as an infant culture, which over time and through hard labor achieves its aesthetic emancipation, is a conceit common to many colonial situations around the world, such as America, South Africa, and Aotearoa New Zealand. "A loosely chronological overview of Canadian literary production reveals a pattern of development," writes Marta Dvorak, "namely an initial period of imitation or emulation of metropolitan norms, then a configuration or shift towards assimilation, and finally – in a desire to forge a distinctive national culture – a reconfiguration or revaluation of that which had been considered marginal."[28] The Australian poet Judith Wright traces the same teleology in *Preoccupations in Australian Poetry* (1966), describing the settler poets of her generation as the first to express a quintessentially Australian point of view, "no longer as transplanted Europeans, [...] but as men with a present to be lived in and a past to nourish it."[29] It matters little that Wright believes she is describing actual movements in Australian cultural history, whereas Taylor admits his framework is an explanatory "trope," or indeed that their respective milestones fall at different dates; the overall shape of Wright, Goodwin and Taylor's historical arcs are near identical.[30]

In more recent decades, this developmental paradigm has begun to show signs of age. "Many presume that, today, great Australian writers do not need to be distinctly or vocally Australian," writes Nicholas Birns in *Contemporary Australian Literature: A World Not Yet Dead* (2015). "[I]n some quarters," he continues, "a collective Australian identity has become an embarrassment."[31] In acknowledgment of the confines of national literature as a category, postcolonial scholar Michael Griffiths adopts the concept of "~~Australian literature~~," to denote the ways "in which thinking 'Australia' is a necessary but insufficient condition for considering this settler-colonial political, legal, economic, social, and imaginary construct – and thinking it otherwise."[32] Yet, despite these methodological schisms and critical reorientations, the central ideal of national literary studies, the contention that there is a formative link between literature and the place of its composition, continues to inform much scholarship, albeit in more covert or sublimated ways. Take, for instance, Tony Hughes-d'Aeth's *Like Nothing on this Earth: A Literary History of the Wheatbelt* (2017), an ambitious study of writers working in and around Western Australia's fertile agricultural country, or Elizabeth Ellison and Donna Lee Brien's edited collection, *Writing the Australian Beach: Local Site, Global Idea* (2020), which includes essays ranging from the "coastal gothic" to filmic representations of the beach in Australian life.[33] Hughes-d'Aeth conceives of his scholarship not within a national but an ecocritical frame:

> The fact that country does not coincide exactly with bioregion – though they often speak to each other – opens up deeper epistemological differences that remain to be negotiated. No one is necessarily clamouring for a rebooted Jindyworobak syncretism, but there might yet be some value in a genuine dialogue about the spiritual (or in the current parlance, *more-than-human*) value of environment.[34]

Following Paul Giles, we might label Hughes-d'Aeth's grounding assumption an "isomorphic fallacy," an academic conceit that seeks to "encompass a particular bounded territory" and to "treat that space as emblematic of a particular kind of identity."[35] If Australia is too large, inchoate, and ideologically charged to function as a proper object of disciplinary study, then Hughes-d'Aeth argues that distinct biotas – the Australian wheatbelt, or the beach – might serve as manageable chronotopes of literary-historical attention.

*

The roots of the "isomorphic fallacy" in Australian letters can be traced back to Lawrence's *Kangaroo,* which was intended as the first contribution to an unfinished series of seven novels, each responding to the underlying spirit of one of the seven continents, which Lawrence hoped to visit.[36] "All art partakes in the Spirit of Place in which it is produced," he wrote in the November 1918 issue of the *English Review.* "Every great locality expresses itself perfectly, in its own flowers, its own birds and beasts, and lastly in its own men."[37] Straightforward though these statements may seem, Lawrence's claim must immediately be distinguished from the familiar notion that authors draw inspiration from the natural world (a hollow truism that he would have taken as self-evident). Instead, he argues that to understand literature one must first recognize the environment as an active collaborator, a secret co-author, essentially involved in its creation. Just as climate defines mountains, grasslands, and coastlines so, too, these same natural forces mold authors and their texts.

In *Kangaroo,* the spirit of place concept is mentioned explicitly in a passage recounting a moonlit walk through the South Australian hills, and might also be applied to a scenic description of coastal cliffs and gullies seen from a train window while travelling between Sydney and Thirroul (renamed Mullumbimby in the novel).[38] However, the book's most sustained treatment of the concept is also its most eccentric, and comes when Somers is accused of being a "pommy," an Australianism that Lawrence's narrator defines as follows: "A Pommy is a newcomer in Australia from the old country. *Teacher:* Why did you hit him, Georgie? *Georgie:* Please miss, he called me a Pommy. *Aussie* (with a discoloured eye): Well y'are one, ain'cher? Can I help that ch'are one?"[39] As the subsequent digression goes on to relate, the expression "pommy," used to describe an English tourist or recent settler in Australia, derives from pomegranate in two distinct ways. First, pomegranate – "pronounced invariably [in the Australian accent] pommygranate' – is a near perfect rhyme for immigrant (which, in a "naturally rhyming country [like Australia]," might alone satisfy the "etymologist[s]").[40] But pommy finds its second origin in an enduring visual gag: When first acclimatizing to Australia, Europeans can be recognized by their sunburnt foreheads and their "round and ruddy cheeks."[41] "So we are told," laments *Kangaroo*'s narrator, the English visitor's head swells up like a ridiculous, bright red fruit: "Hence again, pomegranate, and hence Pommy," he adds.[42] That the Australian climate changed Lawrence's body, specifically his blood, was the kind of formative environmental influence the author was anticipating.

Over a number of pages, Somers stews over the term, working through the word's various connotations, finding them slippery, unsettling, difficult to pin down. "Perhaps after all he was just a Pommy, prescribing things with overmuch emphasis, and waiting to feel God-Almighty in the face of unborn events."[43] Here, pommy speaks to Somers' connection to Old World values, to the cultural traditions of his native England, and to his inability to assimilate to a new climate and foreign way of life. Yet, in an almost immediate about-face, the novel offers an opposing perspective (once again voiced by Somers): "I am hopping and hissing like a fish in a frying-pan. Putting too much 'soul' into it. Far too much. When your blood has thinned down, out here, there's nothing but the merest sediment of a soul left, and your wits and your feelings are clear of it."[44] Blood, a quintessential Lawrentian concern, should be read as akin to the human soul or consciousness itself. Pommy here indexes a transformation that Somers is undergoing by the mere fact of being in Australia. Here, the English visitor is less anxious about being cast as an outsider, as someone too rigid in their loyalty to foreign convention, and is instead overcome with a rival concern: that he might in fact not be English enough; that travel has proved his character inconsistent, mutable, that in Australia he has entered a space of conversion.

This conversion – his response to the "spirit of [Australian] place" – is most thoroughly explored through Somers' relationship to Ben "Kangaroo" Cooley, who tries to convince the Englishman to use his pen in the service of his Australian political movement. His persuasive tactics oscillate between sinister, genteel charm and thuggish intimidation. He is a physically imposing presence:

> He was really tall, but his way of dropping his head, and his sloping shoulders, took away from his height. He seemed not much taller than Somers, towards whom he seemed to lean the sensitive tip of his long nose, hanging over him as he scrutinised him sharply through his eyeglasses, and approaching him with the front of his stomach.[45]

It is because of Cooley's S-shaped physique that he is given the nickname "Kangaroo," a creature that Lawrence elsewhere sketches in a poem: "Wistfully watching, with wonderful liquid eyes. / And all her weight, all her blood, dropping sackwise down / towards the earth's centre."[46] Indeed, Cooley's abnormally engorged belly becomes an object of immense fixation for Somers, who is at once attracted and repulsed by its protrusion: "A sort of magnetic effusion seemed to come out of Kangaroo's body, and [Somers'] hand was almost drawn in spite of himself to touch the other man's body."[47] Later, to complete the anthropomorphic metaphor, Somers adds: "you're such a Kangaroo, wanting to carry mankind in your belly-pouch, cosy, with its head and long ears peeping out."[48]

The barely closeted sensuality of this encounter is as surreal as it is undeniable; and themes of homosexual desire have been noted by numerous critics discussing *Kangaroo*.[49] Yet, as James C. Cowan observes, "[m]ale kangaroos *do not* have pouches," and there is also a maternal subtext that has been missed by academic readers.[50] Cooley describes his role as that of an expectant parent, explaining that his stomach is not "Abraham's bosom, but a pouch to carry young Australia in"; it is not a place of safety or refuge, but a womb within which the infant Australian culture can gestate.[51] His followers, he tells Somers, "are my children, I love them. If I'm not to believe in their generosity, am I to believe in your cautious, old-world carping, do you think. I won't!"[52] Throughout the novel, Somers fears that he is being transformed by his Australian experiences, that he will be reborn "with this curious transparent blood of the antipodes, with its momentaneous feelings and its sort of absentness."[53] As an English visitor he feels ill at ease and out of place. To lose this sense of alienation would be to admit his identification with the place, to stop being a visitor and become a settler, to be admitted to the Australian fold.

Lawrence's protagonist ultimately refuses the invitation to become Australian: He leaves the country for good after Cooley is assassinated at a political rally, symbolically shot in the stomach, "[b]ullets in my marsupial pouch," as the demagogue puts it in a deathbed letter to his departing friend.[54] But *Kangaroo*, an Australian novel by a British author, which has often been rejected on grounds of its faulty local credentials, has also perversely, as Peter Beilharz writes, left behind a legacy of "Australian intellectuals searching for the *genius loci* [...] that made us special in the face of European decline and the rise of mechanical civilisation in America."[55] *Kangaroo*, argues Beilharz, was instrumental in expressing what would become Australia's national literary character. Put another way, Lawrence's novel was foundational in establishing the aesthetic terms of its own exclusion from Australian literature.

*

If *Kangaroo* chafes (as much as it shapes) the mold of Australian literature, might Lawrence's novel instead be read alongside the Australian novels of other writer-visitors? Each of these authors can be seen to grapple with the same problem: how to reconcile their existing conception of literature with dislocating experiences away from home. Prior to his career as a novelist, Joseph Conrad worked as a merchant mariner and made four visits to Australia, experiences that he later recorded in memoir and short stories.[56] The strongest statement about Australia in his published oeuvre occurs in his late biographical essay, "On Geography and Some Explorers" (1924), in which he recounts how, while master of the iron barque *Otago* in 1888, he sailed up the east coast of New South Wales and Queensland, following the same route taken by Captain Cook and the *Endeavour* in 1770, or as Conrad puts it, "stepping in the very footprints of geographical discovery."[57]

Kanga Creek: An Australian Idyll (1922), the only work of fiction by British sexologist Havelock Ellis, is a loosely autobiographical story of how in 1870s the sixteen-year-old Ellis worked as a schoolteacher in New South Wales, and experienced all the agony and ecstasy of adolescence.[58] Published in 1922, the year before Lawrence's Australian novel, Ellis' idyllic romance raises the interesting question of what Australian literary modernism might have looked like had *Kanga Creek,* rather than *Kangaroo,* served as a founding document. Robert Louis Stevenson visited in 1890, and Sydney appears as a setting in his adventure novel *The Wrecker* (1892). Inspired by Stevenson, Marcel Schwob, the cult French author of *Le roi au masque d'or* [*The King in the Golden Mask,* 1892], followed the British novelist's example. He sailed to Australia, but the experience left him bitterly disappointed: "The voyage [was] mournful," the coastline "*horrible*" and, as he wrote in a letter to his wife dated February 1902, "[t]he crest of a bay in Tasmania is topped with a horrible pelt of black, naked, rigid, trees, whose branchless trunks stand on end as though in dread."[59]

After Lawrence's visit in 1922, the canon of visitor-novelists writing on Australia expands to include: Georges Perec (in 1981), Michel Butor, (in 1968, 1971, and 1976), and Haruki Murakami (in 2004), among many others. Perec and Butor were both resident scholars at the University of Queensland; Perec worked on his final, unfinished novel *53 jours* (*53 Days,* published posthumously in 1989), and Butor wrote an experimental text titled *Courrier des Antipodes* (*Letters from the Antipodes,* 1978). Murakami visited to fulfill a book contract to report on the 2000 Sydney Olympics: "You're probably wondering why I have come all this way just to see the Olympics?' he writes in シドニー! [*Sydney!,* 2004]. "If I think about it, I've never really been interested in the Olympics. Some time ago I came across a sentence in an American novel where the author wrote, "It's as boring as the Olympics."'[60] In a rare moment of elation, Murakami recalls Cathy Freeman's victory in the 400-meter event: "It moved everybody. I closely witnessed what it was like to melt something in a human. The most beautiful and the most charming moment in this Olympic Games."[61]

48

It could be argued that, since Lawrence's visit in 1922, the significance of the international traveler in Australian literature has waned, that the tyranny of distance between Australia and the globe that facilitates the visitor-novel has been defeated by the "quickening mobility of people and capital and technology," that the "timeless obstacles, imposed [...] by wide oceans and high mountains and long deserts, are being lowered."[62] "[A]ny place that you can get to by jet," observes the historian and naturalist George Seddon, "is unlikely to be very different from the place you just left."[63] Yet, even as the advance of globalization threatens to homogenize world culture and literature, the borders of the Australian nation-state seem a particularly durable institution. This irony takes on a particularly violent tenor in the life and writing of Kurdish-Iranian journalist, poet, and film producer Behrouz Boochani. In *No Friend but the Mountains* (2018), a novelistic memoir composed through a stream of clandestine WhatsApp messages, Boochani writes of his imprisonment on Manus Island, a victim of Australia's policy of indefinite mandatory detention for refugees arriving by boat without a visa. "What is a border?," asks Boochani. "My whole life has been impacted by the concept of 'border'."[64] His predicament is brought into stark contrast by the comparative freedom and mobility of his writing and ideas: In 2019, *No Friend but the Mountains* won Australia's most lucrative literary award – the Victorian Prize for Literature. As Louis Klee writes: "Behrouz Boochani's testimony has elevated him to a paradoxical position. Today he may be the most significant political voice in a country he has never visited."[65] Boochani represents, in a sharp way, the clarity of vision that can occur when you observe a place in which you are an absolute outsider.

The heterogenous anti-canon of visitor-novels cannot collectively be named a tradition, at least not in the intolerant sense that a category such as "Australian literature" aims to shape. As is implied by this idiosyncratic and disconnected group of figures (Trollope and Perec, Stevenson and Murakami, Conrad, and Boochani), the works of the visitor-novelists do not collectively present a neat arc away from the inauthentic visions of a *jardin exotique* toward authentic settlement in place, as presented by Wright and Taylor. Instead, in these novels, we encounter a series of landfalls, or what American literary historian Wai Chee Dimock has called a "criss-crossing set of pathways, open-ended and ever multiplying, weaving in and out of other geographies, other languages and cultures."[66] In *Through Other Continents: American Literature Across Deep Time* (2006), Dimock steps outside the spatial boundaries of the US to discover Henry James meditating, along with Veronese and Plutarch, on Alexander's victory in the Battle of Issus (333 BCE); Ezra Pound's treatment of world culture in *The Cantos* (1922–1962); and Robert Lowell's use of Horace to express his opposition to the Vietnam

War. Dimock proposes a new paradigm for American literary studies, one that seeks to wrench Americanists out of their habit of thinking within the confines of national geography. Instead, she takes a *longue durée* view and wonders "[w]hat would American literature look like restored to a [...] scale enlargement along the temporal axis that also enlarges its spatial compass?"[67] It is a question with even grander implications for a comparatively young, geographically remote discipline like settler Australian literature.

Dimock's key insight is that all places – whether cultural centers (like postwar America) or relative peripheries (like Australia) – are habitually provincial in their inwardness, ignorant of the "input channels, kinship networks, routes of transit, and forms of attachment – connective tissues binding America [or Australia] to the rest of the world."[68] In an essay from 1974, Australian art historian Terry Smith identified this intractable tension as the "The Provincialism Problem."[69] Considering the projection of the New York art market in the 1970s, Smith argues that New York is itself also provincial – even though, when viewed from the outside, it can seem like an aggrandizing universal. To argue against provincialism is merely to confirm it, insofar as it operates as a kind of "projection" that is evidenced all the more by the attempt to overcome it. Instead, rejecting its logic requires a cutting of the gordian knot: a more thoroughgoing appreciation of how centers and peripheries are co-constituted, each requiring the other not only to reflect, but to buttress, their position in global culture. Lawrence's *Kangaroo*, perhaps unwittingly, exemplifies this gesture: "giving back to Australians the provincialism which they had also invented."[70]

Notes

1 See Justin Clemens, "First Fruits of a Barron Field," *Critical Quarterly*, 61.1 (2019), pp. 18–36.
2 Henry Savery, *Quintus Servinton: A Tale Founded upon Incidents of Real Occurrence*, ed. Cecil Hadgraft (Brisbane: Jacaranda Press, 1962), p. 263.
3 Marcus Clarke, *Marcus Clarke*, ed. Michael Wilding (St. Lucia: University of Queensland Press, 1976), p. 33.
4 Brian Elliott, "Review of *Quintus Servinton: A Tale Founded upon Incidents of Real Occurrence* by Henry Savery," *Australian Literary Studies*, 1.1 (1963): pp. 70–72 (p. 72).
5 E. Morris Miller, *Australian Literature from its Beginnings to 1935* (Melbourne: Melbourne University Publishing, 1940), p. 1.
6 Miller, *Australian Literature*, p. 11.
7 Miller, *Australian Literature*, pp. 966–971.
8 Graham Huggan, *Australian Literature: Postcolonialism, Racism, Transnationalism* (Oxford: Oxford University Press, 2007), p. 11.

9 Benedict Anderson, *Imagined Communities: Reflections on the Origin and Spread of Nationalism* (London: Verso, 2006; 1983).

10 See Ken Gelder and Rachael Weaver, *Colonial Australian Fiction Character Types, Social Formations and the Colonial Economy* (Sydney: Sydney University Press, 2006), pp. 19–27.

11 Andrew Taylor, *Reading Australian Poetry* (St Lucia: University of Queensland Press, 1987), p. 21.

12 Taylor, *Reading Australian Poetry*, p. 10.

13 Brigid Rooney, *Suburban Space and the Australian Novel* (London: Anthem Press, 2018), p. 24.

14 Peter Beilharz, "Tocqueville in the Antipodes? Middling Through in Australia, Then and Now," *Thesis Eleven*, 65 (2001): pp. 51–64 (p. 56).

15 Katharine Susannah Prichard, "Lawrence in Australia," *Meanjin*, 9.4 (1950): pp. 252–259 (p. 252).

16 A. D. Hope, "D. H. Lawrence's *Kangaroo*: How It Looks to an Australian," in *The Australian Experience: Critical Essays on Australian Novels*, ed. W. S. Ramson (Canberra: Australian National University Press, 1974), pp. 157–173 (p. 162).

17 A. D. Hope, "Australia," in *The Penguin Book of Australian Poetry*, eds. John Tranter and Philip Mead (Ringwood: Penguin, 1991), p. 16.

18 Hope, "D.H. Lawrence's *Kangaroo*," p. 166.

19 A. A. Phillips, "The Cultural Cringe," *Meanjin*, 9.4 (1950): pp. 299–302 (pp. 299–300).

20 Geoffrey Dutton, *Out in the Open: An Autobiography* (St Lucia: University of Queensland Press, 1994), p. 90.

21 Susan Lever, "D. H. Lawrence's Australian Experiment," *Inside Story*, October 21, 2015: https://insidestory.org.au/dh-lawrences-australian-experiment/.

22 Michael Heyward, "A Classic is a Terrible Thing to Waste," *Text Publishing*, January 24, 2012: www.textpublishing.com.au/blog/a-classic-is-a-terrible-thing-to-waste.

23 Making a slight irony of Heyward's earlier article, in 2018 *Kangaroo* was republished as a Text Classic.

24 D. H. Lawrence, *Kangaroo*, ed. Bruce Steele (Cambridge: Cambridge University Press, 1994), p. 109.

25 Peter Conrad, "Sydney, Not the Bush," in *Best Australian Essays 2000*, ed. Peter Craven (Victoria: Black Inc, 2000), pp. 418–432 (p. 422).

26 Taylor, *Reading Australian Poetry*, p. 9.

27 Ken Goodwin, *A History of Australian Literature* (London: Macmillan, 1986), p. 5.

28 Marta Dvorak, "Fiction," in *The Cambridge Companion to Canadian Literature*, ed. Eva-Marie Kröller (Cambridge: Cambridge University Press, 2004), pp. 155–176 (p. 155).

29 Judith Wright, *Preoccupations in Australian Poetry* (Melbourne: Oxford University Press, 1966), p. xxii.

30 Taylor, *Reading Australian Poetry*, p. 10.

31 Nicholas Birns, *Contemporary Australian Literature: A World Not Yet Dead* (Sydney: University of Sydney Press, 2015), p. 21.

32 Michael R. Griffiths, *The Distribution of Settlement: Appropriation and Refusal in Australian Literature and Culture* (Perth: University of Western Australia Press, 2018), p. 23.

33 See Tony Hughes-d'Aeth, *Like Nothing on this Earth: A Literary History of the Wheatbelt* (Perth University of Western Australia Press, 2017); Elizabeth Ellison and Donna Lee Brien (eds.), *Writing the Australian Beach: Local Site, Global Idea* (London: Palgrave Macmillan, 2020).

34 Tony Hughes-d'Aeth, "Thinking in a Regional Accent: New Ways of Contemplating Australian Writers," *Australian Book Review* 426 (2020): pp. 24–26 (p. 26).

35 Paul Giles, *Virtual Americas: Transnational fictions and the Transatlantic Imaginary* (Durham, NC: Duke University Press, 2002), pp. 6–7.

36 Frieda Lawrence to Adelle Seltzer, November 10, 1923, in D. H. Lawrence, *The Letters of D. H. Lawrence*, eds. Warren Roberts, James T. Boulton, and Elizabeth Mansfield (Cambridge: Cambridge University Press, 2002), IV, p. 384.

37 D. H. Lawrence, *Studies in Classic American Literature*, eds. Ezra Greenspan, Lindeth Vasey, and John Worthen (Cambridge: Cambridge University Press, 2003), p. 167.

38 Lawrence, *Kangaroo,* pp. 13–15, 75–79.

39 Lawrence, *Kangaroo,* p. 147.

40 Lawrence, *Kangaroo,* p. 147. Indeed, this explanation is sufficient for the celebrated philologist Sidney J. Baker, who, in his landmark study *The Australian Language* (1945), writes: "'Immigrant' gave us *jimmigrant,* and although that last term has become obsolete [...] it provoked the rhyming slang *pomegranate* and that led to *pommy.*" Sidney J. Baker, *The Australian Language* (Melbourne: Sun Books: 1970), p. 379.

41 Lawrence, *Kangaroo,* p. 147.

42 Lawrence, *Kangaroo,* p. 147.

43 Lawrence, *Kangaroo,* p. 147.

44 Lawrence, *Kangaroo,* pp. 147–148.

45 Lawrence, *Kangaroo,* p. 108.

46 D. H. Lawrence, *The Poems*, ed. by Christopher Pollnitz (Cambridge: Cambridge University Press, 2013), p. 345.

47 Lawrence, *Kangaroo,* p. 138.

48 Lawrence, *Kangaroo,* p. 210.

49 See, for example, Murray S. Martin, "*Kangaroo* Revisited," *D. H. Lawrence Review* 18.2 (1985–1986): pp. 201–215; Howard J. Booth, "D. H. Lawrence and Male Homosexual Desire," *The Review of English Studies*, 53.209 (2002): pp. 86–107.

50 James C. Cowan, *D. H. Lawrence: Self and Sexuality* (Columbus: Ohio State University Press, 2002), p. 86.

51 Lawrence, *Kangaroo,* p. 122.

52 Lawrence, *Kangaroo,* p. 131.

53 Lawrence, *Kangaroo,* p. 148.

54 Lawrence, *Kangaroo,* p. 322.

55 Peter Beilharz, "Robert Hughes and the Provincialism Problem," *Reflected Light: La Trobe Essays*, eds. Peter Beilharz and Robert Manne (Melbourne: Black Inc, 2006), pp. 90–111 (p. 93).

56 See Joseph Conrad, *The Mirror and the Sea & A Personal Record*, ed. Zdzisław Najder (Oxford: Oxford University Press, 1989); Joseph Conrad, "A Smile of Fortune," *Twixt Land and Sea*, ed. J. A Berthoud (Cambridge: Cambridge University Press, 2008), pp. 9–77.

57 Joseph Conrad, *Last Essays*, eds. Harold Ray Stevens and J. H. Stape (Cambridge: Cambridge University Press, 2010). For a full account of Conrad's *Endeavour* re-enactment see Brendan Casey, "Cook, Conrad and the Poetics of Error," *JASAL: Journal of the Association for the Study of Australian Literature* 20.2 (2020): pp. 1–12.

58 See Havelock Ellis, *Kanga Creek: Havelock Ellis in Australia*, ed. Geoffrey Dutton (Sydney: Picador, 1989).

59 Marcel Schwob, as quoted in Victoria Reid, "Marcel Schwob and Robert Louis Stevenson: Encounters in Death and Letters," in *Franco- British Cultural Exchanges, 1880–1940*, eds. Andrew Radford and Victoria Reid (London: Palgrave Macmillan, 2012), pp. 131–150 (p. 148).

60 Haruki Murakami, as quoted in Leith Morton, *The Alien Within: Representations of the Exotic in Twentieth-Century Japanese Literature* (Honolulu: University of Hawai'i Press, 2009), p. 197.

61 Haruki Murakami, シドニー!, trans. Tets Kimura, typescript.

62 Geoffrey Blainey, *The Tyranny of Distance: How Distance Shaped Australia's History* (Sydney: Pan MacMillan, 2001), p. 361.

63 George Seddon, *Selected Writings*, ed. Andrea Gaynor (Carlton: Latrobe University Press, 2019), p. 66.

64 Behrouz Boochani, *No Friend but the Mountains*, trans. Omid Tofighian (Sydney: Picador, 2018), xx.

65 Louis Klee, "Cannibal Island: The Story of Refugee Incarceration Told Through WhatsApp," *Times Literary Supplement*, 6065, June 28, 2019: www.the-tls .co.uk/articles/manus-prison.

66 Wai Chee Dimock, *Through Other Continents: American Literature Across Deep Time* (Princeton: Princeton University Press, 2006), p. 3.

67 Dimock, *Through Other Continents*, p. 3.

68 Dimock, *Through Other Continents*, p. 3.

69 Terry Smith, "The Provincialism Problem," *Artforum* 8.1 (September 1974): pp. 54–59.

70 Beilharz, "Robert Hughes and the Provincialism Problem," p. 105.

3

PAUL GILES

Settler Colonial Fictions

Beyond Nationalism and Universalism

In his contribution to the *Penguin New Literary History of Australia* (1988), Peter Pierce lamented what he called "[t]he stasis of Australian literary historiography," the way it had become trapped in a self-perpetuating loop between "radical nationalists" who advocated the promotion of specifically Australian cultural values and "universalists" whose view of Australian literature was shaped by Eurocentric "accents of Oxbridge."[1] As Pierce acknowledged, the position of "each side" was always "less coherent than it has been in the interests of the other to pretend," but this tired opposition has led over the years to many oversimplifications of the subject.[2] The purpose of this chapter is not only to consider how settler colonial fictions contributed to the emergence of Australian literature in the second half of the nineteenth century but also to scrutinize some of the methodological assumptions and dilemmas involved with the subject's institutionalization.

The term *settler* (as in "Old Emigrant Settler') was already a cliché in Australia by the 1820s, and "settler colonialism" has itself been described by Lorenzo Veracini as "a largely Australian developed category," one that brings together domestic settlement with the politics of colonial authority.[3] "For Patrick Brantlinger, such domesticity might be seen "almost to parody" imperialism, transposing its power structures into diminutive local forms.[4] Marcia Langton aptly remarked that it is now impossible to consider white Australian literature "as if none of the brutality, murder and land clearances occurred," and there is a clear parallel with recent revisionist criticism on nineteenth-century US literature, which, under the influence of Toni Morrison and many others, has reconstructed the American literary canon to highlight blind spots around categories such as "freedom" that were once thought to epitomize a national style in the frontier romances of James Fenimore Cooper, Herman Melville, and Mark Twain.[5] Yet just as Morrison evoked a richer and more multifaceted account of nineteenth-century US culture, so it is possible to reimagine nineteenth-century Australian literature within an enlarged, multidimensional critical framework.

One characteristic of Australian literature of this time is an imaginative blurring of categories, both generic and substantive. In Oliné Keese's *The Broad Arrow* (1859), set largely in Tasmania, it becomes difficult to distinguish settlers from convicts or convicts from slaves. The narrator comments acerbically: "though Mrs. Evelyn would sign an anti-slavery document with heartfelt abhorrence of the system, she in habitual theory was as much a slave-holder as any 'Down Southern'."[6] Published after the abolition of transportation, Keese's interest is more in the cultural legacy of this system. Scenes from Norwell's earlier life continue to haunt the dissolute army officer when he arrives in Australia to seek the woman he seduced and caused to be wrongly transported: he thinks of how the past "rises, like a ghost, before me."[7] This Janus-faced quality, looking in two directions simultaneously, also typifies Australian settler colonial fictions. These fictions, as Dorice Elliott observed, paradoxically embody an ontologically "unsettled status," looking back nostalgically to the familial "home" as well as forwards to prospects of material comfort and security.[8] Many nineteenth-century Australian novels feature an ironic situation of upper-class people preserving their genteel customs while adapting to life in rougher surroundings. In Mary Theresa Vidal's *Bengala; or Some Time Ago* (1860), which Elliott described as "an Austenesque comedy-of-manners," the Veseys, former residents of Bath, respond negatively to a polite question about whether they "begin to feel settled."[9] "'Why—hem—aw—settled? why, hardly. . .' 'O, we're in a horrid rummage!,' said Mrs. Vesey, interrupting her husband. 'It is indeed nothing short of one of Hercules' labours to make this place habitable'."[10] Vidal's comedy depends again upon a blurring of categories, where drawing-room conversation is transposed to an alternative sphere.

Though Vidal spent five years in Australia in the early 1840s as an Anglican minister's wife, most of her life and career were spent in England, and it is important to recognize that settler colonial fiction was at this time a popular part of English literary culture. Just as Australian literature has suffered from attempts to identify what was "really Australian" in the cultural heritage, as H. M. Green said in 1961 echoing a nationalism promoted by Vance Palmer and others, so English literature has been unduly circumscribed by the historical tendency to regard colonial scenarios as marginal to what F. R. Leavis called the "great tradition" of the English novel.[11] In fact, as Tamara S. Wagner has written, by "the mid-nineteenth century 'English' literature had become an increasingly global phenomenon," with novels set in Australia, whose settler population had risen from 12,000 in 1810 to 1.25 million in 1860, attracting widespread interest.[12] In his "General Editor's Foreword" to the Colonial Texts series, inaugurated in

1986, Harry Heseltine declared a primary aim of the series was to contribute "to the understanding of the literary culture of Australia's colonial period," but this tended to overlook how "Australia's colonial culture" was always imbricated in a wider discursive network.[13] Much Australian literary criticism in the modern era has been shaped in one way or another by Miles Franklin's *Laughter, Not for a Cage* (1956), which contains brilliant insights into particular writers and is of great interest in relation to Franklin's own fiction, but as literary criticism is severely compromised by the author's polemically nationalist agenda, which led her to dismiss most nineteenth-century fiction for insufficient "Australianness."[14] In *Following the Equator*, written after his visit to Australia in 1895, Mark Twain cited the work of Rosa Praed, Marcus Clarke, Ralph Boldrewood, and others in his description of Australia's "brilliant and vigorous literature."[15] Such approbation makes Green's style of critical self-immolation – "there is no attempt to make out that what is considered first rate by Australian standards is necessarily first rate by the standards of a greater literature" – appear all the more anomalous.[16]

Twain's remarks are especially pertinent if we consider alternative genealogies for nineteenth-century Australian literature, other than the familiar colonial context. In his pioneering 1856 overview of Australian literature, *The Fiction Fields of Australia*, Frederick Sinnett was not complimentary about the fiction of Alexander Harris, declaring that *The Emigrant Family* (1849) "possesses comparatively little merit as a novel."[17] Sinnett found Harris' work to be "full of very graphic descriptions of bush life and operations," but lacking in the portrayal of "human character" that he considered to be a "universal" value.[18] But settled characters were never Harris' priority, either artistically or philosophically. He managed to evade court martial in 1825 for deserting the British army by fleeing to Australia, where he spent sixteen years, before converting to Christianity and returning to England. He then, in 1851, migrated to the United States, where he lived for several years in Wisconsin and became an American citizen, before dying in Canada in 1874. Harris' Australian writings are suffused not by colonial proprieties or characterization, but by landscape and metaphysics. In his first novel, *Settlers and Convicts* (1847), the narrator comments on how the "free emigrant" is often confused with the convict and "free persons" arrested "on suspicion of being bushrangers," and these crossovers are not merely an indictment of bureaucratic bungling but an intimation of how, in a larger sense, settlers and convicts should be regarded as analogous rather than antithetical classifications.[19] Within "the still wilderness" of the Australian landscape, the sense of man's "conspicuous littleness is irresistible," and this leads Harris to evoke a frontier world that is ontologically unsettled, in a way redolent more of Puritan and Transcendentalist traditions in American literature than the sociable temper of British Victorian fiction.[20] Harris' autobiography, "Religio Christi," refers to the guidance of "the Unseen Hand" and of "a yet mightier chart of God's ways, the starry universe."[21] It also cites the influence on his thinking of Jonathan Edwards and Timothy Dwight, recalling, in particular, reading "the System of Theology delivered as a course of lectures by Dr. Dwight of Yale College, Connecticut, at a house of a friend, a clergyman in Sydney."[22]

The idea of Dwight's teachings being influential in New South Wales might seem strange, but it testifies to the principles of incongruity and displacement that permeate Harris' writings. The hero of *The Emigrant Family* is Martin Beck, "a fine and rather handsome young man of American-negro descent," who claims his "parents were Yankees," though we are told this is merely an attempt to "sustain in his own mind [...] propinquity to a civilized people," with his parents in fact being "blacks of American birth" who had been sent as convicts to Van Diemen's Land "from different parts of the British Islands."[23] Nevertheless, American "smartness" and "love of gain" drive the "active, restless and impulsive" Beck, with the narrative charting a course from an ordered colonial society to a more mercurial frontier world, one that interrogates the whole notion of "arrangements [...] set down as permanently settled."[24] Beck's professional abilities "compelled homage," but he comes to find himself increasingly isolated, a picaresque hero pitted against a more traditional social fabric.[25] Beck's mixed heritage reflects not only on "the felon population" but also the issue of "blacks" in Australia, and when a warrant is out for the arrest of "Martin Beck, alias Black Beck," this introduces a third term into the familiar colonial dialectic of white settlers against black "savages."[26] The novel itself is an exercise in generic crossover, mixing fact and fiction but striving through footnotes to attest to the basis of these imaginative scenes in verifiable reality. In 1989, Dorothy Green said it was "easy to misunderstand Harris unless one grasps the fact that he looked at life from the point of view of a citizen of the world, uninterested in national boundaries," and his portrayal of the articulate Beck makes for what Ian Duffield has called a "highly unusual" treatment of race, one that conforms neither to American stereotypes of the slave nor Australian models of indigence.[27] Though Henry Kingsley's *The Recollections of Geoffry Hamlyn* (1859) became canonized as the classic novel of this colonial period, Harris' fiction portrays a less Anglophile and more unsettled, adventurous world.

One of the daughters of a British colonist in *The Emigrant Family* complains that "men have a joy in strife of every kind, that it is in their nature to struggle with the elements," and Harris' fiction portrays a male frontier world, one in which domestic quietude plays only a minor role.[28] The gender politics of settler colonial fiction are, however, amply addressed in the work of Catherine Helen Spence, whose fictional emphasis is on the "mundane" and "ordinariness" rather than the sensational.[29] Spence published, in 1876, one of the best early critical essays on George Eliot, applauding the English novelist for her "sense of just proportion," the way she balances the allure of romance against a broader cultural framework so as to elucidate the long-term consequences of human behavior within a world whose moral dimensions are mixed rather than melodramatic.[30] Eliot was so impressed by Spence's essay that she wrote the Australian author a note of apology for having treated her dismissively when Spence visited her London home in March 1866, remarking on how Spence's piece had "gratified" her by its "laying of the finger on the right spot, which is more precious than praise."[31] Spence's own fiction shares some of these aesthetically stringent qualities, aspiring not to reflect a picturesque version of the country – "the gaunt shepherd with his starving flocks and herds," as she put it – but rather (in an echo of Matthew Arnold) "to see Australia steadily and see it whole."[32]

Spence received a fair amount of critical attention, with Sinnett calling her first work *Clara Morison* (1854) "[d]ecidedly the best Australian novel" of its era.[33] Like Vidal's *Bengala*, Spence's novel was published by J. W. Parker of London in its two-volume series, with Vidal noting in her book's dedication the interweaving of continuity and transition that characterized this genre: "though life is the same in one hemisphere as another, the accidental and surrounding circumstances vary, and there is a more rapid and continual change in a new colony."[34] Spence's own aim was always to combine representation of interiority with a wider social compass, so as to adumbrate how the process of settlement involved steady progression in both private and public realms. *Clara Morison* starts with a young girl's forced migration from Scotland to Adelaide, and it allows the reader access to her emotional life through personal journals and letters, but the novel's trajectory involves characters finding their "place" not only within family life but also in relation to the gradual maturation of the "dear colony, where we have all grown up together," as Annie Elliot describes it. South Australia is the protagonist of *Clara Morison*, with the narrator noting how Adelaide has always been free from convicts and comparing it favorably to the turbulence of "that horrid Victoria" during the gold rush, where "convulsion has unfixed everything."[35] Spence's preferred model was a secularized version of the allegorical journey in John Bunyan's *The Pilgrim's Progress* (1678), described in her *Autobiography* as a "great work," where gradual move-ment along a difficult path would lead ultimately to a state of fruition.[36] Like Eliot in *Middlemarch* (1871–1872) reimagining Christian teachings through the secular framework promoted at this time by Higher Criticism of the Bible, Spence appropriates a paradigm of redemption in metaphorical terms, as an analog to fulfillment of the settler colonial passage. This is why Spence's fiction places so much emphasis on coming to Australia "not to make our fortunes and leave the colony forthwith," as Margaret Elliot says in *Clara Morison*, "but to grow up and settle in it," adding that Australia "shall soon be an important nation."[37] Spence's expansive fictional narra-tives consequently seek to reconcile different strands of emigrant experience within a global framework.

Spence thought her "best novel – the novel into which I put the most of myself" to be not *Clara Morison*, but *Gathered In*, originally serialized in the *Adelaide Observer* from September 1881 to March 1882, but not pub-lished in book form until 1977.[38] *Gathered In* is another transhemispheric novel that moves between Scotland and Australia, and again its focus is not on contingency but on pattern, the way truth emerges through and across time. The hero, Kenneth Oswald, is ultimately "gathered in" to his fam-ily inheritance, despite being born illegitimate, and this exemplifies one of Spence's recurring themes, an explicit rejection of the "Calvinistic theol-ogy" that would categorize sexual transgression as inevitably ruinous.[39] In Spence's own interpretation, at least, her utopian novel *Handfasted*, written in 1879, failed to find favor when she entered it for a *Sydney Mail* prize competition because of its advocacy of "handfasting," the early Scottish custom involving a trial marriage of a year and a day, something Spence considered "too dangerous" for respectable Australian society.[40] Having abandoned in 1855 the Presbyterian religion of her childhood and turned instead to a more emollient Unitarianism, she addressed throughout her fiction the displacement of Puritan tenets into humanistic precepts. In *Mr. Hogarth's Will* (1865), whose plot turns on an estate left to Hogarth's ille-gitimate son Francis, the patriarch's niece declares "we should not condemn a man for life on account of something done, or, as in this case, only pro-posed, when very young, and in circumstances of temptation which you and I, perhaps, can scarcely appreciate."[41] There is an intertextual quarrel here with Nathaniel Hawthorne – Hogarth's niece Jane is said to be "not of the slight ethereal style which Mr. Hawthorne admires, but rather of the healthy, well-developed flesh-and-blood character of British feminine beauty" – and this exemplifies how Spence's fiction always engages intellec-tually with American as well as British fiction.[42] Indeed, in *Clara Morison* the courtship between Reginald and Clara takes place almost exclusively on the lexical playfields of literary criticism, as they come to realize their mutual preferences and antipathies in readings of various Victorian writers. Rather than just seeking to describe an Australian environment after the fashion of travel narratives, Spence was seeking to create a discursive mediation of various social, political, and cultural issues through antipodean perspectives for a global audience.

In her *Autobiography*, Spence recalls discussing the question of "heredity" with Boston writer Oliver Wendell Holmes and objecting to "the fatalism of heredity as being about as paralyzing to effort as the fatalism of Calvinism."[43] Heredity is a key question for Spence, as indeed it is for many Australian settler colonial novelists, and this issue often manifests itself in the way their narrative trajectories move simultaneously backwards and forwards in time. Spence's utopian fictions – *Handfasted*, and *A Week in the Future*, which was originally serialized in the *Centennial Magazine* in 1889 – are a mixture of Scottish heritage and social radicalism, with Spence paying tribute in her *Autobiography* to the influence on this work of Charlotte Perkins Gilman, "a cultured Bostonian, living in San Francisco," whom she met on her 1893–1894 lecture tour of the United States.[44] Fariha Shaikh has commented on how, "ironically," it was only when Spence was introduced to the family of abolitionist William Lloyd Garrison in America that, as she put it, "I began to be a little ashamed of being so narrow in my views on the coloured question"; but this actually speaks to a larger contradiction throughout Spence's work, whereby her progressive politics were crossed with a scientific belief in heredity and racial heritage.[45] Spence's important work in the fields of feminism and electoral reform – she was one of the pioneers of the transferable vote system, which still operates in Australia to this day – should not detract from her fictional accomplishments, which abound in dialectical tensions rather than unilateral polemic. She has not been particularly well-served by editors: even the modern edition of *Handfasted* chooses to omit one entire chapter "Salt Lake City," which is crucial to the book's comparative representation of the Mormon religion, because of what the editor Helen Thomson deemed "its unnecessary prolixity."[46] Thomson chose also to omit from *Handfasted* dialogue that "seemed unnecessarily wordy and immaterial to the novel as a whole," but in fact the manifold complications inherent in Spence's fictions are crucial to their integrity as literary works.[47]

The aesthetic status of nineteenth-century Australian fiction has always been a vexed question. Walter Besant estimated that the number of readers in the English-speaking world expanded from 50,000 in 1830 to 120 million by the late 1890s, and many jeremiads appeared around this time about the destructive effects of market commodification on literary standards. Besant's

1884 lecture "Fiction as One of the Fine Arts" maintained that the popular middlebrow novelist was the proper heir of the great Victorian tradition and that he or she should offer the world entertainment and "a cheerful countenance," but this elicited as riposte Henry James' essay "The Art of Fiction," published the same year, which argued for the novel as an art rather than a craft.[48] Most recent accounts of nineteenth-century Australian fiction, however, have emphasized its place within the marketplace, with more attention to questions of circulation and the economics of publishing rather than textual complications. Katherine Bode's recent focus on "serialized fiction" in Australian newspapers, for example, is driven in part by principled rejection of "a selective canon of great works."[49] This fits with an Australian academic tradition of cultural studies, influenced by Pierre Bourdieu, which has taken issue with "the assumption that literature comprises a special kind of writing that is to be considered aesthetically," an idea dismissed by Tony Bennett as no more than a "form of elite self-fashioning."[50]

Yet not all Australian novelists were so avowedly egalitarian. Though she always had an eye for commercial self-interest, Ada Cambridge was one writer of this era overtly dedicated to the pursuit of literature as a high art form rather than just a commodity. She was an almost exact contemporary of Henry James – James was born in 1843 and died in 1916, Cambridge born in 1844 and died in 1926 – and just as James tried carefully to curate his own posthumous reputation through meticulous authorial revisions in the New York edition of his novels, so Cambridge wrote to her publisher George Robertson in 1924 asking him to guard her "literary remains," with an eye not so much on money but what her biographers called her "place in the literary canon."[51] With typical playfulness, Cambridge in A Woman's Friendship (1889) named one of the protagonist's horses "Henry James Junior."[52] Cambridge successfully serialized her novels in Australian newspapers from 1872, but, as she subsequently observed, she became "almost the first author" to benefit from the International Copyright Act passed by the United States in 1891, which guaranteed royalties to non-resident authors.[53] After being taken up by William Heinemann and other publishers in the 1890s, writing books for a global marketplace became her priority. Her work was thus widely read not only in Britain but also in America, where she was regarded as a British author with Australian connections.

Such versatility speaks to the qualities of an author who, like James, created her fictional worlds out of comparison and transposition between different geographic and philosophical states. Born in Norfolk, Cambridge married an English clergyman, George Cross, and her first works, published before her emigration with Cross in 1870, were two books of devotional verse. After her move to Australia, however, she became interested in exploring a rhetoric of blasphemy, with her subsequent volume of poems, *Unspoken Thoughts* (1887), raising skeptical questions about the nature of orthodox belief in a world where "the infinite, empty darkness," as her poem "Despair" puts it, threatens to become overwhelming.[54] Strongly influenced by the heterodox temper of Arthur Hugh Clough, whose work she cited in many of her novels, Cambridge developed an aesthetic that drew on the original theological connotations of perversion, a mode involving the opposite of religious conversion, swerving away from established truth into more deviant pathways. Jonathan Dollimore theorized "the perverse dynamic" as having "its origins in, or exists in an intimate relation with, that which it subverts," so that perversion, both theological and sexual, is "often perceived as at once utterly alien to what it threatens, and yet, mysteriously inherent within it"; and it is this unsettling double state that is adumbrated in Cambridge's novella "The Perversity of Human Nature" (1887), where the characters find themselves divided between strict moral principles and contrarian impulses.[55]

Cambridge's novel *Fidelis* (1895) chronicles "another instance of that perversity of human nature which is like a natural law," and all of her fiction encompasses such symbiotic divisions: between England and Australia, between Christian orthodoxy and agnosticism, between feminist independence and what "The Perversity of Human Nature" calls the "dependence of her sex upon the strong arm and the strong will."[56] Her work represents in significant ways the vacillating nature of gender relations and cultural politics at the turn of the twentieth century, with her last novel, *The Making of Rachel Rowe* (1914), portraying women caught between competing pressures of higher education and domesticity in a world where the Suffragettes have become active. In her 1913 essay "Hobbled," Cambridge declares herself to be "a woman's woman," and "even – though I detest the term – a woman's rights woman," and she deplores the tendency of "tangled" fashions such as "chiffons" to restrict women's freedom.[57] Nevertheless, this feminist agenda is always framed within a formal rhetoric of structural ambiguity and self-deprecating humor. *Materfamilias* (1898), a retrospective narrative in the first person by a grandmother chronicling three generations of family life over the course of emigration from England and settlement in Melbourne, is also an extraordinarily innovative account not only of how class and gender issues have historically evolved but also of their mediation by inevitably flawed and partial understandings. This is a satirical narrative that interrogates the premises of its own satirical objectification, while raising ethical questions about such potentially dehumanizing styles of art. There is an experimental quality to Cambridge's novel, a self-reflexivity epitomized here by its internal representation of a cyclorama depicting the unfolding of history at the 1888 Centennial Exhibition in Melbourne. Portraying marriage as a trial over time, and chronicling how fortunes change over the seasons of life, *Materfamilias* anticipates the style of Virginia Woolf not only in its gender dynamics but also in its spatial and temporal reach.

Lorna Sage declared in 1999 that Cambridge was firmly established "as a major figure of late nineteenth-century Australian literature," but, even in an era when such long novels are unfashionable, it is odd that Cambridge's work is not better known in the Anglophone literary world as an important point of transition between Victorian realism and modernism.[58] Her range of allusion is as probing as in any of the writers influenced by the Aesthetic Movement, who were her contemporaries and peers. *A Mere Chance*, which was serialized in 1880 and appeared in book form in 1882, refers explicitly to Thomas Hardy and Dante Gabriel Rossetti, and it frames its representation of the heroine as a "perverse child" through an exposure of psychological and erotic contradictions turning on power relations and the tensions arising between inheritance and independence. As Rachel says here: "nature makes us with many capacities. Some of them counteract the others."[59] Like her compatriots Catherine Martin and Rosa Praed, Cambridge continually returns to the "[s]trange mysteries of heredity," as one of the characters puts it in *Path and Goal* (1900), a "hereditary design" that becomes a formative force even in deviations from it.[60] Indeed, heritage might be identified as one of the defining tropes of nineteenth-century Australian fiction, just as the frontier, in however convoluted and ambivalent a form, is always a shadowy presence in nineteenth-century American fiction.

Yet for Cambridge this heritage, both familial and cultural, is always crossed by alternative conditions of a new country and a new century, and it is this perpetual oscillation between alternative perspectives that forms the fulcrum of her work. Many of her novels feature travel between continents and hemispheres, but such geographic displacement can be understood not just empirically but also metaphorically, as indicative of the way her scenarios introduce antipodean distance as a corollary to philosophical alienation, an estrangement from realms of the familiar. In her essay "The Lonely Seas" (1911), Cambridge depicts travel as an ethical imperative, saying it is "the delusion of the unthinking, who have never slipped their moorings, that the deep-sea voyage is but a careless runaway from home and duty," while arguing that the "sweep of vision" associated with a journey allows the traveler to "perceive something of the relative proportion of things, and, amongst them all, your place."[61] Such a "sweep of vision" also characterizes *Path and Goal*, with the lovers reunited after many years apart achieving a final *Liebestod* in the Pacific Ocean, where their ship reels under the storm "like a boy under punishment trying to get away from the whip" as the lovers recognize "that they were quite alone and helpless in that apparent infinity of sea."[62] There is also a specific reference in this climactic scene to Edgar Allan Poe – "it was like Poe's story of the Pit and the Pendulum, they said – like dying a hundred deaths" – and this attests to Cambridge's familiarity with Poe's aesthetic of transgression and reversal, as outlined most famously in his story "The Imp of the Perverse" (1845).[63]

Cambridge's fiction thus combines the legacy of *Sturm und Drang* romanticism with a paradoxical idiom of containment, with her work energized by the way these forces clash against each other. She much admired Wagner's music, but perhaps the closest figure to her in literary terms was William Dean Howells, who similarly engages with residual styles of idealism – particularly, in his case, the legacy of New England transcendentalism – but then characteristically recalibrates them according to the demands of economic and social prudence. In her final published essay "Nightfall" (1922), which made an audacious case for euthanasia, Cambridge paid tribute to Howells, saying that "[s]piritually, I had walked beside him since the long-ago days when his first publications came to Australia."[64] Howells had died in 1920, and it was appropriate that Cambridge's essay should have appeared in *Atlantic Monthly*, a journal he edited for several years. Like Howells, Cambridge's compulsive focus on the material world – furniture, decorations, urban environments – arose not just out of a desire for photographic realism, but from a broader perception of the limits of idealism and how material goods necessarily interpose themselves within more rarefied designs. This, again, is another version of the perverse aesthetic, demystifying religious or spiritual orthodoxy into its worldly corollaries, so as to highlight intellectually the primacy of matter over spirit.

Despite her own English family background, Cambridge during the latter part of her life "read almost exclusively American literature."[65] She also sent copies of her novels to James Carleton Young for his bibliographic collection, adding in the inscription to her 1922 gift of *Path and Goal* that she was pleased the novel was finding a home in the United States, "where I have long believed that the standards of literary culture, workmanship & taste are the highest & most stable of any in the world."[66] This suggests again Cambridge's concern for her own posthumous position in the literary canon, but it also implies, as we saw with Alexander Harris, how it is more productive to consider Australian settler colonial fictions in a triangular relation to both Britain and America, rather than merely in a postcolonial dialogue with English traditions. Despite being widely read in her own lifetime, Cambridge has been more or less ignored by scholars of English Victorian literature, and this might be attributed not only to their own circumscribed academic fiefdoms but also to the unwillingness of Australian scholars to read these works within the context of Anglophone World Literature. Australian fiction of the nineteenth century is a rich field, but it is one only properly understood in comparative rather than nationalistic terms. It also needs readers willing to invest time in the twists and turns of narrative, the slow forms of gradually unfolding developments in plot and character, rather than contenting themselves merely with the flatter facts of circulation figures or digital computations of word counts. Nineteenth-century Australia represents a world increasingly distant in time if not in space, and it is one not easily accommodated within the affective agendas of "creative writing" that increasingly dominate English studies in Australian universities. Literary history always properly involves the study of alterity as well as homology, and, as the distinguished American literary scholar Robert S. Levine remarked, rather than works that "resonate with their own affective lives [...] there is much to be said for writings that pull readers out of their worlds to expose them to something that is quite other."[67] In this sense, settler colonial fictions should be recognized for their provocations and alien qualities, just as early Australian literature itself is a field ripe for critical reappraisal.

Notes

1 Peter Pierce, "Forms of Australian Literary History," in *The Penguin New Literary History of Australia*, ed. Laurie Hergenhan (Ringwood: Penguin Australia, 1988), p. 85.

2 Pierce, "Forms of Australian Literary History," p. 85.

3 Ken Gelder and Rachael Weaver, *Colonial Australian Fiction: Character Types, Social Formations and the Colonial Economy* (Sydney: Sydney University Press, 2017), p. 117; Lorenzo Veracini, "'Settler Colonialism': Career of a Concept," *Journal of Imperial and Commonwealth History* 41.2 (2013): pp. 313–333 (p. 323).

4 Patrick Brantlinger, *Rule of Darkness: British Literature and Imperialism, 1830–1914* (Ithaca: Cornell University Press, 1988), p. 132.

5 Marcia Langton, "*Well, I Heard It on the Radio and I Saw It on the Television ...*" (Sydney: Australian Film Commission, 1993), p. 46. See also Toni Morrison, *Playing in the Dark: Whiteness and the Literary Imagination* (Cambridge, MA: Harvard University Press, 1992).

6 Oliné Keese, *The Broad Arrow: Being Passages from the History of Maida Gwynnham, a Lifer*, ed. Jenna Mead (Sydney: Sydney University Press, 2019), p. 335.

7 Keese, *The Broad Arrow*, p. 335.

8 Dorice Williams Elliott, "Unsettled Status in Australian Settler Novels," in *Victorian Settler Narratives: Emigrants, Cosmopolitans and Returnees in Nineteenth-Century Literature*, ed. Tamara S. Wagner (London: Pickering and Chatto, 2011), p. 37.

9 Elliott, "Unsettled Status in Australian Settler Novels," p. 37.

10 Mary Theresa Vidal, *Bengala, or Some Time Ago*, ed. Susan McKernan (Kensington, NSW: New South Wales University Press, 1990), p. 46.

11 H. M. Green, *A History of Australian Literature, Pure and Applied* (Sydney: Angus & Robertson, 1961), p. 93; F. R. Leavis, *The Great Tradition: George Eliot, Henry James, Joseph Conrad* (London: Chatto and Windus, 1948).

12 Tamara S. Wagner, "Introduction: Narrating Domestic Portability: Emigration, Domesticity and Genre Formation," in *Victorian Settler Narratives: Emigrants, Cosmopolitans and Returnees in Nineteenth-Century Literature*, ed. Tamara S. Wagner (London and New York: Routledge, 2011), pp. 1–22 (p. 2); James Belich, *Replenishing the Earth: The Settler Revolution and the Rise of the Angloworld, 1783–1939* (New York: Oxford University Press, 2009), p. 83.

13 Harry Heseltine, "General Editor's Foreword," in Vidal, *Bengala*, p. viii.

14 Miles Franklin, *Laughter, Not for a Cage: Notes on Australian Writing* (Sydney: Angus & Robertson, 1956), p. 86.

15 Mark Twain, *Following the Equator: A Journey Around the World* (New York: Oxford University Press, 1996; 1897), p. 214.

16 Green, *History of Australian Literature*, p. xviii.

17 Frederick Sinnett, *The Fiction Fields of Australia*, ed. Cecil Hadgraft (St Lucia: University of Queensland Press, 1966), p. 42.

18 Sinnett, *The Fiction Fields of Australia*, pp. 32–33.

19 [Alexander Harris], *Settlers and Convicts; or, Recollections of Sixteen Years' Labour in the Australian Backwoods* (Carlton: Melbourne University Press, 1953), pp. 78, 226.

20 [Harris], *Settlers and Convicts*, pp. 186, 179.

21 Alexander Harris, "Religio Christi," in *The Secrets of Alexander Harris*, ed. Grant Carr-Harris (Sydney: Angus & Robertson, 1961), p. 167.

22 Harris, "Religio Christi," p. 176.

23 Alexander Harris, *The Emigrant Family: or, The Story of an Australian Settler*, ed. W. S. Ransom (Canberra: Australian National University Press, 1967), pp. 28–29.

24 Harris, *The Emigrant Family*, pp. 39, 156, 26.

25 Harris, *The Emigrant Family*, p. 69.

26 Harris, *The Emigrant Family*, pp. 271, 39, 308, 258.

27 Dorothy Green, "The Road Not Taken," *Southerly* 49.3 (1989): pp. 288–299 (p. 290); Ian Duffield, "Alexander Harris's *The Emigrant Family* and Afro-black People in Colonial Australia," in *The Black Presence in English Literature*, ed. David Dabydeen (Manchester: Manchester University Press, 1985), p. 71.

28 Harris, *The Emigrant Family*, p. 59.

29 Fiona Giles, *Too Far Everywhere: The Romantic Heroine in Nineteenth-Century Australia* (St Lucia: University of Queensland Press, 1998), p. 44.

30 C. H. Spence, "George Eliot," *Melbourne Review* 1 (1876): pp. 146–163 (p. 147).

31 C. H. Spence, "George Eliot's Life and Works," *Melbourne Review* 10.39 (1885): pp. 217–244 (p. 219).

32 Catherine Helen Spence, *An Autobiography* (Adelaide: W. K. Thomas, 1910), p. 97.

33 Sinnett, *Fiction Fields of Australia*, p. 34.

34 Vidal, *Bengala*, 3.

35 Catherine Helen Spence, *Clara Morison: A Tale of South Australia During the Gold Fever* (Kent Town: Wakefield Press, 1994), I, p. 229; II, p. 142; II, p. 137.
36 Spence, *Autobiography*, p. 62.
37 Spence, *Clara Morison*, II, pp. 255–256.
38 Spence, *Autobiography*, p. 55.
39 Catherine Helen Spence, *Gathered In: A Novel*, eds. B. L. Waters and G. A. Wilkes (Sydney: Sydney University Press, 1977), p. 43.
40 Spence, *Autobiography*, p. 63.
41 Catherine Helen Spence, *Mr. Hogarth's Will* (Ringwood: Penguin Australia, 1988; 1865), p. 191.
42 Spence, *Mr. Hogarth's Will*, p. 48.
43 Spence, *Autobiography*, p. 73.
44 Spence, *Autobiography*, p. 70.
45 Fariha Shaikh, *Nineteenth-Century Settler Emigration in British Literature and Art* (Edinburgh: Edinburgh University Press, 2018), p. 192; Spence, *Autobiography*, p. 73.
46 Helen Thomson, "Preface," in Catherine Helen Spence, *Handfasted*, ed. Helen Thomson (Ringwood: Penguin Australia, 1984), ix.
47 Thomson, "Preface," p. ix. For a fine analysis of the importance of the chapter omitted from the published novel, see Nan Bowman Albinski, "*Handfasted*: An Australian Feminist's American Utopian," *Journal of Popular Culture* 23.2 (1989): pp. 15–31.
48 Nigel Cross, *The Common Writer: Life in Nineteenth-Century Grub Street* (Cambridge: Cambridge University Press, 1985), pp. 206, 215.
49 Katherine Bode, *Reading by Numbers: Recalibrating the Literary Field* (London: Anthem Press, 2012), pp. 2, 4.
50 Tony Bennett, "Sociology, Aesthetics, Expertise," *New Literary History* 41.2 (2010): pp. 253–276 (p. 264).
51 Elizabeth Morrison, "Editor's Introduction," in Ada Cambridge, *A Woman's Friendship* (Kensington: New South Wales University Press, 1988), p. xxix; Margaret Bradstock and Louise Wakeling, *Rattling the Orthodoxies: A Life of Ada Cambridge* (Ringwood: Penguin Australia, 1991), p. 218.
52 Cambridge, *A Woman's Friendship*, p. 59.
53 Ada Cambridge, Letter to George Robertson, March 4, 1923, as cited in Elizabeth Morrison, "Introduction," in Ada Cambridge, *A Black Sheep: Some Episodes in his Life* (Canberra: Australian Scholarly Editions Centre, 2004), p. xli.
54 Ada Cambridge, *Unspoken Thoughts*, ed. Patricia Barton (Canberra: Australian Defence Force Academy, 1988), p. 45.
55 Jonathan Dollimore, *Sexual Dissidence: Augustine to Wilde, Freud to Foucault* (Oxford: Oxford University Press, 1991), pp. 33, 121.
56 Ada Cambridge, *Fidelis* (Canberra: Mulini Press, 1997), p. 123; Ada Cambridge, *The Perversity of Human Nature* (Sydney: Sydney University Press, 2004), p. 34.
57 Ada Cambridge, "Hobbled," *North American Review* 197.688 (1913): pp. 392–404 (pp. 393, 398).
58 Lorna Sage, *The Cambridge Guide to Women's Writing in English* (Cambridge: Cambridge University Press, 1999), p. 108.
59 Ada Cambridge, *A Mere Chance* (London: Richard Bentley, 1882), pp. 67, 76.

60 Ada Cambridge, *Path and Goal* (New York: Appleton, 1900), pp. 195, 179.
61 Ada Cambridge, "The Lonely Seas," *Atlantic Monthly* 108.2 (1911): pp. 95–100 (p. 96, p. 100).
62 Cambridge, *Path and Goal*, p. 326.
63 Cambridge, *Path and Goal*, p. 336.
64 Ada Cambridge, "Nightfall," *Atlantic Monthly* 130.2 (1922): pp. 231–234 (p. 231).
65 Bradstock and Wakeling, *Rattling the Orthodoxies*, p. 209.
66 Elaine Zinkhan, "Ada Cambridge: A Poetry Manuscript and Holograph Inscriptions in America, Formerly Part of the James Carleton Young Collection," *Bibliographical Society of Australia and New Zealand Bulletin* 14.4 (1990): pp. 120–140 (p. 123).
67 Robert S. Levine, "Reimagining 1820–1865," in *Timelines of American Literature*, eds. Cody Marrs and Christopher Hager (Baltimore: Johns Hopkins University Press, 2019), p. 143.

4

MICHAEL R. GRIFFITHS

White Writing, Indigenous Australia, and the Chronotopes of the Settler Novel

> *... to suggest the passage of time to readers of the white race (which has always measured time by events) through the minds of black people (whose history was, from our point of view, very uneventful, and who never had any very strong conception of time at all) is a task which I feel may be quite impossible!*
> – Eleanor Dark to W. A. R. Collins, January 20, 1941[1]

The passage of time, as represented within the Australian novel, is an issue of much concern, especially when we consider the representation of Aboriginal people by non-Indigenous writers. As Johannes Fabian has shown, when European discourses such as anthropology (and literature perhaps, too) construct their "other," they often do so by emplacing this other as never sufficiently coeval and therefore fixed within the distant past – or, as is the case for novelist Eleanor Dark, here, "never [having] had any very strong conception of time at all."[2] In this sense, Dark's comment suggests that capturing Aboriginal forms of life within the mode of time proper to the novel, especially the historical novel, is an impossibility.

While Dark's characterization of the Aboriginal experience of time as without a sense of the "event" in the European sense smacks of being both negatively defined and essentialist, it is true that even a non-Indigenous observer of Aboriginal culture as astute as the anthropologist W. E. H. Stanner found it difficult to compare and translate the terms of how eventfulness is meaningfully understood within the two cultures. In his 1953 essay "The Dreaming," he opened by suggesting:

> A central meaning of The Dreaming is that of a sacred, heroic time long ago when man and nature came to be as they are; but neither "time" nor "history" as we understand them is involved in this meaning. [...] A blackfellow may call his totem, or the place from which his spirit came, his Dreaming. He may also explain the existence of a custom, or law of life, as causally due to The Dreaming. [...] Although, as I have said, The Dreaming conjures up the notion of a sacred, heroic time of the indefinitely remote past, such a time is also, in a sense still part of the present.[3]

Warraimaay historian Victoria Grieve-Williams calls attention to problems of translation in rendering the Arrernte word *altjira rama* as "dreaming" given that *altjira* also means "the eternal." Whether "Dreaming" is the best translation or not, in this sense, the concept *altjira* is directly related to a theory of time and temporality.[4] While Dark's apparent intention was to avoid writing an Indigenous sense of time she could not or did not know, this humility carries problematic implications all the same. Dark's assertion that Aboriginal culture and people "never had any very strong conception of time at all" reinforces an exoticist idea of the Indigenous untimely, one not unlike the eschewal of the coeval found in Fabian's diagnosis of anthropology. The Dreaming (*altjira rama*) is clearly a sense of time, albeit a radically different one than that of European culture. Therefore, Dark's sense that European conceptions of history and traditional Aboriginal understandings of time require an act of translation (perhaps impossibly so) is more grounded in the reality of the situation. The Dreaming and related senses of time are not, then, eternal in some ephemeral and abstract sense, as is intimated in the title of Dark's novel, *The Timeless Land* (1941). Rather, they are conceived according to a unique sense of temporality that emphasizes the relation between past, place, and present. A conception of the Australian novel and its representation of indigeneity and of Aboriginal people thus benefits not only from a sense of racial thought and the history of colonization (though these will be indispensable) but also from a conception of time and its cultural incommensurabilities. I will return to Dark as one of my exempla, but I want to remain with this question of time as an indicator of cultural difference. In other words, I am interested in time as a concern in the construction, translation, and dissemination of Aboriginal culture to white readers through the medium of the Australian novel.

To touch on the question of time in the novel is inevitably to invoke Mikhail Bakhtin's notion of the chronotope. Bakhtin defines the chronotope as "the intrinsic connectedness of temporal and spatial relationships that are artistically expressed in literature."[5] In one sense, Bakhtin's notion of chronotope is simply a synonym for setting in place and time. The complication arises in that such a conception immediately takes on related framing devices such as genre, cultural context, and the conceptual scheme that they together reproduce. The historical novel, for instance, has a radically distinct sense of time (and place) to that of a novel set entirely within the approximate time of its writing. The historical novel therefore evokes the sense of a remote past setting, and as such, there is always a possibility of multiple senses of time and of place cohabiting within the one novel. As Bakhtin puts it: "[c]hronotopes are mutually inclusive, they co-exist, they may be interwoven with, replace or oppose one another, contradict one another or find themselves in ever more complex interrelationships."[6] This sense of "mutually inclusive," "co-exist[ing]" chronotopes might inform our sense of white writing about Indigenous Australia, especially in light of a caveat like Dark's about the perceived difference in temporal sensibilities across settler and Indigenous worldviews. While there may indeed be culturally specific understandings of time between European and Indigenous Australian cultures, such caveats as Dark's draw attention to European settler *conceptions of Indigenous time* more than to the reality of Indigenous ontologies. A number of scholars, including Marcia Langton, Bob Hodge, Vijay Mishra, and Elizabeth Povinelli, have explored the way the concept of Aboriginality can be constructed in a tense dialectical relationship with settler discourse about Indigenous people and things.[7] The image of Aboriginality or Aboriginalism that we encounter in the white Australian novel is an artifact of settler conceptions, desires, and fantasies about Indigenous people.[8] As such, we are often dealing, in the Australian novel, with a series of chronotopes of indigeneity that render the fantasies of white Australians about time, the past, the land, and Aboriginal people. This chapter proceeds to observe several examples of white writing about Indigenous Australia with the lens of each particular chronotope in mind.

The Nineteenth Century

As Katherine Bode has recently observed, one strong premise in Australian literary studies about white Australian representations of Aborigines in the nineteenth century is that authors did not engage with Indigenous characters to any great degree. She writes: "beginning in the nineteenth century, fiction replicated the legal lie of *terra nullius* by not depicting Australia's original inhabitants."[9] Where this *is* the case, critics have turned to ideas of the gothic, the uncanny, and other such generic tropes to represent the present-absence of Aboriginality. While there is certainly a strong current of gothicism in Australian literature and a potent sense of the uncanny, Bode nonetheless suggests that postulations of the absence of Aboriginal characters and representations in nineteenth-century Australian fiction are exaggerated.[10] Drawing on an innovative method of digital humanities scholarship, combined with a rich and extensive repository of nineteenth-century Australian fiction (predominantly short fiction) published in newspapers and other periodicals, Bode surveys numerous patterns in the depiction of Aboriginal characters in colonial Australian fiction. She suggests that Aboriginal characters are abundant in nineteenth-century fiction, if often representing racist clichés and stereotypes. According to Bode's useful summary:

Much more frequently, the unsettled colonial condition is evoked by depicting, not repressing, the Aboriginal presence [...]. These characters are generally presented in friendly and harmonious though inequitable, relationships with colonists: for instance, teaching them about bush foods, guiding them through the bush, looking after stock, or simply spending time around the station. Such Aboriginal characters are roughly drawn sketches or stereotypes – the childlike native, the lazy black, the harmless primitive – and their purpose in these narratives is to assist, and thereby justify, the colonial mission.[11]

Bode also names the experience of representations of "attacks by Aborigines and bloodshed" as a not infrequent plot point within these colonial fictions.[12] She concludes that, while Aboriginal people are not always represented kindly, "the presence of Aboriginal people is not denied or repressed" in Australian colonial fiction but, we can add, these representations are instead distorted.[13]

Nonetheless, the traditionally canonical Australian novels of the late nineteenth century engage scantily with Aboriginal presence. The 1874 version of Marcus Clarke's *For the Term of His Natural Life* does not engage with Aboriginal characters or presences. Strikingly, this is the case even though Clarke was dealing with the chronotope of massacre and frontier conflict and set the novel in part in Port Arthur in the late 1820s and early 1830. This was the moment of the Black War in lutruwita (Tasmania), which saw Aboriginal people resisting colonization (if ultimately unsuccessfully). Andrew McCann observes that Clarke was "well aware of Tasmania's bloody history."[14] He wrote a series of articles on lutruwita which, amidst all else, mention the "extermination known as the Black War." *His Natural Life* – the longer serialized version of the novel – does contain a paragraph that explicitly references Indigenous presence in the colony and the Black War in particular. It reads as follows:

two years before, the great attack upon the blacks – known as the Black War – had taken place, but by 1830, the once dreaded natives, reduced to 600 souls, were objects of pity, rather than terror, and the expedition against them remembered almost as a matter of history, so rapidly had the colony progressed in civilisation and importance.[15]

Clarke's ironic tone is palpable particularly around the notion of "civilization" – all but placed in inverted commas – and its heightened sense of its own "importance." But irony can still reinforce the temporality of inevitability, loss, and Indigenous doom. As such, the underlying trope of pity in Clarke's most famous work portrays a sense of affective but disengaged sympathy with Indigenous plight, but also (as McCann implicitly notes) the sense that the colonial elimination of the Aboriginal population is a condition for modernity's emergence. Here modernity as a chronotope emerges at the expense of an Indigenous population "remembered almost as a matter of history."

Where Clarke's shorter fiction would include Aboriginal characters – as in the short satire "King Billy's Troubles: Or Governmental Red-Tapeism," Aboriginal characters like the titular King Billy become a device for parody of colonial bureaucracy. In the story, the station-owner protagonist must go all the way to the London colonial office simply to request that Aboriginal inhabitants of his district be supplied with breeches – a nod to Victorian proprieties. But perhaps the most sustained depiction of an Aboriginal character in the nineteenth-century Australian novel appeared in 1888 with Rolf Boldrewood's *Robbery Under Arms*. The novel follows the adventures of Dick Marston and his brother Jim, who join the bushranger gang of a mysterious anti-hero named simply "Captain Starlight" (his real name is not even known at the novel's end by the jury of Marston's final trial).[16] The novel equates the ability to track with an Aboriginality that it suggests is subject to appropriation by whites:

> My name's Dick Marston, Sydney-side native. I'm twenty-nine years old, six feet in my stocking soles, and thirteen stone weight. Pretty strong and active with it, so they say. I don't want to blow – not here, any road – but it takes a good man to put me on my back, or stand up to me with the gloves, or the naked mauleys. I can ride anything – anything that ever was lapped in horsehide – swim like a musk-duck, and *track like a Myall blackfellow* [my italics]. Most things that a man can do I'm up to, and that's all about it.[17]

As well as this inaugural, appropriative self-comparison, a crucial aspect of the novel is that Starlight has a loyal "half-caste" sidekick and constant member of his gang: "Warrigal." In this way, *Robbery Under Arms* may be the first Australian novel to feature a major Aboriginal character. In one way, Warrigal is multifaceted, both deeply devoted to Starlight and jealously guarding his privileged position in the gang from newcomers such as Dick and Jim. While this seeming complexity suggests a psychologically rich character, the novel repeatedly tropes the "halfe-caste" sidekick as canine – a loyal dog to Starlight's anti-heroism.[18] As Starlight himself says, late in the novel, "[n]o dog was ever more faithful than he has been to me all through till now; but I was vexed at his having sold Dick and poor Jim."[19] This kind of racist portrayal is ubiquitous (as Bode shows) in nineteenth-century short fiction – for example, the "treacherous black" and the "noble savage."

The sense of treachery is amplified given that it is the way the plot finally reaches its climax. It is precisely Warrigal's disdain for Dick and Jim that leads to Starlight's death near the novel's end. Warrigal tips off the police to a plan the two have to escape to Queensland and lead a quiet life. But Starlight, becoming cognizant of this betrayal, rides back from his own escape to assist the betrayed members of his gang, leading to a shootout with the police that leads to the deaths of Jim and Starlight. To this point, there is little hint in the book of any alternate Indigenous chronotope of the kind hinted at in the provocation from Dark with which I began. When Warrigal rides into the scene of the gunfight, shortly after Starlight's death, he hands Dick Marston a revolver and insists: "'You shoot me, Dick Marston; you shoot me quick', he says. 'It's all my fault. I killed him – I killed the Captain. I want to die and go with him to the never-never country parson tell us about – up there!'"[20] Here we encounter a limited attempt to conceive a non-Indigenous sense of time (Christian, with its reference to the teachings of the "parson") alongside an Aboriginal sense of time and even that of the Dreaming as Warrigal conceives the Christian sense of afterlife as a passage to "never-never country." This is, of course, syncretic, but a fairly unsatisfying syncretism since it is situated in the larger linear realist narrative of the remainder of the novel. But Boldrewood's text attempts in a halting way to evoke Aboriginal conceptions of life, death and time involving difference; this effort bears little syncretic fruit.

The Twentieth Century

Boldrewood's "half-caste" Warrigal may have been a fairly one-dimensional antagonist. But he was not yet a representation of an aggregate, a social problem or a failure in government policy. Nor was there yet a discourse through which he could be known in his racial and cultural being, such as anthropology, for example. Fifty years later, Xavier Herbert's Norman Shillingsworth – protagonist of his 1938 novel *Capricornia* – would be a rounded, complex character, albeit with a fraught relation to his own Aboriginality. His very journey allegorizes a struggle against government policy and with its potential forms. Clearly, a transition in white depictions of Aboriginal characters and concerns takes place with (roughly) the turn of the twentieth century. What was the source of this transition?

The first decades of the twentieth century saw an explosion of anthropological and government investigation into such social effects as the so-called "half-caste problem" – that is, an exploding population of people of mixed descent. This phenomenon threw into doubt the long-standing settler colonial belief that the Aboriginal people were a "doomed race."[21] In 1896, reflecting on his observations as part of the Horn Scientific Expedition, the biologist and influential early Australian ethnographer Walter Baldwin Spencer wrote that "[i]n contact with the white man the aborigine is doomed to disappear."[22] Seventeen years later, Spencer would be one of the first to note a counter-valent tendency in the demography of Aborigines: the increasing number of people of mixed descent. "The question of half-castes," he wrote, "is a somewhat difficult one to deal with [...]. [I]t is sincerely to be hoped that as the country becomes more populated, the pro-portionate number will become less."[23] After increased investigation into the question of Aboriginal population, particularly in remote areas of the Commonwealth such as the Northern Territory – with its small and precari-ous white population – by the 1920s it had become clear that the population of people of Aboriginal descent was in fact increasing. By 1937, at the first Commonwealth Conference of Chief Protectors, demographic questions would again preoccupy the proceedings. Commonwealth Chief Protector Cecil Cook noted at that time that: "The number of half-castes in certain parts of Australia is increasing."[24] In the nineteenth century, Aboriginal people and, in particular, "half-castes" had been a social fact; in the twenti-eth century, they were increasingly being considered a social problem.

Discursive responses to this perceived crisis took multiple forms. In 1941, Norman Tindale, ethnologist at the South Australian Museum, asserted that "[t]he aborigines of South Australia are a dying remnant, but the half-castes who replace them are increasing in numbers and need attention and care."[25] He went so far as to assert that the expedition's findings were "[s]ufficient to indicate that the half-castes replace vanishing fullbloods in short time and appear to be steadily increasing at a rate probably greater than among any other type of the general population."[26] Anthropology and policy came together to form a discourse about the proper mode of governance over the lives of Aboriginal people. Australian States and Territories formalized their policies into Aborigines acts, such as in 1897 in Queensland, 1905 in Western Australia, and 1910 in the Northern Territory. The prospect of a rising half-caste population was received, at first, as a threat and a poten-tial crisis, one that would lead to the increased removal of mixed-descent Aboriginal children that produced what was later recognized as part of the Stolen Generations.

In the early twentieth century, the expertise on Aboriginal people acknowl-edged by white Australians was less than that of Aboriginal people themselves, consigned as they were to the status of either the supposedly primitive "full blood" or the aberrant "half-caste." Rather, authority to dispense knowl-edge on Aboriginal people's customs and way of life lay with anthropologists and policymakers. It was in this context that authors such as Herbert, Dark, and Katharine Susannah Prichard wrote their novels. The authority held by anthropologists and native administrators was not lost on any of these authors who, indeed, often claimed verisimilitude in their representations through the veridiction of such "liberal," "progressive" experts. Prichard, in the "Foreword" to the first edition of her 1928 novel of miscegenation in northwest Australia, *Coonardoo: The Well in the Shadow*, recounts that:

> Before *Coonardoo* was printed in the *Bulletin* I asked Mr Ernest Mitchell to read the M. S. Mr Mitchell is Chief Inspector of Aborigines for Western Australia. He has had thirty years' experience of the aborigines and no one in this country has wider knowledge and more sympathetic understanding of the Western and Nor'-West tribes. Mr Mitchell suggested an omission and several changes of spelling, but said that he could not fault the drawing of aborigines and conditions in *Coonardoo*, as he knew them.[27]

Ellen Smith has, for instance, explored the relation between Prichard's long engagement with the Australian Communist Party and the permutations of social realism within the latter's novels and drama.[28] However, in this paratext at least, the accuracy of the novel is avowed principally through its verification by a government native affairs department employee. Further, it is not only Mitchell's expertise and "knowledge," but also his affective connection to Aboriginal people – his "sympathetic understanding" that is emphasized.

Herbert also engaged with native affairs as a discourse and as a government department. He wrote to his publisher and editor, P. R. Stephensen, in the mid-1930s to declare that he "dream[ed] of being made a patrol officer, so that I may go right home to the old people and become one of them."[29] For Herbert, a government position in the native affairs administration equates to the possibility of connecting to, becoming part of and appropriating the position of an Aboriginal subject. In 1935, he won the position of superintendent of Darwin's Kahlin Compound for Aborigines. Herbert asserted his authority through his familiarity with anthropological discourse on Aborigines. In 1936, perhaps to advance his own position, he wrote to his friend Arthur Dibley in Sydney and revealed his scheme to auto-didactically study anthropology in order to convince Sydney University Professor of Anthropology A. P. Elkin to award him the University's Diploma of Anthropology Course. He writes to Dibley that when he inquired about the Diploma: "I had in mind the thought that if anything worthwhile is to be done for the Aborigines the men who will be appointed will most likely be Anthropologists. I feel sure that If I had a Diploma of Anthropology I could bluff my way into a permanent post."[30] While it was by "bluff" that Herbert seemed eager to carry it off, here the authority of anthropology, like that of native affairs, structures the possibility of what can be known by white people about Aboriginal people. As we shall see, it also structures his novel. Like Prichard and Herbert, Dark acknowledges in the front matter to *The*

Timeless Land: "For my descriptions of aboriginal life and customs I have found material in the works of Professor A. P. Elkin, Dr Phyllis Kaberry, Dame Mary Gilmore, Dr Herbert Basedow, Mrs Daisy Bates C. B. E. and others."[31] The Australian novel had reached a stage at which the expertise of the anthropologist and the native administrator had become paramount. Yet this would also be challenged by the communism of Gilmore (and Prichard herself), even as Phyllis Kaberry's work with Aboriginal women would develop work that contact-era ethnographers (such as Baldwin Spencer) could not touch. In particular, Kaberry's capacity to engage with Aboriginal women's business deconstructed the sense held at the time that Aboriginal culture was entirely patriarchal. These discourses would indeed also determine the sense of time engaged with in the novel.

Herbert's *Capricornia* presents an interesting case study: its curious sense of time is a chronotope of mythicism giving way to the bite of true satire. A third of the way through the novel, Oscar Shillingsworth, uncle of the novel's "half-caste" protagonist, argues with his stockman Peter Differ, whose very name codes difference from the social norm. Through the novel, Differ becomes marked as a spokesman for Herbert's own vision of the acceptance of miscegenation and of mixed-descent children within white society. In this early scene of debate, he positions the possibility of an ethics of miscegenation within the context of the "half-caste problem" that we saw identified by figures like Baldwin Spencer and Tindale. Differ declares to Shillingsworth:

> You're like the majority of people in Australia. You hide from this very real and terrifically important thing, hide it, and come to think after a while that it doesn't exist. But it does! It does! Why are there twenty thousand halfcastes in the country? Why are they never heard of? Oh my god![32]

There are a number of such dialogues – often involving Differ – throughout the novel. They engage with an ethics of responding to miscegenation, particularly as it responds to carnal relations between white men and Aboriginal women. Yet the "half-caste problem" comes also to structure the novel as a whole.

As Sean Monahan has suggested, "[l]ooked at as a conventional novel of bourgeois realism, the first half of *Capricornia* is perplexing," precisely because it takes until the second half to focus its attention entirely and properly on its "half-caste" hero Norman Shillingsworth.[33] Monahan suggests that the reason for this apparent lack of focus lies in an attempt "not [only] to tell the story of a single hero but to tell the story of a country."[34] Monahan further suggests that the first part of the novel, spanning chapters 1 to 5, tells a mythic story of early settlement.[35] Take the following lines, where Herbert's narrator describes the settlement of Capricornia:

It was beginning to look as though the land itself was hostile to anyone but the carefree nomads to whom the lord gave it, when a man named Brittins Willnot found the site of what came to be known as the town of Port Zodiac, the only settlement of any size that ever stood permanently on all the long coastline.[36]

Here we see the sense of the apparently mythic tone to the settlement of a seemingly inhospitable place, inflected by the Dickensian invocation of the white founding figure "Brittins Willnot' – a satirical troping of the imperialist assumption of settlement's foundations in the naming of a character. In telling what the novel itself calls the country's "unofficial early history" with the early settlement of the fictionalized northern Australia called "Capricornia," along with the narratives of mythic white bridging characters such as the larger-than-life fisherman Ned Krater, the novel produces a view of early settlement and contact between settlers (in the most literal sense) and Aborigines as part and parcel of a kind of foundational time of settlement.[37] As Monahan's taxonomy of *Capricornia* has it: the "second section of the novel (Chapters 7–15) examines the flawed world created by the initial failure of the white invaders to respond properly to Australia," in particular the failure to properly care for and find a place for the rising number of half-castes whose fates are dramatized.[38] Chief amongst these are Tocky Lace – the illegitimate daughter of Humboldt Lace, the government Protector of Aborigines and, of course, Mark Shillingsworth's abandoned son Nawnim (meaning "no name') whom the boy's Uncle Oscar eventually – on realizing how limited and harmful the various government compounds and facilities for half-caste children are – takes responsibility for and names Norman. The final section recounts the tragedy of the novel: Norman, on returning an educated adult, a trained engineer, to Capricornia finds no acceptance as a person of mixed descent. Believing himself to be a Javanese prince and not at all Aboriginal, he at first behaves haughtily to the Aboriginal characters he meets before learning the truth, which leads him to retreat into the bush.[39] This leads Norman eventually to father a child with Tocky, even as both she and the child are tragically found dead at the novel's final denouement.

Two things might become apparent from this brief summary of a long and complex novel. First, the further problem appended to the "question of half-castes" in Australia's north is the failure of assimilation. For Herbert, the tragedy is that color prejudice and broader racism mean that no matter how educated or socially and culturally "uplifted" (as the phrase went), a person of mixed parentage such as Norman can find little or no acceptance in Australia, and particularly its wild north. The second feature to become apparent might be recognized as formal: Herbert establishes the tragic, perhaps preordained dimension of this failure of (what he sees as) positive assimilation through the precession of the three chronotopes of the novel. These are made up of a mythic origin to settlement, the historic past during which so much miscegenation (or as the novel names it, "comboism") takes place, and finally, the tragic moment of the present wherein, as a consequence of the events of the past, the half-caste hero is still left outside society, lacking acceptance. Herbert would of course, eventually reverse this logic in *Poor Fellow My Country* (1975) with the story of his again mixed-descent hero Prindy who attempts to follow his "own road" by reconnecting with the Dreaming and his very Aboriginality. Even this solution, of reconnection with culture, is not something Herbert can foresee, and ultimately this effort in the later novel also fails tragically. But this contrast allows us to note the stark distinction between the early Herbert's prescriptive view of Aboriginal justice (the assimilation and education of Aboriginal people) and his later one (the right of Aboriginal people to reconnect with their culture), even as he can envision neither effort being successful.

Eleanor Dark's *The Timeless Land*, published only a few years after *Capricornia*, moves even further back in time and place, to the early settlement of Sydney harbor. Dark, as we saw in my opening epigraph taken from a letter to her London publisher William Collins, worried over the implications of a suggestion of Collins' to consider rewriting the prologue of *The Timeless Land* from the perspective of key Aboriginal characters. As Dark's biographers Barbara Brooks and Judith Clark summarize it:

> In her first draft of *The Timeless Land*, Eleanor started with a long prologue about the existence of this continent in the European imagination before 1770 when it was nothing more than a "rumour, a guessed-at mystery, a will o'-the-wisp to adventurers, a blank space on the maps of the greedy world". She described how Ptolemy marked it on his map as the Unknown Land, and merchants from India and Arabia traded with islands to the north, hearing rumours of a rich unexplored territory. When she sent Collins the manuscript in 1940, he was concerned about the length [...] and suggested that she cut her prologue, and some of the letters to settlers [...]. He suggested that the arrival of the whites could be seen from Bennilong and his father's point of view.[40]

Dark's concern turned upon a sense of the distinct sense of place and (in particular) time arising from Aboriginal culture as opposed to European culture. "It seems to me," she wrote:

> very important to get this suggestion of the age of the country, and the centuries during which the blacks inhabited it before the whites even knew of its existence. To incorporate this in the story through the eyes of Bennilong and his father as you suggest would, I agree, preserve the unity of the book better – but it presents some formidable difficulties.[41]

At this point, she lays out the "difficulties" highlighted within my epigraph. These principally bear on time. Her concern is that white readers "measured time by events," whereas she understood Aboriginal people to have "never had any very strong conception of time at all" – at least not in the sense of the historical, event-based time that she attributed to her readership.

While the sense of time that Dark wished to convey in her draft prologue – of Australia's chronotopic place within a series of European events – was abandoned, the sense that, to her European characters, Australia was supposed to be mired in timelessness was captured at key points:

> Governor Phillip stood on the deck watching the twilight sink into night, and struggled with an illusion. There was no sense of Time here. To-night was it Now, or a thousand years ago? Where was it in the life of a man which gave him that reassuring sense of the passage of Time? On his little journey from the cradle to the grave, how comforting to feel that Time moves forward with him – how chilling, how strange, how awesome, to feel, as one felt here, that Time was static, a vast, eternal, unmoving emptiness through which the tiny pathway of one's life ran from darkness into darkness and was lost![42]

In this way, Dark was unable to conjoin her narrative of the coming to Sydney harbor of the eventful time of Western history with her account of this temporality as she had envisaged for her draft prologue. But while she chose to heed her publisher's advice and cut the Western narrative of Australia's place in the precession of world events, she would nonetheless, as in this passage from Phillip's perspective, paint Australia as atemporal, steeped in the timelessness that bestowed upon her novel its title.

As we have seen, the occasional depiction of Aboriginal characters within the nineteenth-century novel gave way to a whole chronotope of indigeneity vested in claims to ethnographic authenticity within early twentieth-century novels. Patrick Wolfe has suggested that invasion is a structure and not an event.[43] The temporality of settlement in Herbert's first five "mythic" chapters of his *Capricornia* might suggest a certain *event* of colonization as taking up a discrete period of time – perhaps the equivalent of the *Arrernte* concept of the Dreaming (however problematic this may be). Nonetheless, the effects of this moment of settlement as it is depicted in both *Capricornia* (and, indeed, arguably the *Timeless Land* trilogy) reverberate through what follows in each novel. The fact that novelists such as Herbert or Dark are aware that the events they wish to paint give way to settler colonial structures also suggests that the effort to maintain an idea of Western/European eventfulness and Indigenous timelessness becomes unsustainable in the Australian novel since it depicts white settlers and Aboriginal contact. As I opened by suggesting, *altjira rama* is not timelessness – the absent other of Western history – but rather a rich conception of time, place and being. This depiction conveys a chronotope of separation, an eschewal of the coeval (*pace* Dark). As time marches on, white engagements with Aboriginality have both echoed and corrected this tendency – made matters better as well as worse.

Notes

1 Eleanor Dark to W. A. R. Collins, January 20, 1941. Eleanor Dark Papers, Mitchell Library, MLMSS 4545, Box 25.
2 Johannes Fabian, *Time and the Other: How Anthropology Makes its Object* (New York: Columbia University Press, 2014; 1983).
3 W. E. H. Stanner, "The Dreaming (1953)," in *The Dreaming & Other Essays* (Melbourne: Black Inc, 2010), pp. 57–72 (p. 57).
4 Vicki Grieves, "Aboriginal Spirituality: A Baseline for Indigenous Knowledges Development in Australia," *The Canadian Journal of Native Studies* 28.2 (2008): pp. 363–398.
5 Mikhail Bakhtin, *The Dialogic Imagination: Four Essays*, ed. Michael Holquist, trans. Caryl Emerson and Michael Holquist (Austin: University of Texas Press, 1981), p. 84.
6 Bakhtin, *The Dialogic Imagination*, p. 232.
7 Marcia Langton, *"Well I Heard It on the Radio and I Saw It on the Television":
An Essay for the Australian Film Commission on the Politics and Aesthetics of Filmmaking by and about Aboriginal People and Things* (Sydney: Australian Film Commission, 1993); Elizabeth Povinelli, *The Cunning of Recognition: Indigenous Alterities and the Making of Australian Multiculturalism* (Durham, NC: Duke, 2002).
8 See Michael R. Griffiths, *The Distribution of Settlement: Appropriation and Refusal in Australian Literature and Culture* (Press University of Western Australia Press, 2018), pp. 9–14.
9 Katherine Bode, *A World of Fiction: Digital Collections and the Future of Literary History* (Ann Arbor: University of Michigan Press, 2018), p. 176.
10 For a key example of writing about Australian fiction in terms of the gothic, see Ken Gelder, "Australian Gothic," in *The Routledge Companion to Gothic*, ed. Catherine Spooner and Emma McEvoy (London: Routledge, 2007), pp. 115–123. See also Ken Gelder and Jane Margaret Jacobs, *Uncanny Australia: Sacredness and Identity in a Postcolonial Nation* (Melbourne: Melbourne University Press, 1994).
11 Bode, *A World of Fiction*, p. 177.
12 Bode, *A World of Fiction*, p. 177.
13 Bode, *A World of Fiction*, p. 177.
14 Andrew McCann, *Marcus Clarke's Bohemia: Literature and Modernity in Colonial Melbourne* (Melbourne: Melbourne University Press, 2004), p. 197.
15 Marcus Clarke, as cited in McCann, *Marcus Clarke's Bohemia*, p. 197.
16 Rolf Boldrewood, *Robbery Under Arms* (Sydney: New Holland, 2008), p. 439.
17 Boldrewood, *Robbery Under Arms*, p. 6. Emphasis added.
18 Cf. Boldrewood, *Robbery Under Arms*, p. 420.
19 Boldrewood, *Robbery Under Arms*, p. 436.

20 Boldrewood, *Robbery Under Arms*, p. 438.

21 Russell McGregor, *Imagined Destinies: Aboriginal Australians and the Doomed Race Theory 1890–1939* (Carlton: Melbourne University Press, 1997), p. 63.

22 Walter Baldwin Spencer, as cited in McGregor, *Imagined Destinies*, p. 61.

23 Walter Baldwin Spencer, *Preliminary Report on the Aboriginals of the Northern Territory* (Melbourne: Government Printer, 1913), p. 21.

24 *Aboriginal Welfare: Initial Conference of Commonwealth and State Aboriginal Authorities* (Canberra: Government Printer, 1937), p. 10.

25 Norman B. Tindale, *Survey of the Half-Caste Problem in South Australia* (Adelaide: Royal Geographical Society [South Australian Branch], 1941), p. 67.

26 Tindale, *Survey*, p. 101.

27 Katharine Susannah Prichard, "Forward to the First Edition," in *Coonardoo* (Sydney: Angus & Robertson, 1956; 1929), p. v.

28 Ellen Smith, "Different Workers: Political Commitment and Subaltern Labour in Katharine Susannah Prichard's Brumby Innes," *Journal of Postcolonial Writing* 51.6 (2016): pp. 648–660.

29 Xavier Herbert, *Letters* (St Lucia: University of Queensland Press, 2002), p. 70.

30 Herbert, *Letters*, p. 64.

31 Eleanor Dark, *The Timeless Land* (Melbourne: Fontana Books, 1973; 1941), p. 6.

32 Xavier Herbert, *Capricornia* (Sydney: Angus & Robertson, 1975; 1938), p. 82.

33 Sean Monahan, *A Long and Winding Road* (Perth: University of Western Australia Press, 2003), p. 35.

34 Monahan, *A Long and Winding Road*, p. 35.

35 Herbert, *Letters*, p. 64; Monahan, *A Long and Winding Road*, p. 36.

36 Herbert, *Capricornia*, p. 2.

37 Herbert, *Capricornia*, p. 1.

38 Monahan, *A Long and Winding Road*, pp. 39–40.

39 Elspeth Tilley, *White Vanishing: Rethinking Australia's Lost-in-the-Bush Myth* (Amsterdam: Rodopi, 2012).

40 Barbara Brooks with Judith Clark, *Eleanor Dark: A Writer's Life* (Sydney: Pan Macmillan, 1998) p. 350.

41 Eleanor Dark to W. A. R. Collins, January 20, 1941. Eleanor Dark Papers, Mitchell Library, MLMSS 4545, Box 25.

42 Eleanor Dark, *The Timeless Land* (Melbourne: Fontana Books, 1973; 1941), p. 55.

43 Patrick Wolfe, "Settler Colonialism and the Elimination of the Native," *Journal of Genocide Research* 8.4 (2006): pp. 387–409.

5

EVELYN ARALUEN

Mabo, Mob, and the Novel

The Post-*Mabo* Turn

The recent periodization of a "post-*Mabo*" turn in Australian literature has been presented by scholars as a defining re-evaluation of the relationship between settler Australia and Aboriginal peoples. The Australian postcolonial school of critique popularized by Bill Ashcroft and colleagues in the early 1990s emphasizes the 1988 bicentenary of invasion, and the handing down of the 1992 *Mabo v. Queensland (No 2)* High Court decision as transformative events in Australian political and cultural identity.[1] On June 3, 1992, the Australian High Court recognized the claim of the Meriam people, a group of Torres Strait Islanders led by Koiki Mabo, over the islands of Mer, Dauar, and Waier. In the popular imagination, this ruling (which I discuss in more depth below) is thought to have overturned the legal fiction of *terra nullius* and to have provided the foundation for native title claims in Australia.[2] The subsequent creative and scholarly writing attending to this "post-*Mabo*" turn paradigm is nominally demarcated by a recognition of *terra nullius* as a legal and cultural injustice, an acknowledgment of the history of violent dispossession of traditional owners, and, theoretically, a renewed emphasis on the possibility of ethical community, which is generally rendered through symbolism and gesture as opposed to material political transformation. Each of these elements is explored with varying levels of commitment to a critique of settler-coloniality, whiteness, and the culpability of contemporary Australians in the ongoing oppression of Aboriginal peoples and Country. The postcolonial school of critique explores this renegotiation of settler and Aboriginal subjects and experiences through a logic of shared oppression, distinguished by multiple modernities of colonization.

While the specific implications of the *Mabo* case have received cursory framing from Australian literary scholars since the early nineties, there is comparatively little scholarship that connects the work of settler writers to prenative title land rights policies or struggles. In 2009, Ken Gelder and Paul Salzman argued that where pre-*Mabo* Australian literature is defined by the silencing of Aboriginal histories alongside the invocation of "nostalgias for a fully embodied mode of white settler occupation," post-*Mabo* literature thematizes Aboriginal dispossession alongside "white panic [over property] ownership and belonging."[3] More specific framing of a post-*Mabo* literary turn was then advanced by Kieran Dolin in 2014, structured around shifts in white Australian literary frameworks of "envisioning" land following the High Court's *Mabo* judgment. Dolin examined writing by Dorothy Hewett, Alex Miller, and Andrew McGahan, and peripherally Kate Grenville's *The Secret River* (2005), as shifting sites in "the interplay between the language of law and discourses of topography" in contemporary settler Australian fiction. Liliana Zavaglia's 2016 *White Apology and Apologia: Australian Novels of Reconciliation* extended upon the explicit emphasis of land and property of these previous approaches, and advanced another point of eventfulness in former Prime Minister Kevin Rudd's 2008 Apology speech:

> Together with *Mabo* and the *Apology*, the novels also reveal this conflicted drive as a tension that arguably came to define this period. This tension fluctuates between a reconciliatory impulse of sorrow for Indigenous historical loss and the defensive desire to offer exits for white culture from the ongoing demands of a violent settlement history. This book examines how these novels exhibit this tension as a twinned register of white desire, which performs what I describe as a double movement of apology and apologia, reflecting the shifting states of white culture in the process of reconciliation.[4]

Zavaglia further contextualizes the literature of this period with the influence of the Hawke Labor government's 1991 Council for Reconciliation Act, the History Wars, John Howard's dismantling of Aboriginal rights platforms, and conservative politician Pauline Hanson's paranoid fantasies of "white" persecution. She reads novels by Alex Miller, Andrew McGahan, Kate Grenville, and Gail Jones through the framework of "perpetrator trauma," informed by the historian Dominick LaCapra's research on trauma, absence, and loss in post-apartheid South Africa and post-Nazi Germany.[5] As Zavaglia demonstrates through her analysis, these novels stage historical conflicts of land theft, slavery, and genocide through interpersonal settler-Aboriginal encounters in a double gesture of grief and defense, and generally linger on themes of absence and haunting. In the conflation of Aboriginal suffering with settler guilt and discomfort, such approaches follow LaCapra's conditions for "melancholic paralysis," which unproductively obfuscates the actual histories of dispossession and displacement and reaffirms the centrality of settler anxieties over Indigenous experiences.[6] Across *White Apology and Apologia: Australian Novels of Reconciliation* there is an awareness that the symbolic resolutions offered in novels insufficiently attend to the material and political demands of reconciliation.

Most recently, Geoff Rodoreda has sought to offer a comprehensive interrogation of settler and Aboriginal literary approaches to *Mabo* and native title in *The Mabo Turn in Australian Fiction* (2018). He argued that the post-*Mabo* category's emergence is ultimately defined by the liminal condition of the settler body between the supposedly distinct spaces of the bush and the colonial frontier. This liminal subjectivity is epitomized by the opening of David Malouf's 1993 novel *Remembering Babylon*, which Rodoreda describes as a point of origin for a reimagined sense of national identity brought on by *Mabo*:

> [T]he Mabo decision of 1992 altered the notion of what it meant to be a settler Australian. Non-Indigenous Australians were finally confronted with a new narrative about the occupation and settlement of Australia: no, Australia was not a *terra nullius*, an empty land belonging to no one, settled peacefully by the British, from 1788; the land, already occupied by nations of peoples, was taken from its original inhabitants. Aboriginal people were dispossessed, often violently so, of their rights to land. More than any other event in Australia's history, the Mabo decision has challenged previous ways of thinking about land, identity, settler belonging and history.[7]

In this paradigm, the common law refutation of *terra nullius* is positioned as a revolutionary event. For Rodoreda, the *Mabo* decision has both political and cultural implications, and has fundamentally transformed not only the broader political and cultural landscape of Australian society but also the conditions of settler subjectivity. Rodoreda's argument is predicated on the assumption that *Mabo* was understood or responded to by settlers through meaningful acceptance and action and was then readily translated into literary fiction. He proposes several typological tropes and distinguishes between settler and Aboriginal approaches through the linked but ultimately oppositional positions of "post-*Mabo*" and "beyond-*Mabo*." Post-*Mabo* fiction for Rodoreda is writing by non-Aboriginal authors that acknowledges or thematizes, in whole or in part, prior and continuous Aboriginal occupation and possession of the land. It is writing that seeks to dispute the myth of *terra nullius* and critically scrutinizes colonialism in Australia and the often-violent dispossession of Aboriginal peoples. In "Beyond-*Mabo*" fiction, Aboriginal authors challenge *Mabo*-based approaches to land management, prioritize Aboriginal epistemological and custodial relationships to land, and assert broader values of Indigenous sovereignty. He further defines First Nations texts such as Melissa Lucashenko's *Mullumbimby* (2013), Alexis Wright's *Carpentaria* (2006), and Kim Scott's *Benang* (1999) as "sovereignty novels," concerned less with thematizing grief and loss and more with challenging the implication of British sovereignty made explicit by the High Court of Australia's determination in 1992.

These approaches to the ambivalent signifier of post-*Mabo* operate in the wider context of affective signifiers of settler subjectivity. Most arguments for the significance of post-*Mabo* fiction as a category do so in the form of periodization, positioning the emerging genre as a signifier of a new ethical condition of settlement. It should be acknowledged that *White Apology and Apologia* is structured by periodization, but gives a fuller account of the political and cultural conditions acting upon the affective aspects of Reconciliation, complicating the claim that post-*Mabo* literature might be read as an explicit response to legal reforms regarding place and property. Rodoreda's claim in *The Mabo Turn in Australian Fiction* – that these literary formations predate the official legalities but are structured by the same impulses – emphasizes that post-*Mabo* and beyond-*Mabo* are not solid temporal descriptions, but rather forms of interpretation and rhetoric that "both reflect *and* agitate a changed way of thinking that non-Indigenous Australians have had to come to terms with in relation to understandings of Aboriginal attachment to land and an Indigenous presence in Australian society."[8] According to this argument, in which "post" describes a sense of contestation, and not chronology, the post-*Mabo* novel both argue for and instantiates a new settler accommodation of Indigenous presence.

This genealogy of the post-*Mabo* novel identifies a series of tropes and conventions that claim to articulate unsettlement and rupture with the colonial past. However, as Aboriginal responses to the genre demonstrate, these practices continue to reify and reinscribe settler-colonial legal and cultural structures that entrench Aboriginal dispossession. As such, the post-*Mabo* genre requires examination as a site of fundamental structural repetitions, as well as one of apparent or rhetorical fissure.

Settler Moves to Innocence

Properly situated in the history of settler Australian literary forms, the post-*Mabo* genre purports to represent a reformed and newly ethical national polity that obviates, obscures, and exculpates the ongoing oppression and deprivation of Aboriginal peoples, boasting an ethical condition that we, as Aboriginal people, are still denied.

Following Michael Griffiths' argument in *The Distribution of Settlement: Appropriation and Refusal in Australian Literature and Culture* (2018), I argue that the post-*Mabo* genre is yet another demonstration of the settler-colonial culture's predication on structures of repetition and eventfulness.[9] The formal singularity that authors and scholars of post-*Mabo* fiction emphasize to instantiate the bicentenary, *Mabo* and more recently the *Uluru Statement from the Heart* (2017) as significant moments of acknowledgment and reconciliation have their roots in earlier pastoral and frontier traditions of writing place and landscape in Australia. Tropes of colonial melancholy, bush gothicism, fetishization, and the sublime act upon the post-*Mabo* novel of the late twentieth- and early twenty-first century with as much imaginative authority as can be found in the modernist, pastoral, and frontier literatures of the previous centuries. Reading this emphasis as a transformation of older colonial logics, rather than a psychic or ethical drive propelled by a changing political landscape, we are able to contextualize a genealogy to these aesthetics that sheds greater light on post-*Mabo* fiction's two primary political functions: an appeal for symbolic resolution of settler-Aboriginal relations in the self-effacing refusal of material closure, and the fundamental appropriation of Aboriginal spirituality upon which this resolution is itself predicated.

Arguably this constitutes an evolution or a sophistication of the same logics that have, since invasion, structured settler responses to, and representations of, Aboriginal land and its custodians. The ostensible deep content of the Australian national literary character – summarized by John McLaren as "the hostility of the landscape to man's efforts to tame it" – moves anxiously around Aboriginal presence in cosmic, embodied, and negated forms.[10] As Affrica Taylor has observed, narratives of exploration, discovery, settlement, and struggle that emphasize white heroism and resourcefulness against the *Unheimlichkeit* of the Australian landscape were mobilized to legitimate a sense of settler sovereignty and right-to-dwelling, but failed to resolve the unhomeliness of the setting.[11] The environmental conditions of the land being incompatible with European modes of agriculture, nineteenth-century colonial poets such as Charles Harpur and Henry Kendall translated the landscape through gothic themes of hostility and hardship in early Australian pastoral poetics. In the hallowed *Bulletin* years of the 1890s, later writers such as Henry Lawson and Barbara Baynton staged forbidding prose tales of estrangement and annihilation against the backdrop of a land fundamentally opposed to humanity and civilization. Their works construct homesteads that concentrate poverty and struggle, and function more to stage the land's cosmic retribution than they do to provide a domestic refuge from the elements. As Jonathan Dunk in his study of early colonial short fiction observes, the deeper grammar of these lonely refuges and crumbling shacks in the bush always speak towards expiation and possession.[12]

As I have argued previously, the Australian pastoral is a site of conflict between the alluring but resistant aesthetics of the land, and the familiar but incompatible languages of the traditional Euro-Western form.[13] Following Paul Kane and Andrew Taylor in their reckoning of the pastoral not as genre but as a series of modes that assimilate natural and human worlds into artistic endeavor, this tension has been mobilized by settler writers and artists for a range of nationalist concerns – most saliently the ongoing articulation and justification for the cultural and geographic boundaries of the colony within, beyond, and against the imperial center.

While the "bush ethos" underpinning these early nationalist texts provides an effective thematic for the psychological condition of exile from the vantage point of the settler convict, it can also be critiqued as a self-dramatizing mythology. With regard to texts such as *The Secret River*, we are right to be suspicious of the overdetermination of the land as haunting and ghostly. As Alan Frost suggests in his study of early New South Wales colonial literature, the Australian literary character has been dominated by an origin narrative historically inconsistent with early settler writings, a useful position for its resistance of the reductive argument that the Australian landscape is somehow psychically responsible for settler crisis in these narratives:

> It seems reasonable to suspect that the personalities of those who expressed the bush ethos may also have shaped it [...]. Might it not be in that taking convicts and the bush as the correlatives for their feelings of isolation and despair, these writers were expressing individual predilections rather than a general historical experience?[14]

The character of an Australian colonial melancholic – most famously identified by Marcus Clarke in his introduction to Adam Lindsay Gordon's *Sea Spray and Smoke Drift* in 1867 – has historically styled itself as the working-class outcast around tropes of economic and cultural displacement.[15] But as Bob Hodge and Vijay Mishra remind us, the settler colonial project of Australia both transported and translated the ambitions and antagonisms of the metropolitan center into the new land, along with the alliances of power and oppression that collaborated against the lawful custodians.[16] If Aboriginal presence is noted in these works, it is a representation predominantly concerned with symbols of atavistic inconvenience to the colonial project, charged with psychic significance in the evocation of a ghostly specter haunting land lost to Aboriginal people, but which ultimately clears space for the discovery and cultivation of that land by the appropriate settler. Hodge and Mishra have explored this double premise as the "Aboriginal archipelago" of simultaneously refusing to acknowledge Aboriginal presence in social space, while conjuring up emblematic tropes of Aboriginal spiritual presence in disembodied forms. Although one strategy seems to suggest a more ethically considerate response, they

argue that each of these tropes enacts a form of violence – the former erasing Aboriginal people from literature, and the latter from history, into the
mythic void of the Dream Time – itself a simultaneously inaccurate and
appropriative formulation.[17]

These drives persist in contemporary Australian fiction today. In literary
terms, they enact what Patrick Wolfe has theorized as the colonial "logic
of elimination," wherein the genocidal erasure of Indigenous peoples facilitates the acquisition of land for the establishment of the settler colony,
whilst settlers simultaneously cultivate a symbolic return of the native to
demarcate the colony's point of departure from the imperial center.[18] This
return is imagined through strategies of settler nativism and fantasies of
adoption into Indigenous cultural spaces, practices, and languages, and
through artistic performances of settler heroism and reconciliation with the
grateful survivors. This structure corresponds neatly with what Eve Tuck
and K. Wayne Yang have described as "settler moves to innocence": a range
of intellectual evasions of settler complicity in the colonization of Indigenous
peoples.[19] This includes notions of settler nativism and fantasies of adoption
into Indigenous land and cultural traditions on purely symbolic terrain.

The success of this pastoral maneuver in pre-federation tropes gives way
to a motif of haunting in modern Australian fiction, observed by Hodge
and Mishra in several modernist novels and significantly palpable in the
post-*Mabo* genre. Where Harpur, Kendall, and Lawson curated Aboriginal
graves in their arcadian glens to anchor the doomed-race theory popularized by Darwin, modern novelists write of bones surfacing beneath colonial
homesteads as in Andrew McGahan's 2004 novel *The White Earth*, or of
haunted suburban landscapes of Tim Winton's 1998 novel *Cloud Street*. As
Griffiths contends, these tropes and formations return and are recycled in
the contemporary literary imaginary at "the interface between elimination
and appropriation," where Aboriginal presence and culture is variously celebrated, mourned, fetishized and erased in "a mode of appropriation that
would appear to conjure a false Indigenous presence that is available to colo-
nisers."[20] In the literary imagination of a post-*Mabo* but never post-settlement
Australia, both celebration and mourning can function as consolidations,
rather than unsettlements of the colonial logics of elimination described by
Wolfe. A critical differentiation inheres in the object, rather than the sentiment of these rituals. Is the sorrowful past lamented as part of a process of
healing and restorative justice involving contemporary Indigenous communities, or rather a ritual of expiation for the settler? Griffiths continues:

> In this way, settler appropriation is structured around the, at turns,
> quasi-celebration, appropriation, and fetishisation of Aboriginal culture and

country that accompanies and bolsters the lived experience of invasion and theft that has structured the settler colony since contact. Imperialist nostalgia is melancholic and such melancholic nostalgia is the psychic structure of guilt aimed at the exculpation of the settler subject. By imagining appropriation as a tribute to Aboriginality, the melancholic and nostalgic character of this particular form of settler common sense makes fetishism a psychic alibi for theft.[21]

These forms of elimination, curation, appropriation, and replacement circulate through a quality Griffith describes as "artifactuality" – extending the appeals to authority and structures of circulation from which anthropological representations of Indigeneity gain their influence on literary contexts.[22] These historical processes and traditions contribute to a moral landscape in which representations of settler guilt, or colonial melancholy regarding Aboriginal presence, must be regarded with extreme hermeneutic suspicion. Griffiths further notes that these disingenuous tropes seem to inhabit, replicate, and disseminate a curiously deceptive temporality:

> The spectre of past essences emergent from the settler colonial canon and its archive means rendering any authenticity a vanishing impossibility, consistently out of reach of those settler and Indigenous subjects whose identification it nonetheless solicits. And it is important to note: this vanishing image reproduces the double time of settler-colonial melancholia. Just as settler-colonial futures are premised on elimination, so artifactuality attempts to foreclose the possibility of comporting identity to the authenticity that the traces of the archive invents and insists upon.[23]

In the post-*Mabo* novels of writers like Grenville and McGahan, the domestic tranquility of the settler fantasy is disrupted by haunting and spiritual retribution. Yet no attempt is made to encounter Aboriginal presence in agential, embodied, and material ways. In these narratives, the colonial homestead, built on an interchangeable foundation of rock engravings, burial sites, or massacre grounds, is rendered structurally and cosmically unviable under the weight of settler guilt. Although these novels attempt to dramatize the realization that the settler is not the heroic possessor of the land, they nonetheless seek through expiation and catharsis to occupy a position of ethical equanimity on country not functionally dissimilar from possession. These symbolic gestures are often framed in ancestral or atavistic terms: a melancholy scenery of petroglyphs or burial sites without living descendants to tend them. Read generously these traces might constitute an attempt to situate ancestral and immemorial presence in the land, against assumptions of *terra nullius*, but I'm more inclined to agree with Dunk's suggestion that:

> The discursive elisions and contradictions within that desperately national textual body which have been symptomatically interpreted by a certain Freudian

emphasis of postcolonial criticism – as tremors of conscience within the settler mind – can and should be read as subsequent and more sophisticated functions of those colonial logics, and not as failures or limitations thereof.[24]

Where the various modes of the colonial pastoral construct a nativized identity from the labor of conflict against a hostile landscape, in the post-*Mabo* novel the excavation of colonial sins from the (apparent) total silence of *terra nullius* is itself the labor of belonging. As it has been since its earliest origins in Australian literature, mourning and melancholia is a ritual of settler possession.

Mabo and Mob

The main point of dissonance for the Aboriginal reader of the settler post-*Mabo* novel has less to do with formal integrity, and more with the dramatic departure from the legal, political, and cultural realities of the *Mabo* judgment and the subsequent Native Title Act 1993 for Aboriginal and Torres Strait Islander communities. What does it mean for our invaders to be so psychically and creatively invested in a myth of our reconciliation, when it is predicated on the endless literary restaging of our dispossession?

Writings from Aboriginal scholars such Aileen Moreton-Robinson, Megan Davis, Larissa Behrendt, Irene Watson, Phillip Falk, and Gary Martin have sought to emphasize that *Mabo* and native title represents only one aspect of the broader discourse and lived experience of Indigenous sovereignty in Australia. Long before native title was formalized by the 1993 Act, Aboriginal people were working and agitating for the right to their land, with the first formal petition for the return of land dating back to Maria Lock's letter to Governor Darling in 1832, very shortly after the first novel was published in Australia, Henry Savery's *Quintus Servinton: A Tale Founded upon Incidents of Real Occurrence*. The popular cultural interpretation of *Mabo* as an explicit refusal of *terra nullius* neglects decades and, indeed, more than two centuries of resistance to invasion and settlement, as well as overemphasizing the legal status of *terra nullius*, which emerged itself not as law but rather discourse in the 1980s in a context of agitation towards emerging land rights debates. When *terra nullius* was "overturned" by the High Court in 1992, and native title recognized as being held by traditional owners from the islands of Mer, Dauar, and Waier in the Torres Strait, it was significantly on the basis of records of continued agricultural practice, reflecting the Lockean emphasis on agricultural cultivation as defense for the invasion and subsequent settlement of Aboriginal and Torres Strait Islander lands.[25] While recognizing the pernicious and dehumanizing racial discourse of settler coloniality, which degraded Indigenous people to the status of savages, it is refusing the claim that the British had legal priority to the land, which lies at the heart of the land rights struggle in Australia.

As Indigenous rights researcher Richie Howitt demonstrated in 2006, the incommensurable tensions between the legal and cultural achievements of *Mabo* and native title stem from the Australian High Court's "sleight-of-hand" in defining the co-existence of Indigenous and non-Indigenous forms of possession and occupation:

> Having reduced the robust and ancient jurisdictions of the Dreaming to the fragility of "native title," the High Court introduced a slippery notion of "co-existence." This notion was not an acknowledgement of the co-existence of Indigenous and non-Indigenous interests in particular places, but an abstract conceptualisation of legal interests in property that could exist together. It was this abstract conceptualisation which was used to address the persistent presence of Aboriginal people in cultural landscapes that were now possessed by new owners whose title was predicated on the imaginary of terra nullius.[26]

The function of native title was never to provide robust and efficient legal frameworks with which to assert Indigenous sovereignty and support the return of invaded lands and waters to custodians, but rather to further entrench the power of the settler colony to extend benevolence to the native subject. Contrary to its popular representation native title is in many senses antithetical to meaningful land rights – it is an alienating and legalistic process in which traditional law and custom is controlled and regulated by the state. As Moreton-Robinson has famously declared, *Mabo* and the subsequent Native Title Act of 1993 invented "a rule of extinguishment that did not exist under common law," which required an Indigenous investment in patriarchal whiteness for its success:

> Pursuant to the *Mabo* decision and the subsequent Native Title Act 1993, Indigenous people are in effect trespassers in the land until they prove their native title. The law places the burden of proof for native title on the Indigenous people to demonstrate to courts of law controlled by predominantly white men. Since courts regard the written word as more reliable than oral testimonies, all claimants must be able to substantiate their oral histories with documents written by white people, such as explorers, public servants, historians, lawyers, anthropologists, pastoralists, and police. These documents are often in conflict with Indigenous representations; lawyers and judges usually seek to resolve the disjuncture by introducing the texts or oral testimonies of additional white experts. Thus, patriarchal whiteness sets the criteria for proof and the standards for credibility.[27]

Moreton-Robinson's emphasis on the textuality of native title is a key consideration in the settler-colonial literary response to native title. As has been shown, much of the literary commentary generated by or involved with the *Mabo* era fails to recognize that the *Mabo* decision constituted an acknowledgment, rather than a statement of accountability, of something always known to Aboriginal people. Settler novels overtly concerned with indexing the significance of *Mabo* in a structure of eventfulness are almost invariably overdetermined by an ongoing process of artifactuality distant from Indigenous realities, including the many injurious effects of native title on Indigenous communities. Native title requires laborious, expensive, and traumatic processes to prove prior and continuous occupation, and when it fails, as it so often does, communities are left devastated and divided by the process. Settler colonial fantasies of reconciliation and forgiveness in the post-*Mabo* novel are thereby predicated on the explicit erasure of Aboriginal lived realities.

Return to Country

As Ali Gummilya Baker and Gus Worby remarked in their study of *Mabo*'s impact on Aboriginal identity and writing, where contemporary Aboriginal novels are concerned, "Mabo now means to be seen as well as heard."[28] In light of the complex and at times hostile relationships many Aboriginal and Torres Strait Islander communities have with the native title process, an expanding body of Indigenous writing in Australia has been reflecting on and engaging with the complexity of the native title process, and the fundamental indignity of seeking the recognition and ratification of ancient law/lore through callous colonial processes. Where the settler post-*Mabo* novel's engagement with the broad symbolism of the *Mabo* era has continued to manifest in tropes of ghostliness and mourning, Aboriginal novelists such as Tara June Winch and Melissa Lucashenko have been embracing and emphasizing themes of language restoration, spiritual connection, and the rehabilitation of native ecosystems and interrogating the fragility, failing, and limitation of native title and its impact on Aboriginal communities and individuals. Novels such as Winch's *The Yield* (2019) and Lucashenko's *Mullumbimby* (2013) and *Too Much Lip* (2018) center Aboriginal community experience in their depiction of native title processes, and privilege restoration and renewal of country over legal or symbolic forms of repossession. Often enough reconnection is not staged in terms of political sovereignty, but rather the acknowledgment of intergenerational traumas from dispossession and displacement and the role that country plays in healing.

Settler colonial investment in guilt, melancholia, reconciliation, and other modes of non-Indigenous belonging through the post-*Mabo* novel seeks to resolve cultural traumas in symbolic terms and are underpinned by a fundamental misinterpretation of the legal and psychological implications of the land rights movement and subsequent native title legislation. Even if a shift to more realistic representations of the post-*Mabo* era in contemporary Aboriginal novels could resolve these failed projects, this is not an Aboriginal problem to solve.

Notes

1 See Bill Ashcroft, Gareth Griffiths, and Helen Tiffin, *The Empire Writes Back: Theory and Practice in Post-Colonial Literatures* (London and New York: Routledge, 2002; 1989).
2 For a brief overview, see Aileen Moreton-Robinson, ""Our Story Is in the Land": Why the Indigenous Sense of Belonging Unsettles White Australia," *ABC Religion & Ethics* 9 November 2020: www.abc.net.au/religion/our-story-is-in-the-land-indigenous-sense-of-belonging/11159992.
3 Ken Gelder and Paul Salzman, as cited in Geoff Rodoreda, *The Mabo Turn in Australian Fiction* (Oxford: Peter Lang, 2018), p. 22.
4 Liliana G. Zavaglia, *White Apology and Apologia: Australian Novels of Reconciliation* (Amherst, NY: Cambria Press, 2016), p. 2.
5 Zavaglia, *White Apology and Apologia*, pp. 15–16. See also Dominick LaCapra, "Trauma, Absence, Loss," *Critical Inquiry* 25.4 (1999): pp. 696–727.
6 Zavaglia, *White Apology and Apologia*, p. 205.
7 Rodoreda, *The Mabo Turn in Australian Fiction*, p. 3.
8 Rodoreda, *The Mabo Turn in Australian Fiction*, p. 6.
9 Michael R. Griffiths, *The Distribution of Settlement: Appropriation and Refusal in Australian Literature and Culture* (Perth University of Western Australia Publishing, 2018), p. 5.
10 John McLaren, "The Image of Reality in Our Writing," *Overland* 27–28 (1963): pp. 43–47 (p. 45).
11 See Affrica Taylor, "Settler Children, Kangaroos and Cultural Politics of Australian National Belonging," *Global Studies of Childhood* 4.3 (2014): pp. 169–182.
12 Jonathan Dunk, "Short Fiction Short Nation: The Ideologies of Australian Realism," *Australian Literary Studies* 33.3 (2018): pp. 1–19.
13 See Evelyn Araluen, "Snugglepot and Cuddlepie in the Ghost Gum," *Sydney Review of Books,* February 11, 2019: https://sydneyreviewofbooks.com/essay/snugglepot-and-cuddlepie-in-the-ghost-gum-evelyn-araluen/.
14 Alan Frost, "What Created, What Perceived? Early Responses to New South Wales," *Australian Literary Studies* 7.2 (1975): pp. 185–205 (p. 204).
15 Marcus Clarke, *A Colonial City*, ed. by I. T. Hergcnhan (St Lucia: University of Queens land Press, 1972), pp. 361–365.
16 See Bob Hodge and Vijay Mishra, *Dark Side of the Dream: Australian Literature and the Postcolonial Mind* (Sydney: Allen & Unwin, 1991).
17 Hodge and Mishra, *Dark Side of the Dream*, p. 30.

18 Patrick Wolfe, "Settler Colonialism and the Elimination of the Native," *Journal of Genocide Research* 8.4 (2006): pp. 387–409.
19 Eve Tuck and K. Wayne Yang, "Decolonisation is not a Metaphor," *Decolonisation: Indigeneity, Education and Society* 1.1 (2012): pp. 1–40.
20 Griffiths, *The Distribution of Settlement*, p. 6.
21 Griffiths, *The Distribution of Settlement*, p. 9.
22 Griffiths, *The Distribution of Settlement*, pp. 10–11.
23 Griffiths, *The Distribution of Settlement*, pp. 11–12.
24 Dunk, "Short Fiction Short Nation," p. 1.
25 According to Locke's influential argument in *Two Treatises on Government*, individuals come to possess a "parcel of land" by "improving" it through labour. See John Locke, *Two Treatises of Government*, ed. Peter Laslett (Cambridge: Cambridge University Press, 2005), II.33. James Tully's revisionary argument from his 1991 essay "Rediscovering America" has been influential on the scholarship, especially in Canada. See James Tully, *An Approach to Political Philosophy: Locke in Contexts* (Cambridge: Cambridge University Press, 2009).
26 Richie Howitt, "Scales of Coexistence: Tackling the Tension Between Legal and Cultural Landscapes in Post-Mabo Australia," *Macquarie Law Journal* 5 (2006): pp. 49–64 (p. 51).
27 Aileen Moreton-Robison, *The White Possessive: Property, Power, and Indigenous Sovereignty* (Minneapolis: University of Minnesota Press, 2015), p. 69.
28 Ali Gumillya Baker and Gus Worby, "Aboriginality Since Mabo: Writing, Politics, and Art," in *A Companion to Australian Literature Since 1900*, eds. Nicholas Birns and Rebecca McNeer (Rochester, NY: Camden House, 2007), pp. 16–40 (p. 22).

6

EMMETT STINSON

Publishing the Australian Novel

The material networks of the publishing industry determine how contemporary literature circulates in Australia. Book history is an established method of Australian literary studies, and critics such as Elizabeth Webby have been analyzing material literary production since the 1970s, but the study of the publishing industry is comparatively new. As David Carter has argued, publishing studies is a "floating discipline, attached uncertainly to communications, literary studies, book history, writing and business studies."[1] While publishing studies might form part of the "material turn" in Australian literary studies,[2] most Australian researchers also train students for work in the industry; publishing studies thus entails a theory-praxis nexus more like creative writing than traditional literary studies. Publishing forms the conditions of possibility for Australian literature: Even in an age of self-publishing, the overwhelming majority of culturally significant books are produced through the industry itself. The publishing industry exerts its influence over popular, critical, and scholarly reception in various ways: by selecting the manuscripts that will be published, by editing them to conform with what editors believe to be audience expectations, by distributing them to specific networks of retail outlets, and by marketing books in specific ways and contexts that signal their genre, form, and intended audience – which often shapes a book's subsequent reception. Moreover, the larger dynamics of the field of publishing have a direct effect on how literature is produced. The growth of the modern, bureaucratized Australian publishing house during the twentieth century enabled modes of cultural nationalism – or what Mark Davis has termed the "literary paradigm"[3] – that served to codify notions of Australian literature. But the increasing economic rationalization of international conglomerate publishers, which has only accelerated under what Mark McGurl has termed the "Age of Amazon,"[4] has also threatened traditional business models for literary publishing, which has had significant effects on both the way that literature circulates and how authors support themselves financially.

Paradigms for Analyzing the Publishing Industry

There are two overlapping paradigms for analyzing how publishing and editing influence literary production: The first draws on literary sociology, and the second on material analyses in book history. The vast majority of literary sociology extrapolates from Pierre Bourdieu's investigations of French literary cultures. For Bourdieu, literature was a "field," which, as John R. W. Speller has argued, emerges from "historical process of autonomisation and differentiation" such that the "'rules of the game' which determine the relative positions and possible position-takings of all the agents involved in each particular field" are generated internally, rather than being determined by external notions of value, such as economics, political influence, or other forms of power.[5] Bourdieu states that those who "occupy the dominant positions" in the field will "manifest their independence with respect to external powers, political or economic" to demonstrate their autonomy.[6] Fields need to be understood according to their internal logic, which arises out of the competitive struggles of agents who seek to determine its value structure; sociological analyses need to consider "not only the material production" of literary works, but also the "production of the value of the work," which requires understanding of how prestige operates within the field.[7] For Bourdieu, the literary field is bifurcated by two "poles" that represent rival notions of value: "the pole of pure production, where the producers tend to have as clients only other producers (who are also rivals)" and "the pole of large-scale production, subordinated to the expectations of a wide audience."[8] The pole of production is "autonomous" and suspicious of "immediate success"; this area of the field relies upon prestige, or symbolic capital, which is important because it is the "capital of consecration" that has the power to turn works into classics that will accrue value over time.[9] The pole of large-scale production is "heteronomous" and includes publishers and writers for whom "success is in itself a guarantee of value," and who seek to produce bestsellers that will sell immediately, but whose long-term success is more uncertain.[10]

Crucially, for Bourdieu, there is a polar alignment of authors and their publishers, editors, critics, and other various intermediaries: "publishers of the avant-garde and producers of bestsellers agree in saying that they would inevitably run into trouble if they ventured to publish works objectively designed for the opposite pole of the publishing space."[11] While these different fields of production (authors, publishers, critics, and so forth) are not isomorphic, they share homologous notions of value. For this reason, Bourdieu argues that the sociology of literature must consider "not only the direct producers of the work" but also the "producers of meaning and value of the work – critics, publishers, gallery directors and the whole set of agents whose combined efforts produce consumers capable of knowing and recognizing the work of art as such."[12] This is so because intermediaries shape the reception of the work in the process of mediation, and, for this reason, production and reception cannot be disentangled.

The second model is drawn from the field of book history and relies upon Robert Darnton's account of the book "communications circuit that runs from author to the publisher (if the bookseller does not assume that role), the printer, the shipper, the bookseller, and the reader."[13] This account offers a method for examining the mediation and reception of books as they move from author to reader. Moreover, like Bourdieu, Darnton links production with reception by arguing that the "reader completes the circuit" in influencing "the author both before and after the act of composition."[14] Darnton's account has recently been updated to account for digital technology by Claire Squires and Padmini Ray-Murray in their "digital publishing communications circuit," which acknowledges that "radical disruptions and disintermediations that are occurring in the digital age."[15] As Squires and Ray-Murray argue, traditional publishing activities are being undertaken by new agents, such as self-publishers who market and distribute their own work. Other traditional agents, such as printers, have become entirely disintermediated from digital sections of the value chain. There are also new players in the industry, including technology companies like Amazon, which is now arguably more influential than the older publishing conglomerates. As a result, books now circulate through more various pathways than in Darnton's model, and any material analysis must acknowledge this new variability. The Bourdieusian' and the book history models, however, share the notion that a book's reception and its perceived value among both industry professionals and readers is heavily dependent upon the process of production and mediation. From this perspective, critical investigations of publishing and editing practices are useful because they illuminate these conditions of possibility and clarify how individual works engage with and rely upon specific networks and individuals who shape the field of literature itself. Moreover, sociological analysis promises, at least in theory, to elucidate how different notions of literary value are created and imbued within social networks of agents and institutions.

Editors and Publishers in the Australian Literary Field

Editors are often popularly imagined as pedants who draw red lines through grammatical errors and awkward phrases. While this detailed work, known as copyediting, remains important, many editors primarily engage in larger tasks, such as commissioning (selecting manuscripts to be published by a publishing house), developmental editing (working with authors to develop manuscripts under contract), and structural editing (helping authors to improve issues of structure, pacing, coverage, and tone). Moreover, this editorial work is often undertaken by people who may be called an "'editor,' a 'senior editor,' a 'publisher,' or, in some cases, a 'publishing manager.'"[16] Elizabeth Weiss, for example, has noted that her role as publisher at Allen & Unwin frequently included aspects of commissioning and developmental editing, including "bringing projects to the publishing house, working on developing projects with authors and keeping an overview of books which are being written, are in production or have been published, basically all through their lives."[17] Editors working in these roles determine what is published, and also act as the first readers of a text, offering suggestions for revision based on anticipated audience reaction. In general, the role of editors in Australian literary production has not been adequately studied, aside from memoirs by such editors as Hilary McPhee, Michael Wilding, and Craig Munro, and a monograph on Beatrice Davis. As Alice Grundy has argued, the scholarly investigation of editing can reveal that "most beloved works are not the product of a solitary writer in a garret but of their interactions with the creative and commercial forces that surround the book's publication."[18] Editors and publishers, in the process of selecting and developing works, often function as the mediation point between the creative and the commercial.

Beatrice Davis remains the most significant editor in the history of Australian publishing. Davis started at Angus & Robertson in 1937, very likely becoming Australia's "first full-time book editor."[19] She was arguably the most influential tastemaker in local publishing over the next forty years, and became "the bridge that spanned modern Australian literature from Miles Franklin to Tim Winton."[20] Davis is particularly important for her contributions to Australia's literary cultural nationalism; she co-founded the anthologies *Coast to Coast* and *Australian Poetry* to provide a prominent venue for Australian writing in 1941, brought the literary journal *Southerly* in-house at Angus & Robertson in 1944, and was a judge of the inaugural Miles Franklin Award in 1957, which was awarded to Patrick White's *Voss*.[21] While Davis played a crucial role in discovering important local talent and training a new generation of Australian book editors, she also inhabited a publishing industry entirely unlike today's conglomerates: "until the early 1960s A&R was more like an old-fashioned university liberal arts department than a modern publishing company."[22] Significantly, Davis' "department was not intended to be commercial" and she was "not responsible for preparing the budgets for books."[23] Her role was to select works that had literary merit, a function that has increasingly become peripheral for large publishers.

Perhaps the next most significant editors in Australia were, in fact, a team: Diana Gribble and Hilary McPhee, who founded the independent publisher McPhee Gribble in 1975. Although comparatively short-lived (the company was sold to Penguin in 1989), the company's legacy rests on its reputation for discovering important Australian literary voices during a time of significant investment in national culture. The company is best known for its publication of Helen Garner's *Monkey Grip* in 1977 and remains associated with an urbanized, bohemian literary culture mostly located in Melbourne; the company occupied a three-story townhouse on 203 Drummond St in Carlton, near the University of Melbourne and, according to Gribble, "an in-house creche became part of the business and coped with (or promoted) a mini-explosion of babies on the premises."[24] In a sense, however, this also mirrored the publishers' interests in feminism explored in works such as *Monkey Grip* and Gabrielle Carey and Kathy Lette's *Puberty Blues* (1979).

McPhee Gribble cultivated the symbolic capital of a hip independent publisher, while also partnering with major publishers to ensure financial stability. The company's early books were underwritten by "providing editorial and packaging services to William Heinemann and the University of Queensland Press."[25] While Gribble calls their decision to license the paperback of *Monkey Grip* to Penguin "a mistake," this partnership may have secured a larger market for Garner.[26] In the 1980s, the company balanced its literary list with commercial work, providing "children's pages for *Women's Weekly*" and a children's series for Penguin, and outsourcing services to other publishers.[27] Moreover, a co-publishing agreement negotiated with then-director of publishing for Penguin, Brian Johns, "largely enabled" the expansion of McPhee Gribble's list.[28] After Johns' departure from Penguin in 1987, however, the agreement faltered, and – as a result of other financial difficulties, McPhee Gribble was ultimately sold to Penguin in November of 1989, and McPhee left Penguin in 1992. Gribble would go on to found Text Publishing, which, under the direction of Michael Heyward and Penny Hueston, would become one of Australia's leading independent publishers.

The University of Queensland Press (UQP) has had several well-known editors, including Frank Thompson, who was arguably responsible for establishing UQP as a literary publisher. Craig Munro remains particularly notable for his work editing Peter Carey, his long tenure at the publisher, his publication of extensive memoirs about his experiences, and his own contributions to scholarship on books and publishing. Munro worked at UQP from 1971 until 2005, serving as publishing manager for much of his time there. Munro edited debut books by Peter Carey, Olga Masters, and Murray Bail, and also edited work by David Malouf, Barbara Hanrahan, Roger McDonald, and Rodney Hall.[29] The press was able to follow "its own enlightened literary path at a time when other Australian imprints were being hoovered up by conglomerates"; being located within a university environment may have made it more hospitable to the bohemian writers orbiting the press in the 1970s, such as Michael Wilding, Michael Dransfield, and Frank Moorhouse.[30] UQP served as a model for future independents in many ways: As early as 1975, it was already trading international rights, selling work into other markets, and buying overseas titles to reprint locally, which is still an important revenue source for Australian publishers such as Text and Scribe.[31] Munro became publishing manager in 1983, and Carey's UQP novels such as *Oscar and Lucinda* (1987) drove sales with Booker Prize and Miles Franklin wins. As with McPhee Gribble, a co-publishing arrangement with Penguin enabled the press to expand its fiction list, but the commercial environment of the "recessionary 1990s" proved difficult; their close relationship with Penguin ended, and a "lack of ongoing funding support" from government became a critical problem.[32] By the late 1990s, the press was "struggling to compete in a tough commercial marketplace dominated by book chains and global publishing conglomerates."[33] Carey also left the press on good terms in 2002 after three decades. It remains an important publisher of Australian fiction and poetry.

Ivor Indyk and Evelyn Juers founded the press Giramondo in 1995, and one could argue that it has become the most significant Australian literary publisher of the last twenty-five years. Giramondo has published major works by established authors such as Alexis Wright, Brian Castro, Gerald Murnane, Judith Beveridge, and Jennifer Maiden, while also working to increase broader recognition of their work. Giramondo has also published debut or new works by the next generation of significant writers, including Fiona Wright, Luke Carman, Michael Mohammed Ahmad, Felicity Castagna, Lisa Gorton, Michael Farrell, and Keri Glastonbury. Giramondo publishes literary forms that most large publishers would see as commercially unviable, including books of poetry, literary essays, and short stories. The press is located at the Writing and Society Research Centre (WSRC) of Western Sydney University and has sought to feature authors from Western Sydney – traditionally seen as an area comprised of working-class people and recent migrants, who have often been excluded from Australian literature. Giramondo has launched a series of original literary translations (unusual in Australia) and has announced the third run of its literary journal *HEAT*. Indyk was also central in the creation of *The Sydney Review of Books,* which has quickly become one of Australia's premier outlets for reviewing and intellectual literary discourse. A crucial difference between Giramondo and many similar publishers is its focus on the backlist, or older titles that remain in print: many Giramondo titles may not sell well initially but have longitudinal sales from being assigned in high schools and universities.

There are many other editors and publishers who have influenced Australian literature in significant ways. Susan Hawthorne and Renate Klein, for example, founded Spinifex Press in 1991, and it has been an important venue for publishing literature that engages with radical feminism. Magabala Books has been crucial for commissioning and publishing works by Aboriginal and Torres Strait Islander authors since 1987. And there are many contemporary editors closely associated with literary publishing, even given the increasing \ commercial demands of the market, such as Aviva Tuffield, Mandy Brett, Alice Grundy, Kent McCarter, David Winter, and Terri-ann White, among many others. Despite the difficulties caused by both global competition and the increasing power of Amazon, literary editing continues to influence readers and critics by determining what is published and how, even if most of this work takes place behind the scenes.

The Decline of Literary Publishing?

One of the key questions among scholars of Australian publishing and editing over the last fifteen years involves literary publishing's increasingly marginal relationship to the publishing industry. Mark Davis has offered the strongest articulation of this argument, proposing that the publishing industry has seen the decline of a literary paradigm that organized postwar publishing. For Davis, the literary paradigm was a project of "cultural nationalism, funded by progressive governments" which was dominant from the 1960s through the 1980s and sought to create "a national literary canon, centred on leading writers of the Whitlam generation and those perceived to be their heirs."[34] But cultural nationalism weakened with bipartisan support for a neoliberal agenda of financialization and deregulation in the 1990s, with the result that "by the early 2000s almost no major Australian publisher was aggressively seeking or promoting new literary fiction at the forefront of their lists."[35] Conglomerate publishers maximized profits and focused on bestselling books, which are typically works of genre fiction, celebrity biographies, cookbooks by well-known chefs, and books about sports, rather than literary novels.[36]

Davis' argument appears to have been substantiated empirically. Jan Zwar, David Throsby, and Thomas Longden, for example, have noted that the Macquarie University study of publishers "estimated that literary books comprise roughly 5% of trade sales, and less than half of these comprise Australian-authored literary works."[37] The Macquarie University report on Australian authors noted that more than 30 percent of literary authors had seen a decline in incomes over the past five years.[38] According to Zwar, "most literary titles – apart from those by high-profile authors – have print runs of

2,000–4,000 copies."[39] This means that most works of literary fiction are so-called "midlist" titles, which is to say works that sell but in such small amounts that they only break even or return a small profit. Recent research by Tracey O'Shaughnessey and Brigid Magner, which employs two decades of sales and income data from Nielson BookScan, demonstrates that "royalties and advances for midlist authors are shrinking," that "there is less 'discoverability' of titles through bookshops" for midlist titles, and that the "seemingly constant quest for the bestseller within the publishing industry is doing nothing to encourage heterogeneity" among titles being published.[40] While O'Shaughnessey and Magner's analysis does not single out literary titles, the increased difficulties faced by midlist titles affect most literary authors.

Other scholars, however, have described the changing relationship between literature and publishing in very different ways. Beth Driscoll, for example, has charted the rise of a "new middlebrow" that complicates the Bourdieusian antinomy between commercial success and literary prestige.[41] Driscoll defines the middlebrow as "middle-class, reverential towards elite culture, entrepreneurial, mediated, feminized, emotional, recreational, and earnest."[42] Driscoll notes "a constant tension between art and commerce animates middlebrow culture" whose "commitment to increased accessibility is twinned with an awareness of the commercial opportunities offered by an expanded market for cultural products."[43] The tension here reflects the Bourdieusian distinction between symbolic and economic regimes of capital, but the middlebrow opts for both: "The dream of the literary middlebrow is to secure both cultural legitimacy and commercial success."[44] This is particularly evident in middlebrow institutions like The Booker Prize or Oprah's Book Club, which seek to be both accessible, mass events and to promote notions of literary quality. But this also means that the middlebrow's relationship to literary publishing is somewhat contradictory: While it may be reverent toward the prestige of literary works, its institutions are not really geared to support the midlist works that constitute the majority of literary publishing.

David Carter has re-examined the nexus between commerce and quality in slightly different terms. He argues that "Bourdieu's analysis of the avant-garde opposed to bourgeois taste and institutions (and to the mass or popular) has limited explanatory power for the contemporary Australian literary field."[45] Nonetheless, Carter notes that "the opposition between commercial and cultural imperatives" continues to play an important role in literary production despite the "greater blurring of high and popular categories that critics – and publishers – have noted."[46] Carter, however, argues that the opposition between autonomy and heteronomy now "operates internally within the larger houses, especially in relation to fiction" rather than being a divide between different kinds of agents and institutions, and, as a result, Carter argues for viewing trade publishing itself as "a relatively autonomous field," which is organized around two major understandings of value, the economic and the symbolic, with most books appealing to one category, and a few that can appeal to both.[47] Carter grounds this analysis in a survey of fiction publishing – which is not the same as literary publishing – and notes that fiction is in good health and diversifying across different kinds of publishers and genres. Ultimately, he argues for literature as a "dispersed, disaggregated field" that combines "commodity, industry, professional or aesthetic practice, ethical or pedagogical technology, leisure, entertainment, policy object and national space" and that this "diversity [is] better captured in a more flexible notion of 'Australian writing' than restricted notions of Australian literature."[48] In arguing for the removal of the term "literary," which has been subsumed within a broader array of practices that nonetheless "contribute to a 'vibrant reading and writing culture'," Carter's analysis redescribes Davis' decline as an expansion of different novelistic forms beyond traditional parameters of the literary.[49]

Stuart Glover's analysis of four different debut fictions – Hannah Kent's *Burial Rites,* Graeme Simsion's *The Rosie Project,* Chris Somerville's *We Are Not the Same Anymore,* and Balli Kaur Jaswal's *Inheritance* – examines the changing literary field in qualitative terms. Glover notes that the first two of the books are bestsellers, which have been promoted to large audiences, and the publisher-generated promotional materials are explicit sales pitches: "Any pretence that writing and publishing are not fundamentally commercial gives way in the face of an avalanche of boosterish public relations material."[50] Glover notes that the second two titles were printed in "short runs by small publishers and their marketing materials emphasise the book's literary and cultural value."[51] Despite these differences, all display what he calls "market credentialism," a term that includes "peer blurbs," as well as "shortlistings, prizes won, fellowships, teaching appointments, and creative writing degrees completed."[52] Glover emphasizes the importance of creative writing programs for publishing outcomes among Australian authors: "completing a graduate-level program does measurably improve one's chances of making it between hard or soft covers" with "30 percent of all masters-level projects and 50 percent of all doctoral-level projects" going on to be published.[53] Glover suggests that this is so because creative writing programs are increasingly taking on an editorial function, because they are "selective" and "offer an unusually rich editorial experience [...] from the time you propose your project, to confirmation, to mid-candidature, to final review, not to mention examination."[54] Such projects, as a result of this attention, are "unlikely to be wholly incompetent," but they may suffer from a lack of ambition, since "no one is taking any crazy chances."[55] Indeed, Glover argues that all four works, despite spanning commercial and literary poles are aesthetically very similar:

"These books are unities. They display an awareness of form and genre. They avoid 'bad' writing as we generally understand it: their prose is not prolix, overstated, florid, convoluted or inelegant."[56] The implication is that division between commercial and literary forms of writing is less stark than it appears.

Quantitative analysis of literary publishing and noncommercial forms, however, does suggest that real differences exist among publishers and publishing networks. My survey of literary publishing in 2012 suggested that large Australian publishers produced only twenty-seven works of literary fiction, while just eight of the more prominent small publishers were responsible for seventy-three literary titles.[57] Moreover, the recent resurgence in the publishing of single-author short story collections – a generally unprofitable form with a few notable exceptions like Nam Le's *The Boat* (2008) and Maxine Beneba Clarke's *Foreign Soil* (2014) – has been driven almost entirely by small publishers.[58] Australian poetry is overwhelmingly produced only by small publishers, such as Cordite, Giramondo, UQP, and Puncher & Wattmann. All this suggests that small publishers have become overwhelmingly responsible for the mediation of Australian literature, while larger conglomerates focus on more profitable genres and commercial fiction.[59] But this also decreases the potential audience for readers of literature, because small publishers primarily sell into one segment of the bookselling market, which is the independent bookstore.[60] While Australia's independent booksellers are unusually robust and comprise about 30 percent of the local bookselling market, they are also concentrated in urban areas. Small publishers have more difficulty being stocked by chain stores (such as Collins and Dymocks) and are rarely stocked by so-called Discount and Department Stores, such as Kmart and Target; these two sectors, which small publishers might not sell into at all, comprise nearly 60 percent of the market. Thus, the Bourdieusian distinction between the commercial and avant-garde poles of the literary field does need to be updated: "in the current moment it is literature itself that circulates among a field of producer-consumers" and thus comprises the pole of pure production.[61] While contemporary literature "has taken on the cultural form of avant-garde," it "lacks the avant-garde's aesthetic program" and has not "*elected* to be 'underground'"; instead, literature has been pushed into this state by "large-scale changes in global economics, cultural policy, management paradigms, reading habits, and the dynamics of the publishing industry" that have resulted in "literature's increasing marginalisation" in the Australian market.[62] There are signs, however, that small publishers are beginning to be recognized as the primary mediators of Australian literature, since major literary awards – the Miles Franklin Award, the Prime Minister's Literary Award for Fiction, and the Stella Prize – have all been dominated by small press titles in recent years.[63]

Ivor Indyk has described the small publisher as existing in a "province" at "at the far edge of trade publishing [...] its titles scarcely known to the general reader, and bought by few, its existence dependent on what is more like a subsistence economy than the profit-driven commercial economies of the multinationals [...] that dominate our publishing landscape."[64] While this might seem like hyperbole, Indyk's discussion of sales figures emphasizes the tight margins of Giramondo's kind of literary publishing. The press' "poetry books sell around 200 to 300 copies each, regardless of the stature of the poet," which is also true of literary essays and translations.[65] Memoirs and novels "might sell between 1000 and 1500 copies" and "only a Miles Franklin listing or a CBCA Young Adult award is likely to make any difference to this."[66] For a large publisher, however, a successful novel would usually sell 6,000 copies or more.[67] Prizes are no guarantee of increased sales: Indyk notes that Brian Castro's *Blindness and Rage* (2017) "won a Prime Minister's Award and earnt its author [...] an amount of money many times greater than the income from all his preceding books combined," but in the next six months, "the book itself sold only fifty copies."[68] But Indyk also clarifies that success is measured differently for a small press such as Giramondo, since, for small literary publishers, "time out here has its own way of passing, in large silent stretches between the book and its reception, if it has one."[69] This is because the literary publisher is motivated not by the goal of immediate sales but a "belief in posterity."[70] This reflects one of Bourdieu's own insights about publishers traditionally aligned with the avant-garde, such as the Parisian publisher Les Éditions de Minuit, who published *En attendant Godot* [*Waiting for Godot*] in 1952, but had to wait five years for the title to hit 10,000 sales.[71] Posterity, for the small publisher, is not simply conceptual, but actually has an economic corollary in longitudinal sales, or what publishers call the "backlist." Part of the difficulty for publishers is that the viability of the backlist – the name for those no longer new but still in-print titles that continue to sell reliably – has been undermined in various ways in the current bookselling environment. This is a significant concern for the ongoing viability of smaller literary publishers, especially at a moment when conglomerate publishers have more limited investments in Australian literature.

Equity, Diversity, and Australian Publishing

Another key area of contestation within notions of Australian literary publishing has involved questions of equity, diversity, and inclusion. Julianne Lamond has articulated this historical concern with literary value, saying that "ideas about what high culture is [...] have been shaped in large part by modernism," which "formed itself in opposition to a notion of feminised, rapacious, disastrous popular culture," that often included the kinds of books read by women in this period.[72] While this claim seems problematized by the existence of so many exemplary female modernists (such as Virginia Woolf, Gertrude Stein, Djuna Barnes, H. D., Christina Stead, Katherine Mansfield, and Clarice Lispector), there can be no doubt women have been systematically denied symbolic recognition and excluded from institutions of literary prestige. As Alexandra Dane argues, while "women have long been present in the Australian literary field," they have been "excluded from legacy-making institutions" and have thus been "routinely denied the opportunity to enter the collective public cultural memory."[73] Dane analyses a dataset of more than 36,000 authors over a fifty-year period to examine how they have interacted with key taste-making institutions, including book reviews, literary festivals, and literary prizes. One of her findings is that, despite Davis' claims for the decline of the literary paradigm, "symbolic capital within the field of cultural production [...] is *increasingly* dependent on a group of institutions dedicated to identifying and celebrating literary works."[74] For this reason, internal activism for equity within these institutions is necessary for change.

The catalyst for action in Australia was the shortlist announcement for the 2011 Miles Franklin Award, which included no women. This emphasized the prize's lack of equity, since it had historically awarded the prize at a ratio of three male winners for every female winner. A group of prominent female authors, editors, and book industry professionals responded by establishing The Stella Prize (after Miles Franklin's first name), an annual prize for books written by female-identifying and non-binary authors, which began in 2013. This activism appears to have had a significant effect on major literary prizes: from 2011 to 2020, the Miles Franklin went to eight women and two men, and the Prime Minister's Literary Award for fiction went to seven women and five men (there were joint winners on two occasions). During that same span, the Miles Franklin has also been won by three Indigenous authors. This suggests that literary prize judges are now taking inclusiveness very seriously. As part of its broader mission, the Stella Prize also initiated its annual "Stella Count," modelled on the VIDA Count in the US, which seeks to look at books reviewed by gender. As Melinda Harvey and Julianne Lamond have argued, it appears that the Stella has had a decisive influence here, as well: "In 2018, 49% of all reviews surveyed are of books written by women, up from 40% in 2012."[75] They note that this means that "field as a whole is now almost at parity" and that "the act of counting actively shifts the gender balance of literary journalism in Australia."[76] There have also been long-standing calls for greater inclusiveness in relation to race and ethnicity, and literary journals, such as *The Mascara Literary Review, Peril,* and *Liminal* continue to lead the charge on these issues alongside literary collectives, such as Sweatshop in Western Sydney.

Contemporary Australian publishing is a transmedia industry worth more than $2 billion in Australia and includes trade publishing, educational publishing, technical and "grey" publishing, and rights sales across international borders and media forms. It is a specialized industry with complex divisions of labor. Literature, as a fact, is increasingly economically marginal within the publishing industry, but it still holds an important cultural place, and many influential cultural institutions and industry members still believe in the central importance of Australian literature. But literary works are increasingly produced by smaller publishers, who have less capacity to market works broadly, fewer connections to mass media, and usually can only access one segment of booksellers. These publishers have also historically been excluded from literary prizes, though this appears to be changing significantly. It may be for these reasons that, even in an increasingly networked world in which barriers to entry have been reduced for self-publishers, authors, as Dane has noted,[77] actually appear to be more reliant than ever on taste-making institutions such as reviews, festivals, and literary prizes for recognition.

Notes

1 David Carter, "The Literary Field and Contemporary Trade-Book Publishing in Australia: Literary and Genre Fiction," *Media International Australia* 158.1 (2016): pp. 48–57 (p. 49).

2 Philip Mead, *Networked Language: Culture and History in Australian Poetry* (North Melbourne: Australian Scholarly Publishing, 2008), p. 1.

3 Mark Davis, "The Decline of the Literary Paradigm in Australian Publishing," in *Making Books: Contemporary Australian Publishing*, ed. Anne Galligan and David Carter (St Lucia: University of Queensland Press, 2007), pp. 91–108.

4 Mark McGurl, "Everything and Less: Fiction in the Age of Amazon," *Modern Language Quarterly*, 77.3 (2016): pp. 447–471.

5 John R. W. Speller, *Bourdieu and Literature* (Cambridge: Open Book Publishers, 2011), p. 79.

6 Pierre Bourdieu, *The Rules of Art: Genesis and Structure of the Literary Field*, trans. by Susan Emanuel (Cambridge: Polity, 1996), p. 61.

7 Pierre Bourdieu, *The Field of Cultural Production: Essays on Art and Literature* (New York: Columbia University Press, 1993), p. 37.

8 Bourdieu, *The Rules of Art*, p. 121.

9 Bourdieu, *The Rules of Art*, p. 148.

10 Bourdieu, *The Rules of Art*, p. 147.

11 Bourdieu, *The Rules of Art*, p. 165.

12 Bourdieu, *The Rules of Art*, p. 37.

13 Robert Darnton, "What Is the History of Books?" *Daedalus* 111.3 (1982): pp. 65–83 (p. 67).

14 Darnton, "What Is the History of Books?" p. 67.

15 Claire Squires and Padmini Ray-Murray, "The Digital Publishing Communications Circuit," *Book 2.0* 3.1 (2013): pp. 3–24 (p. 19).

16 Diane Brown, "Commissioning," in *Paper Empires: A History of the Book in Australia: 1945–2005*, eds. Craig Munro and Robyn Sheahan-Bright (St Lucia: University of Queensland Press, 2006), pp. 191–194 (p. 192).

17 Brown, "Commissioning," p. 191.

18 Alice Grundy, "The Crystal Mirror or the Book That Wasn't," *Sydney Review of Books*, September 28, 2020: https://sydneyreviewofbooks.com/essay/the-crystal-mirror/.

19 Jacqueline Kent, "Beatrice Davis," in *Paper Empires: A History of the Book in Australia: 1945–2005*, eds. Craig Munro and Robyn Sheahan-Bright (St Lucia: University of Queensland Press, 2006), pp. 177–81 (p. 178).

20 Kent, "Beatrice Davis," p. 178.

21 Kent, "Beatrice Davis," p. 178. For the details on White's win, see David Marr, *Patrick White: A Life* (North Sydney: Vintage, 2008; 1991), pp. 304–305.

22 Kent, "Beatrice Davis," p. 180.

23 Kent, "Beatrice Davis," p. 180.

24 Dianna Gribble, "McPhee Gribble," in *Paper Empires: A History of the Book in Australia: 1945–2005*, eds. Craig Munro and Robyn Sheahan-Bright (St Lucia: University of Queensland Press, 2006), pp. 108–110 (p. 108).

25 Gribble, "McPhee Gribble," p. 108.

26 Gribble, "McPhee Gribble," p. 108.

27 Gribble, "McPhee Gribble," p. 109.

28 Gribble, "McPhee Gribble," p. 109.

29 Craig Munro, *Under Cover: Adventures in the Art of Editing* (Brunswick: Scribe Publications, 2015), p. 3.

30 Munro, *Under Cover*, p. 18.

31 Munro, *Under Cover*, p. 119.

32 Munro, *Under Cover*, pp. 178–179.

33 Munro, *Under Cover*, p. 241.

34 Davis, "The Decline of the Literary Paradigm," pp. 93–94.

35 Davis, "The Decline of the Literary Paradigm," p. 94.

36 Davis, "The Decline of the Literary Paradigm," p. 97.

37 Jan Zwar, David Throsby, and Thomas Longden, "How to Read the Australian Book Industry in a Time of Change," *The Conversation*, October 14, 2015: https://theconversation.com/how-to-read-the-australian-book-industry-in-a-time-of-change-49044.

38 Jan Zwar, David Throsby, and Thomas Longden, "Industry Brief No. 4: Changes in Authors' Financial Position," *Macquarie University* October 2015: www.businessandeconomics.mq.edu.au/__data/assets/pdf_file/0003/360714/4_Changes_in_Authors_Financial_Position.pdf.

39 Zwar, Throsby, and Longden, "How to Read the Australian Book Industry."

40 Brigid Magner and Tracy O'Shaughnessy, "Monstering the Midlist: Implications for Author Income and Publishing Sustainability," *Australian Humanities Review* 66 (2020): pp. 10–43 (pp. 36–37).

41 Beth Driscoll, *The New Literary Middlebrow: Tastemakers and Reading in the Twenty-First Century* (Basingstoke: Palgrave Macmillan, 2014).

42 Beth Driscoll, "The Middlebrow Family Resemblance: Features of the Historical and Contemporary Middlebrow," *Post 45*, July 1, 2016: https://post45.org/2016/07/the-middlebrow-family-resemblance-features-of-the-historical-and-contemporary-middlebrow/.

43 Driscoll, "The Middlebrow Family Resemblance."

44 Driscoll, *The New Literary Middlebrow*, p. 141.

45 Carter, "The Literary Field and Contemporary Trade-Book Publishing in Australia," p. 49.

46 Carter, "The Literary Field and Contemporary Trade-Book Publishing in Australia," p. 50.

47 Carter, "The Literary Field and Contemporary Trade-Book Publishing in Australia," p. 50.

48 Carter, "The Literary Field and Contemporary Trade-Book Publishing in Australia," p. 56.

49 Carter, "The Literary Field and Contemporary Trade-Book Publishing in Australia," p. 56.

50 Stuart Glover, "So Many Paths That Wind and Wind," *Sydney Review of Books*, October 4, 2013: https://sydneyreviewofbooks.com/essay/so-many-paths-that-wind-and-wind/.

51 Glover, "So Many Paths That Wind and Wind."

52 Glover, "So Many Paths That Wind and Wind."

53 Glover, "So Many Paths That Wind and Wind."

54 Glover, "So Many Paths That Wind and Wind."

55 Glover, "So Many Paths That Wind and Wind."

56 Glover, "So Many Paths That Wind and Wind."

57 Emmett Stinson, "Small Publishers and the Emerging Network of Australian Literary Prosumption," *Australian Humanities Review* 59 (2016): pp. 23–43 (pp. 30–31).

58 Emmett Stinson, "Short Story Collections, Cultural Value, and the Australian Market for Books," *Australian Humanities Review* 66 (2020): pp. 46–64 (p. 59).

59 Stinson, "Small Publishers and the Emerging Network of Australian Literary Prosumption," p. 31.

60 Stinson, "Small Publishers and the Emerging Network of Australian Literary Prosumption," p. 32.

61 Stinson, "Small Publishers and the Emerging Network of Australian Literary Prosumption," p. 36.

62 Stinson, "Small Publishers and the Emerging Network of Australian Literary Prosumption," p. 37.

63 Emmett Stinson, "Small Publishers, Symbolic Capital and Australian Literary Prizes," *Book Publishing in Australia: A Living Legacy*, eds. Aaron Mannion and Millicent Weber (Clayton: Monash University Publishing, 2019), pp. 208–229.

64 Ivor Indyk, "Publishing from the Provinces," *Sydney Review of Books*, February 18, 2020: https://sydneyreviewofbooks.com/essay/publishing-from-the-provinces/.

65 Indyk, "Publishing from the Provinces."
66 Indyk, "Publishing from the Provinces."
67 Stinson, "Small Publishers and the Emerging Network of Australian Literary Prosumption," p. 32.
68 Indyk, "Publishing from the Provinces."
69 Indyk, "Publishing from the Provinces."
70 Indyk, "Publishing from the Provinces."
71 Bourdieu, *The Rules of Art*, p. 143.
72 Julieanne Lamond, "A Fool's Game? On Gender and Literary Value," *Sydney Review of Books*, March 18, 2019: https://sydneyreviewofbooks.com/essay/a-fools-game-gender-literary valuc/.
73 Alex Dane, *Gender and Prestige in Literature: Contemporary Australian Book Culture* (Switzerland: Palgrave Macmillan, 2020), pp. 11–12.
74 Dane, *Gender and Prestige in Literature*, p. 187.
75 Melinda Harvey and Julieanne Lamond, "2018 Stella Count," *The Stella Prize*: <https://thestellaprize.com.au/the-count/2018-stella-count/>.
76 Harvey and Lamond, "2018 Stella Count."
77 Dane, *Gender and Prestige in Literature*, p. 187.

PART II

Authorships

7

FIONA MORRISON

"Rich and Strange"
Christina Stead and the Transnational Novel

> Full fathom five thy father lies;
> Of his bones are coral made;
> Those are pearls that were his eyes;
> Nothing of him that doth fade,
> But doth suffer a sea-change
> Into something rich and strange.
> – "Ariel's Song," The Tempest

On a Sydney morning in late March 1928, Christina Stead boarded *The Oronsay*, a vessel of the Orient Line on its return journey to the Tilbury Docks, Port of London. Inbound from the Port of Brisbane, the new turbine steamer was set to continue Melbourne–London via the Indian Ocean and the Suez Canal, an itinerary that British clippers and steamships had used on the Australian run since it became possible in 1869. This return circuit represented a journey home for the steamship and crew, but whether it was a voyage "in" or "out" for the young Australian woman was less clear. With the strangely bifocal habitus of a colonial child educated in an Anglophone tradition, Stead did feel the pull of affiliation and recognition from the imperial center, and her transnational mobility articulated the complexities inherent in colonial–peripheral movement from Sydney to London in the mid-to-late 1920s. This is dramatized in an early short story, "Night in the Indian Ocean," which is based on Stead's expatriate voyage and focuses on a sequence in which vessel and passengers are becalmed in the nocturnal heat of the Arabian Sea, caught midway between Sydney and London. This suspension highlights and contests the fiction of the seemingly natural diffusionist structure of the established colonial world system in which the British colonial-imperial "charge" traveled vigorously outward from center to periphery, across oceanic circuits established by the shipping of people, mail, and cargo. Stead's story dramatizes the scene of transnational mobility as a telling interplay between stasis and movement, incarceration and freedom, concentration and diffusion, orientation and disorientation. Further, the central "scene" of a displaced and disordered English heiress and her young Australian minder represents enduring elements of Stead's narrative vision, including her fearless representation of human ecosystems that cohere around dynamic struggles for power, autonomy, self-expression, or survival. Speech and capital are the vital and energetic resources of these ecosystems and Stead's forensic and critical interest in how these dramatic forces work (often with a specific interest in oppression and resistance) make her one of the most important and original political women writers of the twentieth century. Her artistic vision encompassed detailed work on her Australian past and, without demur, the many places in the world in which she found herself or to which she gravitated.

Her novels and short stories still read as astonishingly original; the synergies and disruptions of national and international literary influence and setting produced novels that are beautifully described by Ariel's fittingly marine epithet of "rich and strange," where "strange" carries the meaning of exceptional and astonishing, as well as that which is situated outside the known or local. Christina Stead's expatriate career was characterized by continuous mobility and long duration. Her fiction traversed several continents (Europe, North America, Australia) and multiple national and political contexts. The archive of her work encompasses the juvenilia of her school and university years from 1916 to the posthumous publication of her masterpiece, *I'm Dying Laughing*, in 1986 and the collection of her short stories *Ocean of Story* (1987). Transnational mobility created the conditions for an extraordinary body of work, but it also created challenges around critical assessment that have lingered (not least practical matters of multiple addresses, publishers, and agents). Aspects of literary classification and stable reputation have not been a matter of settled opinion, though importance and even genius are usually agreed upon. Stead finds a productive place in the canons of Australian transnational writing, which includes writers such as Henry Handel Richardson, Martin Boyd, and Shirley Hazzard, but she must also be included in the canon of twentieth-century women novelists whose work was restlessly compelled by the ongoing provocations of both politics and aesthetics, including Jamaica Kincaid, Toni Morrison, Nadine Gordimer, Muriel Spark, Doris Lessing, and Rebecca West. This essay introduces another navigational coordinate for Stead, one that collocates aspects of her antipodean origin and transnational movement with questions of literary style and form. Like Fernand Braudel on the Mediterranean, Édouard Glissant and Derek Walcott on the Caribbean, and Paul Gilroy on the Atlantic, Stead was a pioneering writer of the oceanic South.[1] From her short story, "A Night in the Indian Ocean" (the late 1920s) to the Sydney harbor setting of her first novel, *Seven Poor Men of Sydney* (1934), and from her epic vision of the

Pacific in the "Sea-People" prologue and "Island Continent" first section of *For Love Alone* (1944) to the foreword to her edited selection of short stories, *Great Stories of the South Sea Islands* (1955), Stead brought her inheritance as the daughter of a marine biologist and her oceanic perspective to bear on fictional prose. Stead's oceanic vision constitutes a key Australian example of what Kerry Bystrom and Isabel Hofmeyr have recently called "hydro-colonial poetics," which connects to aspects of Stead's prose style as well as her keen understanding of economic and political flows of commodities and power.[2] In late 1968, *The Kenyon Review* published a short personal essay by Stead as part of its annual "International Symposium on the Short Story," which Stead opens with an alignment with the Global South: "I love *Ocean of Story*, the name of an Indian treasury of stories."[3] Stead refers here to the Sanskrit *Kathasaritsagara*, or *The Ocean of the Streams of Stories*, an eleventh-century collection of Indian folktales and legends compiled by a Kashmiri poet called Somadeva from a much earlier text known as "the great story' (the *Brihatkatha*, 200–500 BCE). A complex frame-tale treating the life of a Kashmiri prince holds the springs and rivers of story together as an "oceanic" set of tales. The overlay of marine and narrative form is intriguing, where "ocean" is the figure for epic collection or compendium and "stream" conveys the multiplicity of story. In Stead's own account of the importance of the short story, the tale was a pure natural water resource, endlessly generative and unstoppable, always rising, flowing and gathering alluvial power: "But there it was, the ocean of story, starting out in the drops, drops of hill-dew, or sweat on the mountain's brow, running down, joining trickles from the rocks [...] broadening and sounding deep and moving in its fullness toward the ocean of story."[4] The story compendium collects the "million drops of water that are the looking glasses of all our lives."[5] Here and elsewhere in the essay, Stead explains the short story form, and indeed the human impulse to storytelling, through a system of marine metaphors.

This marine genealogy of the tale informs Stead's account of coming to writing as a young child in the "water hemisphere." Raised first within sight of Cape Solander and Botany Bay and then on the shoreline of Sydney harbor, Stead claims "I was born in the ocean of story or on its shores."[6] After her return to Australia in the 1970s, Stead told this story of her vocational origin in the sea many times: "And the sea – we were all closely connected with the sea. It was part of our lives. Now the sea is a continent with no passports; it's a country in itself. We felt we belonged to the sea. It wasn't a question of leaving Australia, nothing to do with that at all."[7] On this account, Stead's view of citizenship was inevitably worldly; she naturally belonged to both Australia and the world via the ocean and its sea-roads, and her transnational movement and transnational writing were ordained

by geography. Transoceanic citizenship, artistic vocation, and artistic practice meet in Stead's presentation of ocean, river, and stream as the essential figures of narrative form and literary style. In the 1970s, pursuing her
"sea-woman" account of her writing life, Stead explained the impact of
early scientific training by her father in impartial marine examination. This
informed the strong orientation of her writing to "record" objectively the
action of natural ecosystems and the Darwinian struggle for survival: "when
you're a little girl and you like an aquarium and you see fish doing this and
that and snails and so on, you don't criticise and say they should do something else [...] they are, they exist that way, and that is the only way to see
things truly."[8] Thus, marine or aquatic elements connect and describe three
significant aspects of Stead's writing: the scientific naturalist's vision of the
ecosystem and its realities, the importance of vital materiality, and the aesthetic impact of presence in the form of immersion or saturation.

   Movement, vitality, passion, and appetite are all aspects of vital life that
underpin Stead's marine aesthetics. Negative manifestations of these phenomena also appear in the form of seductive vitalities, libertine passions,
artistic facility, and compulsive hunger. For Stead, the only truly destructive
antonyms for the drives of life were stagnation and stasis, which appear
dialectically in her novels as provincial suffocation, domestic incarceration,
suburban boredom, stultified desire, and the iron imprisonments of poverty
and political oppression. Thus, movement and stasis are a pivotal dyad in
Stead's work, where mobility is associated with life and stasis with destruction. This importance of life and movement also frames aspects of Stead's
style, which is characteristically immersive: plot is often episodic, and
description and speech can be torrential. In Stead's prose, rushing energy or
building rhythm is privileged over stylistic decorum or balance. As we can
see from her essay on the short story, Stead was devoted to what Walter
Benjamin called the "living immediacy" of storytelling.[9] In the early 1940s,
when she was preparing to teach a course in creative writing in New York,
Stead made several statements about the creative process and literary style
that illuminate this preference. In early 1942, she commented in a letter to
her stepmother Thistle Harris (also a marine biologist) that: "the sensuality,
delicacy of literature does not exist for me; only the passion, energy and
struggle, the night of which no one speaks, the creative act."[10] In an interview in the same period, she claimed that "the essence of style in literature,
for me, is experiment, invention, 'creative error' [...] and change: and of its
content, the presentation of 'man alive'."[11] Stead's focus on the dynamic
presentation of "man alive" declares the primacy of character in her fiction.
In her notes for creative writing teaching, Stead identified the "novel of
strife" as the kind of open, turbulent, and grotesque form that might house

the dramatic urgency of the "man alive."[12] This was an intrinsically political form in which characters vied with each other for mastery, self-expression, or freedom. Almost thirty years later, Stead repeated the creative significance of character (personality), situation (ecosystem), and interpersonal drama: "sometimes I start with a situation, sometimes with a personality. I never question or argue. I'm a psychological writer and my drama is the drama of the person."[13] Tracing Stead's marine aesthetics across a publication span of more than fifty years (1934–1986), this essay will examine Stead's work in three distinct periods: early (1928–1935 in London and Paris), middle (1935–1947 in the United States, mainly New York) and late (1948–1986 in Europe, England and Australia, including posthumous publication). These phases can be summarized in this way: The ambitious modernist experiment of the early period shifts through the Popular Front years to a greater realist focus in the American years, which altered again in the early Cold War to reveal fascinating deformations of the novel. This chapter will highlight a key text in each period, and provide some points of orientation and connection.

Into the World (1928–1935)

Critical work on Stead's earliest reading and writing has illuminated her emergence as a writer. Hazel Rowley's 1993 biography suggests that Stead's early reading ranged from the marvels of European fairy tales to the marvels in the writings of Darwin.[14] As she grew, Stead's reading and writing retained this aspect of combination. European realism (mainly French), modern European theatre (Ibsen and Strindberg), and European philosophy (Nietzsche and Bergson) became significant. Her family's alignment with the nationalist-socialist 1890s was of equal importance. Stead knew and loved the Australian vernacular classics such as Henry Lawson's short stories, A. B. "Banjo" Paterson's poems, and the broad vernacular comedy of Steele Rudd. Joseph Furphy, Miles Franklin, and Henry Handel Richardson provided different examples of the realist novel about Australia. She read Brennan, Slessor, and the Lindsays in the nineteen-teens and twenties and these Australian writers and artists were particularly important for the different kinds of balance each struck between the influence of Australia and of Europe. In the midst of this colonial-transnational reading, Stead's own writing began to emerge.[15] Stead continued to write through the early 1920s and we know that David George Stead took a collection of Stead's short stories to the Australian publisher, Angus & Robertson, in early 1925. Robertson declined to publish and advised publication first in England.[16]

The feedback was clear: For Stead to succeed as a writer, access to overseas publishers and markets was essential. Stead saved singlemindedly for three years to earn her own "travelling scholarship" so she could follow to London the academic men and wealthier female students she had met at the University of Sydney in the early 1920s. As well as publishers, Stead sought congenial artistic and political milieus and wider worldly experience.

With the already layered and unsettled cultural heritage of a colonial artist to hand, Stead moved to London, which she disliked, and then to Paris, where she embraced avant-garde praxis and literary modernism with obvious recognition and zeal. In touch with the international community of the avant-garde in Paris and building on work she has shaped while still in Sydney, Stead wrote one of the most important Anglophone novels to combine modernist aesthetics, Left politics, and the matter of the settler-colonial periphery: *Seven Poor Men of Sydney*. Her first novel poses this question: "Who can tell what minor passions running in the undergrowth of poor lives will burst out when a storm breaks on the unknown watershed? There is water in barren hills and when rain comes they spurt like fountains, where the water lies on impermeable rocks."[17] Stead later recalled her project in this way:

> At Sydney Girls High School, I had my first serious project, based on a footnote in the textbook of European history we used. The footnote referred to the *Lives of Obscure Men* and this appealed to me markedly [...] a sort of counter Who's Who [...]. I did eventually do something of this sort. My first novel was called *Seven Poor Men of Sydney*.[18]

Her "counter" history is a group novel about seven proletarian workers associated with the printing trade. The "men," attached by trade, politics, and family ties, traverse the Sydney cityscape and assorted suburban locations in the nineteen teens and twenties as they wrangle passionately with poverty, education, family, trauma, and self-expression. As well as declaring the centrality of marginal experience at the semi-periphery, political economy, and poverty, the theme of the obscurity of the poor but talented is an interesting announcement of the antipodean writer on the world stage. It was a work that Marxist economist and writer William Blake (Bill Blech), Stead's lover in these years and then lifelong partner, described as having "mountain peaks."[19]

The Sydney setting delivers a groundbreaking example of the use of the colonial-provincial scene as both marvelous (poetic) and quotidian (realist).[20] A near-contemporary Australian critic, M. Barnard Eldershaw (a pseudonym of Marjorie Barnard and Flora Eldershaw), saw the lineaments of this dual commitment in Stead's first novel, but could not process its meaning: "It is not fantasy in the world of fantasy, but fantasy in a world of reality and reality in a world of fantasy. The Historical mingles with the imaginary, the real with the unreal in bewildering confusion, and the author behaves as if both worlds, or all worlds, were of the same value."[21] Although an account of surrealism would have assisted Barnard Eldershaw, the transnational combinations of this novel are complex and contain the poetic and realist, the modernist visionary and the proletarian vernacular, and the Australian and the European. Stead's bold commitment to these doubled modalities delivered a work that, even now, reads like a lightning strike in the domain of Australian fiction. Stead opens the novel in the vein of a modernist verse drama; the reader is reminded of both early Slessor and Yeats:

> *Fisherman's Bay. First days of the first poor man.*
> *An October's night's dream.*
> *A Stirring sermon has no effect on an ill-fated hero.*[22]

The bay lies at the southern end of the entrance to Sydney harbor. The spring night's dream seems briefly Shakespearean, but the modernist scene contextualizes an "ill-fated hero" (the "first poor man" in the "first days") and describes a nightmarish vision of the industrialized signal world centered on the "enormous spectral pole" that presides over the city, which in turn resides beneath "the yellow rim of the great sub-tropical moon."[23] The binding ties of religion hover, though the whole scene is restless with the "movements of ships and storms" as the narrative point of view strays inexorably seaward, the light sweeps from the south, to the city, then north, and further out to the Tasman sea:

> The hideous low scarred yellow horny and barren headland lies curled like a scorpion in a blinding sea and sky. At night, house-lamps and ships' lanterns burn with a rousing shine, and the headlights of cars swing over Fisherman's Bay [...]. From the signal station messages come down of the movements of ships and storms [...]. In dark nights, from the base of that enormous spectral pole which points up any distance into the starry world, one looks down on the city and the northern harbour settlements, on the pilot lights in the eastern and western channels, and on the unseen dark sea, where the lighthouse ray is lost beyond the horizon and where ships appear though the waves, far out, lighted like a Christmas Tree, small, and disappearing momentarily.[24]

Stead moves effortlessly from this expressionist-surrealist vision of the Sydney harbor headland (from "blinding sea and sky" to "unseen dark sea") to the materialist world of shipping, its aleatory circulation of world capital and the ruinous consequences for the exploited labor upon which the system rests. A central tension between movement and stasis is first staged here:

> Early in the morning, through the open window, the people hear the clatter of anchors falling into the bay, and the little boys run out to name the liners waiting there for the port doctor, liners from Singapore, Shanghai, Nagasaki, Wellington, Hawaii, San Francisco, Naples, Brindisi, Dunkirk and London, in the face of all these old stone houses, decayed weatherboard cottages, ruinous fences, boathouses and fishermen's shanties.[25]

Stead's command of the details of the economic life of the harbor city is matched by her command of the working world of the printing business that was so important to the maintenance of the colonial port city. This life is recreated through the vivid details of working life, especially a virtuosic inclusion of everyday speech of the working-class "men." The vernacular orality in *Seven Poor Men of Sydney* is primarily associated with the city life, with politics, with print media and its circulation, with the world of work and the machinations of capital. However, there are some speeches of striking poetic power made from quasi-pastoral suburban locations, too, such as Kol Blount's extraordinary elegy for Michael Bagenault at the end of the novel. Imaginatively engaged with Michael's suicide at the Gap (returning to the southern headland), the paralyzed and stymied Kol Blount produces a sea vision of the island continent that challenges and decries the atrophy and waste of the working men and women's lives. Through this memorial, the novel circles back to its own beginning at the entrance-exit point of transnational travel and unites the poetic and the realist at the elegiac registration of stasis despite struggle.[26]

Written in Paris at various points during 1931–1933, *The Salzburg Tales* (1934) is a collection of short stories based on Stead's experiences at the Salzburg Festival in 1930, though it is another early work that includes writing completed in Sydney prior to expatriate departure. Characters from different nations join in a structure of mobile and transnational storytelling familiar from *The Canterbury Tales* (1392). Gothic and quotidian elements structure this compendium of tales told by visitors to the Festival, but again it is the vibrant and ambitious deployment of character through speech that is striking, here in short-form fiction. Stead's first publication was greeted by warm reviews hailing an imaginative and original new voice. Rowley reports that *The Times* called Stead a "writer of many gifts," with "an altogether admirable command of the fantastic" and that the *Times Literary Supplement* commented that "Miss Stead" was "a writer of unusual interest."[27] Rebecca West responded that the collection "has its own wild charm, and obviously a work of a strong and idiosyncratic talent."[28] Where *The Salzburg Tales* celebrates the theatrical vocality and diversity of another of Stead's shifting collective, *The Beauties and the Furies* (1936) continues Stead's engagement with politics and modernism in the complex system of the city, but this time the setting is the City of Light itself and the genre is romance. The narrative and stylistic energy of this novel lie in the movement and motives of its complex (and political) Parisians rather than the faux rebellious English lovers and sojourners (harbingers of Stead's category of "fake radical"). Stead is more interested in passion in the sense of struggle than any clichéd writing about international romance.

1934 was Stead's final year in Paris. It was a year in which the question of the responsibility of the politically committed writer, a question already energized by the advent of the Great Depression, gained greater political urgency. Three key Popular Front writers' congresses focused on this question: in Moscow (August 1934), New York (April 1935), and Paris (June–July 1935). Following Moscow's avowal of socialist realism as the key anti-fascist aesthetic in 1934, the New York and Paris congresses declared realism the central element of Popular Front aesthetic work, rejecting modernism as bourgeois and unhelpful. While Stead read the papers of the Soviet and American Writers' Congresses, she attended the Paris Congress as the secretary of the English delegation. She wrote an analysis of the Congress that appeared in the July 1935 issue of the British communist periodical *The Left Review* as "The Writers Take Sides." She contended in this piece that the ideal of the leftist writer was to "enter the political arena, take lessons from workmen and use their pen as the scalpel lifting the living tissues, cutting through the morbid tissues, of the social anatomy."[29] Her use of this time-honored trope indicated that she was not just thinking about her fiction as a discursive product, but how her fiction performs as discourse. In the work after the Congress in 1935, we begin to see Stead's swing toward critical realism and away from more symbolic or expressionist modes of writing, though her restless experimentation with speech, character, genre, and the novel form did not falter. In particular, *House of All Nations* (1938) rises to meet a particular challenge: How to represent the rising dominance of fascist demagogues in Europe? Drafted in Paris, London, and New York, the novel was finished in Spain at the outset of the Civil War. Based on Blake and Stead's working years at the Travelers Bank in Paris (1929–1934), the novel dramatizes the ecosystem of a corrupt and then failing international bank in Paris in the early 1930s.

Although it is a huge novel, *House of All Nations* sees a reduction of scale from the cityscape to one institution (the bank as "house" or brothel), and shapes narrative action to revolve around a central character – in this case a criminal of great vitality and charm. This is a critical change in the structure of Stead's fiction and one that remains for the balance of her career. The novel is characteristically immersive in detail but reveals a new kind of narrative structure in the shape of 104 cinematic scenes, which indicates an awareness of John Dos Passos' "camera eye" technique. A shift away from an expressionist mode of description is also obvious, as is the related intensification of character-construction through speech. The Banque Mercure is an edifice made of speech, which suggests that talking (and swindling), rather than money, is the material base of the bank. In this system, a criminal bank director is surrounded by and holds together a collective of men. "A robber by instinct, sharpshooter of commerce by career, nourished by corruption," Jules Bertillon drives the epic, episodic, and ethnographic account of the bank's collapse in 1931–1932.[30] As a worldly account of shady international capital in bed with fascism, it is an essential novel of the 1930s.

The American Years

By 1935, Stead and Blake fled the collapse of Travelers Bank and made their way, via Britain and Europe, to the capital of American capital – New York City. The late Stead of 1974 remembered, perhaps with an overlay of nostalgia: "the Thirties was a terrific convulsion in the U.S.A., and the whole of society was in a ferment, nobody really knew which way the society was going. Oh, it was a terrific epoch, very thrilling."[31] Stead's sojourn in America's "terrific epoch" lasted from mid-1935 until early 1947. She produced five novels that addressed the matter of the United States in the Depression, the war years, and the early Cold War: *The Man Who Loved Children* (1940), *Letty Fox: Her Luck* (1946), *A Little Tea, A Little Chat* (1948), *The People with the Dogs* (1952), and *I'm Dying Laughing* (1986). *For Love Alone* was published in 1944, and although it is a transnational novel set in equal parts in Sydney and London, it was inspired in part by Stead's short stint at MGM in Los Angeles in 1942–1943, and so it plays a small part in the American sequence. *The Man Who Loved Children* is Stead's domestic allegory of political domination, humiliation, and resistance. The Pollit Georgetown and Annapolis family homes index the downward mobility of the Great Depression in America. In these homes, male narcissism and patriarchal domination are met with a dogged and complex resistance from both mother and eldest daughter of the family home. This plot is clearly sourced in Stead's own childhood, but the importance of the sophisticated political allegory of American New Deal politics makes purely autobiographical readings difficult.[32]

Joining Australian source material to American settings and American literary and political history, *The Man Who Loved Children* indicates a new command of the structure and potential of the novel form. Here is an excerpt describing a summer's day in the second Pollit residence, "Spa House," located in Annapolis on the river. This structurally echoes the first summer's day sequence in the novel ("Sunday is a Funday") and even though further poverty, greater oppression, and the true nature of a fascist father have now become apparent to the mother and children of the house, the physical environment of the Annapolis house on the river is characterized by Stead's eye for the natural world. Here we see her inclination for building prose rhythm and her grasp of material vitality:

> Sam's birthday began in a lovely morning, and everyone got up early. There was dew on everything, the cedar-waxwings were eating the mulberries, and there was the sound of a bombardment from the corrugated iron roof of the new shed, where the wasteful little wretches, in their hundreds, threw down scarcely tasted berries. There was a haze over everything, dew on the anthills, and the determined, brilliant wasps were at work, scratching wood fibre off the old wooden bench with a light rasping sound, zooming dizzily and plastering with a do-or-die air.[33]

Despite the lyrical representation of natural phenomena here, Stead's work with the human system addresses the unhomely home as a political situation collocating a variety of oppressed subjects. Women and children bear the brunt of oppression, but the proletariat and the racial subject are allegorized in these portraits. A seemingly genial father, Sam Pollitt, dominates this domestic fiction. Stead's portrait of Sam Pollitt as "Mr. America" and the "man about the house" is centered on her prodigious rendition of American vernacular speech, though travestied verbal performances of all kinds litter Sam's oppressive vocal omnipresence and ironize his links to the democratic associations of America he loves to cite. His vocal dominance, energetic and often virtuosic, overwhelms individuality, creativity, and finally the possibility of a separate sense of self.[34] In the following scene, Henny has just given birth to a sixth child (with stepdaughter Louie, her tally is seven), and Sam abrogates this labor without hesitation:

> And I am myself so ill, Looloo-girl, that I can hardly rejoice as I always do at the birth of a child. The great glory of man, the great glory of the flaming forth of new stars, the glory of the expanding universe, which are all expressed in our lives by the mystery, wonder, and tragedy of birth have always thrilled me beyond expression. And here I lie, with bones of jelly. It did for me, Looloo.[35]

Sam's captive homemade audience must bear witness to the endless vocality of the man who loves himself. The reader, like Sam's family, is incarcerated at close quarters with these bravura rhetorical performances of hypocrisy and self-delusion. It is the "surround sound" of Sam's voice that charms, disturbs, and imprisons – the dominance of this voice consistently underwrites an actual lack of economic or social freedom to leave.

For much of the novel, Sam's verbal and physical dominance is challenged by the vital undercurrent of gothic realism and grotesque materiality that surrounds the description and registers of Henny Pollitt, Sam's "spitfire" wife and mother of his many children. If Sam associates himself with idealism, Henny is associated with an earthier understanding, with folklore and everyday realities:

> "He lives," said Henny to herself, in her bed, "in a golden cloud floating about over a lot of back alleys he never sees; and I'm a citizen of those back alleys, like a lot of other sick sheep. I'd like to pull the wool off his eyes, but I don't dare. He'd take the children away from me; I'd be branded, hounded – I know his Lordship."[36]

In her position as an heiress who made a poor marriage, Henny is connected to an accumulation of aging treasures and luxuries in the privacy of her room and harrowing (though ultimately ineffective) verbal tirades in the "public sphere" of the larger house. Treasure and tirade furnish her attempts to hold the line against the rising tide of debt, poverty, and related destruction of privacy and dignity at the hands of her husband. Her stepdaughter recognizes her stepmother's gendered position within this impossible structure, absorbs the abusive ranting that she intuits springs from this oppression, and thus plots an alternative course toward freedom from her incarceration. Louisa Pollitt is Sam's eldest child and, in the space between domineering father and vituperative stepmother, her experience represents the embattled development of the artist-as-female-adolescent. Where Henny is defined by the impossible questions of household debt and economic survival, Louie becomes defined by the questions of self-expression, freedom, and revenge. Since she cannot contest her father on the grounds of the spoken voice, Louie turns to imaginative writing, where Sam has no purchase at all. Already a reciter of quotations and teller of children's tales, Louie moves into writing when inspired by the wider world of a good high school and her newfound desire for her English teacher, Miss Aiden. Louie's first writing is passionate writing about love ("The Aiden Cycle" sonnet sequence), but her most effective composition is a play designed as political resistance. At the nadir of family poverty and traumatic uproar, Louie writes a playscript in coded language for herself and her siblings to perform. She calls it "Tragos Herpes Rom," and it is based on Shelley's "The Cenci," which stages the daughter's resistance to patriarchal tyranny. The play's idiosyncratic language and vision (and its oblivious patriarchal target) mean that it fails as a political intervention, but it defines the seminal moment in which the daughter makes her claim to be the Shelleyan artistic subject with the power to name, represent, define, and desire.

Soon after the doomed performance of Louie's play, a breaking point arrives in the mired battleground of the Pollitt family. Resistance from the exhausted Henny and demoralized Louie is finally overwhelmed by Sam's determination to dominate all available bodies. Late in the second half of the novel, when the inexorable downward mobility and ensuing poverty prompted by his narcissism has become its most severe, Sam decides to boil down a marlin to recover its oil for use about the house. The inescapable smell of the boiled marlin offers a visceral allegory for political and emotional exhaustion, dehumanization, and dissolution that arises from unyielding oppression:

> The effluvia of the fish, all that could be conveyed by air, were seeping again round the house, for the storm was passing away at last, and all that remained was the flickering of the sky, fringes of rainy cloud, and the pools of water underfoot. The water in the creek was lapping high too. It seemed to Sam that nature was licking at his feet like a slave, like a woman, that he had read of somewhere, that washed the feet of the man she loved and dried them with her hair.[37]

The super-saturation of this "effluvia" robs the children and wife of their small remaining freedom from the regime of the father. They are imprisoned in a universe that privileges a domestic tyrant whose fantasies of enslavement mirror his actual enslavement of his own family. The intense materiality of this sequence in the realm of smell recalls Stead's astonishing work on the acoustic and olfactory details of family life. Ever unsentimental, Stead insists on the reality that the mother and daughter's relieved flight or tragic escape leaves the petty tyrant of the domestic *polis* to thrive on the continued labor of other subjugated women and his remaining children.

Louie's escape at the end of *The Man Who Loved Children* and Teresa's flight from Australia toward love and freedom in *For Love Alone* can be set against a very different kind of mobility and freedom in *Letty Fox*. These three novels can be read as an informal trilogy treating the subject of young women in modernity, and a shifting thematics of mobility and stasis inform all three. *For Love Alone* is significant for its transnational staging of the two worlds of Australia and England, though it is most remarkable for the power and originality of Stead's rendition of Sydney in the 1930s. The vital materiality and saturated erotics of Stead's description of Sydney is anticipated in the famous Prologue ("The Sea People") to Part I, where "the skies are sub-tropical, crusted with suns and spirals, as if a reflection of the crowded Pacific Ocean, with its reefs, atolls, and archipelagos."[38] This island of plenty is identified as a "great Ithaca," naming it as the powerful island to which the seafaring Odysseus will return. The power and priority of the mighty Pacific is mapped across the Ionian and Aegean seas, decades before Derek Walcott made a similar comparison between the Caribbean and the Aegean.

Sydney harbor is initially the stage for a creative young woman's "mad love" – persistently associated with water – that cannot be contained in the provincial society or patriarchal home in which she finds herself. In Part I, we find Teresa in her room near the sea before her libidinal potential has been mired in the miserable traps laid for her by the sadistic Jonathan Crow:

> Her room, the door ajar, invited her, blazing to her [...] the door and window open made her stand still on the landing for a few moments as she looked into her room, trembling with expectancy [...]. It was the hot intolerable hour, the hour when in hot countries the sun begins to embrace the earth and crush it with his weight; when he changes everything in it.[39]

As Part I progresses, however, Teresa moves away from erotic plenitude and self-discovery toward self-denial when she sets herself a regime of working and saving to fund her journey to London. Teresa wants to leave her provincial milieu in a bid to be free and love as a fully passionate subject and artist, so she chooses a remote love object to energize and strengthen her quest into the world, undertaken not under the transgressive sign of ambition, but instead the quest for love. Ironically (and this is the fundamental tension of Stead's narrative), Crow, the "dark" love object that powers movement from near and far, is also a source of stagnation and deformation. We see this darkly charismatic monster often in Stead's work in the form of the charismatic narcissist (Oliver Fenton, Sam Pollitt, Andrew Hawkins, Robbie Grant, Nellie Cotter), but this story of the creative woman who barely survives an exploitative and nonreciprocal love is also a story of determination, of a narrow escape into the world and restitution through the recognition of a truly worldly and openly loving man. If Teresa is the young woman in modernity who negotiates the world of sex and love in the realm of romance, Letty, her "sister" does so with a streetwise *picara*'s eye on the main chance in the streets of New York City.

In New York City, the circulation of stories and commodities and the restlessness of economic survival and libidinal progress are facets of urban experience captured by Stead in her portraits of the New York *picara* with her feet in the radical 1930s (*Letty Fox: Her Luck*), the wartime financier-libertine (*A Little Tea, A Little Chat*), and the postwar dilettante (*The People with the Dogs*). Stead's New York trilogy offers various iterations of the picaresque character and picaresque narrative, paying a particular attention to gender and the way in which market forces and alienation are negotiated by women. Setting sail, casting off, costing, and loading freight, sizing up other ships, bringing other ships to harbor, sea roads and sea lanes – this was the commercial and piratical figure system of Stead's New York trilogy, which comprises an under-read Australian and transnational engagement with a great American city as it was becoming a world cultural and economic capital (1935–1946). The New York novels, which are distinctly the product of the New York war years from 1941, coalesce around the energetic rogues and wanderers at their various centers, but at the heart of the trilogy sits Stead's keen question about a lack of system or properly coherent theory of political action. Stead refers to *libertinage* in the context of Letty's behavior, and here she indicates not so much the required curtailment of libertine desire and bohemianism as much as the countervailing need for a political theory and political discipline. Letty's capacity to extract herself from the system of economic alienation in the marriage market will rest on finding a way of reading or theorizing her situation rather than simply responding to events or cashing in on the "chic" or fad of Left radicalism, an element of political hypocrisy that Stead despised. So, Stead's critique of "no system" (no proper Marxism) starts with "the error of female riot" (sex mobilized to secure marriage) in *Letty Fox*, and works into a larger satire of fake New York radicals. This critique progresses, as the war draws to a close and moves into McCarthyite America, to the grim portrait of the dehumanizing reification of sexual and economic relations in *A Little Tea, A Little Chat*, only softened a little by the recollection of New York in *The People with the Dogs* from the precarious locus of postwar Europe. In flight from growing McCarthyism in the States, Stead and Blake set sail for Europe again in early 1947 with relief and hope, but the Cold War meant that the old political and artistic habitus of Europe was a mirage. The vitality that a return to Europe should have produced for them did not eventuate. They settled down in very poor circumstances in suburban England after 1955. This produced a long stasis in Stead's writing.

Negation and its Discontents (1947–1986)

Cotter's England (1966), *The Puzzleheaded Girl* (1967), *The Little Hotel* (1973), *Miss Herbert (The Suburban Wife)* (1976), and *I'm Dying Laughing* (1986) comprise the works of Stead's late period, though there is an argument for placing *The Puzzleheaded Girl* with the American sequence. Given the gap in publication between 1952 and 1966, we can see that the seminal moment in the third stage of Stead's writing life was the reissue of *The Man Who Loved Children* in 1965, twenty-five years after its first publication. Randall Jarrell's long introductory essay to the 1965 reissue claims *The Man* as the great neglected masterpiece of family life in world literature. His impassioned case for Stead led her to be rediscovered in the United States and England and finally published in Australia. International publishers began to publish her immediate postwar writing, which started to appear from 1966.

It is worth noting that, while Stead's later period of composition seems to span the years 1948 to 1986 (with a hiatus in 1952–1966), it is more accurate to say that much of what constitutes Stead's late novels were materially conceived and drafted in the period 1948–1953. Broadly speaking, the late work emerges from this early Cold War block, with some intermittent bursts of work for publication, or, in the case of *I'm Dying Laughing,* posthumous assemblage. The coda structure resists Hazel Rowley's view that Stead's late work reveals the impact of depression and aging. In fact, it might be more useful to think about heavy political sadness, difficult economic and political choices, and loss of audience for the Left writer in the Cold War. Edward W. Said suggests that the key term for the "late" work is *catastrophe*, which connotes a "turn" as much as disaster, and this applies rather well to Stead's political and artistic situation after 1947. In line with the fate of the Left in the West after 1945, Stead's focus on the stories of fake or lazy radicals moves into sustained portraits of outright bad faith, political hypocrisy, and a "natural history" of political betrayal and its ecosystems. Although Stead's late work can be difficult and discordant, the "catastrophe" she doggedly sought to record has left us with two different masterworks: the vibrant but unfinished *I'm Dying Laughing* (1950/1986) and the craggy and uncompromising *Cotter's England* (1953/1966). The "lateness" of these two works has multiple meanings: the idea of that which is chronologically late in a career, and a quality of irremediable aftermath or of being "too late." There is an additional lateness concerned with the extended time between production and reception, and this identifies a certain way in which Stead's work is actually "out of time," since significant gaps exist between the scenes of writing and of reading, and the Left affiliation that had sustained Stead and Blake was also out of step in the West.

The signature vitality of Stead's prose continues into her late work, even as her ethnographic drive to tell the truth of the Cold War moment on both sides of the Atlantic moves her inexorably into darker, less structured renditions of people, place, and things. We see an increase in the strife, drama, and struggle anticipated by *A Little Tea, A Little Chat,* where the effort to capture the "man alive" amounts to a representation of domination that is uncomfortably immersive. It is notable, too, that central characters of the key late works are women writers whose one-time radicalism and failed political commitment is anatomized alongside their failed creativity. In *Cotter's England*, in particular, it is as though the novel has become a pure recording device to report the truth of what has been intimately seen and heard about female exploitation, self-deception, and political hypocrisy in Cold War Britain. Verbal charm and political charisma are part of Nellie Cotter's power, but even more than Sam Pollitt and Robbie Grant, aggression, compulsion, and mania inform and disturb this portrait of the political woman and her unfortunate familiars. It is the profundity of the progression from vitality and committed political work into bad faith, moral degeneration, and involuted stasis that gives *Cotter's England* its position as Stead's final major work published in her lifetime.

I'm Dying Laughing is the last published work in Stead's oeuvre. There is some reason to think of it as the culminating work of the American sequence, but Stead found it difficult to finish and thus it is read as her great last work. *I'm Dying Laughing* is based on the marriage and careers of Ruth McKenney and Richard Bransten, whom Stead knew well from the late 1930s and who struggled with themselves, their marriage, and their politics in the pressure cooker of American early Cold War contexts. The central character of the novel is Emily Wilkes, a Midwestern woman who is a very successful and wealthy writer of comedy – a humorist. She is also a committed and effective communist from the 1930s to the early Cold War. With her pithy insight and comic vision, Emily Wilkes saw the reality of American political identity with rare clarity and verve, including her own complicity in the machinery of contradiction:

> 'Isn't our history all struggle, all terror, all bloodshed; and at the same time, all hooraying, all success? America the Golden [...]. Other countries have history; we have nothing but contradictions. We haven't even got a system; or if we have, no one knows what it is. American get-ahead, that's the only system we know.'[40]

Emily Wilkes embodies the dynamics of crisis and contradiction as the writer who earns a living from comedy but yearns to tell the tragic truth. As the long and verbally torrential novel unfolds in tidal waves of speech and writing, Wilkes continues to hold both possibilities open through a kind of personal inflation of body and textual production, but experiences increasing artistic, moral, and political derangement through her transgression of all meaningful limits in an historical period of seemingly impossible choices.

I'm Dying Laughing is one of Stead's most important novels, not least because it is one of the rare Anglophone literary accounts of the complex abandonment of the Left by the Left in the early Cold War by a writer who kept the faith. It is at once a work about the necessity of political commitment and the maintenance of a redoubtably individual perspective. As *I'm Dying Laughing* works through questions of art, political affiliation, historical development, and the fate of the radical generation of the 1930s, it retraces the lineaments of Dreiser's *An American Tragedy* (1925), a book openly alluded to in *I'm Dying Laughing*. Thus Stead's late masterwork is a tragic novel about a comic author who yearns to write tragedy. I would argue that tragedy, rather than travesty and farce, was the mode that Stead wanted to engage, but the very political history with which she was involved continued to unfold around her, making the purchase required by tragedy difficult without resorting to historical allegory, as Arthur Miller had done. *I'm Dying Laughing* marshals the extraordinary political and artistic tensions of the period between the mid-1930s and mid-1950s. Though unfinished, the work signals the ambition and capacity of Stead's "mature subjectivity" to "render disenchantment and pleasure," though her complex transnational career and the ways in which canons of literary value were construed after World War II never really afforded Stead the chance of the "hubris and pomposity" that might need to be stripped away.[41]

From a childhood on the shore of the sea of stories in the early days of the twentieth century to a posthumous collection of tales, *Ocean of Story* in 1985, Stead's career can be viewed as one of restless negotiations of the novel form, transnational authorship, and political transnationalism. The coordinates that stabilized her impressive movement through the great capital cities of modernity did not alter: She was interested in politics and the fate of the oppressed, she felt bound to tell the truth of the world she witnessed (and this included the truth of modern women's lives), and she invested in the identity of the "sea-woman" as a way of negotiating her international mobility.[42] Stead's worldly work was acutely grounded in her Australian upbringing and her sense of both nation and region: Australia provided material to which she returned again and again, as evidenced in the late, uncollected stories about Australia in *Ocean of Story*. However, her artistic ambition was such that she extended her writerly vision into the world and wrote about where she was situated with a moral urgency and insatiable curiosity about "the drama of the person" that is evident even in the uncompromising works of her late period. In the twenty-first century, we continue to find ways to address and explain what is clear about Christina Stead: She is one of Australia's great writers and one of the most important political women writers of the twentieth century. Her combination of unsentimental geopolitical critique and fearless literary aesthetics grew from her ambitious claim to be a female mariner – an Australian Odysseus – whose citizenship of the country of the ocean extended to an epic desire to write what she had seen and where she had traveled.

Notes

1 Meg Samuelson and Charne Lavery, "The Oceanic South," *English Language Notes* 57.1 (2019): pp. 37–50 (p. 37).

2 Kerry Bystrom and Isabel Hofmeyr, "Oceanic Routes: (Post-it) Notes on Hydro-Colonialism," *Comparative Literature* 69.1 (2017): pp. 1–6 (p. 3).

3 Christina Stead, "England," *Kenyon Review* 30.4 (1968): pp. 444–450 (p. 444).

4 Stead, "England," p. 449.

5 Stead, "England," p. 449.

6 Stead, "England," p. 444.

7 Christina Stead, in Rodney Wetherell, "Interview with Christina Stead," *Austra lian Literary Studies* 9.4 (1980): pp. 431–448 (p. 432).

8 Stead in Wetherell, "Interview," p. 441.

9 Walter Benjamin, *Illuminations* (New York: Harcourt Brace Jovanovich, 1968), p. 83.

10 Christina Stead to Thistle Harris (her father's widow) 4.1942, in Christina Stead, *A Web of Friendship. Selected Letters. 1928–1973*, ed. R. G. Geering, (Pymble, New South Wales: Angus & Robertson, 1992), p. 94.

11 Christina Stead as cited in "Christina Stead," *Twentieth Century Authors: A Biographical Dictionary of Modern Literature*, eds. Stanley J. Kunitz and Howard Haycroft (New York: Wilson, 1942), p. 1275.

12 Susan Lever, "Christina Stead's Workshop in the Novel: How to Write a 'Novel of Strife'," *JASAL: Journal of the Association for the Study of Australian Literature* 2 (2003): 81–91.

13 Jonah Raskin, "Christina Stead in Washington Square," *London Magazine* 9.2 (1970): pp. 69–77 (p. 75).

14 Hazel Rowley, *Christina Stead: A Biography* (Port Melbourne: Minerva, 1994).

15 Margaret Harris, "Christina Stead's Earliest Publications," *Australian Literary Studies* 31.6 (2016): www.australianliterarystudies.com.au/articles/christina-steads-earliest-publications.

16 Rowley, *Stead*, p. 61.

17 Christina Stead, *Seven Poor Men of Sydney* (North Ryde: Angus & Robertson, 1990; 1934), pp. 2–3.

18 Christina Stead, *Ocean of Story: The Uncollected Stories of Christina Stead* (Ringwood: Penguin, 1986), pp. 496–497.

19 Stead, "Interview with Rodney Wetherell," p. 447.

20 Peter Kirkpatrick, "Walking Through Seven Poor Men of Sydney," *JASAL: Journal of the Association for the Study of Australian Literature* (1999): pp. 62–67.

21 M. Barnard Eldershaw, *Essays in Australian Fiction* (Melbourne: Melbourne University Press, 1938), pp. 165–166.

22 Stead, *Seven Poor Men of Sydney*, p. 1.

23 Stead, *Seven Poor Men of Sydney*, p. 1.

24 Stead, *Seven Poor Men of Sydney*, p. 1.

25 Stead, *Seven Poor Men of Sydney*, p. 2.

26 See also Fiona Morrison, "Modernist/Provincial/Pacific: Christina Stead, Katherine Mansfield and the Expatriate Home Ground," *JASAL: Journal of the Association for the Study of Australian Literature* 13.2 (2013): pp. 1–12.

27 Quoted in Rowley. *Times*, January 30, 1934, p. 9 (unsigned); *Times Literary Supplement,* February 15, 1934, p. 106.

28 West is quoted in the back of Peter Davies' edition of *Seven Poor Men of Sydney*, published in October 1934.

29 Christina Stead, "The Writers Take Sides," *Left Review* 1.2 (1935): pp. 453–462 (p. 454).

30 Christina Stead, *House of All Nations* (North Ryde: Angus & Robertson, 1988; 1938), pp. 93–94.

31 Anne Whitehead, "An Interview with Christina Stead," *Australian Literary Studies* 6.3 (1974): pp. 230–248 (p. 244).

32 Essential reading here is Louise Yelin, "Fifty Years of Reading: A Reception Study of *The Man Who Loved Children*," *Contemporary Literature* 31.4 (1990): pp. 472–498.

33 Christina Stead, *The Man Who Loved Children* (Harmondsworth: Penguin Books, 1970; 1940), p. 404.

34 Joseph Boone makes this argument very powerfully in "Of Fathers, Daughters and the Theorists of Narrative Desire: At the Crossroads of Myth and Psychoanalysis in *The Man Who Loved Children*," *Contemporary Literature* 31.4 (1990): pp. 512–541.

35 Stead, *The Man Who Loved Children*, p. 277.

36 Stead, *The Man Who Loved Children*, p. 133.

37 Stead, *The Man Who Loved Children*, p. 446.

38 Christina Stead, *For Love Alone* (Sydney: Angus & Robertson, 1966; 1944), pp. 1–2.

39 Stead, *For Love Alone*, p. 100.

40 Christina Stead, *I'm Dying Laughing*, ed. R. G. Geering (New York: Henry Holt, 1987), p. 21.

41 Edward W. Said, *On Late Style: Music and Literature Gainst the Grain* (London: Bloomsbury, 2006), p. 107.

42 Christina Stead to Stanley Burnshaw, June 10, 1965, in *A Web of Friendship*, p. 172.

8

CHEN HONG

Sexuality in Patrick White's Fiction

Patrick White, the winner of the Nobel Prize for Literature in 1973, has long been acclaimed as a great modernist Australian writer. A versatile writer of novels, short stories, plays, and poems, White has been celebrated by various critics and academics as a "visionary and rationalist," a "powerful cultural critic," and even a "prophet from the desert."[1] Though no political radical, he was a revolutionary in another sense. He definitively put modernism on the map in Australia, which up until then had largely been dominated by more conventional novelists and poets, such as Xavier Herbert, Henry Handel Richardson, and A. D. Hope. Deeply preoccupied with the universal questions of the human existence and its discontents, as well as the ways to transcend various mortal limitations, White rooted his works in the specificities of Australia, while also making his characters and settings a microcosm of humanity at large. His fiction is both cosmopolitan and "concerned to draw the exact curve of the specific sensibility of his own time and nation."[2] But White is perhaps known less for his distinctive understanding of human nature than for his contrarian way of life. In spite of being widely recognized as a literary giant, a celebrity, and, in his later life, an influential public figure, he remained a pessimistic eremite, hardly concealing his scorn for Australia's mundane surroundings – "this abominable country" – and its philistine people, whom he described variously as "vegetables" and "vipers."[3]

Nonetheless, the characteristic that exerted the greatest impact on his life and his writing is, I believe, his homosexuality. White unswervingly ascribed his literary talents to his sexual inclination, declaring to Geoffrey Dutton: "If I am anything of a writer it is through my homosexuality, which has given me additional insights."[4] Yet even with these forthright personal avowals, there was, until recently, little sustained critical attention to sexuality in White's fiction. The most notable exception here is David Marr's remarkable biography *Patrick White: A Life* (1991), but for a long time, one was almost as likely to find critical perspectives marred by homophobic presumptions (such as David Tacey's Jungian approach) as readings that illuminatingly explored how White's sexuality informed his writing.[5] On the one hand, critics were afraid that the supposed universality of White's writing – his status as "anything of a writer" – would be compromised by an undue focus on his particular sexuality.[6] On the other hand, some critics, such as Simon During in his controversial, "pseudo-theoretical reading of White as an Eliot-style aristocratic high-modernist," present White as deliberately complicating his "grand metaphysical inquiries with sanguine physicality" (as Jonathan Dunk points out in a critique of During).[7] In either case, the supposed particularity of sexuality was perceived as undercutting universal themes.

This situation has thankfully changed somewhat in the last two decades, especially due to the growing influence of queer theory in Australian studies.[8] Anouk Lang has argued that White's modernist formal innovation is itself queer, while Elizabeth McMahon has questioned how we might "read the graphesis of homosexuality" in White's 1979 novel, *The Twyborn Affair*.[9] This work has opened exciting avenues for research. Though writers such as James Joyce and D. H. Lawrence have long been recognized as important influences on White, less attention has been paid so far to how White's modernist influences were queer from the start. It would be easy to think of White agreeing with the provocative title of Diana Souhami's *No Modernism Without Lesbians* (2020): His first novel, *Happy Valley* (1939), was written "very much under the influence of Gertrude [...] she helped form me," by which he means Gertrude Stein, from whom *Happy Valley* takes its "decorative patterning, [...] rhythmic repetitions and paratactical touches of phrasing."[10] (When departing from one of his lovers, Pepe Mamblas, it was "a copy of Stein's *The Autobiography of Alice B. Toklas*" that he gave him "to read on the return journey to Paris").[11] It is funny to think, too, that White's novels issued from "a magnificent desk with wide, shallow draws and red linoleum top" designed especially for him by the important gay artist Francis Bacon (when White couldn't bring it back to Australia, he had a copy made).[12] As interesting as such details are, this chapter sets out not simply to trace queer connections, but to explore the relationship between Patrick White's sexuality and its literary expression in his novels.

Sexuality is essential to literary creativity and expression. It would be impossible to deny this today, especially given how literary theory and literature have been irrevocably shaped by psychoanalytic theory and its legacies. Sigmund Freud famously attended to literary and artistic works, tracing how sexuality had shaped, for example, the artistic pursuits of Leonardo da Vinci.[13] In the years since Freud's field-defining insights, numerous literary theorists, such as Leo Bersani, have sought to connect "sexuality, psychoanalysis, and aesthetics."[14] But sexuality is not only ascribable to literary articulation. It can also exist in conjunction with an artist's cultural, political, and social interests. Perhaps the best foundation for this claim is Judith Butler's argument in her foundational text of queer theory, *Gender Trouble* (1990). According to Butler, identity categories such as "gay" and "straight" tend to be "instruments of regulatory regimes, whether as the normalizing categories of oppressive structures or as the rallying points for liberatory contestations of that very oppression."[15] Thus, the culturally endorsed, normative "self" of heterosexuality, as well the marginalized "other" of homosexuality, coexist to formulate a unique interplay of fluid identity and desires. We could add, in light of Eve Kosofsky Sedgwick's *Epistemology of the Closet*, that there is also a duality, even multiplicity, of sexual identity in a homosexual person's life.[16] In the system of compulsory heterosexuality, a homosexual person may have to confine and conceal their sexual preference and orientation into a reclusive realm – the so-called closet – where innermost secrets are kept. But more than that, an artist's fluid subjectivity often finds expression in a complex and disguised manner.

There can be no simplistic dichotomy of "in" or "out" of the closet for an author such as White. White is generally said to have "come out" with *Flaws in the Glass* (1981) and it is indeed with this book that his sexuality was first noted in reviews. When the Nobel prize was announced in 1973, it was seen as the first award for an Australian writer, but White was not considered alongside other gay, lesbian, or bisexual Nobel winners for literature (such as André Gide, Selma Lagerlöf, or Thomas Mann). Such a genealogy did not exist at that point.[17] A nationalist interpretation of White's work was far more evident (something that reflects the Nobel Prize's terms of conferral: White was credited as having "introduced a new continent into literature").[18] *The New York Times* noted that White had "become the first Australian author to receive such international acclaim," but said of his private life only that he was a "reticent man."[19] His partner, Manoly Lascaris, was not mentioned. Conversely, after White's sexuality became visible, his reputation was eclipsed in the Anglophone world. Although this may have had to do with other factors, such as the natural downturn in fortunes once a writer has died, or the emergence of younger, more postmodern writers such as Peter Carey, White's heyday in the Global North and the visibility of his sexuality have been at inverse variance. He is a famous writer who happened to be homosexual, not a famous queer writer.

Yet to look only at the surface profession and acknowledgment of White's sexuality is to miss the subtlety at play in his fiction. In all his writing, there is a complex interplay of concealment and openness – a network of nuances, implications, and complications.[20] "The line between inside and outside of the closet is not," as McMahon puts it, "clear, easily identified, or stable."[21]

Even a novel such as *The Twyborn Affair*, with its sexually indeterminate protagonist, can be both "the most explicit in regard to a lived practice of sexuality" and "simultaneously the most veiled and the most figurative on this subject," as McMahon demonstrates.[22] These multiple and compounded levels mean that readings of White's novels very often reveal as much, if not more, about the reader and their values than they do about the novels. As readers, we can pivot between the extremes of "the *alazon*, the Imposter, who boasts of more than she knows," and "the *eiron*, the Ironical Jester, who feigns ignorance and who knows much more than he reveals."[23] In some cases, as with White's second novel, *The Living and the Dead* (1941), the reader may even be exasperated by their epistemic advantage vis-à-vis the novel's enduring closetedness. Marr even suggests that: "Had White been able to state Standish's predicament bluntly, the end of *The Living and the Dead* might have been the opening pages of a more profound novel."[24] But no matter what kind of sexual preferences we read into a given novel, sexual relations, identities, and images in White's fiction can only be understood as multifarious. We find this, for instance, in the deeply concealed angst of White's characters – a melancholy that may reflect the repressive social scheme that has imposed sexual and cultural inhibition and restrictions. To elucidate this, I sketch how three typical categories of sexuality – heterosexuality, bisexuality, and homosexuality – become representative of White's depiction of the sexual sufferings of his characters.

Heterosexuality

In earlier novels such as *The Tree of Man* (1955) and *Voss* (1957), heterosexuality is represented in a relatively "conventional' way. But even here, there is an obvious inability on the part of both White's male and female characters to fully pursue their satisfaction – "satisfaction" meaning not only sexual gratification, but also spiritual and personal fulfillment. *The Tree of Man*, which first brought White to general attention after his return from Europe to Australia, was intended to fill what he famously called "the Great Australian Emptiness," a term that White used to describe the peculiar nihilism of settler Australian culture.[25] A story of "living and dying," *The Tree of Man* discloses a certain ambivalence, we might say, in the representation of sexuality.[26] This is particularly evident by the way White depicts the novel's two protagonists, Stan Parker and his wife Amy Fibbens Parker. A heterosexual couple, Stan and Amy's relationship is by no means an ordinary matrimony. They never fully understand each other, and live in two different perceptual worlds, as opposite as the fire and flood that at different times menace their settlement.

In the case of *Voss*, Voss and Laura Trevelyan, though clearly in love with one another, are prevented from having any physical intimacy by various impediments that are beyond their ability to overcome. The relationship develops into a platonic, telepathic affair, with Laura in the city of Sydney and Voss out in one of Australia's inland deserts. We could consider this the "optimal" depiction of a heterosexual relationship in White. Deprived of bodily, sensual contact, it instead becomes ethereal. But Laura continues her love affair with Voss even after his death. This otherworldly romance, beyond the confines of lived experience, also exceeds compulsory hetero-sexuality. And so, the seemingly ordinary heterosexual relationship, from acquaintance to courtship to marriage, is also never corporeal. Voss and Laura's verbal and carnal interactions exist only through telepathy, halluci-nation, and dreams. This is not to say that their affair is only supernatural, but that it surpasses the natural way of life. After all, Patrick White says that, in writing *Voss*, he wanted to "marry Delacroix to Blake."[27] The pas-sion, fervor, voluptuousness, and eroticism – all these homosexual elements in nature under the disguise of heterosexuality – carefully intertwine with the expressiveness of Delacroix's undulating, imprecise, even violent brush-strokes, alongside the strange, mystic pronouncements of Blake's poetry. Perhaps the most significant similarity between *The Tree of Man* and *Voss* emerges here: in the protagonists' relationship with nature. The Jungian critic David Tacey claims in this connection that: "Parker found his deity reflected in the natural world around him, but for Voss the ideal image is always somewhere else, somewhere mysterious, remote, out of reach."[28] Nature, in this way, serves both as the medium for the protagonists' rela-tionship and the outlet for them to let loose their subsumed passions.

Bisexuality

In White's works, bisexuality is also a matter of inhibition and expression. White had a deeply embedded apprehension about the attitudes of others, espe-cially his readers, towards his homosexuality. If readers, as he once put it in a letter to the film director Joseph Losey, "realise they have been spurred on by a homosexual [...] [then] a lot of them will think they have been duped."[29] Were we to treat these words candidly, then the ubiquitous androgynous fig-ures in White's work could be read as a strategy of simultaneously expressing and concealing homosexual desire. White's later fiction, especially, is populated by a plethora of physically and psychologically androgynous characters. We could put this down to White's awareness of his own inability to incorporate the socially and culturally endorsed and encouraged sexual preference into his personal and literary experiences. But we might also read it as a principled artistic rejection of the heterosexual binary – a refusal to arbitrarily divide his understanding of humanity into femininity and masculinity.

White was fond of saying that *The Aunt's Story* (1948) was his favorite among his novels. Theodora, the protagonist of *The Aunt's Story*, is a solitary and outwardly unattractive spinster. She has an emblematic mustache – what White calls her "humiliating fringe."[30] Theodora displays male characteristics in ways that would have been immediately recognizable in the period, such as wearing boots and trousers. When she is in women's clothes, she is said to walk "fast [...] with the long strides that made them say as Theo Goodman was some bloke in skirts."[31] In fact, she is almost asexual, and holds to the conviction that life should not be "conditioned by sex."[32] The barrenness of the social landscape of Sydney makes her an outcast in both the social and sexual sense, while her self-imposed exile to Europe only intensifies her sexual solitude. Detached, ostracized, and ultimately institutionalized, Theodora becomes desexualized: She exists instead beyond the common differentiation of femininity and masculinity.

Homosexuality – arguably sexuality itself – is mostly touched upon or hinted, often in metaphoric allusions, in White's earlier novels. In *The Twyborn Affair*, by contrast, sexuality becomes a central theme. In *The Twyborn Affair*, the protagonist, Eudoxia/Eddie/Eadith is a polymorphous, androgynous person – alternately a woman, a man, and a woman, shifting gender as the narrative shifts location (between France, Australia, and London). This shifting sexuality is White's first explicit attempt to explore the connection between sexuality and the volatility of personal identity. The transformation of Eudoxia/Eddie/Eadith is as much a journey toward self-realization as self-annihilation. In her relationship with Angelos Vatatzes, Eudoxia achieves a sexual duality that helps her explore the transcendental dimension of existence. Angelos gives her both physical realization and spiritual enlargement. Reality and ideal thus become mixed, helping to reach an ambivalence that is a way to achieve oblivion in the present, disguise the real, and seek the mystic and sublime. Sexual ambivalence thereby becomes a portal to other kinds of ontological ambivalence, as Eddie in Australia tries out both heterosexuality and homosexuality in search of a "true" identity. Eddie's sexual escapades with both Marcia Lushington and Don Prowse lead him/her to London, where Eadith's brothel serves as a sexual laboratory for the residents, the customers, and Eudoxia/Eddie/Eadith him/herself to understand the relativity of an individual's identity. Androgyny in White's other works is often very carefully veiled, occasionally betraying only by traces, nuances, and delicate indications.[33] In the *Solid Mandala* (1966), Waldo Brown's attempt to shed the restrictions of his masculine persona by donning his mother's ballroom dress could be interpreted as a protest against a cultural archetype of sexual identity. Drag, then, offers a particularly fruitful way to explore self-identity, while also negotiating acceptable forms of social recognition and cultural tolerance.

Homosexuality

White often thought of homosexuality as a condition visited upon him. He never flaunted his sexual orientation. It was seldom something that friends could easily and openly canvas and discuss with him. Nevertheless, homosexuality had a profound and undeniable influence on White's writing. Remarking on the relation between literary creativity and sexuality, he declared that: "[a]s a homosexual I have always known what it is to be an outsider. It has given me added insight into the plight of the immigrant – the hate and contempt with which he is often received."[34]

White started his life as a writer in an age when homosexuality was still taboo in many Western countries. Social pressures and discrimination made him cautious about revealing traces of his homosexuality in his life and his writings. In Simon During's analysis, such reluctance on his part is "partly because gay pride seemed actually to increase the importance of sexuality to personality and life as a whole, partly because he had internalized his own homosexuality both as a 'disease' and as feminizing, and partly too because it was easy to exaggerate the fear surrounding the closet and the silence it imposed."[35] According to this view, references to same-sex intimacy in White's writing are often implicit and obscure. The important exception here is *Flaws in the Glass*, a striking counter-example occurring in the following passage:

> Perhaps because a rare commodity, water played a leading part in my developing sexuality. I was always throwing off my clothes to bathe, either at the artesian bore during a pause from mustering, the water ejaculating warm and sulphurous out of the earth, or in the river flowing between the trunks of great flesh-coloured gums, to a screeching, flick-knife commentary by yellow-crested cockatoos, or at night in the hollow below the homestead if a good season had turned it into a lagoon. Here I was joined by the men who worked about the place, whose company I enjoyed without becoming their equal. The way to the lagoon was stony. I once found a pair of old high-heeled shoes amongst the junk dumped in the bathroom. I wore them, tottering across the stones till reaching the acquiescent mud, the tepid water of the lagoon. My companions turned the shoes into a ribald joke, acceptable because it was something we could share. We continued joking, to hold more serious thoughts at bay, while we plunged, turning on our backs after surfacing, spouting water, exposing our sex, lolling or erect, diving again to swim beneath the archways made by open legs, ribs, and flanks slithering against other forms in the fishy school, as a flamingo moon rose above the ashen crowns of surrounding trees.[36]

In his fiction, however, White's deliberate encoding of homosexuality entices acts of decipherment, thus positioning the reader in an epistemologically active position. The very fact that White's writing is confined creates a space for readerly transgression.

White certainly did not extoll Australian "mateship" – that fabled male camaraderie shared by farmhands and workers in the Australian bush tradition. Nor did he venerate the beauty of male physique, though he does, from time to time, lavish attention on some minor bodily detail, such as the hair on a man's wrists. Nonetheless, we find allusive, obscure, and camouflaged instances of homosexuality across White's work. One memorable example can be found in *Voss*. The expedition team is an all-male community, compromised of members with ambivalent sexual orientations. In the terms of Sedgwick's *Between Men*, it is a "homosocial" group.[37] The team venturing into the Australian desert is secluded and reclusive. In a sense, we watch them edging away from mainstream culture into a wasteland – towards the masochistic release of the final impersonality of destruction. (It may be worth noting here that White described himself as "soaked in Rimbaud,"[38] a queer icon and French poet who declared that the poet need become "a *seer*, by a long, immense and reasoned *disordering of all the senses*," and yet gave up poetry aged twenty, undertook dangerous trading journeys in East Africa, and died at only thirty-seven.[39] Rimbaud not only provides a model for Le Mesurier in *Voss*, but for the central journey of *Voss* itself.) Though their "exploring" of course fails in its colonial sense, in another, more interesting sense, it achieves the masochistic pleasure of "losing and dissolving the self," perhaps even, as Bersani writes, "*re*discove[ring] the self outside the self" in a kind of "spatial, anonymous narcissism."[40] In another sense, though, White's treatment of this group is ambiguous. We could say that the expedition is a triumph of homosexual desires, but the fact that it ends in tragedy signifies the death wish of compulsory heterosexuality. The all-male group, led by the would-be *Übermensch* Voss, is a kind of escape for his homosexual characters, too. Although the adventure ends up in tragedy, it is homosexuality, latent and disguised, that helps men "make contact with their primordial, quasi-unconscious nature (which is what their quest into Australia's interior signifies). Homosexuality in *Voss* belongs to the closet, but at the same time it is primordial for men."[41] The same could be said of the friendship between Mordecai Himmelfarb and Alf Dubbo in *Riders in the Chariot*, where their erotic affinity is not at all named but is impalpably present.

In some novels and short stories, White tries to explore his own sexual dilemma through domineering mother figures. In Marr's biography, White's mother Ruth is presented as equivalent to Mrs. Goodman in the *Aunt's Story* and Mrs. Polkinghorn in the short story "The Letter." For

Tacey, who insists on translating this into Jungian terms, the experience of a strong mother figure is accompanied by the physical and psychological absence of a father. It is true that many of White's characters struggle to achieve sexual and therefore personal identity, and that mothers are the dominant presence in their life. In this sense, the family structure is like an enclosure inhibiting the protagonists' sexual and social explorations. This can even have an incestuous subtext, as though the family enclosure were implosive and inwardly collapsing. Nevertheless, personal formation cannot be achieved by simply escaping all constraints. Though the death of Theodora Goodman's mother, for instance, frees her from the gendered burdens of family life, her journey could, to follow Tim Anderson's suggestion, be thought of as the attempt to create "a shell against Australian reality."[42]

In White's later works, notably *The Solid Mandala*, siblings are bound together in bewildering ways that render precise individuation impossible. Arthur and Waldo Brown, the two twin brothers in the novel, could be read as the reflection of the different facades of one individuality. As White put it in *Flaws in the Glass*: "I see the Brown brothers as my two halves."[43] "[I]n most of White's fiction," as John Colmer speculated, "the characters are fragments and variations of the author's self."[44] But we might also read White's novel against his own statements here: a sexual fascination flows between the two brothers, and this incestuous desire plays directly into Waldo's murder of Arthur. In this way, *Solid Mandala* could be viewed as an elegiac depiction of preadolescent enclosure.

Conclusion

Around the time of *The Tree of Man*, White wrote to his publisher, Ben Huebsch:

> I don't know whether other authors experience what I do: a feeling that they may be writing a secret language that nobody else will be able to interpret. Consequently the strain is very great until one discovers it is intelligible to someone else. And this time the strain has been increasing over four years.[45]

For White, writing was always bound up with the simultaneous revelation and writing-over of secret meanings. Reading, understanding, and interpreting White's novels also involves an act of readerly becoming. The reader must strive to become an interpreter who can discern and reveal the encoded, the disguised, the euphemistic, the implied. White's purposeful inarticulation of his sexual identity needs textual and intertextual close reading and uncovering.

White had tried to define and locate, hence declare, his sexuality, but he still remained reticent in writing about homosexual notions and practices, and many of his characters are ambiguous in declaring their sexual preferences. In other words, many of his novels were written "from the closet," remaining constrained within the structure of socially and culturally sanctioned tradition. But precisely for this reason, the psychological features of his characters are exquisitely described and styled, while the reading experience becomes a process of discovering and uncovering coded secrets charged with private significance. As Peter Wolfe pointed out in 1983, White was not a conventional realist. Despite the conceptual heft and intricate storytelling of his fictions, "No social historian he."[46] And despite his close reading of writers such as Joseph Conrad, William Faulkner, and James Joyce, he was not a modernist along those lines. An Australian writer who forsook the expatriate journeys made by so many of his contemporaries, he distinctly disidentified with Australian nationalism. At the core of all these contradictions is a private selfhood communicable in fiction alone.

Building on Marr's biography, recent criticism on White has finally given us a better view of White's personal life, particularly his relationship with his life partner, Manoly Lascaris. This relationship can be seen in refracted ways in many of White's fictions – the apposition of narcissistic Waldo and compassionate Arthur in *The Solid Mandala,* the character of Angelos Vataztes in *The Twyborn Affair*, and the relationship of Eirene Sklavos and Gilbert Horsfall in the posthumously published *The Hanging Garden.* A memoir by Vrasidas Karalis and critical work by Shaun Bell has made clear the centrality of Lascaris to an understanding of the Nobel Laureate's life and work.[47] A new wave of critical scholarship also flourished in the 2010s, culminating in Christos Tsiolkas's 2018 reappraisal of White's work. Tsiolkas noted that he had been "able to work for most of two decades as a writer without the need or the desire to engage with" White's work.[48] This was reflective of a general reticence about White across Australian culture in the two decades after his death. Perhaps, as Tsiolkas put it, the "vitriolic" attitude of White towards "so many aspects" of Australia was being returned in kind.[49] But Tsiolkas's powerful defense of White's achievement is an indication of a small renaissance of critical interest in White's work.

White remains the most celebrated Australian writer in history. He is also the best-read and most researched Australian novelist, always with new and ever more aspects for readers to appreciate, and for academics and critics to scrutinize and discuss. This status is inseparable from the moment, in 1973, when the Swedish Academy awarded him the Nobel Prize. The citation commended him for his "epic and psychological narrative art which has introduced a new continent into literature."⁵⁰ But this psychology is not simply that of his characters. When we bear in mind the complexity of sexuality in White's fiction, it could mean the psychology of his readers, too.

Notes

1 Dorothy Green, "Patrick White: A Tribute," in *Patrick White: A Tribute*, ed. by Clayton Joyce (North Ryde: Angus & Robertson, 1991), pp. 1–6 (p. 1); Simon During, *Patrick White* (Melbourne: Oxford University Press, 1996), p. 9; John McLaren, *Prophet from the Desert: Critical Essays on Patrick White* (Melbourne: Red Hill Press, 1995), p. i.

2 William Walsh, "Fiction as Metaphor: The Novels of Patrick White," *The Sewanee Review* 82.2 (1974): pp. 197–211 (p. 198).

3 Patrick White, *Letters*, ed. David Marr (Sydney: Random House, 1994), pp. 274, 339.

4 White, *Letters*, p. 537.

5 For an account of the homophobic elements in David Tacey's criticism, see Rick Wallach, "On the Limits of Archetypal Criticism," *Antipodes* 6.2 (1992): pp. 133–138.

6 For a good articulation of this problem, see Brigid Rooney, "Public Recluse: Patrick White's Literary-Political Returns," in *Remembering Patrick White: Contemporary Critical Essays*, ed. Elizabeth McMahon and Brigitta Olubas (Amsterdam: Rodopi, 2010), pp. 3–18 (p. 5).

7 Jonathan Dunk, "Review of Bridget Grogan, Reading Corporeality in Patrick White's Fiction," *Commonwealth Essays and Studies* 42.0 (2019): 1–3 (p. 2). See During, *Patrick White*, pp. 71, 77.

8 See Ian Henderson, "Knockabout Worlds: Patrick White, Kenneth Williams, and the Queer Word," in *Patrick White Beyond the Grave: New Critical Perspectives*, ed. Ian Henderson and Anouk Lang (London: Anthem Press, 2015), pp. 181–192; Guy R. Davidson, "Displaying the Monster: Patrick White, Sexuality, Celebrity," *Australian Literary Studies*, 25.1 (2010): pp. 1–18.

9 Anouk Lang, "Queering Sarsaparilla: Patrick White's Deviant Modernism," in *Patrick White Beyond the Grave*, pp. 193–204; Elizabeth McMahon, "The Lateness and Queerness of The Twyborn Affair: White's Farewell to the Novel," in *Remembering Patrick White*, pp. 77–94 (p. 88).

10 Peter Craven, "Jackeroo Epic," in *Happy Valley* (London: Vintage, 2013), pp. ix–x. See also Diana Souhami, *No Modernism Without Lesbians* (London: Head of Zeus, 2020).

11 David Marr, *Patrick White: A Life* (Sydney: Random House, 1991), p. 164.

12 Marr, *White*, p. 169.

13 Sigmund Freud, *Leonardo da Vinci: A Memory of his Childhood*, trans. Alan Tyson (London and New York: Routledge, 2001).

14 Leo Bersani, *Is the Rectum a Grave? and Other Essays* (Chicago: University of Chicago Press, 2010), p. ix.

15 Judith Butler, "Imitation and Gender Insubordination," in *The Lesbian and Gay Studies Reader*, ed. Henry Abelove, Michèle Aina Barale, and David M. Halperin (New York and London: Routledge, 1993), pp. 307–320 (p. 308).

See also Judith Butler, *Gender Trouble: Feminism and the Subversion of Identity* (London and New York: Routledge, 1999; 1990).

16 See Eve Kosofsky Sedgwick, *Epistemology of the Closet* (Berkeley: University of California Press, 2008; 1990).

17 Valerie Beattie notes that White has often been omitted from anthologies of gay writing. See Valerie Beattie, "In Other Words: Homosexual Desire in the Novels of Patrick White" (PhD thesis, University of Edinburgh, 1996), pp. 4–5.

18 "The Nobel Prize in Literature 1973," The Nobel Prize: www.nobelprize.org/prizes/literature/1973/press-release/.

19 Alvin Shuster, "Nobel for US Economist; Australian Writer Chosen," *The New York Times*, October 19, 1973, p. 1.

20 Patrick White, *Flaws in the Glass: A Self-Portrait* (London: Jonathan Cape, 1981).

21 McMahon, "Lateness and Queerness," p. 87.

22 McMahon, "Lateness and Queerness," p. 87.

23 Gillian Rose, Love's Work: A Reckoning with Life (New York: Schocken Books, 1995), p. 114.

24 Marr, *White*, p. 194.

25 Patrick White, "The Prodigal Son," in *Patrick White Speaks* (London: Penguin, 1992), pp. 13–17 (p. 15).

26 Marr, *White*, p. 282; White, *Letters*, p. 118.

27 White, *Letters*, p. 106.

28 David Tacey, *Patrick White: Fictions and the Unconscious* (Melbourne: Oxford University Press, 1988), p. 69.

29 White, *Letters*, p. 545.

30 Patrick White, *The Aunt's Story* (London: Vintage, 1994; 1948), p. 18.

31 White, *The Aunt's Story*, p. 67.

32 White, *The Aunt's Story*, p. 32.

33 See also Jinlong Liu, "Ideal Identity Arises from Bricolage: Identity Issues in Patrick White's *The Twyborn Affair*," *Comparative Literature: East & West*, 3.1 (2019): pp. 68–78.

34 White, as cited in Marr, *White*, p. 248.

35 During, *Patrick White*, p. 71.

36 White, *Flaws in the Glass*, pp. 51–52.

37 See Eve Kosofsky Sedgwick, *Between Men: English Literature and Male Homosocial Desire* (New York: Columbia University Press, 2015; 1985).

38 White, *Letters*, p. 217. See John Beston, "Patrick White and Rimbaud," *Commonwealth* 27.2 (2005): pp. 99–110.

39 Arthur Rimbaud, "To Paul Demeny," in *Selected Poems and Letters*, trans. Jeremy Harding and John Sturrock (London: Penguin, 2004), pp. 237–239 (pp. 238–239).

40 Bersani, *Is the Rectum a Grave?*, p. 175. Emphasis added.

41 During, *Patrick White*, p. 75.

42 Tim Anderson as quoted and glossed in Lang, "Queering Sarsaparilla," p. 198.

43 White, *Flaws in the Glass*, p. 146.

44 John Colmer, *Patrick White* (London: Methuen, 1984), p. 33.

45 White, as cited in Marr, *White*, p. 299.

46 Peter Wolfe, *Laden Choirs: The Fiction of Patrick White* (Lexington: University Press of Kentucky, 1983), p. 1.

47 Shaun Bell, ""Greece – Patrick White's Other Country": Is Patrick White a Greek Author?," *JASAL: Journal of the Association for the Study of Australian Literature* 14.5 (2014): pp. 1–14; Vrasidas Karalis, *Recollections of Mr. Manoly Lascaris* (Sydney: Brandl & Schlesinger, 2009).

48 Christos Tsiolkas, *Patrick White* (Melbourne: Black Inc, 2018), p. 4.

49 Tsiolkas, *Patrick White*, p. 4.

50 Marr, *White*, p. 535.

9

LOUIS KLEE

Constellational Form in Gerald Murnane

In December 2017, during his address to a small conference at the Goroke Golf Club, Gerald Murnane held out a sheet from an exercise pad on which he had drawn a configuration of five interlinked polygons (Figure 1). Noting its likeness to a solar system, to the "starry firmament overspreading" a landscape, and to townships linked by road networks and railway lines, he explained that it was a diagram illustrating his method of writing fiction. It shows, he said, "the way in which many of the pieces of fiction literally took *shape* in my mind before I began [...] writing."¹ Someone in the audience, hastily sketching the shape in his notebook, later called it "a wobbly parallelogram," but with the typescript before us, we could more pedantically fix it as an "arrangement or disposition of five objects so placed that four occupy the corners, and the fifth the centre."² By coincidence, this is the definition of Thomas Browne's "quincunx": a lattice of five points that Browne identifies in his discourse *The Garden of Cyrus* (1658) as the "fundamental figure" of the order of things, evident in everything from the structure of gardens, the shapes of butterflies and moths, and the seeds of pine trees through to human monuments and constellations.³ Browne concludes his treatise by imagining it continuing in the minds of those waking as he falls asleep: "To keep our eyes open longer, were but to act our *Antipodes*."⁴ In the antipodes – the place where Murnane delivered his address "The Still-Breathing Author," the place he has never left – this same pattern emerges not as the basic structure of the universe, but as something that holds for him an even greater reality: It illuminates the associations between the persistent images in his mind; what he calls the "literary equivalent of subatomic particles."⁵

While Murnane brandished his diagram at Goroke for an audience of mostly scholars and critics, the same shape is composed by a narrator in *Emerald Blue* (1995) instructing an imagined student in his fiction-writing course.⁶ "In Far Fields" begins with the narrator writing out several sentences in the presence of this conjectured student. Each sentence corresponds

148

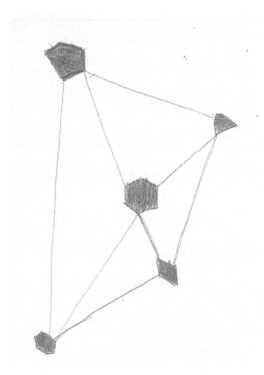

Figure 1: Murnane's Polygon © Gerald Murnane

to an image in his mind. These images "emanate," in the words of another of Murnane's narrators, a feeling that is "persistent, intense, and sometimes troubling, and yet, at the same time, promising."[7] "[W]ordlessly," they compel him: "*Write about me in order to discover my secret and to learn what a throng of images as yet invisible, lie around me.*"[8] The writer assigns each sentence to a distinctly colored manila folder ("blue, orange, yellow, and buff or plain," and so on) and "strews" the pages on the carpet of his office floor, stooping, letting himself become absorbed in the task of ordering them.[9] He then returns to his desk, shuts the folders in a drawer, and begins to write according to the pattern he has divined. The student is still beside him, watching.

Perhaps more than any straightforward pedagogical purpose – and I suspect that there is still interesting scholarship to be done in elucidating the connection between Murnane's "pedagogical reflection," as Luke Carman calls it, and his late fiction – this performance aims to inculcate an ethos.[10] What motivates it is the narrator's conviction that "any person paid to teach other persons how to write pieces of fiction should be able, in the presence of any number of those other persons, to write the whole of a previously unwritten piece of fiction and to explain [it] at the same time."[11] This may seem an idiosyncratic, possibly even perverse demand. But it arises from a deeply held belief in an immediacy and intimacy only possible in fiction. The writer must be able to define and enact their method simultaneously, not just for the student standing over their shoulder, but also for a reader, who, if they press beyond the first pages of "In Far Fields," will find a story consisting of a system of tenacious images that proceeds not by stream of consciousness but "by following the stream system."[12] Many of Murnane's stories share this sense of unfurling from their own exegesis. This is true, above all, of A Million Windows (2014), which is at once a book-length tract on a "theory of fictional narration" and an exhibition of the same theory that speculatively assembles the narrators of Murnane's previous fictions into a "colony of writers."[13] Yet even Murnane's less obviously self-reflexive fictions set out in the spirit of "In Far Fields." "[M]y mind," as the narrator reminds his student, "consisted only of images and feelings; [...] a diagram of [it] would resemble a vast and intricate map with images for its small towns and with feelings for the roads through the grassy countryside between the towns."[14]

This constellational mode of writing fiction is the single most important continuity in Murnane's authorship. From his earliest book Tamarisk Row (1974), with its narrator who yearns for the "true meaning" in assortments of marbles, in "precious streaks and tints," ever awaiting the secret of "one fateful formation" to be revealed to him, through to Border Districts (2017), with its narrator who withdraws to a remote township to "record my own image-history," Murnane has been profoundly and obsessively devoted to investigating the emotionally charged topography of his personal mental imagery.[15] A writer, he has often said, quoting Robert Bly, "must learn to trust his obsessions" – and for Murnane these obsessions are "the landscapes or the human faces or the melodies or the panels of coloured glass in doors or window or the sets of racing colours or the aviaries of birds or the passages of prose in books and magazines" that appear again and again across his oeuvre.[16] Often these networks of association extend beyond a single fiction, only materializing "long after the piece has been finished," when a later work helps him to "understand an image in an earlier piece."[17] Brendan Casey, by way of Marcel Proust, has described this as "retrospective illumination" in his exceptional study of Murnane's late fiction – an "ulterior unity," a "vital and not logical" connection between fragments that emerges in an epiphanic flash – while Ivor Indyk characterizes it more as an accretive and proactive "return to images [that] clearly have a charge which [Murnane] didn't – or couldn't – elaborate on fully in earlier attempts."[18] Both accounts acknowledge that, in the words of "The

Breathing Author" (2001), "the whole enterprise of my fiction-writing" constitutes "an effort to bring to light an underlying order – a vast pattern of connected images – beneath everything that I am able to call my mind."[19] In the "The Still-Breathing Author," with his diagram in hand, Murnane adds: "*Meaning*, for me, is *connection*. A thing has meaning [...] when it has a connection to another thing."[20]

Many aspects of this vision are already evident in Murnane's earliest fiction, *Tamarisk Row*. Published when he was thirty-five years old, *Tamarisk Row* is nestled in the imagination of Clement Killeaton, a schoolboy from a working-class Catholic family in a rural Australian town. Killeaton's father is so hopelessly committed to gambling on horse races that the threat of financial ruin hangs relentlessly over the family. But *Tamarisk Row* is also a treasury of vivid images, undisclosed secrets, and imagined worlds – perhaps it is even "the Great Code of Murnane's imaginative iconography."[21] Significantly, the contents of Clement's mind are accorded the same reality as the "so-called actual events on the surface of a well-known planet" as Murnane writes in the book's preface.[22] For though it is narrated in the third person, *Tamarisk Row* is told in the spirit of an older man who, as a Murnanian narrator says of Jung, "set out to play again his favourite childhood games in the hope of learning about himself something of much value."[23] The decision to depict Clement's mental universe in this way was Murnane's first major breakthrough as a writer. According to his biographer, Shannon Burns, it came when he was reading Günter Grass's *Die Blechtrommel* [*The Tin Drum*] (1959). Murnane realized that "the contents of people's minds can be reported on the same level as the things that people see with their eyes. That hit me like a thunderclap."[24] In his later fiction, as we shall see, the world of the mind is not simply of equal reality, as it is in *Tamarisk Row*, but elevated higher still.

The other crucial feature of *Tamarisk Row* is that it first establishes Murnane's devotion to the grammatical sentence. On the sentence, Murnane is blunt: The sentence alone is "a unit of meaning."[25] He holds his own sentences in particularly high regard. As he declared in an interview: "My sentences are the best-shaped of any sentences written by any writer of fiction in the English language during my lifetime."[26] On another occasion, he wrote to the *London Review of Books* to censure Frank Kermode's loose attribution of the term when referring to a "sequence of clauses and phrases" in Thomas Pynchon.[27] Superlatives aside, Murnane's sentences are one of the most unmistakable elements of his fiction. In his later fiction especially, his sentences replace pronouns and proper names with situated epithets and tags, being animated, as Teju Cole speculates, by an attempt to "give in each sentence an account of the circumstances that led to that sentence."[28]

The outcome is "a meticulous and testimonial quality that [...] mimics the process of thought."[29] In the words of Ben Lerner, this creates a paradoxically "plain and elaborate" prose rhythm, evident especially in its repetitive "chains of prepositions (of, on, of, on)."[30] By Murnane's own analysis, his best sentence is an almost chiastic one from *Landscape with Landscape* (1985) – "I hear from myself a voice I have wanted for a long time to hear" – while some of his longest and most flamboyant occur in *Tamarisk Row*, where the sentence bears the weight of associative pattern-making, their "integrative function" being intimately linked to Clement's striving to make sense of connections.[31] This is especially evident in those sentences that deal with the sequences of racehorses, where the dizzying syntax enacts "not even an actual straining, staring racehorse" but a stochastic, almost abstract "knot of what he might have called compressed mental imagery."[32] Consider, for instance, the following lengthy sentence from *Tamarisk Row*, which depicts Clement gazing at the altar in St Boniface's church:

> Alternatively drifting down towards the levels of air where the whispered prayers of knelling people pass on the first stage of their devious journeys through its baffling network, and billowing up towards the colourless slopes where the elaborate robes of the least of the angels and saints might sometimes trail carelessly past, the maze of filmy pathways, one remote corner of which is more complex and multifarious than the pattern of the streets in any unvisited city or the tracks of cattle or hares or people of long ago through the grasses of inland plains or the sequences of coloured silks at successive intervals of fifty yards in famous staying races on broad racecourses or the whereabouts year after year of the well-knit nests of birds cunningly lodged among dense thickets in a thousand narrow gullies, tempts anyone watching its diffuse pulsating glitter to order his own steps or the involuntary shifting of his features or the spilling over of his unruly thoughts into a semblance of the first irregular but compelling arrangement of laneways in a long vista along whose farthest twinkling tracks not even the wisest or most saintly priest or nun may yet have travelled.[33]

We might say that this sentence describes how the altar's "maze of filmy pathways" tempts the onlooker to reorder their gestures and thoughts. Yet it embeds this description in such a vertiginous visual array of lively and incongruous contextualizing details and possible analogs that it does not so much reconstitute a pattern as, in Murnane's words, "call into being [...] a mental space that might eventually expand until I [find] myself confused, disoriented, lost even, among details of my own devising."[34]

Important as these stylistic continuities in Murnane's authorship are, we can discover as much by attending to a conspicuous discontinuity. For fourteen years, between the publication of *Emerald Blue* in 1995 and *Barley*

Patch in 2009, Murnane gave up writing fiction (at least publicly), publishing only a few short stories, later included in his *A History of Books* (2012), and a collection of essays, *Invisible Yet Enduring Lilacs* (2005). In 2007, in an important survey of Murnane's work, Paul Genoni remarked: "It appears likely that Murnane has published his last major fiction."[35] But two years after Genoni's sober prognosis, Murnane made a remarkable return to fiction, publishing a sequence of stylistically integrated late works: *Barley Patch* and the concurrently drafted *A History of Books*, followed by *A Million Windows*, and his self-declared final work, *Border Districts*.[36] After *Border District*'s publication, Murnane announced: "I am no longer a writer, as that word is usually understood. You might say of me, as someone said of Thomas Hardy [...], that I've been *delivered* of my books."[37]

These late works have brought Murnane renewed critical attention and international acclaim. While it remains true that his fiction has never attained the commercial publishing success of several other Australian writers of his generation – a fact has fed the persistent journalistic cliché that he is "the greatest living English-language writer most people have never heard of"[38] – he has exerted a subtle influence on contemporary fiction, most notably on writers like Lerner and Cole. He has also found himself celebrated in unlikely quarters, such as by the Canadian poet Lisa Robertson, who describes being "completely amazed and convinced" when coming across one of his books in Toronto.[39] "[W]hen I read Murnane," she says, "I am not in a narrative, I am in a structure of consciousness that is inventing its own terms of relation with the world. It's not a representation of experience, it is experience."[40] We may also speculate that the self-reflexive way Murnane's late fiction responds to the earlier Derridean and post-structuralist readings of his work accounts for something of its striking elective affinity with the "Theory Generation" writers, as Nicholas Dames labels Lerner and Cole; writers whose novels "satirize [continental philosophy and 'Theory'] with unease."[41] (In a similar spirit, while playing an elaborate epistolary prank on his most prominent, Derridean critic, Imre Salusinszky, Murnane commented: "we are keen rivals in some ways").[42] The way Murnane's fictions refract his autobiography through the devices of "*considered narration*" – a form defined by the scrupulous candor of the narrative voice – even gives it a surprising kinship with contemporary autofiction.[43]

Murnane's hiatus also raises difficult questions for critics. While the reasons that prompted him to give up fiction are most readily explained by a combination of pragmatic factors – critical neglect, the vicissitudes of his publishers, the demands of caregiving, and the impossible ambitions of his sprawling, abandoned manuscript *O, Dem Golden Slippers* – the stylistic rift between his early and late works is marked enough that Murnane's "post-break" writing is now, as Indyk has it, "asserted confidently as a critical fact."[44] Murnane himself has consistently pushed back against those critics who read "an orderly progression" into his writing, while acknowledging that "trends and developments can be found."[45] Typically critics divide his work into three periods: first, a supposedly "realist, Catholic phase," comprised of *Tamarisk Row* and *A Lifetime on Clouds* (1976) (the latter a section of *A Season on Earth* [2019], which has only recently been unearthed and published in its entirety); second, his "major phase," beginning with the shift to the first-person in *The Plains* (1982), then becoming "entrenched" in the interlocking *Künstlerroman* of *Landscape with Landscape*, and culminating in his most revered and intricate fiction *Inland* (1988); finally, the late phase, in his more essayistic and elegiac post-hiatus fictions, with their cautiously loquacious narrators, each of whom, to borrow a phrase from Teju Cole, has "a suggestive and imprecise identification with [the] author."[46]

For Murnane, however, the most important break in his oeuvre arrived before the hiatus. "At some time [...] while I was writing *Inland*," as he puts it, "I felt no longer reluctant to have my fiction recognised for what it truly is: an honest account by an utterly reliable narrator of what most presses on him at the time of writing."[47] This explains the most intriguing aspect of Murnane's hiatus: His late fiction performatively incorporates and anticipates the interval of *not-writing* into writing itself as a way of powerfully enacting the principles that spur the will to fiction. Indeed, the decision to give up writing was first announced in the final short story of *Emerald Blue*, "The Interior of Gaaldine," which terminates with the words: "The text ends at this point."[48] "The Interior of Gaaldine" offers an oblique rationale for Murnane's subsequent silence, but one that remains "so carefully coded," as Indyk argues, that "it would have been a miracle if anyone understood."[49] It is in *Barley Patch*, the book that marked Murnane's return to fiction, that he offers the most in-depth and complex consideration of the reasons for writing and not writing, beginning from its opening words: "*Must I write?*"[50] Like "In Far Fields," the narrator of *Barley Patch* teaches fiction-writing at a university, and once each year he reads the advice from Rainer Maria Rilke's *Briefe an einen jungen Dichter* [*Letters to a Young Poet*] (1929) to his students, urging them "to question themselves from time to time as Rilke would have had them do. I then said it would be no bad thing if several at least of the persons present were to decide, at some time in the future, in the stillest hour of their night, that they need no longer write fiction."[51] While never learning if any of his students abandoned writing, in the autumn of 1991, "on a bustling afternoon rather than during a still night," the narrator himself resolves to give up fiction.[52] While most of *Barley Patch* provides a digressive series of responses to another question – "*Why had I written?*" – the reason he gave up writing stems not from a lack of faith in fiction but, to the contrary, because he had not valued fiction highly enough.[53] In a passage that not only decodes, but re-enacts the encrypted message of "The Interior of Gaaldine," the narrator of *Barley Patch* returns to a scene from *Tamarisk Row*, noting that "the chief character saw in his mind from time to time certain fictional personages whose district was bounded on one side by tamarisk trees."[54] Murnane is here taking inspiration from a diary entry of Emily Brontë, which concerns the people of Gondal discovering the interior of Gaaldine.[55] Like Brontë's diary, Murnane's narrator adds that he should have written that the "people of the tamarisks were of a mind to discover the interior of the barley patch."[56] While this passage may seem riddling, it is immediately explained by an analogy to the Russian writer Ivan Turgenev, who once (in a passage Murnane most likely borrows from Henry James) dreamed of his characters petitioning him to write about them.[57] Just as Murnane's narrator falls silent upon entering a "country on the far side of fiction," he remarks that "Turgenev had wrongly interpreted what he seemed to see while he slept."[58] Turgenev's characters "stood on the outermost border of their native territory and pleaded with the writer of fiction not to try to write about them but to put away his writing and to join up with them: to become an inhabitant of their far-reaching countries or continents."[59] For the narrator of *Barley Patch*, true fiction makes us realize not that characters are "real" like us but rather, as T. S. Eliot once remarked, that we might aspire *to be real like them*, "a creature like [fiction's] creatures."[60]

In this way, *Barley Patch* expresses the fundamental conviction that drives Murnane's late fiction: the belief, everywhere expressed after the rift he describes while writing *Inland*, that "*there is another world but it is in this one*"; that the world of fiction holds an even greater reality than the everyday world; that the everyday world is interesting only "insofar as it provides me with evidence for the existence of another world"; that, finally, "the so-called actual and the so-called possible [...] come to be indistinguishable in the sort of text we call true fiction."[61] In an influential essay, J. M. Coetzee calls this Murnane's "radical idealism" – radical because Murnane is willing to affirm even the most extreme ramifications of this view, referring, for instance, to the theories of Charles Darwin as "baseless speculation," or pronouncing, over a beer with Shannon Burns at the Goroke Hotel, that "Materialists and Marxists who think the world is just a mass of guts and brains and stuff are just fucking dolts."[62] Murnane is not proposing a philosophical system here (he even goes so far as to state, "I may be unable to think abstract thoughts"), but professing an absolute belief in what can be attained through the *practice* of examining the associations between his personal mental imagery.[63] In this way, what at first seemed like routine counsel – writers must trust their own obsessions – takes on a more magisterial significance: "rightly or wrongly," irrespective of the reasons why an image remains in his mind, the narrator of *Barley Patch* must be deferential to its promise of deeper truth.[64]

On this basis, Murnane's fiction has often been described, by sympathetic critics and detractors alike, as a solipsistic endeavor.[65] If, as Schopenhauer once said, solipsism means ensconcement in an impenetrable blockhouse of the mind, then for Murnane it seems like a monologue issuing from the monastic enclosure of an ideal memory house (as in his short story "Stone Quarry"), where the writer seeks to patiently reconstruct truths glimpsed obliquely "from the sides of my eyes."[66] Yet this view of Murnane omits something vital to his fiction. Certainly, Murnane writes not realist but idealist fiction, but his is an idealism of the ideal reader.[67] The writer's solipsism is intimately bound to what Cole, in a letter to Murnane, calls "the reader's solipsism"; the feeling that, as we read Murnane's fiction, we are his "only reader"; that the text's associations are intimately addressed to us.[68] Each reader, Cole continues:

> feels, in stony disregard of the facts, that the author writes for him alone. The work feels personal, feels, in fact, like a letter, written by one person, singular, intended for another, singular. [...] In this specific sense, you have for many years now been writing directly to me – this is not the first letter that has passed between us but, rather, a belated response to the many I received from you in the form of your published writing and failed to answer.[69]

Reading Cole's correspondence, we are not far from the opening of *Inland*, where the reader is situated voyeur-like over the text, as if it were an intercepted letter. But such a position of compromised reading gestures negatively to the second half of *Inland*, where Murnane's narrator pursues his fleeting intimacy with "the girl from Bendigo Street" by addressing the whole novel as though it were a letter to her.

The reader and the writer can only connect indirectly, then, through the medium of fiction. This renders fiction "a sort of miracle as a result of which invisible entities are made aware of each other through the medium of the visible."[70] Murnane is here transforming an idea he takes from Proust, from whom he claims to have "borrowed most of my theories about literature [...] especially [the] notion of *le moi profond*."[71] For Proust, the "deep self," as distinct from the "external self" that is present in habitual and social life, can be expressed only through fiction's mediacy.[72] Murnane finds the impetus for this deep self in "the passage of fiction that has affected more than any."[73] In the final volume of *À la recherche du temps perdu* [*In Search of Lost Time*] (1913–1927), Marcel, Proust's narrator, stumbles on an uneven-paving stone and is struck by a quick succession of involuntary memories that he deems "real without being actual, ideal without being abstract," and in which "the permanent and habitually concealed essence of things is liberated and our true self [*vrai moi*], which seemed [...] to be dead [...] is awakened."[74] Marcel realizes the writer's vocation as "a more profound reality, in which our true personality finds expression that is not afforded it by the activities of life."[75] (As if in understated tribute to Proust, all three of the images that the narrator of *Barley Patch* hopes to connect in his projected work of fiction are already vividly present in *À la recherche du temps perdu*: the uncurling of a protruding frond, a loose strand of hair on a forehead, and the undulating movement of seaweed.)[76] But the narrator of *Inland* does not seek the metaphorical resurrection of the true self so much as an intermingling of the reader and writer in a space beyond death. In *Inland*, the reader and the writer are, in a sense, interred "in land" together as "sleepers in that quiet earth."[77] These words, borrowed from the conclusion of *Wuthering Heights* (1847), are quoted in the final sentence of *Inland*, but in their original context they describe the narrator's graveside musing on the posthumous reunion of Catherine and Heathcliff's bodies.[78] The narrators of Murnane's fiction, from *Inland* onwards, are written for "a few readers of good will, or perhaps for only one such reader whom he wishes never to meet but only to approach by means of his writing"; or perhaps even as a letter written by someone who is dead to a "young woman [who] remains alive in order to go on reading what I could have never written."[79] The paradoxical nature of intimacy is best encapsulated in a sentence from *A Million Windows*: "I, the narrator, would dread to feel that we are separated by even these sentences."[80] *These sentences* are what makes it possible for the writer to impart to the reader what matters most, and yet they also serve as a permanent reminder of an imperfect medium – writing – which is premised on deathlike silence and separation.

There are many more beguiling conundrums in Murnane's fiction that fall beyond the scope of this brief essay. We might continue, for instance, as Samantha Trayhurn does in an insightful piece, by examining how the narrator in Murnane's post-hiatus fiction can only attain access the world of ideal through being imagined by a sympathetic reader.[81] Then there is the question of what to do with the conspicuous fact that this ideal reader is gendered as female, such that "the 'real' (mundane) and the real (ideal) world maintain themselves in a tension of erotic reciprocity," as Coetzee writes – something that plays out in the late fiction's baroque patterns of nested narratives, metaleptic intrusions, and recurrent images of dehiscence.[82] Similarly, while the late works often read like "a kind of instruction manual for how Murnane would like an ideal reader to engage with his work," this strikingly counterpoints with the narrator's own way of reading.[83] In *Barley Patch*, the narrator calls himself "an erratic reader," a "wilful reader," who strays from the novels he reads, delighting in fashioning his own dwelling in some remote and neglected corner of the book, or else extrapolating out from one imperfectly remembered image. Much like A. C. Bradley in his readings of Shakespeare, Murnane's narrators read as if to "inhabit the possible worlds of the text."[84] His fictions thus seem to demand one kind of reader while demonstrating another, though both, we might speculate, are driven by trust – trust in the association of images and in the reader of goodwill, receptive to sharing in it.[85] Inciting the reader to join him in a fiction that strays along digressive paths of feeling and tarries with powerful images is one way, Murnane argues, of "allowing the reader freedom."[86]

There is also room for further investigation into how this associative intimacy is charged with emotional freight. This affective dimension has been well articulated in recent scholarship, most artfully in the work of Indyk, Casey, and Brigid Rooney. It provides a welcome corrective to past readings that treated Murnane's fiction as a form of metafiction in which "our deepest feelings are only kinds of grammar."[87] In "The Provincial Imagination," Indyk illustrates how the post-hiatus fictions impart feelings "so fraught with implication that [they] require the embedded realities of recursion, or multiple associations of a sequences of images, to absorb [their] ramifications."[88] This recovery of the affective dimension of Murnane's associative method has opened exciting directions in the scholarship (although, if applied too insistently, it does come with the risk of reducing Murnane's fiction to what James Wood elsewhere calls "a kind of male sentimentality of reticence").[89] However, I believe that there is much interesting work on Murnane still to come. Besides a few all too easily dismissed polemics, there has been little critical work on the political and ethical stakes of Murnane's fiction.[90] How, for instance, would his insistence that there is "no such thing as 'Time'," that "we experience only place after place" compare with the discussions of chronotopes and temporality in the other chapters of this volume?[91] There are also paradoxes about a writer who professes faith in the ontological existence of characterological beings while himself writing a fiction populated with very few characters in the traditional sense. What to make of the fact that Murnane's narrators can at once scoff at "ignorant authors" who claim "the purpose of fiction is to create believable characters," while himself holding characters in fiction to be the highest reality?[92] Strikingly, Murnane (or, rather, the narrators of his late fiction) seeks to join his characters not by housing them in his fiction, but by turning his fiction into a prolonged reflection on the nature of characterhood and fiction itself. Perhaps the answers to such questions will begin with the vast and meticulously arranged archive that Murnane speaks of as a letter to "a reader of the future."[93]

Notes

Thank you to Shannon Burns and Brendan Casey for useful comments on this essay.

1 Gerald Murnane, "The Still-Breathing Author," in *Gerald Murnane: Another World in This One*, ed. Anthony Uhlmann (Sydney: Sydney University Press, 2020), pp. 165–179 (p. 168).

2 Tristan Foster, "Scenes from Gerald Murnane's Golf Club," in *Gerald Murnane: Another World in This One*, ed. Anthony Uhlmann (Sydney: Sydney University Press, 2020), pp. 9–11 (p. 11); *Oxford English Dictionary*, s. v. "quincunx". Murnane sometimes notes that these shapes vary between his works, with book-length works requiring "extensive charts" and short works presenting themselves "as three-dimensional *structures*, often transparent and containing further sorts of complexity." He sometimes refers to these shapes as "constellations." See Gerald Murnane, *Last Letter to a Reader: Essays* (Sydney: Giramondo, 2021), pp. 50, 62.

3 Thomas Browne, *The Works of the Learned Sr Thomas Brown, Kt. Doctor of Physick, late of NORWICH* (London: Tho. Basset, Ric. Chiswell, Tho. Sawbridge, Charles Mearn, and Charles Brome, 1686), III, p. 26. I am also paraphrasing the more elaborate list provided in W. G. Sebald, *Die Ringe des Saturn. Eine englische Wallfahrt* (Frankfurt: Eichborn Verlag, 1995) p. 29/*The Rings of Saturn* (London: Vintage, 2002; 1995), p. 21.

4 Browne, *Works*, III, p. 52.

5 Murnane, "The Still-Breathing Author," p. 178.

6 Gerald Murnane, "In Far Fields," in *Stream System: The Collected Short Fiction of Gerald Murnane* (New York: Farrar, Straus and Giroux, 2018), pp. 247–295 (p. 247).

7 Gerald Murnane, *A Million Windows* (Sydney: Giramondo, 2014), p. 181.

8 Murnane, *A Million Windows*, p. 181.

9 Murnane, "In Far Fields," p. 253; Murnane, "The Still-Breathing Author," p. 166.

10 Luke Carman, "To the Eye Untrained," in *Gerald Murnane: Another World in This One*, pp. 13–28 (p. 15).

11 Murnane, "In Far Fields," p. 248.

12 As cited in Imre Salusinszky, *Gerald Murnane* (Oxford: Oxford University Press, 1993), pp. 95–97.

13 Murnane, *A Million Windows*, p. 132, p. 174.

14 Murnane, "In Far Fields," pp. 248–249. See also Gerald Murnane, *Barley Patch* (Sydney: Giramondo, 2009), p. 222.

15 Gerald Murnane, *Tamarisk Row* (Sheffield: And Other Stories, 2019), pp. 44, 51, 105; Gerald Murnane, *Border Districts* (Sydney: Giramondo, 2017), p. 25.

16 Murnane, "The Still-Breathing Author," p. 168; Murnane, *Border Districts*, p. 11.

17 Murnane, "In Far Fields," p. 255.

18 Marcel Proust, *In Search of Lost Time*, trans. by C. K. Scott Moncrieff and Terence Kilmartin (London: Vintage, 2000), V, pp. 176–177; Brendan Casey, "The Reader of Goodwill: Gerald Murnane's Late Fiction" (unpublished Honours dissertation, University of Melbourne, 2015), p. 43; Ivor Indyk, "What Kind of Literary History Is A History of Books?," in *Gerald Murnane: Another World in This One*, pp. 153–163 (p. 159). See also Murnane, *Last Letter*, pp. 99–100.

19 Gerald Murnane, "The Breathing Author," in *Invisible Yet Enduring Lilacs* (Sheffield: And Other Stories, 2020), pp. 137–164 (p. 141).

20 Murnane, "The Still-Breathing Author," p. 169.

21 Saluszinsky, *Gerald Murnane*, p. 7.

22 Murnane, "Foreword," in *Tamarisk Row*, pp. 7–10 (p. 9).

23 Murnane, *Barley Patch*, p. 208.

24 Shannon Burns, "The Scientist of his own Experience: A Profile of Gerald Murnane," *Australian Book Review* 373 (August 2015): www.australianbookreview .com.au/abr-online/archive/2015/158-august-2015-no-373/2636-the-scientist-of-his-own-experience-a-profile-of-gerald-murnane-by-shannon-burns.

25 Murnane, *Last Letter to a Reader*, p. 34.

26 Tristan Foster, "Eight Questions for Gerald Murnane," *3:AM Magazine* , April 21, 2015: www.3ammagazine.com/3am/eight-questions-for-gerald-murnane/.

27 Gerald Murnane, "Letter to the Editor," *The London Review of Books*, March 22, 1990: www.lrb.co.uk/the-paper/v12/no3/frank-kermode/that-was-another-planet.

28 Teju Cole, "Transcript of Teju Cole's Letter to Gerald Murnane," *Music & Literature* 3 (2013): pp. 1–3 (pp. 2–3).

29 Cole, "Transcript," p. 3.

30 Ben Lerner, "A Strange Australian Masterpiece," *The New Yorker*, March 29, 2017: www.newyorker.com/books/page-turner/a-strange-australian-masterpiece.

31 Salusinszky, *Gerald Murnane*, p. 10. See also Murnane, *Last Letter*, pp. 41, 90, 94–96.

32 Murnane, *Barley Patch*, p. 210.

33 Murnane, *Tamarisk Row*, pp. 98–99.

34 Murnane, "The Still-Breathing Author," p. 173.

35 Paul Genoni, "Gerald Murnane," in *A Companion to Australian Literature since 1900*, ed. Nicholas Birns and Rebecca McNeer (Rochester, NY: Camden House, 2007), pp. 293–304 (p. 302).

36 Murnane notes having thought of other books as his last book, such as *A History of Books*. See Murnane, *Last Letter*, p. 90.

37 Murnane, "The Still-Breathing Author," p. 166.

38 Mark Binelli, "Is the Next Nobel Laureate in Literature Tending Bar in a Dusty Australian Town?," *The New York Times*, April 1, 2018: www.nytimes .com/2018/03/27/magazine/gerald-murnane-next-nobel-laureate-literature-australia.html.

39 Lisa Robertson, "'Reading Is Like Dreaming': An Interview with Lisa Robertson," *The Sydney Review of Books*, March 21, 2022: https:// sydneyreviewofbooks.com/interview/lisa-robertson/.

40 Robertson, "'Reading Is Like Dreaming'."

41 Nicholas Dames, "The Theory Generation," *n + 1* 14 (2012): pp. 157–168 (p. 160).

42 Gerald Murnane, "Letter to Sandra Moore" [January 8, 1992], University of Melbourne, *Scripsi* Archive, 105/26 Box 26.

43 Murnane, *A Million Windows*, p. 15. See Timothy Bewes, *Free Indirect: The Novel in a Postfictional Age* (New York: Columbia University Press, 2022).

44 Indyk, "What Kind of Literary History Is *A History of Books*?," p. 154. On the reasons for Murnane giving up fiction see Ivor Indyk, "The Provincial Imagination," *Music & Literature* 3 (2013): pp. 45–56 (p. 54).

45 Murnane, "The Still-Breathing Author," p. 170.

46 Nicholas Birns, "Review of Grounded Visionary: The Mystic Fictions of Gerald Murnane by Brendan McNamee," *The Powys Journal* 30 (2020): pp. 204–208 (p. 206); Anthony Uhlmann, "Introduction," in *Gerald Murnane: Another World in This One*, pp. 1–7 (pp. 1–3); Shannon Burns, "Truth, Fiction and True Fiction," in *Gerald Murnane: Another World in This One*, pp. 29–36 (pp. 29, 33). The quote from Teju Cole appears in *Known and Strange Things: Essays* (London: Faber & Faber, 2016), p. 70.

47 Murnane, "The Still-Breathing Author," pp. 171–172.

48 Murnane, "The Interior of Gaaldine," in *Stream System*, pp. 437–469 (p. 469).

49 Indyk, "The Provincial Imagination," p. 51.

50 Murnane, *Barley Patch*, p. 3.

51 Murnane, *Barley Patch*, p. 4.

52 Murnane, *Barley Patch*, p. 4.

53 Interestingly, Murnane suggests that these italicized questions issue not from the narrator, but from his ideal reader. See Murnane, *Last Letter*, p. 79.

54 Murnane, *Barley Patch*, p. 252.

55 Brendan Casey has observed that Murnane's reading of Brontë's diary differs from the standard critical understanding of the passage. On the standard reading, the Gondals, from a northern island in Europe, are "discovering," in the colonial sense, the interior of a South Pacific island near Australia, whereas in Murnane's interpretation fictional characters are finding a fictional world. See Brendan Casey, "Murnane and His Precursors," Lecture Course at the Melbourne School of Continental Philosophy, January 10, 2022 to February 7, 2022.

56 Murnane, *Barley Patch*, p. 253.

57 Henry James, "The Portrait of a Lady," in *The Art of the Novel: Critical Prefaces by Henry James* (Chicago and London: University of Chicago Press, 2011), pp. 40–58 (pp. 42–43).

58 Murnane, *Barley Patch*, p. 254.

59 Murnane, *Barley Patch*, p. 256.

60 T. S. Eliot, as cited in Sophie Ratcliffe, *On Sympathy* (Oxford: Clarendon Press, 2008), p. 56.

61 Gerald Murnane, *Inland* (Champaign: Dalkey Archive Press, 1988), p. 100; Murnane, *Stream System*, p. 466; Murnane, *A Million Windows*, p. 140.

62 J. M. Coetzee, "Reading Gerald Murnane," in *Late Essays* (Sydney: Knopf, 2017), pp. 259–272 (p. 263); Murnane, "The Still-Breathing Author," p. 176; Murnane in Burns, "The Scientist of his own Experience."

63 Murnane, *Invisible Yet Enduring Lilacs*, p. 153.

64 Murnane, *Barley Patch*, p. 61.

65 Salusinszky, *Gerald Murnane*, pp. 57–58.

66 Arthur Schopenhauer, as quoted in Jean-Paul Sartre, *L'être et le néant: Essai d'ontologie phénoménologique* (Paris: Gallimard, 1943), p. 268; Murnane, *Border Districts*, p. 50. It would be interesting to compare this strand of Murnane's work to medieval monasticism, especially silent orders, and apophatic theology.

67 On the "idealist novel" see Naomi Schor, "Idealism in the Novel: Recanonizing Sand," *Yale French Studies* 75 (1988): pp. 56–73.

68 Cole, "Transcript," p. 1. See also Murnane, *Last Letter*, p. 89.

69 Cole, "Transcript," pp. 1–2.

70 Murnane, *Stream System*, p. 544.

71 Gerald Murnane, "Transcript of Gerald Murnane's Long Letter to Teju Cole," *Music & Literature* 3 (2013): pp. 5–15 (p. 9).

72 Marcel Proust, *Contre Sainte-Beuve* (Paris: Gallimard, 1971), p. 222.

73 Murnane, *Barley Patch*, p. 99.

74 Proust, *In Search of Lost Time*, IV, p. 224.

75 Proust, *In Search of Lost Time*, V, p. 174.

76 On these images cf. Murnane, *Barley Patch*, pp. 73–74, pp. 77–78; Proust, *In Search of Lost Time*, I, p. 12, V, pp. 283–284, II, pp. 583–584, VI, p. 232.

77 Murnane, *Inland*, p. 169.

78 Emily Brontë, *Life and Works of Charlotte Brontë and Her Sisters* (London: Smith, Elder and Co, 1873), V, p. 306.

79 Murnane, *A Million Windows*, p. 132; Murnane, *Inland*, p. 163.

80 Murnane, *A Million Windows*, p. 33.

81 Samantha Trayhurn, "'Images and Feelings in a Sort of Eternity': Gerald Murnane's Ideal Female Reader," in *Gerald Murnane: Another World in This One*, pp. 37–43 (p. 39).

82 Coetzee, "Reading Gerald Murnane," p. 267.

83 Trayhurn, "'Images and Feelings in a Sort of Eternity'," p. 41.

84 Ben Masters, *Novel Style: Ethics and Excess in English Fiction since the 1960s* (Oxford: Oxford University Press, 2017), p. 85.

85 Murnane, *Barley Patch*, pp. 6, 19.

86 Gerald Murnane with Will Heyward, "An Interview with Gerald Murnane," *Music & Literature* 3 (2013): pp. 19–27 (p. 24).

87 Salusinszky, *Gerald Murnane*, p. 103.

88 Indyk, "The Provincial Imagination," p. 48.

89 James Wood, "Getting to the End," *The New Republic* May 21, 2007: https://newrepublic.com/article/64041/getting-the-end.

90 The critique most often cited and rebutted by scholars is in Ken Gelder and Paul Salzman, *After the Celebration: Australian Fiction 1989–2007* (Melbourne: Melbourne University Press, 2009), pp. 131–132. In *Last Letter to a Reader*, Murnane very briefly considers, and offers a reply to, a "disapproving comment" from a reviewer who claimed (in Murnane's words) that he "seemed unaware that a different sort of landscape had preceded the Australian landscape that I wrote about so often and that a different sort of people had occupied that landscape." See Murnane, *Last Letter*, p. 121. Perhaps noteworthy in this connection is Murnane's friendship with Paul Carter. See particularly Gerald Murnane, "Living in a New Country: History, Travelling and Language by Paul Carter," *Australian Book Review* 147 (1992): www.australianbookreview.com.au/abr-online/archive/1992/522-december-1992-no-147/8261-gerald-murnane-reviews-living-in-a-new-country-by-paul-carter.

91 Murnane, *Last Letter*, p. 6. On Murnane and chronotopes, see also Merve Emre's suggestive comments in Merve Emre, "The Reclusive Giant of Australian Letters," *The New Yorker*, August 1, 2022: www.newyorker.com/magazine/2022/08/01/the-reclusive-giant-of-australian-letters.

92 Murnane, *Last Letter*, p. 37.

93 Murnane, "The Breathing Author," p. 161.

IO

BRIGID ROONEY

Helen Garner's House of Fiction

I fantasised again and again our street with its centre parking metres, the
green carpet in the hall, the flattened square of sunlight that hit the wall
of the first landing on the stairs, and my room with its blue floor and
thin red curtain, oh the joy of going home, it choked me in the throat.
   Not a person.
   A place.[1]

The writing of Helen Garner (*b.* 1942) weaves across fiction and nonfiction. Excluding recent collections of previously published stories, Garner has produced six books under the sign of "fiction." Her first, the full-length novel *Monkey Grip* (1977), is reputedly the first to emerge from second-wave feminism in Australia. After *Monkey Grip* came fiction that varied in length, mood, and structure: *Honour & Other People's Children* (1980), *The Children's Bach* (1984), and *Postcards from Surfers: Stories* (1985). Garner also published the two screenplays she wrote at this time – *The Last Days of Chez Nous & Two Friends* (1992) – for films directed by Gillian Armstrong and Jane Campion, respectively. This fiction-writing period seemed to end with Garner's most experimental work, *Cosmo Cosmolino* (1992), until the late-arriving sixth novel (or, more strictly, novella) *The Spare Room* (2008), which reprises and recasts long-standing themes and concerns. In the last three decades, Garner has largely switched to nonfictional prose in both essay and book form, a second career phase launched by *The First Stone* (1995), a book about a campus scandal that arguably eclipsed *Monkey Grip* in celebrity and notoriety. Thereafter came four books of selected essays and nonfictional writings, as well as two more book-length works of reportage: *Joe Cinque's Consolation* (2004), and *This House of Grief* (2014). Most recently, Garner has published three edited volumes of her diaries.

   The apparent split in Garner's oeuvre between fiction and nonfiction is belied by the consistency of her narrative style: Garner's distinctive voice is carried by the energy, intimacy, and intensity of the prose, by carefully wrought storytelling structures, and by the consistency of her preoccupations. Garner frequently returns, in the words of *The First Stone*'s subtitle, to "questions of sex and power" as these play out in different contexts. Her book-length works of nonfiction enter the theatrical space of the courtroom, while in fiction the focus is the house, a dynamic, formative space for interior life and expressive action, and for the relationships and ethical quandaries of characters. To focus on the house in Garner's fiction, as this essay does, is to engage a longer history of representations associating the novel with the domestic interior, extending from how the domestic realm is figured in fiction, to the role of novel-reading itself in the formation of interior life and subjectivity, and in the reproduction of the middle-class family unit.[2] Garner's fiction can be read with and against this literary heritage, since her stories fashion "new configurations of family" via the revisionary model of the shared, communal household – a model Garner herself experienced in Melbourne in the 1970s.[3] The communal household, with its individual freedoms and shared, collectivist projects, accommodated countercultural values loosely, if contradictorily, drawn from libertarianism and feminism. In Garner's fiction, the putting into practice of these values may be attended by ambivalent feelings.

Eleanor Hogan's 1995 reading of several of Garner's fictions identifies a homology between the body of the (feminist) woman and the household in which she lives.[4] Yet in these fictions, the idealized communal household, with its heyday in the early 1970s, is rarely encountered in the narrative present. More often, it resides in, and represents, a golden past, while characters grapple with its memory and legacy in their fallen, compromised present. Near the end of *Cosmo Cosmolino*, having returned at last, Alby stands in Sweetpea Mansions, summoning the "picture of the household folded in his mind" that he had carried with him "as an image of the way a life might be lived":

> Even now, though, years after he had *been saved*, the house still visited him in dreams; and while its layout would metamorphose in a multitude of ways, revealing here a bright attic he had somehow never noticed, there a splendid prospect of rivers and pastures out a window which had previously given on to a brick wall, it was always the same house: he knew it every time and entered it with joy.[5]

The house in Garner's fiction manifests the mythic, oneiric qualities identified by Gaston Bachelard, who writes, in *The Poetics of Space* (1958), that in dreams "the various dwelling places of our lives co-penetrate and retain the treasures of former days."[6] It also derives its potency from being sited at the junction of personal experience and wider history. Garner's representation of share houses maps, for instance, onto the historical moment of the "return to the city" that occurred in both North America (notably led by Jane Jacobs) and Australia during the 1960s and 1970s. In this period, a tertiary-educated, middle-class generation abandoned the outer postwar suburbs of their childhood, gravitating instead to older working-class and newer migrant neighborhoods close to the center of cities. This seeming rejection of middle-class suburbia was embodied in the countercultural share house, with its communal, collectivist orientation. In general terms, life in such a household was characterized by sexual freedom and openness to experimentation with drugs; the privileging of creative self-expression and the refusal of menial conformity; and revised forms of coupledom and childrearing. These features were shaped by an eclectic combination of libertarian and feminist ideas linked to broadly countercultural, anti-patriarchal, or anti-bourgeois orientations. Ironically, however, and as work by Emily Potter and Kirsten Seale suggests, the cultural heritage vested in the "Monkey Grip house" – the house in which Garner's book is reputed, rightly or not, to have been written – participates within socioeconomic cycles of gentrification and inflation of real-estate values.[7] In this light, share houses in Garner's fiction and more generally can be apprehended less in relation to their refusal of suburban or bourgeois lifestyles and more as reflecting and advancing the interests of an upwardly mobile professional class that helped to reproduce the individualist and consumerist lifestyles of global late capitalist and urban modernity.

Ethical questions – touching on privacy, creative or artistic license, and the appropriation, consumption, or commodification of the lives, stories, and circumstances of others – can haunt the writing of realist fiction, which leans heavily on such resources for substance, plausibility, and verisimilitude. Such questions are especially salient in relation to Garner's writing practice, as she has on occasion acknowledged. Her fiction not only reinvents her own experience in communal households, but also draws on that of her friends and acquaintances in terms she has herself recognized as being risky.[8] The ethical dilemma for the novelist in drawing from and recasting the lives of intimate others – housemates, friends, and lovers – finds some analogy with tensions produced by the collision between principles of personal and artistic freedom and communal ideals. Share houses seem to promise freedom from bourgeois convention and from private property, but their practical tensions, conflicts, and contradictions are less easily resolved. Garner's fiction both focuses on and enacts these contradictions and collisions. The household, in short, is the recurring and fundamental context for the exercise of a problem around which Garner's writing circles – one summarized by Bernadette Brennan as: "how should one balance the desire for personal freedom with ethical responsibility."[9]

Monkey Grip's reputation as Australia's breakthrough, second-wave feminist novel may be undeserved since the honor probably belongs to the lesser-known, bravely explicit lesbian feminist novel *All that False Instruction* (1975) by Kerryn Higgs. But *Monkey Grip*'s immediate popular impact (seen in the rapidity of its adaptation for film), its lasting iconicity, and its role in inaugurating the so-called women's decade (the 1980s) in Australian fiction are incontestable. For contemporary Australian writer Charlotte Wood, *Monkey Grip* "represented the wresting of Australian literature away from the grip of conservative old men into the hands of radical young women."[10] Complicating its reception, however, were rumors of the novel's provenance in its author's diaries. From the outset, *Monkey Grip* rode the boundary between autobiography and fiction, seeming both to reveal and conceal its author-protagonist, and anticipating Garner's move to "auto-fiction" in *The Spare Room*. The act of keeping a diary, figured in the narrative itself, may be correlated with Nora's teasing fear – or desire – that others in the house will "snoop," as she herself in fact does.[11] This swerve away from yet flirtation with exposure is suggested by the cover of the first edition of *Monkey Grip*, with its photo, taken from just above, of a woman riding a bicycle. The woman's face is hidden, but her distinctive floppy hat and floral dress match a contemporaneous photo that identifies the woman as Garner herself.[12] While the figure of the diarist in the communal house internalizes the writer in her house of fiction, *Monkey Grip*'s cover both reveals and conceals its protagonist as author.

As a chronicle of daily happenings and intimate emotions told in the manner of a diary, *Monkey Grip* lacks a classical narrative shape of climax, denouement, and resolution. Kerryn Goldsworthy has observed how, despite its popular acclaim, the novel met with some initial critical resistance not only on account of its provocative content (explicit drug-taking, non-monogamous sex, absence of conventional moralizing), but also because of its narrative form. *Monkey Grip*, however, only *seems* shapeless. Its formal features emulate the flow between inner feelings and environment: The sign at the Fitzroy swimming pool that gives the opening chapter its title of "Acqua Profunda" (sic) not only refers to "deeper waters" but also hints at the fluidity of the prose. In both sharp detail and dreamy drifts, we follow the days of single mother Nora, the novel's thirty-three-year-old narrator-protagonist, as she moves through her passionate affair with drug-addicted Javo. At various intervals, Nora takes up with other lovers, amid mothering her young child Gracie, integrating herself into successive households, managing on welfare and scraps of work, and moving about freely, on foot, by bike, or – in jaunts beyond Melbourne – by car, train, or plane. Nora's almost perpetual motion – walking, riding, and making love – affords a kinesthetic quality to the novel, amplifying the restlessness of self and desire. In the process, from its immersive, daily perspective on the inside of bedroom or house, *Monkey Grip* radiates outwards from countercultural Melbourne's inner northern suburb of Fitzroy to the small holiday town of Merimbula on the New South Wales south coast, south to Hobart, and north to Sydney. In the narrative background is a significant temporal marker. The year – as we learn – is 1975, with its December election bringing a controversial end to the era of Prime Minister Gough Whitlam, which had been marked by progressive legislative reform, rapid social transformation, and massive injections of funding for education and the arts.

The opening of the novel looks back to the golden age of the "old brown house on the corner" in which there "were never enough chairs for us all to sit up at the meal table": "It was hunger and all sheer function: the noise, and clashing of plates, and people chewing with their mouths open, and talking, and laughing. Oh, I was happy then. At night our backyard smelt like the country."[13] Early in the narrative, this first "brown house" is sold and its household dispersed: "Some wept, some raged, some shrugged and went off searching," says Nora, who temporarily retreats into an acid-induced dream state, in which "I became part of the room and the curtains were part of my skin rippling smoothly like ribs of sands on the Sahara."[14] The integral relation between the interior self and house is figured: "When I left that house, ragged ends of myself would be left hanging."[15] In Sydney, at the furthest distance from home, Nora is flooded by images of her Melbourne house – its daily square of sunlight in the stairwell, and her room, "with its blue floor and thin red curtain, oh the joy of going home, it choked me in the throat."[16] Nora is drawn back "[n]ot [by] a person" but by "a place."[17]

The choking grip of "place" suggests its intricate entanglement with characters. Javo is a place as well as a person, a visually striking assemblage of architectural features with his lean body and lantern head, in which the relative brilliancy or fadedness of his blue eyes provides Nora with a gauge of how stoned he is at any given time. When Javo is jailed in Bangkok, Nora becomes dry and hungry, as if thirsting or hollowing out. His return is drought-breaking.[18] The title, "monkey grip," is frequently glossed in the cover blurbs of various editions as referencing the addictive character of the Nora-Javo relationship: "The harder they pull away, the *tighter* the *monkey grip*." Addiction, in *Monkey Grip* – whether to ecstatic lovemaking or drugs – is theme and driver of the narrative but is not pathologized.

Rather, it joins a spectrum of experimental behaviors subject to nonjudg-mental record, holding at bay the otherwise standard novelistic injunction to *Bildung* ("development"). Nora simply survives and moves past her addiction to Javo, perhaps only temporarily. What is borne in on us by the narrative, however, is the way their intense, addictive love is bound up with the allure of destruction.

Drifting through and beyond the golden time of the communal house, with its conviviality, warmth and free love, the narrative registers ambiv-alence and contradiction. The more troubling aspects of collectivist, liber-tarian modes of coupledom and parenting are the focus of Garner's next work of fiction, *Honour & Other People's Children* (1980), a pair of novel-las that return to the communal household in terms that both recall and diverge from *Monkey Grip*. Published in one volume, the two stories pres-ent entirely different groups of characters. Yet they are unified in theme and design, perhaps figuring the adjacency of separate houses in the same street, or rooms within the one large house. The novellas both concern couple rela-tionships yet also mirror each other in their focus on relationships between women within, or with respect to, heterosexual coupledom, the household, and parenting. Garner shifts away from the immersive first-person narra-tive of *Monkey Grip* to a more detached, observing third-person narration that – in what becomes a signature device – seamlessly switches focalization from character to character, generating multiple perspectives. Collective households and their heady energies now appear far-off, as each story teases out lingering difficulties in the later lives of their inhabitants.

As Goldsworthy notes, the gap between theory and practice registered in *Monkey Grip* now opens up to "swallow up children."[19] "Honour" traces the inadmissible yet palpable tensions between Frank's lover Jenny and his former wife, Kathleen. Caught in the middle is Florence (Flo), Kathleen and Frank's daughter. Jenny and Kathleen are ostensibly friendly, but Jenny finds Kathleen's relatively unimpeded access to the house that Frank and Jenny inhabit discomforting, as she does Kathleen's continued assumption that Frank himself is still, in some sense, her emotional property. Kathleen's expec-tation of continued access to her ex-husband's intimate lifeworld is partly conditioned by feminist and collectivist principles, but feelings of resentment gnaw away. Kathleen's calm response to Frank's request for a divorce, as merely a "formality," is met by an unbidden, visceral reaction: "[s]ome splinter-self in the depths was twisting in protest: what about *me*?"[20]

The turning point occurs when Kathleen – invited to join Flo and the couple while they holiday at a family beach shack – arrives while they are out. Finding the place locked, Kathleen impulsively breaks in and makes herself at home. When the others return, emotions are stretched taut: Jenny can barely conceal her anger, Kathleen is struck with shamed recognition, and the shocked Flo is caught in adult turmoil. Two images crystallize the state of relations but hold resolution at bay. In a café, as Kathleen and Frank discuss divorce, a sobbing Flo maintains her "honour" by sitting firmly on her hands "so neither of her parents could seize one and sway her into partiality."[21] This image of the child at the fulcrum has its counterpart in the closing image. Guided into place by Flo, Kathleen and Jenny sit at either end of a seesaw. Tentatively, they draw level to its balancing point, in what could be read as rapprochement or stalemate: "They hung in the dark, airily balancing, motionless."[22]

A bone-chilling sadness pervades the second, longer novella, "Other People's Children." This narrative zeroes in on Ruth and Scotty, two women who share a house with the gentle Alex, a musician. The house, a melancholy fragment adrift from the communal past, has seen better days: "The stillness of the dry yard crept in through the back door. A cricket scraped in the mint round the gully trap."[23] Ruth flees the neglect of her first marriage and scrapes by as the single parent of two children. In compulsive repetition, Ruth heads into the arms of working-class socialist and heartless chauvinist Dennis, who refuses to live with her in case it cramps his political activities. The unhappy Ruth directs her disavowed shame and anger at her housemate Scotty, feminist and former high-school teacher, who emerges as lonely, childless by choice (after abortions and a tubal ligation), but now yearns for connection with Ruth's children. She is rebuffed, and the ideal of collective parenting, its anti-patriarchal spirit and promise of communal access to "other people's children," is devastatingly hollowed out. The story ends with the two women, each having endured struggles with men, gendered roles, and loneliness, facing off in the kitchen. Despite Scotty's entreaties, Ruth is fixed in fury. The two women break into open hostilities, indulging in damaging, liberating rage. The story's final image is of disembodied voices, distending the space of the kitchen and cancelling each other out in their cacophony. The image violently recasts the seesaw configuration at the end of "Honour": "A mouth formed words. 'Now we can leave each other alone'. 'I can accept that', said another, low, a thousand miles away."[24]

The sadness and pent-up fury of "Honour" and "Other People's Children" accede to the comedic spirit of Garner's next novella, *The Children's Bach* (1984), although it, too, has dark or shadowy strands. Fulsomely praised by reviewers and attracting rich scholarly readings,[25] *The Children's Bach* is perhaps Garner's most exquisitely crafted fictional work. It approaches the household in a different key, this time centering on the suburban family, and setting unspoken female desire against the *longueurs* of patriarchal monogamy. Garner's portrait of the Fox family is neither celebratory nor damning.

Though political (feminist) implications are suggested, they are held in abeyance in favor of nonjudgmental scrutiny. In their cozily rounded "burrow" of a house live the members of the Fox family – comprising the dominating, conservative yet likeably warm-hearted Dexter; the loyal, capable, quietly discontented Athena; and their two sons, Arthur and Billy (a child with an unspecified intellectual impairment).[26] Their routines are put to the test with the arrival of Dexter's former lover, the chic and childfree urbanite Elizabeth, who, in the wake of her mother's recent death, has her adolescent sister Vicki in tow. This set of familiar strangers, including Elizabeth's current lover, playboy and musician Philip (father to Poppy), brings the outside world into the Fox family home, unleashing chaotic desires that make "the edifice" tremble.[27]

In an opening ekphrasis that prefigures the novella's arc from chaos to restoration, a "torn and stained" photo of the poet Tennyson with his wife and two young sons hints at subterranean tensions in the otherwise ideal family.[28] Stuck on the kitchen wall but forever at risk of peeling off, the picture is always saved and returned to position. The marriage of Dexter and Athena is affectionate but oppressive. The overbearing Dexter, trenchantly opposed to modern things, ironically falls into the immoral world he despises. Athena – named for the goddess of "war and needlecraft" – is at first seen from the outside, from the viewpoint of other characters (notably the newly orphaned adolescent Vicki), but the passage of her emotions and desires defines the plot, placing her at the center of things.[29] Waylaid by hidden discontents, by the thwarting of desire entailed in marriage, Athena is charmed and seduced by the morally vacuous Philip. Having broken free of her bonds and achieved an external perspective, however, she voluntarily returns. The narrative concludes in anticipatory, subjunctive mood as Athena restores order to the domestic realm.

The polyphonic, seamlessly focalized third-person narration of *The Children's Bach* produces libidinal currents. As we follow Athena to the bus stop or shops, for example, the narrative veers off into rhapsody or fantasy without signaling its departure from the quotidian. The prose moves sinuously through compact scenes and vignettes, and through the perspectives of characters in rapid succession. We follow characters and their thoughts as they venture alone, in pairs or groups, beyond the house into the city, its shops and cafes, to parks and nightclubs, and the cemetery. Some of the novella's most vivid images – such as the pet rabbit released from its little hutch into an open paddock where "it crouched shuddering between tussocks under the huge blank sky" – amplify the emotional resonance of mundane, domestic things.[30] *The Children's Bach* is both musical in form and architectural in its vision, its hidden pockets fanning out into distances. The novella's form is mimetic of the ways in which interior selves are entangled with porous, mutable, and dynamic spaces.

In her next book, *Postcards from Surfers* (1985), a collection of short stories, Garner experiments by diversifying character types and scenarios, all the while returning to and examining questions about gendered roles and relations, sometimes probing the limits of feminism. Brennan remarks on the proliferation in these tales of sexually magnetic but unfaithful "Philip" figures – of whom the most developed example was the musician in *The Children's Bach*. Several stories exercise the emotional freight and legacy of difficult parent-child relationships.[31] The title story tells of its narrator's visit to her parents' holiday house in the beachside town of Coolangatta at the southern end of the Gold Coast. This yields a portrait of the mother's compliant passivity, which is contrasted with the dominating crudity of the father, a former wool classer with big blunt hands, who seems simultaneously shrewdly capable, and obtusely self-serving. The enigmatic, unapproachable father, last seen gazing at the ocean from the very edge of his property, is the foregrounded counterpart (and perhaps explanation) of the distantly enigmatic and uncaring lover Philip, to whom the narrator addresses but does not send her postcards.

Garner's experimentation with form reached its zenith in *Cosmo Cosmolino* (1992), the last work of fiction she would publish for many years. With its lost souls, otherworldly beings, and unusual design (two shorter stories buttressing a longish novella), *Cosmo Cosmolino* challenges the classificatory bounds of both realism and the novel. In mode and language, *Cosmo Cosmolino* might be understood as "baroque" – its less convincing aspects have been seen as "purple prose" with leaps into biblical allegory.[32] Garner disclosed that she had wanted to play with her sentences, loosening and lengthening them – that she was trying to figure out "how to get dream into the texture of the story."[33] Some sequences are breathless, extravagant, rhapsodic, while others elaborate darker emotional tones also threaded through Garner's earlier fiction. One could say that *Cosmo Cosmolino* is *Monkey Grip* recast as nightmare, except that its ending strikes a note of fanciful optimism – recapitulating the prospect of a soon-to-be-restored order that concluded *The Children's Bach*.

Harking back once more to the collective household so comprehensively dismantled in *Honour & Other People's Children*, *Cosmo Cosmolino* undertakes the restoration of its ideals. This is the argument of Eleanor Hogan, for whom *Cosmo Cosmolino* effects the "'spiritualisation' of familiar Garner terrain," a recasting of social relations that "betrays a wish to return to older and more comforting structures," and the desire to subsume difference.[34] Hogan's observations about the return to "more comforting structures" prompt consideration of something else at stake: that is, the way *Cosmo Cosmolino* traces but simultaneously forecloses that persistent ethical dilemma – implicated in *Monkey Grip* and Garner's fiction generally – of the freedom of the writer to take from and reinvent the lives of others. Can the wishful conclusion of *Cosmo Cosmolino* be read in relation to this dilemma?

In the opening story, "Recording Angel," the unnamed narrator tells of her long-time friend Patrick, and his folder of information about her (memories, facts, opinions) lodged deep in his brain. The narrator cannot challenge Patrick's knowledge, as her own long-standing identity and his sense of reality depend on the maintenance of the illusion that he is the privileged knower. Patrick, however, undergoes brain surgery, and the sight of him utterly prostrate and suffering stuns the narrator, who is now guilty, having earlier fantasized about surgically removing the "folder" from his brain. The next story, "The Vigil," concerns the immature Raymond, whose negligence is a factor in the lonely death of his lover, Kim. Forced to attend her funeral, Raymond is intercepted by crematorium workers (two nattily dressed "angels") who bear him down to the furnace, where he is compelled to witness the fiery metamorphosis of Kim's corpse. This punishing scene of hellfire is the unspoken backstory for the saved, weakly evangelistic "Ray" of the ensuing "Cosmo Cosmolino." In the latter, we meet the middle-aged, "unclubbable" and "unwifely" Janet, haunted by a mysterious, shadowy column behind her left shoulder, a characteristic (among others) that identifies her as the unnamed narrator of "Recording Angel."[35] As owner of the decrepit Sweetpea Mansions, a once-lively share house, Janet permits Ray and her new housekeeper, Maxine, to move in. Ray awaits his brother Alby, with whom he plans to begin anew. Maxine – carpenter, eccentric, mystic, and artist – moves into the shed, where she weaves her magic. Plot and event are structured by each character's secret longings: Janet's for communal restoration, Ray's for his brother Alby's approval, and Maxine's for a baby.

A decaying house in a time-warp, Sweetpea Mansions is also a mutating space, "its enfilade of hollow rooms" leading off one another, expanding or contracting around its occupants.[36] Echoing the shape-shifting house is the repeated figure of nested worlds, or worlds within worlds, at the center of which is the nested space of the womb. Worlds open darkly within, behind, above, and beneath. For instance, it is quite possible, given Janet's silent discovery of a "lump" while massaging Maxine, that the "foetus" is a tumor. Inspired to prepare a communal meal for her housemates, Janet visits the butchery with its glass-covered display of trussed pink cuts of meat. In a shadowy room at the shop's rear, Janet glimpses an elderly, blood-bespattered woman, standing by a machine, ceaselessly skinning rabbits. This grim adjacency recalls the spatial configuration in "The Vigil" of fiery furnace beneath trimmed lawns.

Events in "Cosmo Cosmolino" cluster bizarrely. In a dreamlike sequence, Maxine couples with Ray and perhaps, as she believes she is destined to do, conceives their child. Later she stumbles upon Ray's bundle of hard-earned savings from his first-ever job as an unskilled laborer. Roped in by a pyramid scheme, Maxine believes she can make them all rich if only she can supply the requisite one thousand dollars. Her intentions are as honorable as her faith is unshakeable. Taking Ray's entire stash, she leaves in its place the tiny trembling cradle she had fashioned from twigs, an object admired by Janet but puzzling to Ray. Maxine believes it a fair exchange, and though she is swiftly thereafter disabused, with the scheme rorted and Ray's money lost, she blithely trusts all is for the best. And indeed, so it is, for in the end, Maxine takes flight – if not literally or even metaphorically, then certainly inexplicably – springing weightlessly from the floor of her shed to its roof, thence above the houses and into the limitless sky, bearing along her "cosmo cosmolino" (world, little world) and scattering jonquils in her wake. Those below – the earthbound Janet, the robbed and distraught Ray, and his lately arrived brother, Alby – must reconcile themselves to the everyday fallen world. Restoration is implied, however: Janet invites the brothers each to choose a room, reconstituting the collective household.

In *Cosmo Cosmolino*, ambiguous questions seem concentrated in Maxine's theft of Ray's money, the full consequences of which are foreclosed and dispersed by Maxine's elevation into an otherworldly dimension, even as the everyday world carries on. Maxine's theft, her substitution of the cradle, product of her imaginative labor, for Ray's money, is narratively justified given this serves her creative vision. Yet a troubling residue remains, given the haplessness and vulnerability of Ray. Even if read as Ray's punishment for the original sin of uncaring negligence (in "The Vigil"), Maxine's theft induces a moral foreboding not lightly dissolved. These ethics acquire their justification from the prior convergence of Maxine's artistic freedom with her assumed freedom of access to the property of others, in accord with the principles of the collectivist household. As an imaginative enactment, the spirit of Maxine's collectivist appropriation of Ray's money both allegorizes and dispenses with the ethical dilemma of the artist – the writer of imaginative fiction – who feels herself obliged to draw from the intimate lives of those to whom she is attached, whether they agree or not, and feels herself justified in so doing. This intriguing work, with its apparent return to beginnings, performs the symbolic closure of Garner's house of fiction, her fiction of the household, enabling its author to fly free from that invented realm.

Sixteen years later, in 2008, Garner published *The Spare Room*, a work of fiction again centered on a household, though with telling differences. In the intervening time, Garner's books of court reportage, *The First Stone* and *Joe Cinque's Consolation*, both hugely successful and widely admired, attracted controversy. This was not only on feminist grounds but also in response to Garner's harnessing of "new journalistic" techniques that involved inserting her own feelings, stories, reflections, and ruminations into the reporting process.[37] On the one hand, in these works, Garner strove to undercut the illusion of objective truth in order to open out a range of perspectives on vexed issues. On the other, these interventions, coupled with Garner's tendency to side overtly with those she saw as victims, led some to question whether this emotionally heightened, rhetorical approach preempted counterarguments and ethical concerns.[38] Further, it was around this time that Garner – by now established as a nonfiction writer – disclosed that her novel *Monkey Grip* had after all been based, as long rumored, on the diaries she had kept at the time. Eloquently defending her book against the sneer that all she had done was publish her diaries – "As if it were lazy. As if there were no work involved in keeping a diary in the first place: no thinking, no discipline, no creative energy, no focusing or *directing* of creative energy'[39] – Garner circled back to the by-now-familiar ethical problem, dramatized in *Cosmo Cosmolino* and implicated in Garner's court reportage:

> How inextricably we are intertwined! We form each other. We form ourselves in response to each other. It's impossible to write intimately about your own life without revealing something of the people who are close to you. This has always been an ethical problem for me, and it always will be. Scour and scourge my motives as I may, consciousness always lags behind action – sometimes by years. Self-awareness is studded with blind spots. Writing, it seems, like the bringing up of children, can't be done without causing damage.[40]

In their frank lucidity – a lucidity marked, nonetheless, by resolute evasion of the consequences they name – these observations seem relevant to *The Spare Room*, a work based, like much of Garner's writing, on people (friends, family, acquaintances) and events in her own life. In this case, the novella drew on the difficult experience of the three-week stay in her own house of a terminally ill friend.[41] In its renegotiation of the fiction-autobiography nexus, *The Spare Room* is like and unlike Garner's earlier works. Seeking to "own" the irrational anger at the heart of her novella, Garner named her narrator-protagonist "Helen." In an interview, Garner also made it clear that though her story was drawn from life, her decision to write fiction gave her the freedom to invent.[42] Garner's strategy brings her novella close to "autofiction," a strategic blending of factual or referential details with fictive reinvention.[43] Even so, one can imagine the potential hurt, for family and friends, of Garner's portrayal of the "Nicola" figure as someone absurdly and irrationally clinging to alternative therapies, rather than facing the truth of her condition.

In *The Spare Room*, Helen lives alone in her own house, right next door to her daughter's family. This position affords privacy and autonomy whilst enabling pleasurable access to her grandchildren's daily lives. Notwithstanding Helen's manifest generosity, Nicola's visit effects a fundamental intrusion and disruption, and the often ambivalent roles of host and guest shape household dynamics as Helen shifts between unstinting, openhearted generosity and a barely suppressed irritation, mounting to explosive anger. Nicola's affected mannerisms and gushing bravado drive Helen mad, but something more is going on:

> A huge wave of fatigue rinsed me from head to foot. I was afraid I would slide off the bench and measure my length among the cut roses. At the same time a chain of metallic thoughts went clanking through my mind, like the first dropping of an anchor. Death will not be denied. To try is grandiose. It drives madness into the soul. It leaches out virtue. It injects poison into friendship, and makes a mockery of love.[44]

"Death" undermines Helen's capacity for love, friendship, and virtue, that sense of her *self* as good, generous, hospitable, and, indeed, selfless. Nicola's stay, her refusal to behave as a compliant, biddable "patient" and fade away quietly, and the sheer physical extremity of her condition, disrupt Helen's happiness, which in turn depends on the continuity of the mundane world, of that domestic order that is defined by daily intercourse with her grandchildren, with the "surging vitality" of their bodies, and the pleasurably anticipated writers' festival or overseas trip – all those cushioning visions of one's future ceaselessly rolling on. These inconveniences are the foretaste of death, in so far as death strips away the illusion of safety and control from the subject, body, and soul, interrupting and derailing plans, demanding surrender to its implacable processes. It is death, more than Nicola, that is the unwanted guest, inside Helen's own house.

Notes

1 Helen Garner, *Monkey Grip* (Ringwood: Penguin, 1997; 1977), p. 108.
2 See, for example, Ian Watt, *The Rise of the Novel: Studies in Defoe, Richardson and Fielding* (London: Pimlico, 2000; 1957); Karen Lipsedge, *Domestic Space in Eighteenth-Century British Novels* (Basingstoke: Palgrave Macmillan, 2021), p. 2.
3 Bernadette Brennan, *A Writing Life: Helen Garner and Her Work* (Melbourne: Text Publishing, 2017), p. 21.

4 Eleanor Hogan, "Borderline Bodies: Women and Households in Helen Garner's *Other People's Children* and *Cosmo Cosmolino*," *New Literatures Review* 30 (1995): pp. 69–82 (p. 70).

5 Helen Garner, *Cosmo Cosmolino* (Ringwood: McPhee Gribble, 1992), p. 188.

6 See Gaston Bachelard, *The Poetics of Space*, trans. Maria Jolas (Boston: Beacon Press, 1994), p. 5.

7 Emily Potter and Kirsten Seale, "The Worldly Text and the Production of More-Than-Literary Place: Helen Garner's *Monkey Grip* and Melbourne's 'Inner North'," *Cultural Geographies* 27.3 (2019): pp. 367–378 (p. 369).

8 Helen Garner, "I" [essay], *Meanjin* 60.1 (2002): pp. 40–43 (pp. 42–43). See also Brennan, *A Writing Life*, pp. 63–64.

9 Brennan, *A Writing Life*, p. 43.

10 Charlotte Wood, "Helen Garner's *Monkey Grip* Makes Me Examine Who I Am," the *Guardian*, October 25, 2018: www.theguardian.com/books/2018/oct/25/helen-garners-monkey-grip-makes-me-examine-who-i-am.

11 Garner, *Monkey Grip*, p. 145.

12 See accompanying photograph of Garner in Lesley Morgan, "*Monkey Grip* by Helen Garner," *Womanspeak* 3.5 (1978): p. 29.

13 Garner, *Monkey Grip*, p. 1.

14 Garner, *Monkey Grip*, p. 56.

15 Garner, *Monkey Grip*, p. 56.

16 Garner, *Monkey Grip*, p. 108.

17 Garner, *Monkey Grip*, p. 108.

18 Garner, *Monkey Grip*, p. 65.

19 Kerryn Goldsworthy, *Helen Garner* (Melbourne: Oxford University Press, 1996), p. 41.

20 Helen Garner, "Honour" [1980]; reprinted in *My Hard Heart: Selected Fiction* (Ringwood: Penguin, 2000), p. 27.

21 Garner, "Honour," p. 78.

22 Garner, "Honour," p. 83.

23 Helen Garner, "Other People's Children" [1980]; reprinted in *My Hard Heart*, p. 105.

24 Garner, "Other People's Children," p. 193.

25 See for example John Clower, "The Anarchist Craft of *The Children's Bach*," *Australia and New Zealand Studies in Canada* 6 (1991): pp. 55–75; Karen Grandy, "Serving in the Home Guard: Housekeepers and Homemakers in *The Children's Bach* and Dancing in the Dark," *Australia and New Zealand Studies in Canada* 6 (1991): pp. 76–89; Kate Livett, "Ekphrastic Effects in Helen Garner's *The Children's Bach*," *Southerly* 77.3 (2017): pp. 66–82; Nicholas Mansfield, "'A Pleasant, Meaningless Discord': Helen Garner's *The Children's Bach*," *Westerly* 2 (1991): 17–22.

26 Helen Garner, *The Children's Bach* (Ringwood: McPhee Gribble, 1984), p. 10.

27 Garner, *The Children's Bach*, p. 63.

28 See Livett's essay, "Ekphrastic Effects," for full analysis of the uses of ekphrasis in the text.

29 Garner, *The Children's Bach*, p. 38.

30 Garner, *The Children's Bach*, p. 40.

31 Brennan, *A Writing Life*, p. 84.

32 On the "baroque," see Ramona Koval, "Rewind to Ms Garner's Angels," *Sydney Morning Herald*, April 21, 2012: www.smh.com.au/entertainment/books/rewind-to-ms-garners-angels-20120419-1x87r.html; on "purple prose," see Jenna Mead, "Politics, Patriarchy and Death," *Island* 53 (1992): pp. 66–69 (pp. 67–68).

33 Garner, as quoted in Robert Hefner, "Of Angels, Dreams and Jokes," *The Canberra Times*, March 15, 1992, p. 22; Helen Garner, "Dreams, the Bible and Cosmo Cosmolino," in *True Stories: Selected Non-Fiction* (Melbourne: Text Publishing, 2017), pp. 139–143 (p. 143).

34 Hogan, "Borderline Bodies," pp. 79–81.

35 Garner, *Cosmo Cosmolino*, p. 56.

36 Garner, *Cosmo Cosmolino*, pp. 64, 138.

37 As Brennan, among others, observe (*A Writing Life*, p. 132), Garner particularly admired American "new journalist" Janet Malcolm, whom she cites, for instance, in her most recent book of courtroom reportage, *This House of Grief* (Melbourne: Text Publishing, 2014), p. 256.

38 For further discussion of these issues see, for example, Brigid Rooney, "The Sinner, the Prophet, and the Pietà: Sacrifice and the Sacred in Helen Garner's Narratives," *Antipodes* 19.2 (2005): pp. 153–159 (p. 155).

39 The disclosure was given in Garner, "I," p. 40.

40 Garner, "I," p. 43.

41 See Brennan, *A Writing Life*, p. 236.

42 Helen Garner's interview with Shannon Burns, as cited in Brennan, *A Writing Life*, pp. 244–245.

43 See Claudia Gronemann, "Autofiction," in *Handbook of Autobiography/Autofiction*, ed. Martina Wagner-Egelhaaf (Berlin: De Gruyter, 2019), pp. 241–246. See also Nicholas Birns' discussion of the means of distinguishing autofiction from fictional autobiography in "A Registering of Transformations: Alex Miller's *The Passage of Love*," *JASAL* 20.2 (2020): https://openjournals.library.sydney.edu.au/index.php/JASAL/article/viewFile/14307/13146.

44 Helen Garner, *The Spare Room* (Melbourne: Text Publishing, 2008), pp. 88–89.

11

LYNDA NG

Alexis Wright's Novel Activism

In the space of two short decades, Alexis Wright has risen to become one of the most fêted authors in contemporary Australian fiction, celebrated in her homeland as an important Aboriginal voice and hailed overseas as a welcome addition to world literature. Although best known for her breakout novel, *Carpentaria* (2006) and for her "collective biography" of the activist Leigh Bruce "Tracker" Tilmouth, *Tracker* (2017), her body of work puts forward a remarkably consistent and cohesive literary vision that is at once Aboriginal and Australian, modern and ancient, local and yet outward-looking. Wright advances this agenda by challenging the linear, evolutionary perspective established by European ideology that configures the West as literate, civilized, and future-facing, in contrast to Indigenous cultures that were treated, by definition, as primitive, preliterate remnants from the past. Her literary experimentation pointedly draws the reader's attention to the epistemic biases that dictate our very definitions of reality and are used, all too often, to attack the authenticity of Aboriginal culture or to suppress Aboriginal peoples.

A recurring theme in Wright's work is the importance of *sovereign thinking*, which ensures Aboriginal culture is both self-defined and asserted with self-confidence. Indeed, Wright began her career working in the government as an advocate for Aboriginal land and legal rights.[1] Her decision to become a writer, then, betrays a keen understanding of the role played by literature in the construction of cultural norms and national imaginaries. The development of a sovereign Aboriginal literature presents a fierce rebuttal to those who would suggest that literacy amounts to a dilution of Aboriginal culture, or constitutes a marker of Westernization. Such attitudes perpetuate the notion that modernity is the sole provenance of the West, a presumption refuted by an ever-growing body of postcolonial work.[2]

Wright's oeuvre challenges common assumptions about the relationship between orality, the written word, and modernity. The Western novel is generally understood to be both the inheritor and usurper of oral storytelling forms such as the epic, now seen as belonging to a prehistory that antedates the invention of writing. In this manner, the novel's debt to the storytelling techniques of an oral culture is at once acknowledged and neatly bracketed off, as when Mikhail Bakhtin declared that "[w]e encounter the epic as a genre that has not only long since completed its development, but one that is already antiquated."[3] The strong Eurocentric bias that governs this neat division between a premodern orality and a modern, script-based literacy is made manifest, however, when we turn to an author such as Alexis Wright, whose literary experimentation is so clearly influenced by her knowledge of a living, oral storytelling culture. Wright envisages the novel not as a capstone to oral techniques, but rather as an extension of an oral literature capable of positing an Aboriginal-inflected modernity.

Conventional forms of literary analysis view the novel – a printed document – as a textual artifact that bears the residue of an oral past. This is evident in critical responses to Wright's fiction, which routinely focus on the musicality of her language; emphasize the mythic or folkloric dimensions that would qualify her as a magical realist author; or speculate as to the inspiration her novels have taken from traditional Aboriginal songlines.[4] Paying attention to these aspects of her work, however, does not do justice to the full scope of Wright's ambition. In this chapter, I suggest that Wright's understanding of an oral tradition as a living art form inspires in her a far more radical impulse – namely, to reconfigure the relationship between reader and writer *off the page*. She does not so much import techniques of oral storytelling into the novel as using the novel form itself to re-enact the relational dynamics of orality. Wright's work demands, then, a new kind of reading, where the text functions as a shared, communal experience capable of transmitting cultural knowledge across the disparate coordinates of author and reader.

In the course of altering the relationship between reader and writer, Alexis Wright challenges categorical divisions between fiction and non-fiction, disrupts Western assumptions about the technological progression from oral to literate cultures, and forces us to reevaluate the ways in which we identify "realism" or "reality." Repudiating the manner in which Western narratives historically configure Aboriginal people as objects, she institutes an important perspectival shift towards an Aboriginal subjectivity that simultaneously repositions us from a Westernized modernity into an Aboriginal-inflected one. Her works challenge the preeminence afforded to the individual in Western literature by introducing a multiperspectival style that is uniquely democratic, ranging not only across different people but also different life-forms.

Aboriginal Literary Activism

For Aboriginal people, the act of writing has always possessed a political dimension that is impossible to separate from the literature itself. In the early days of British settlement, learning English was a strategy for survival, a necessity for negotiating with invaders intent on seizing the land and its resources, thus driving the Indigenous inhabitants towards extinction.[5] With its focus on assimilation, settler colonialism was hardly conducive to the production of Aboriginal literature. It is no surprise, then, that Aboriginal authors only really started to come to prominence after Aboriginal activists began to make strides in the 1960s. Aboriginal women played an influential role in shaping this emerging field. Oodgeroo Noonuccal (formerly known as Kath Walker) became the first Indigenous author to publish a book of poems (*We Are Going*, 1964) as well as the first prose narrative and life story (*Stradbroke Dreamtime*, 1972). Monica Clare's novel *Karobran* (1978), published posthumously, is now widely acknowledged as the first Aboriginal novel. Life writing from Aboriginal women started to establish itself as a significant publishing category in the 1970s; a new milestone was set by Sally Morgan's *My Place* (1987) when it became a national bestseller, proving not only that a wider audience existed for Aboriginal literature but that it could also be profitable.[6]

Life writing was an important vector by which Aboriginal women attained visibility in the broader Australian cultural landscape. It was a genre well suited to capturing the oral dimension of Aboriginal stories as it allowed for the direct transcription of personal yarns into the written form. However, the prominence of life writing also shone a spotlight on the difficulties of authentic Aboriginal self-representation within the confines of a white-dominated publishing market. An element of translation inevitably took place in the transposition of oral accounts to the written form and there were increasing misgivings about the dynamics of having Aboriginal women record their stories, frequently with the assistance of white authors and editors, in order to produce works intended for publication in a market assumed to consist of predominantly white readers.[7] Perhaps most famously, in 1990 the author Mudrooroo accused Sally Morgan of pandering to a white readership and criticized life writing for its complicity in replicating the values and narrative conventions of white culture. Castigating Morgan's work for telling an "individualised story," he suggested that the genre itself was inherently compromised and could not retain the authority and control necessary for establishing a genuine Aboriginal literature.[8]

Aileen Moreton-Robertson's subsequent refutation of Mudrooroo's stance underscores the difficulties of overcoming a white-centered framework when writing in the English-language tradition. Coming to the defense of life writing, Moreton-Robinson suggests that Mudrooroo's very definition of what qualifies as "literature" betrays an internalization of white aesthetics.[9] In their responses, both Mudrooroo and Moreton-Robinson seize on different issues raised by the oral dimension of life writing. Mudrooroo focuses on the way that a speaker naturally alters a narrative to accommodate the listener, whereas Moreton-Robinson asks us to appreciate the political significance of speaking out, an act that in itself recognizes and affirms the identity of Aboriginal women.

It is necessary to review these debates in order to fully appreciate the significance of Alexis Wright's work. As an author, Wright is attuned to the way in which language itself can be implicated in the dynamics of colonial subjugation, most crucially through the power it wields over our interpretation of reality. She shares Mudrooroo's concerns regarding the pitfalls of performing Aboriginality for white audiences, as well as Moreton-Robinson's cognizance of the colonial values that attach themselves to certain literary forms. Reflecting back on her career in 2016, Wright stated: "Why do I write at all? And why do I write what I write? These are questions I wanted to explore while trying to create stories more authentically; and on the other hand I wondered, am I just telling stories I have been conditioned to tell by the stories other people tell about us? How would I free my mind to write differently?"[10] Given that a Westernized perspective designates Aboriginal culture as preliterate and therefore premodern, it is not enough for Wright to simply bend the rules of genre. She seeks instead to challenge the very foundations on which Western literary conventions rest by throwing notions of fiction and nonfiction into disarray.

Wright's frustration with the inadequacy of existing Western literary forms for conveying the Aboriginal experience is evident from the start of her career. After forays into poetry and short stories, Wright announced herself on the Australian literary scene by publishing, in swift succession, the nonfictional *Grog War* (1997), the novel *Plains of Promise* (1997), and the edited collection *Take Power* (1998). This trio of works already manifests Wright's key insight that the only way to create a sovereign literature is to loosen the grip of the colonial attitudes that shape reality itself. On the most fundamental level, this necessitates a realignment of the division normally made between fiction and nonfiction.

In *Grog War*, for example, Wright invents a fictional Aboriginal family to illustrate the pernicious effects of alcohol on the local community in Tennant Creek. This serves a practical function – in the introduction she explains that a fictional guise was necessary to help protect the identities of the people who shared their stories with her, given that "Tennant Creek is a small town with a population of only 3,500 people."[11] But conflating stories also enables Wright to create and sustain characters across the length of the entire book, which in turn gives the reader a chance to develop a deeper, more affective relationship with these people than is typical in the more cursory reportage of a government document. By amalgamating these stories and interpreting them through a fictional lens, she resists the dehumanizing quality of an ethnographic or bureaucratic perspective that quantifies, generalizes, and reduces individuals to mere statistics.

If Wright finds she must resort to a fictional conceit in order to compensate for the limitations of the nonfictional form in *Grog War*, then her debut novel, *Plains of Promise*, pushes with equal force against the constraints imposed by the realist novel. Of all Wright's works, *Plains* gestures most overtly to the genre of life writing and to the expectations concerning the sort of narrative a woman of Wright's generation and background is supposed to tell. It relates an intergenerational story centered around women and the long-term effects caused by state policies that removed children from their families, now referred to as the Stolen Generations. However, unlike conventional examples of memoir or life writing, which must restrict themselves to the stories that an individual can *remember*, Wright uses the fictional license of the novel to explore aspects of life that characters can never know. *Plains* does not so much tell the story *of* Ivy Koopundi, her daughter Mary, and her granddaughter Jessie, as it does the story *around* these individuals. The fictional scope to fill in the blank spaces of personal history takes on particular importance in the Aboriginal context, where government policies deliberately sought to break kinship ties and fracture the interpersonal lines of oral transmission. Wright takes advantage of the possibilities offered by an omniscient narrator to show how the lives of these three women are shaped by other people's decisions and mysterious events regarding Aboriginal law and country that they, as individuals, will forever remain ignorant of.

The ideological expectations bound up in the literary realist mode become starkly apparent when Wright attempts to depict a world that is both modern and steeped in Aboriginal beliefs. *Plains* maintains a realist veneer for the most part, but certain characters are presented as being more attuned to ancestral culture and consequently able to perceive the world differently. Old Dorrie, for instance, is able to communicate with the spirit world and also to understand messages encoded in the winds.[12] Other characters gain access to this alternate, spiritual world when they enter into states of mental impairment. When the Aboriginal youth, Elliot, travels cross-country to make contact with Ivy's original people and collapses near death in the desert, or when the elderly Ivy Koopundi finds herself in the twilight between wakefulness or sleeping, the natural world is revealed to have agency in a manner that is typically discounted by Western realism. Nevertheless, the measure of uncertainty that hovers over these encounters means that a cultural hierarchy between the "real" events that occur in a Westernized modernity and the fantastical or "magical" realm of Aboriginal folklore is maintained.

These skirmishes with an alternate Aboriginal reality are transformed in *Carpentaria* into a fully fledged Aboriginal *Weltanschauung*, where Wright makes a distinct break with all expectations of the realist novel and adapts the English language to serve her own needs fully. Aboriginal beliefs are no longer relegated to the uncertain domain of the semi-conscious but asserted front and center as fact. *Carpentaria* declares the primacy of this ancient belief system by opening with the creation story of the Rainbow Serpent.[13] From this starting point, Wright ensures that an Aboriginal vision permeates every single aspect of the novel: its use of colloquial language; the rhythms of its sentences, which hark back to the songlike nature of oral storytelling; its presentation of story not as belonging to any one person but as a collective endeavor; and its unusual structure, which makes horizontal movements that cut across linear time. It is a novel that makes few concessions to the white reader and insists, instead, that the reader gives themselves over to the radically different perspective offered by an Aboriginal worldview.

In *Decolonising the Mind* (1986), the Kenyan writer Ngũgĩ wa Thiong'o asked how African countries could develop a national literature when working in the language of the colonizers.[14] Ngũgĩ's solution was to reject the colonial language of English in favor of his mother tongue, Gikuyu. Wright, however, finds herself in a different situation since Australia's colonial history, with its policies directed at eradicating Indigenous languages in Australia, has effectively made English her mother tongue. Moreover, the loss of native languages has been used, in the past, to attack Aboriginal peoples for having lost their culture. With *Carpentaria,* Wright effectively claims both the English language and the novel as her own, daring anyone to suggest that either of these would constitute an inauthentic representation of her Aboriginality.

Overturning the premise that the novel is a destination for oral storytelling, Wright suggests that whilst culture is deeply encoded into language it is not necessarily fixed into *writing*. In 2014, she declared: "English is my language because of the history and what I try to do, and I did that in *Carpentaria* in particular, is to write in the way we tell stories and in the voice of our own people and our own way of speaking."[15] By insisting that we recognize oral storytelling as another literary form, Wright effects an important perspectival shift, one that no longer understands the novel as a Western, colonial imposition but rather as a possible continuation of an existing Aboriginal literary tradition. In this tradition, distinct from the Western one, readers are no longer treated as passive recipients of the text but as active listeners, and the positionality of both the author and the reader becomes an important part of the cultural exchange effected by her works. Wright subsequently presents a vision for Australia that centers and acknowledges Aboriginal culture instead of eliding it, and one that also contains an invitation for non-Aboriginal readers to participate. Unlike the linear temporality constructed by Western modernity, Wright's Aboriginal-inflected modernity is not one that relies on exclusion or supersession, but is inherently flexible, expansive, and sustainable.

Silent Intersections of an Apocalyptic Past

Arrernte and Kalkadoon man Charles Perkins, a renowned activist, summed up the immediate impact that English settlement had on Aboriginal peoples by saying: "The apocalypse had begun."[16] This is a sentiment echoed throughout Wright's work, from her declaration on the opening page of *Carpentaria* that "Armageddon begins here" to the postapocalyptic world depicted in her third novel, *The Swan Book* (2013).[17] Settler colonialism aimed to destroy the traditional way of Aboriginal life: Cultural erasure was the key objective for policies of assimilation that took people off their land, separated families, and banned Aboriginal languages from being spoken on missions and in schools. As an oral-based culture, Aboriginality was understood to be particularly vulnerable to these forms of linguistic erasure. By targeting language, white settlers could make their declaration of Australia as *terra nullius* a self-fulfilling prophecy, with the muting of Aboriginal people becoming proof that they did not exist. Against this historical backdrop, literature therefore becomes an important means of counteracting imposed silences and asserting the continuation of Aboriginal culture.

Throughout her oeuvre, Wright emphasizes the strength and tenacity of Aboriginal people who have survived against the odds. She takes care to distinguish between the act of being rendered speechless, frequently by traumatic events, and that of actually being silenced, as in stifled, suppressed, defeated, and extinguished. Characters in her novels may endure such acts of trauma as to leave them speechless, but the recuperative dimension of literature enables Wright to show us that they have not been silenced. This is the case for both Ivy Koopundi in *Plains of Promise* and Oblivia in *The Swan Book*, who suffer violent acts of sexual abuse as young girls. Ivy, raised on a mission, undergoes protracted maltreatment. Preyed on by the mission's reverend, when she falls pregnant he quickly marries her off to an Aboriginal youth; a marriage that will be defined by further violations and mutual hate. At fourteen years of age, she endures a difficult pregnancy only to have her baby removed before she is allowed to hold it.[18] Driven mad by a lifetime of social ostracization, mistreatment, and neglect, Ivy is sent, as an adult, to a psychiatric hospital. Oblivia similarly retreats inwards, becoming mute after she is gang-raped by local boys and left for dead. Though she survives this ordeal, she is transformed into a living mark of shame on the community, her presence an uncomfortable reminder of noxious elements that most people would prefer to forget. Oblivia's speechlessness denotes her symbolic erasure, where even her own parents find it easier to accept her disappearance than to deal with the aftermath of her rape. It is left to Aunty Bella Donna of the Champions, a European climate change refugee who has settled in the area, to eventually rescue Oblivia and give her sanctuary.

These girls are assaulted twice over: first at the hands of men, secondly by the victim-blaming of society. Their inability to speak signals their ejection from normal society, yet their lives are not necessarily diminished by shying away from human contact. Although the voices of Ivy and Oblivia may not be heard in the human world, this does not hold true in the spirit world. Upon her release from the psychiatric hospital, Ivy is visited by a talking dog who she believes to be her host's deceased husband. The quasi-realist mode of *Plains* makes it difficult to tell whether these visitations are real or merely hallucinations, but by dispensing completely with realist conventions in *The Swan Book*, Wright is able to present a lively spirit world that has equal standing as a part of the "real world."

Oblivia hardly interacts with living people but is engaged in constant dialogue with the Harbour Master, an elder who is "an Aboriginal man with an Asian heritage," and his monkey, Rigoletto.[19] The Harbour Master is a frequent visitor when Oblivia lives with Bella Donna, and appears to be a member of the community. It is only when Bella Donna dies and Oblivia is taken by her betrothed, Warren Finch, to live in the city, that he is revealed to have a more indeterminate, spectral status. As Warren Finch and his henchmen, the genies, drive her away from her original country, Oblivia dozes in the car. She dreams about the Harbour Master and he crosses the boundary between dream and reality, entering the car itself, "where he squashes himself on top of the two men and the girl."[20] He returns again when Oblivia is set up in a city apartment on her own, with his monkey in tow. Once we take into consideration the swans that Oblivia rescues and nurses in the apartment, her supposedly solitary existence is in fact very busy and full of distractions provided by these nonhuman companions.

Wright's work challenges long-held beliefs that the novel, as a modern art form, must invariably reflect the isolating experience of the individual in an anthropocentric modernity. Even though her characters turn inward, away from other people, her novels avoid the traps of solipsism that can often accompany what literary theorist Guido Mazzoni has termed "subjective realism."[21] It is significant that, in the aftermath of trauma, both Ivy and Oblivia find refuge in nature. Ivy digs a hole under a eucalyptus tree where her mother had died and it becomes a substitute for her mother's arms: "In time the hole was big enough for her to sit inside it, a cool place to escape the heat. She used to lie in it speaking to the sky."[22] In *The Swan Book*, Oblivia hides herself in the bowels of a eucalyptus tree after her attack and stays there for years, "a decade of being missing," until she is discovered by Bella Donna.[23] When Oblivia emerges, she no longer has any memories of the attack but is, instead, indelibly marked by her sensory memories of living inside the tree. The sensation she has of being pushed into the hole of the sacred tree signifies both her helplessness as a rape victim, as well as the protective hand of the ancestors who guide her to this tree, specifically, the one that is "like all the holiest places in the world rolled into one for us."[24] Ivy and Oblivia may have been taken from and denied the protection of their mothers, but nature reveals herself as an overarching nurturing spirit that steps in to fill the gap.

Individuals are able to draw inner strength from this deep connection with the land because it means that they are never alone. Wright's novels proffer a deeply ecological perspective, one capable of recognizing that the individual exists in relation to the land, animals, and other spiritual creatures in the world. Nonhuman elements are no longer viewed as resources for potential exploitation but presented as equally individualized life-forms or, in the case of weather systems, life forces. It is when characters have their connection with the land severed that they are in danger of losing themselves, alienated and cast adrift in modernity.

This is evident when we reflect on the sad fate of Angel Day in *Carpentaria*, who is in many ways the opposite of Ivy and Oblivia. A woman, not a girl, Angel is not cowed or intimidated by anyone, least of all the men who try to control her. In the Pricklebush, Angel Day is vibrant and forceful, but once she is spirited away to the city, she becomes much diminished in stature. In the city, she is wraithlike: "Every day, Angel Day sneaks away, disappearing through the morning mist like a ghost, leaving very early before the others remove themselves from the tangle of clothes they had crawled into like rats."[25] It is no coincidence that Oblivia's salvation in *The Swan Book* comes through the swans who pursue her and swarm the skies outside her apartment. Her desire to help them overrides her fear of venturing outside, and eventually, when she launches the swans off on their migratory flight home, they provide a beacon from the skies that guides her own journey back. Oblivia's instinct to survive derives from her conviction that she belongs on her country. As Wright has said elsewhere: "Oblivia's mind retains a replicated template of country."[26] Oblivia belongs to the land itself. Her community is that of the life-forms that attach to the land, of which people are but a small part.

A Novel for All Times

The folkloric aspects of Wright's work have led to her frequent identification as a magical realist author, a classification that has likely been encouraged by Wright's own forthrightness about the influence that authors such as Carlos Fuentes, Gabriel Garcia Marquez, Milan Kundera, and Édouard Glissant have had on her work. However, as Alison Ravenscroft has cautioned, the very designation of a work as magical realist can serve to reinforce a binary "that associates indigeneity with magic, irrationality, delusion and dream, and whiteness with realism, reality and rationality, and with consciousness, a wakeful state – despite these critics aiming at something else."[27] It is important to recognize that Wright's work is not simply an Aboriginal variation on magical realist techniques. Her incorporation of orality into the novel forces a reassessment of the form's capacity for a cross-medial translation between oral and written modes, pointing towards possible directions that novels might take in the future.

In 1936, Walter Benjamin mourned the loss of the epic, writing that "[t]he art of storytelling is reaching its end because the epic side of truth, wisdom, is dying out."[28] Benjamin saw the novel as an inherently isolating form whose temporospatial separation of the reader and writer underscored the modern individual's detachment from a wider community. For Benjamin, the epic was a genre whose techniques could be imitated by the novel to some extent but whose significance the novel could never hope to replicate, as Western culture retains only vestigial memories of the interpersonal relationship that once existed between storyteller and listener. Coming as Wright does from a culture that regards oral storytelling as very much an ongoing practice rather than a lost art, her novels understandably challenge these assumptions and reveal the heretofore underappreciated capacity of the novel to accommodate non-Western ontological perspectives.

In fact, Wright uses an oral premise to restore a situatedness to the text, demanding a form of reading that constantly refocuses attention on the positionality of both writer and reader. These qualities have led to her work sometimes being identified as metafictive or postmodern. Yet Wright's deployment of these techniques is intended to do more than simply draw attention to the constructed nature of the text.[29] They are calculated instead to rework effectively the temporal assumptions of the Western novel and provide us with an instructive depiction of Aboriginal ontology. Not content solely to create literary artifacts that mimetically portray an Aboriginal world, Wright also aspires to educate readers so that they have the means to understand such a world. To do so, she must overcome the inherently linear developmental perspective that takes it for granted that orality progresses towards writing (and therefore literature), an assumption that informs Jack Goody's assertion that fictional narratives only arise with the onset of literacy or Walter Ong's suggestion that print technology introduces a sense of finality to the text.[30] As I have shown, Wright contests the manner in which Western culture privileges the category of nonfiction as being a more truthful depiction of "reality." Furthermore, the text for Wright is not a final, authorial document but rather a solicitation of the reader, the starting point for future conversations.

The challenge that Wright's novels present to Western readers becomes especially clear in *The Swan Book* when Oblivia, holed up in The People's Palace, Warren Finch's city apartment, discovers that she is on television. It is a dissonant moment when we are told:

> "Oblivia could not understand how she kept seeing glimpses of herself on the television. The monkey had noticed her first [...] The girl was changed almost beyond recognition, as though Marlene Dietrich's spirit had jumped out of the television and into the girl and then appeared in a news flash where she was standing right beside of all the people on Earth for goodness sake – Warren Finch."[31]

The Oblivia on television is far removed from the girl who rescues swans and moves easily through the streets, unremarked upon. This other, alternative Oblivia, is at ease in public life, traveling the world as Australia's First Lady.

Critical attempts to reconcile this textual schism are revealing in the way they ameliorate its anomalous nature by reincorporating it into a certain familiar logic. Maria Takolander, for instance, describes Oblivia's experiences in the city as taking place in a "supernatural realm" and says that the novel "becomes increasingly hallucinatory after Oblivia's removal from the swamp as the promised wife of Warren Finch."[32] She interprets Oblivia as being "detached from reality and rendered mute."[33] If Takolander chooses to interpret this interlude as a sign of Oblivia's departure from reality, then Brigid Rooney takes the opposite approach and places the locus of reality firmly with Oblivia in The People's Palace. Rooney concludes that the Oblivia on television is an imposter, stating that: "President Warren meanwhile goes on a televised circuit of the nation with fake wife in tow, a duplicate of Oblivia."[34] Whilst both these interpretations are valid, I bring them together here to highlight how realist modes are so deeply embedded in the Western perspective that it is near-impossible to countenance the prospect that both these things might happen at once: that Oblivia experiences life with the Harbour Master and Rigoletto in her apartment, saving swans, and is also, simultaneously, traveling as Warren Finch's constant companion and trophy wife.

Significantly, Wright's narrative does not completely disavow the televised Oblivia. The novel instead states that: "She did not know how it happened, but somehow, a part of her life was being lived elsewhere, with her husband. She came and went into a different life which Warren Finch returned through the television screen."[35] The verity and co-existence of these two concurrent time periods is emphasized by the time pressure Oblivia is under when she leaves the apartment: "Any idea of how to return had not dawned on her yet, although she was keen to return as quickly as possible in case she had to be transformed into Warren Finch's television wife again – because she was forced to go everywhere with him."[36] That she needs to be physically present in the living room, watching herself on television, suggests that the Oblivia focalized by the narrative also has an enduring connection with the image on the screen.

The text's purposeful ambiguity denies the reader any certainty as to which narrative is "real" and which is "imaginary." Wright challenges Western linearity on the deepest structural level here by asserting that time is never resolved. We are asked, instead, to contemplate an Aboriginal concept of "all times." This temporal perspective is fundamental to Aboriginal ontology. Wiradjuri scholar Jeanine Leane reminds us of this in her introduction to *Guwayu – For All Times* (2020), when she writes that "In all First Nations languages, there is a word for all times."[37] The political valency of "all times" is clear – being able to perceive a connection between all times is the first step to being able to recognize a connection between all people and all things. It is an unresolved temporality that restores to the novel the epic's sense of storytelling being at once personal and something far greater than the individual's experience. The philologist Christos Tsagalis describes this as the "oral palimpsest," a deliberate oxymoron that captures the complex intertextual framework that is initiated by orality.[38]

Elsewhere, Jeanine Leane has described Wright's work as "Aboriginal realism" and Wright's success lies in demonstrating how the novel's expansive nature can be utilized to convey completely new cultural perspectives.[39] Even when she is in the city, Oblivia remains attuned to the rhythms and weather patterns of the earth's natural cycles and lives, primarily, in a world populated by ancient spirits and swans. The novel is centered on these aspects of Oblivia's experience and relegates her international travels as the First Lady – what would ordinarily be the focus of a Western novel – to the shadows. Her spectral existence on the television suggests that these events are secondary to the much more significant work that is being done as Oblivia rescues swans and seeks to return to her country.

It is tempting to see Oblivia's splintered selves as the fracturing that occurs after immense trauma and draw analogies to the deeper scars that have been inflicted on Aboriginal culture by a violent history of colonization. With distinct echoes of Oskar in Günter Grass' 1959 novel *Die Blechtrommel* [*The Tin Drum*], Oblivia's growth is arrested. At one point, Aunty Bella Donna of the Champions even tells her: "*Your time stands still.*"[40] Yet the arrested time of Aboriginal culture in Wright's work is not necessarily a blockage in the linear progression of time, but rather a juncture that opens up the many other possibilities that are overlooked or prematurely discounted by a Western perspective. The elliptic qualities that inhere to a concept of *all times* immediately create a more inclusive form of narrative, one that compels the reader to constantly reflect on their own positionality with respect to the shifting geographic and temporal coordinates generated by the novel.

In this configuration of *all times,* we see Wright's true insight into the ways that a return to the principles of orality might heal the rift between humans and the natural world – a rift that Western modernity sees as occurring with the advent of mechanization. After all, in an oral culture the act of storytelling always contains a measure of variation and personalization: To tell a story, a person must make it their own, and each person will tell it in a slightly different way. There is a perspectival flexibility that becomes lost with the reification of the printed text. If Western authors have made the mistake of focusing too much on the transliteration of words themselves – confusing orality with the manner of *how* something is said – Wright returns the emphasis to the intentions behind those acts of speech. Sitting down with someone to tell a story fosters a connection between two individuals. Reading a novel by Wright is not an ethnographic event, but rather an invitation to establish a personal connection with the text and the much broader cultural framework that lies behind it.

Wright's vision of an Aboriginal-inflected modernity dares to suggest that the alienation of the modern individual need not be an inevitable outcome. A sovereign Aboriginal literature does not necessarily exclude non-Aboriginal people from its vision of Australia. Acknowledging *all times* means recognizing the different waves of migration to this country, the possibility of interwoven histories with Indigenous peoples and a communal future. In the past, Wright has said:

> "My personal challenge has always been to develop a literature more suited to the powerful, ancient cultural landscape of this country. It is a journey of imagining our own unique perspective, one that belongs here, and which is the legacy that has been passed down to us through countless generations so that we can know who we are in this place."[41]

Wright speaks specifically about the Aboriginal context, but she could so easily be summing up the function of literature, seen more broadly as an apparatus for establishing interpersonal and intercultural relations across time and space. With this generative approach, the novel no longer signifies a technological break that takes us further away from our folkloric past but is recast, instead, as a literary form that can fortify our connection, as individuals, to the constantly changing world around us. In the most democratic of stances, Wright reminds us acts of listening can be just as important as those of writing.

Notes

1 Philip Mead provides a useful summary of Wright's earlier work as an activist and legal advocate in numerous government departments or Aboriginal agencies. See Philip Mead, "The Injusticeable and the Imaginable," *JASAL: Journal of the Association for the Study of Australian Literature* 16.2 (2016): https://openjournals.library.sydney.edu.au/index.php/JASAL/article/view/11400.

2 Some key examples would be Homi K. Bhabha's analysis of the disjunctive space of modernity in *The Location of Culture*, Simon Gikandi's work on slavery as a constitutive part in the development of modern aesthetics, and the more comprehensive, expanded paradigm of modernity that Laura Doyle captures with her concept of inter-imperiality. See Homi K. Bhabha, *The Location of Culture* (London and New York: Routledge, 2012); Simon Gikandi, *Slavery and the Culture of Taste* (Princeton: Princeton University Press, 2011); Laura Doyle, *Inter-Imperiality: Vying Empires, Gendered Labor, and the Literary Arts of Alliance* (Durham, NC: Duke University Press, 2020).

3 Mikhail Bakhtin, "Epic and Novel," in *The Dialogic Imagination: Four Essays*, ed. Michael Holquist, trans. Caryl Emerson and Michael Holquist (Austin: University of Texas Press, 1981), pp. 3–40 (p. 3).

4 The extent to which Wright's fiction compels a reassessment of the magic[al] realist genre can be seen in Francis Devlin-Glass' discussion of the ways in which Wright "melds satire with a new form of magic realism based in Indigenous knowledge" (p. 392), and Ben Holgate's work on Wright's revivification of magical realism. See Francis Devlin-Glass, "A Politics of the Dreamtime: Destructive and Regenerative Rainbows in Alexis Wright's Carpentaria," *Australian Literary Studies*, 23.4, (2008): pp. 392–407; Ben Holgate, "Unsettling Narratives: Re-evaluating Magical Realism as Postcolonial Discourse Through Wright's Carpentaria and The Swan Book," *Journal of Postcolonial Writing* 51.6 (2015): pp. 634–647.

5 Peter Minter and Anita Heiss pointedly open the *Macquarie PEN Anthology of Aboriginal Literature* (2008) with a letter written in 1796 by Woollarawarre Bennelong to Governor Arthur Phillip. See Bennelong, "Letter to Mr Phillips, Lord Sydney's Steward," in *Macquarie PEN Anthology of Aboriginal Literature*, eds. Anita Heiss and Peter Minter (Montréal: McGill-Queen's University Press, 2008), p. 9.

6 Anne Brewster provides a more comprehensive list of the titles published under the category of Aboriginal women's life writing in her introduction to *Reading Aboriginal Women's Life Stories*. See Anne Brewster, *Reading Aboriginal Women's Life Stories* (Sydney: Sydney University Press, 2015), pp. xxii–xxiii.

7 An instructive reflection on the working dynamics between Aboriginal authors and white editors can be found in Jennifer Jones, *Black Writers, White editors: Episodes of Collaboration and Compromise in Australian Publishing History* (North Melbourne: Australian Scholarly Publishing, 2009).

8 See Mudrooroo Narogin, *Writing from the Fringe: A Study of Modern Aboriginal Literature* (Melbourne: Hyland House, 1990), p. 149. In *Writing from the Fringe*, he says: "In these white productions there is an absence of critical and political comment on the part of the subject, and no analysis of Aboriginal-being-in-Australia – though a deep reading does disclose that existential being structured within the text itself' (p. 151).

9 Aileen Moreton-Robinson writes: "Narogin's critique is spurious because he separates Indigenous women's lives from the Indigenous struggle. He relies on a white patriarchal definition of what it is to be political, thus denying subjectivity as a site of resistance, and he is overly concerned with how the text is written – its form, rather than what is written." See Aileen Moreton-Robinson, *Talkin' Up to The White Woman: Indigenous Women and Feminism* (St Lucia: University of Queensland Press, 2020; 2000), p. 2.

10 Alexis Wright, "What Happens When You Tell Somebody Else's Story?' *Meanjin Quarterly* (2016): https://meanjin.com.au/essays/what-happens-when-you-tell-somebody-elses-story/.

11 Alexis Wright, *Grog War* (Broome, W.A.: Magabala Books, 1997), ix.

12 Alexis Wright, *Plains of Promise* (St. Lucia: University of Queensland Press, 1997), p. 155.

13 Alexis Wright, *Carpentaria* (Sydney: Giramondo, 2006), p. 1.

14 Ngũgĩ wa Thiong'o, *Decolonising the Mind* (London: J. Currey, 1986).

15 Maryam Azam, "Alexis Wright: 'It Was Like Writing a Story to the Ancestors'," the *Guardian*, May 25, 2014: www.theguardian.com/books/australia-culture-blog/2014/may/25/alexis-wright-it-was-like-writing-a-story-to-the-ancestors.

16 Charles Perkins AO, "Aboriginal Australia and Public Administration," *Australia Journal of Public Administration*, 51.2 (1992): pp. 223–233 (p. 223).

17 Wright, *Carpentaria*, p. 1.

18 Wright, *Plains of Promise*, p. 158.

19 Alexis Wright, *The Swan Book* (Sydney : Giramondo, 2013), p. 13.

20 Wright, *The Swan Book*, p. 163.

21 Mazzoni attributes the shift towards a more "subjective realism" to the influence of Jean-Paul Sartre. Guido Mazzoni, *Theory of the Novel*, trans. Zakiya Hanafi (Cambridge, MA: Harvard University Press, 2017), p. 293.

22 Wright, *The Swan Book*, p. 53.

23 Wright, *The Swan Book*, p. 11.

24 Wright, *The Swan Book*, p. 78.

25 Wright, *Carpentaria*, p. 455.

26 Alexis Wright, "The Inward Migration in Apocalyptic Times," *Emergence Magazine*, January 27, 2021: https://emergencemagazine.org/essay/the-inward-migration-in-apocalyptic-times/.

27 Alison Ravenscroft, "Dreaming of Others: Carpentaria and its Critics," *Cultural Studies Review* 16.2 (2010): 194–224 (p. 197).

28 Walter Benjamin, "The Storyteller," in *Illuminations: Essays and reflections*, ed. Hannah Arendt, trans. Harry Zohn (New York: Schocken Books, 2007), p. 87.
29 See, for instance, Arnaud Barras (especially p. 9) and Adeline Johns-Putra. Arnaud Barras, "The Law of Storytelling: The Hermeneutics of Relationality in Alexis Wright's *The Swan Book*," *JASAL: Journal of the Association for the Study of Australian Literature*, 15.3 (2015): https://openjournals.library.sydney .edu.au/index.php/JASAL/article/view/10564/10442; Adeline Johns-Putra, "The Rest Is Silence: Postmodern and Postcolonial Possibilities in Climate Change Fiction," *Studies in the Novel*, 50.1 (Spring 2018), pp. 26–42.
30 Jack Goody, "From Oral to Written: An Anthropological Breakthrough in Storytelling," in *The Novel*, ed. Franco Moretti (Princeton: Princeton University Press, 2006), I, pp. 3–36 (p. 31); Walter J. Ong, *Orality and Literature: The Technologizing of the World* (London: Routledge, 2012), p. 130.
31 Wright, *The Swan Book*, p. 253.
32 Maria Takolander, "Theorising Irony and Trauma in Magical Realism: Junot Díaz's *The Brief Wonderous Life of Oscar Wao* and Alexis Wright's *The Swan Book*," *Ariel: A Review of International English Literature* 47.3 (2016): pp. 95–122 (p. 116).
33 Takolander, "Theorising Irony and Trauma in Magical Realism," p. 117.
34 Brigid Rooney, *Suburban Space, the Novel and Australian Modernity* (London: Anthem Press, 2018), p. 185.
35 Wright, *The Swan Book*, pp. 255–256.
36 Wright, *The Swan Book*, p. 259.
37 Jeanine Leane, "Guwayu – For All Times," *Sydney Review of Books*, August 14, 2020: https://sydneyreviewofbooks.com/essay/leane-guwayu-for-all-times/.
38 Christos C. Tsagalis, *The Oral Palimpsest: Exploring Intertextuality in the Homeric Epics* (Cambridge, MA: Harvard University Press, 2008).
39 Jeanine Leane, "Historyless People," in *Long History, Deep Time: Deepening Histories of Place*, eds. Ann McGrath and Mary Ann Jebb (Canberra: Australian National University Press, 2015), pp. 151–162 (p. 161).
40 Wright, *The Swan Book*, p. 82.
41 Alexis Wright, "The Ancient Library and a Self-Governing Literature," *Sydney Review of Books* June 28, 2019: https://sydneyreviewofbooks.com/essay/the-ancient-library-and-a-self-governing-literature/.

12

JOSEPH STEINBERG

Kim Scott and the Doctoral Novel

I wrote a novel before lunch today
or was it a PhD thesis
I forget.[1]
　　　　　　– Melissa Lucashenko, "Border Protection"

KAYA. *Writing such a word, Bobby Wabalanginy couldn't help but*
smile. Nobody ever done writ that before, he thought. Nobody ever
writ hello or yes that way![2]
　　　　　　– Kim Scott, *That Deadman Dance*

Wet chalk and thin slate. These are the brittle materials that, when paired
with Bobby Wabalanginy's remarkable talent for cross-cultural mimicry,
produce the unprecedented act of phonetic transcription that begins the
acclaimed Noongar writer Kim Scott's historical novel *That Deadman*
Dance (2010). What nobody has ever *written* before is not, of course, the
same as what nobody has ever *said* before: The point of this opening scene
is that, by committing voice to stone, Bobby believes he has become the
first to undertake the monumental task of approximating in letters one
of the more than 250 languages spoken precolonization by First Nations
people in Australia.[3] His literary originality comes about through a process of informed derivation from tradition. What Bobby has written here
marks the advent of a new kind of intercultural literacy, not despite but
because of his writing's conspicuous indebtedness to orality. We need not be
aware of Scott's admiration for Penny van Toorn's *Writing Never Arrives*
Naked (2006), which he read while drafting *That Deadman Dance*, to see
how directly his novel speaks to her claim that "certain traditional orally
grounded Indigenous Australian practices" not only "survived the onset of
literacy" but "may in fact have been secured and reinforced through it."[4]
What reading enables for Scott is the recovery of such practices. In his lyrical essay "I Come from Here" (2011), Scott describes how the archival
labor of "gathering fragments, piecing them together, returning them to

the landscape," of "hunting down our sound" in written records, enables a form of "healing."[5] To which we might add, on the evidence of ground-breaking novels such as *Benang* (1999) and *That Deadman Dance*, that this is a labor that clearly enables Scott's writing. By attending to *That Deadman Dance*'s aesthetic management of these archival labors – which we might more broadly dub the labors of *research* – we can begin to appreciate the novel's originality and representativeness. One of the most striking novelties of our present literary-historical moment is that emerging and established writers alike have found a new patron in the university, where many of them have taken up the opportunity to write a novel in exchange for a research degree. *That Deadman Dance* can and should be understood in relation to this institutional context. It is at once an important milestone in the rise of the doctoral novel and an idiosyncratic reply to the university's reformula-tion of novel-writing as an act of research.

That Deadman Dance might seem an odd choice to illustrate such a claim. As Philip Mead sensibly observes, for a Noongar author such as Scott "'research' is not an invisible and unproblematic practice: it is political, com-munity-based and self-reflexive."[6] Writing itself, as Evelyn Araluen reminds us, "entered Aboriginal life as a vehicle of governmentality and control, and as such will always be marked with these violences."[7] Yet it is precisely this fraught relation to the textual record – as, on the one hand, a bureaucratic technology of assimilation, and on the other, a medium for the reproduc-tion, preservation, and eventually reclamation of oral cultural knowledge by its rightful inheritors – that makes the *impermanence* of Bobby's chosen medium so striking. As if chalk were not perishable enough, he soon aban-dons writing with an implement altogether, instead drawing directly "on the wet slate with his finger."[8] It's a poignant choice, because it means that this extraordinary piece of literary history, his phonetic translation "straight from his mother and father's tongue," *can't* itself be preserved, and thus will never be read by any of Bobby's descendants, for whom his language will become an endangered one.[9] "Nothing of the people he had known, nothing of what they were seeing, thinking" will enter the historical record.[10] His friable medium forms part of the novel's reflection on what Tony Hughes-d'Aeth describes as early contact fiction's "basic postcolonial problem": Even the most revisionist fictions are constrained by the fidelity the genre demands to the longer history of colonization, which means that readers are invariably aware that the fictional "situation does not last."[11] It is unlikely that chalky fingermarks on wet slate will outlast even the rainfall that, by erasing the word "*fine*," Bobby miraculously precipitates.[12] Such a reflexive swerve into the territory of the metaliterary makes it easy to miss the fact that its transience is also what gives Bobby's act of transcription its charge as a historical, and understatedly political, fiction. When written words can so easily escape preservation, who could ever say with absolute certainty that a Noongar of his name *wasn't* the first to attempt such a feat?

There were, after all, many Bobbys. As Scott observes in his family history *Kayang & Me* (2005), co-authored with Wirlomin elder Hazel Brown, "a lot of Noongars on the south coast were given the name [Bobby]" from the 1830s onwards.[13] Neville Green's *Aborigines of the Albany Region, 1821–1898* (1989) is his source for this claim, the many Bobbys it lists often distinguished from each other only by their appended placenames.[14] "Wabalanginy" – translated in *That Deadman Dance* as "all of us playing together" – thus names more than just an ethics of ludic collaboration.[15] It also names this character's nature as a composite performance of moments from numerous real lives, lives in turn structured and guided by inherited stories. This is in pointed contrast to a settler figure like Geordie Chaine, whose dialogue and conduct are at times borrowed more or less verbatim from the writings and doings of his namesake, the Scotsman George Cheyne.[16] Yet Bobby's seminal act of transcription also has more distant antecedents, among them the late-nineteenth-century Minang Noongar author Bessie Flower Cameron, whose letters so inspired Scott that he considered modeling his novel's narration on her voice.[17] There is also a sense in which Bobby's literary labors stand as a corrective to those of Captain Matthew Flinders, the English cartographer who attempted to phoneticize sixteen Noongar words in English.[18] But most of all, Bobby's writing speaks to Scott's sustained engagement with the papers of Gerhardt Laves, a graduate student linguist at the University of Chicago, who became the first person to record Noongar voices in his idiosyncratic version of the International Phonetic Alphabet in 1931.[19] We might say these records, which Scott not only read but workshopped with descendants of Laves' interlocutors, are where Bobby found his voice. Yet this entry in the colonial archive is less something Bobby *writes back to*, in the mode of belatedly resistant intertextuality, than an event he *writes before*.[20] Bobby does on a smaller scale what Laves would later do, but by himself, just under a century prior. It would not be a stretch to see this as an imagining of linguistic sovereignty, in which Bobby defines Noongar's written form on his own terms.

For Bobby is not only a dancer, a storyteller, and a singer. As an imagining of the first Noongar author, he is also a narrative *negation* of Laves; Bobby's writings, were they only extant, would stand as the record of a Noongar voice without the complications of a settler intermediary. Beginning the prologue, Bobby is quite literally the reader's first point of contact: He is both the central character and the author of the novel's first word. In this sense, he takes up the researcher's written authority without forfeiting the so-called informant's knowledge and cultural authenticity. From Laves' point of view as the former, the latter category included Noongar men and women such as Nobbie Brown, George Nelly, Bob Roberts, Moses Waibong, Hughie Williams, and Freddy Windmill/Winmer. Across ten notebooks totaling more than 1,500 pages, plus some 2,500 slips of loose paper, Laves worked with them to document their speech and stories.[21] The memories preserved by this research are internalized by Bobby as a kind of vital organ. He carries "deep inside himself, a story Menak gave him wrapped around the memory of a fiery, pulsing whale heart," a tale reclaimed by Scott from Laves' notebooks and later published separately as *Mamang* (2011).[22] So it is telling that this metaphor also renders these memories markedly transplantable, inheritable as living narrative objects. What their transmissibility reveals is both why Bobby is not bothered by the transience of his chosen medium (why would he think to bind a story behind leather, when he could just wrap it around a memory?) and the subtle analogy between Menak's gift and the novel we hold in our hands. In the ensuing paragraphs, this story will be folded around Bobby's recollection of hearing it told: "Always curious, always brave, you take one step and the whale is underfoot. Two steps more and you are sliding, sliding deep into a dark and breathing cave that resonates with whale song. Beside you beats a blood-filled heart so warm it could be fire."[23]

This reclamation of story is part of *That Deadman Dance*'s contribution to the worthy cause of cultural restoration. But it is also, at the level of craft, an illustration of how this novel's protagonist works as a mechanism for the aesthetic management of a kind of research: that is, for the narrativization of stories reclaimed from Laves' notes and corroborated by the workshopping process. Bobby's approach does differ from that of any conventional researcher on the grounds that it is not retrospective, instead taking place in a proleptic relation to both the novel's narrative and the events he describes, relating "not what had happened but what will."[24] That Bobby "wrote and made it happen," calling forth whales with his words "again and again in seasons to come, starting just here, now," doubles down on the anticipatory relation between his literary endeavors and those of his author.[25] He is not only the prolific creator of much writing, but of writing that itself creates the narrative world he inhabits. Above all, and in a resonantly literal sense, he is therefore a reimagining of the settler researcher as a Noongar creative writer.

Describing Bobby in this way is intentionally anachronistic, but it is a usefully estranging redescription. It allows us to see how Bobby bespeaks the peculiarities of his author's own moment in literary history. *That Deadman Dance* was composed in a specific institutional setting, one that was not available to Australian authors only thirty years ago but has become since the turn of the millennium an increasingly central site of ambitious literary endeavor. Scott's historical novel first took the form of a manuscript titled *A Most Intelajint Kuriositee*, originally submitted as the creative component of his thesis *An Anomalous History and a Noongar Voice: A Literary Investigation of the "Friendly Frontier"* (2009), in order to fulfill the requirements of its author's doctoral degree in creative writing at the University of Western Australia. As the first doctoral novel to win the Miles Franklin Award, *That Deadman Dance* is an object of considerable literary-historical interest. It marks a significant point of intersection between postgraduate creative-writing degrees and the upper echelons of national literary prestige. The award has since gone to two other doctoral novels, Anna Funder's *All That I Am* (2011) and Josephine Wilson's *Extinctions* (2016), an impressive rate of success when one considers the relatively small fraction of published novels that have been the product of a doctorate over the last decade. *That Deadman Dance* is therefore a vital landmark for any account of the doctoral novel's rise in Australia. This is not to imply that Scott was by any means the first Australian novelist to earn a doctorate in creative writing (that distinction is due to Graeme Harper, who did so at the University of Technology Sydney in 1993), nor even the first to do so with what would become a major piece of early contact fiction (an honor owed to Kate Grenville's *The Secret River* [2005], which likewise began life as a doctorate of creative arts at University of Technology Sydney). Nor is it to imply that a comparably suggestive account of the relationship between the discipline of creative writing and the workings of literary prestige could not be unfurled from a book such as Tim Winton's *An Open Swimmer* (1982), the coming-of-age-as-a-dropout novel he wrote under the supervision of Brian Dibble and Graeme Turner at the Western Australian Institute of Technology, which won him the *Australian*/Vogel award for an unpublished manuscript in 1981. Stephen Conte's *The Zookeeper's War* (2007) or Emily Bitto's *The Strays* (2014), doctoral novels which respectively won the inaugural Prime Minister's Literary Award in 2008 and the Stella Prize in 2015, could equally have served as foci for examining the doctoral novel's rise. To tell the story of the institutionalization of the literary novel is to attend to the voices of an extraordinary range of writers who have, at various junctures and with varying degrees of discomfort, counted themselves teachers and students of the discipline known as creative writing.

But I focus on *That Deadman Dance* because it strikingly illustrates how the doctoral degree's reframing of literary writing as an act of research has come to inflect the form of the novels it produces. Scott's fiction has long been a response to its pedagogical contexts: His first novel, the *Künstlerroman True Country* (1993), emerged from his time teaching at a remote government school on Noongar country, as a response to the "disappointment of not finding the country or people [he] came from."[26] Yet *That Deadman Dance* should lay a particular claim to our attention because of the way that Bobby and Scott's writings bookend a long stretch of assimilationist educational history over the course of which, as van Toorn notes, "Aboriginal writing was done under close surveillance in institutions such as schools and mission establishments, where writing was produced to be read by white authorities."[27] *Benang*, which depicts a schoolteacher tying a handkerchief around the mouth of a young Jack Chatalong in order "to accustom him to the absence of his own voice," is a novel acutely aware of the way that schools have historically been places in which instruction in literacy was a way of muting First Nations voices.[28] But *That Deadman Dance* stands as tacit evidence that academic oversight is not necessarily an extension of this dynamic. In the reciprocity of Bobby's education at the hands of Dr. Cross, from whom he learns to write while retaining the right to "put [his words] differently in his own hand," it doesn't take much dialectical ingenuity to discern a trace of the supervisory process his author experienced as a doctoral candidate under the poet-professor Dennis Haskell.[29] In this regard, as in its prologue's imagining of Bobby as a kind of originary creative writer, Scott's historical novel speaks not only to the past, but to the pedagogical relations that are so integral to the literary novel in the age of the university.

The Doctoral Era?

But what exactly do we mean when we talk about literary fiction in the age of the university? Our current literary moment is, in Mark McGurl's influential account, part of *The Program Era* (2009). By the phrase that gives this important monograph its title, McGurl names a period of literary history in which "the university has with the rise and spread of classroom instruction in creative writing [...] become perhaps the most important patron of artistically ambitious literary practice."[30] Though his study's scope is necessarily confined to the US, McGurl's materialist approach to literary history retains much of its descriptive purchase when transposed to an Australian context, albeit with some important caveats.

Program, first off, isn't quite the right word. The Master of Fine Arts (MFA) model, widespread in the US and rightly at the absolute center of McGurl's study, is not the default qualification in Australia, where creative writing BAs, DCAs, and PhDs are far more prevalent than Master of Arts degrees (MAs).[31] *Era* also needs a bit of fine-tuning, as McGurl's dates don't quite correspond While in the US, MFAs proliferated in the postwar decades, it would be more accurate to describe creative writing in Australia as a post-Whitlam phenomenon. Creative writing emerged in Australia over the last quarter of the twentieth century, benefitting immensely from Whitlam's progressive support for tertiary education.[32] With some remarkable exceptions, Australians did not really get with the program during the first few decades of its emergence. One such exception is Christina Stead, who first taught her "Workshop in the Novel" course at New York University in Fall 1943; another is the expatriate poet-critic R. G. Howarth, whose non-credit-bearing "Imaginative Writing Class" at the University of Cape Town was attended from 1957 by a young J. M. Coetzee.[33] By far the most comprehensive account of the discipline's unusual development in Australia is Paul Dawson's *Creative Writing and the New Humanities* (2004), which begins with creative writing's false start in classes at Sydney Teachers' College in the 1940s (taught by no less a luminary than A. D. Hope), before moving through to its flowering over the course of the 1970s and 1980s alongside the rise of literary theory, typically first at colleges of advanced education and institutes of technology and then later at universities.[34] While Macquarie University offered courses in creative writing from as early as 1970, the first sandstone institution to introduce the subject was the University of Melbourne. It did so to the consternation of at least one of its poet-professors: Vincent Buckley categorically refused to teach it, leaving Chris Wallace-Crabbe to deliver classes from 1981.[35] From 1974, the Whitlam government's short-lived abolition of university tuition fees also drew aspiring writers to campus. More experienced authors were recruited by quadrupling funding for the Literature Board of the Australia Council, which at the recommendation of David Malouf proceeded to support a total of 163 writer-in-residencies at tertiary institutions throughout Australia between 1974 and 1988. Among the beneficiaries were such noteworthy names as Thea Astley, Les Murray, and Helen Garner.[36]

Doctoral degrees arrived on campus in 1985, thanks to in no small part to Professor Edward Cowie at the University of Wollongong, in the form of the a doctorate of creative arts (DCA).[37] While, in the UK, Malcolm Bradbury and Angus Wilson's establishment of the first doctoral degree at the University of East Anglia in 1987 was "made possible because of the strong growth of Masters degrees" since they were established there in 1970, in Australia MAs actually came as an afterthought.[38] They were introduced two years after PhDs were when, as the novelist Michael Wilding recalls, he and Dame Leonie put their heads together at the University of Sydney. The University of Technology Sydney "had just announced it would be offering the first Australian graduate course in creative writing next year," so Wilding and Kramer agreed to one up them: "If we put a creative writing component into our pass M.A. for second semester, we could start the first Australian M.A. writing course this year and we could beat them.

'Let's beat them', said Dame Leonie. So we did."[39] Though either outcome in this instance might have been chalked up as a win for the MA, in the long term it is doctoral degrees that have most appealed to Australian writers.

At least to some. Former chair of creative writing Brian Castro, who held the position at the University of Adelaide following the retirement of Thomas Shapcott (appointed Australia's first professor of creative writing in 1997), inveighs in a brilliant jeremiad against what he takes to be the lamentable aesthetic costs of creative writing's institutionalization. The pressure to "write research statements detailing the banalities of our novels' backgrounds, their contribution to research and their significance in the national consciousness" is for him symptomatic of a nationalistic information economy geared toward the "managerialism of content," and it typifies the "betrayal of the intellect by the corporatisation of the institution."[40] Another fiery diatribe, Luke Carman's "Getting Square in a Jerking Circle" (2016), similarly assigns most of "the blame for creating the chasm in our culture from which [...] deluded demi-gods of arts management have arisen" to "the corrupting influence of 'creative writing' courses that serve as cash cows for our beleaguered and fatigued humanities departments," though this claim's ferocity is somewhat mellowed by the fact that Carman himself holds a DCA from Western Sydney University.[41] With equal verve, Tim Winton makes clear his concern with the artistic consequences of such oversight, which he sees in the tumescent presence of "the thesis essay within the novel [...] bulging up, breaking through the surface like a bloating and badly-buried corpse," a return of the narratively repressed that bespeaks a shameless bid for the academic reader's attention.[42]

But though they are by no means unfounded, these reservations should not prevent us from noticing that, for many talented writers today, the pressure to present novel-writing as a kind of research has been at worst a minor irritant and at best in striking accordance with the demands of their chosen form. Michael Mohammed Ahmad, with no less than a decade of training in creative writing under his belt, is firm in his conviction that "a writer needs to engage in creative writing with the same degree of study, investigation and examination that one would need to engage in academic writing, or any other discipline for that matter," an engagement that necessarily "involves *research*."[43] Bundjalung novelist Melissa Lucashenko, who began her DCA at the University of Technology Sydney under the supervision of Debra Adelaide shortly after winning the Miles Franklin Award for her novel *Too Much Lip* (2018), makes a similar claim: "I wanted the 3–4 years of time that the scholarship allows to write intensively. But what I've discovered is an actual joy of researching things I wouldn't have otherwise had the chance to research."[44] Doctoral research's specific generic affordances become apparent once we know her work-in-progress, *Edenglassie*, is a historical novel, a genre in which research starts to look like both an institutional and a compositional necessity. The fruits of careful archival research are similarly on display in Scott's *That Deadman Dance* and Grenville's *The Secret River*. Historical research, more generally conceived, also informs Funder's *All That I Am*, as well as Amanda Frances Johnson's *Eugene's Falls* (2007), Hannah Kent's *Burial Rites* (2013), Christine Piper's *After Darkness* (2014), Rohan Wilson's *To Name Those Lost* (2014), and Ali Alizadeh's *The Last Days of Jeanne D'Arc* (2017), to name just a few examples of conspicuously researched doctoral fictions. Narrating from the beginning of the fifteenth century through to the middle of the twentieth, these novels allow us to see a key factor underpinning Nicholas Birns' claim that historical fiction is "Australia's leading novelistic export."[45] Catalyzed by a set of institutional conditions inadvertently receptive to the production of demonstrably researched historical fiction, this genre also represents the doctorate's primary fictional contribution to the national literary field.

But is the rise of the historical doctoral novel primarily a *national* institutional phenomenon? Or do we need to consider it on a still larger scale? Seen from overseas, the historical novel's symbiotic association with the university might also be understood as a symptom of the genre's change in fortunes within the global economy of literary prestige. As James F. English's important quantitative comparison of bestselling and prize-nominated novels has demonstrated, since around 1980 historical novels have steadily declined in popularity while increasing in prestige, surpassing in the last two decades those set in the present as the most frequent nominees for literary awards. English's sociological account provisionally ties this phenomenon to the Booker Prize's contemporaneous "rise to pre-eminence [...] among the world's fiction prizes," a rise in part sparked by Salman Rushdie's receipt of the prize for *Midnight's Children* (1981).[46] Back within the national frame, we can see how this prize has intersected with the discipline of creative writing by reverse engineering a brief genealogy of recent Australian historical fiction. Scott's dissertation returns to the historian Inga Clendinnen's well-known essay "The History Question" (2006) in a way that establishes *That Deadman Dance*'s continuity with Grenville's Booker-shortlisted *The Secret River*. The published form of Grenville's exegesis, *Searching for the Secret River* (2006), defines her novel's mode of narration as a departure from that of Peter Carey's Booker-winning *True History of the Kelly Gang* (2000), which he wrote while teaching creative writing at an assortment of US colleges.[47] Another line of influence would take us from Grenville back to Thea Astley's *A Kindness Cup* (1974), which she wrote while teaching at Macquarie University, and from there to her close neighbor Thomas Keneally's Booker-shortlisted *The Chant of Jimmie Blacksmith* (1972). Yet another would take us from the doctoral novel that won the Miles Franklin the year after *That Deadman Dance*, Funder's *All That I Am*, to the first Australian novel to win the Booker, Keneally's Holocaust novel *Schindler's Ark* (1982). What this selective lineage suggests is that, although historical novels obviously well predate both the discipline of creative writing and the Booker, the doctoral historical novel's rise to national literary prestige is at some level a permutation of broader generic trends in international prize-giving.

Settler Literacies

I have suggested that the creative writing doctorate's affordances – time to build one's knowledge, access to archives, expert supervisory oversight, and a compulsion to autocritical explication in the form of the exegesis – have all been readily amenable to the production of demonstrably researched historical fiction. For many, Scott included, the doctorate is simultaneously an occasion for the refinement of literary craft. But it has also produced a novel acutely aware that the isolation of detail allows the settler colonial surveyor to manage inhuman scale, and that books remain a way of impressing this landscape into imaginative service:

> We walked to the top of the hill above the village, they said, and saw we were surrounded, one side by ocean, and the other by grey-green bush rolling as far as the eye can see. You might drown in forest, sink and never be seen. Such delicate wildflowers we have seen there, they said, taking comfort in detail that, isolated, might be pressed between the pages of books.[48]

I begin and end this account of the doctoral novel's rise with *That Deadman Dance* not only because of the way it speaks to the affordances of this system of literary production, as a remarkable example of the aesthetic management of research. More than that, Scott's novel allegorizes another aspect of this system: the degree to which institutionalized settler colonial "literacies" continue to set the terms of cultural exchange.[49]

One would be hard pressed to put this point any more candidly than Scott's exegesis does: "the audience for any novel will be predominantly non-Noongar."[50] It is this unavoidable fact of reception that makes Scott wary about the "mere enlistment" of Noongar language, and by extension culture, as a "research tool."[51] What such an enlistment names is a scenario in which the production of historical fiction for a settler audience cannot help but echo the betrayal of reciprocity that precipitates the collapse of frontier relations in *That Deadman Dance*. It names a scenario in which Bobby's coerced signature on a statement at the novel's end, affirming a false history palatable to his settler captors because it omits their lies, murders, thefts, and rapes, comes to resemble Scott's signature on his doctoral dissertation's cover. That is, enlistment bespeaks a symbolic economy in which even the novel's correction of this falsified history functions primarily to provide progressive middle-class settler readers with a narrative affirmation of a truth they likely already believe but largely do not act on – that their existence on the land they occupy is predicated on a history of colonial violence – while making no material difference to the lives of those who count themselves among the Noongar community today. In a far cry from his community-based work of cultural reclamation, Scott's novel highlights how a language used as a research tool risks commodification. Within the late capitalist regime of value that Graham Huggan dubs the system of "postcoloniality," a language used in this way risks becoming but an element within a globalized "system of symbolic, as well as material, exchange in which even the language of resistance may be manipulated and consumed."[52] This is what it means for settler literacies to continue to set the terms of cultural exchange. In the form of bodily *il*literacy on the part of his audience, it's what causes Bobby's concluding performance to fail as a political intervention: Despite his "concession[s] to his audience's sensibility, the ethos of reciprocity his dance enacts is lost on his spectators, and his ambition to "sign a paper with them about how we might live' – a treaty – remains unfulfilled.[53] In this way, Scott's realism lies not only in his depiction of Bobby's situation but also in how he understands and navigates the situation of the contemporary First Nations writer-as-researcher.

Much of *That Deadman Dance* is, in Scott's own words, a depiction of a stretch of early colonial history when Noongar people felt little need to "assert difference, or fit any prescribed notion of identity"; a period when they were "assured of their heritage and who they were, more than able to adopt new cultural forms and forge networks with members of new groups with whom they came into contact, and blind to what subsequent history came to prove so significant: skin-color and other physical markers of race."[54] We can see here another of the affordances of Scott's chosen genre: It allows for the narration of a consciousness with a degree of autonomy *from*, because it largely *precedes*, settler prescriptions of identity. That Bobby "never really had no sense of a single self," that "he never knew himself then as do we, rapidly moving backwards away from one another, falling back into ourselves from that moment when we were together, inseparable in our story and strong," estranges the notion of the individual as a recent arrival before an ancient collective consciousness.[55] Inevitable as this arrival may historically be, and with it the regime that has variously attempted to exterminate, assimilate, and commoditize First Nations cultural difference, novels like Scott's nonetheless return to and reimagine other modes of interpersonal relation. If we want to locate one source of such imaginative returns, a site of relative autonomy from the system of postcoloniality that governs the cultural marketplace, we could do far worse than to begin our search on campus. After all, it was Oodgeroo Noonuccal, who as early as 1975 called on writers to petition the government to set up for Indigenous people "a school for writers," to encourage transnational correspondence between First Nations authors.[56] Almost half a century later, Alexis Wright would echo her sentiment, describing her collective memoir *Tracker* (2018) as "a blueprint for building an independent, Aboriginal-controlled university, one that is tied to land, culture and people."[57] Though Oodgeroo's call remains unheeded and Wright's blueprint unbuilt, *That Deadman Dance* stands as compelling evidence of what even limited forms of institutional autonomy might enable for the novel. Bobby's faith that his settler audience has been "won [...] over with his dance" may at the novel's end seem a false hope, but insofar as Scott's sinuous, recursive historical fiction constitutes an analogous linguistic performance, it intimates that his confidence was not misplaced, just preemptive.[58] Scott's narrative dance should leave us confident that the institutional reformulation of novel-writing as an act of research marks not the novel's decline, but a new set of technical challenges and possibilities to which our finest writers have ably risen, and will doubtless continue to rise.

Notes

1 Melissa Lucashenko, "Border Protection," in *Reading the Landscape: A Celebration of Australian Writing*, ed. by Bernadette Brennan (St Lucia: University of Queensland Press, 2018), pp. 54–55.

2 Kim Scott, *That Deadman Dance* (London: Bloomsbury, 2012), p. 1.

3 See Jakelin Troy, "The First Time I Spoke My Own Language I Broke Down and Wept," the *Guardian*, December 1, 2015: www.theguardian.com/commentisfree/2015/dec/01/the-first-time-i-spoke-in-my-own-language-i-broke-down-and-wept.

4 Penny van Toorn, *Writing Never Arrives Naked: Early Cultures of Aboriginal Writing in Australia* (Canberra: Aboriginal Studies Press, 2006), p. 11.

5 Kim Scott and Eden Robinson, "Voices in Australia's Aboriginal and Canada's First Nations Literatures," *CLCWeb: Comparative Literature and Culture* 13.2 (2011): pp. 1–7 (p. 6).

6 Philip Mead, "Connectivity, Community and the Question of Literary Universality: Reading Kim Scott's Chronotope and John Kinsella's Commedia," in *Republics of Letters: Literary Communities in Australia*, eds. Robert Dixon and Peter Kirkpatrick (Sydney: Sydney University Press, 2012), pp. 137–155 (p. 149).

7 Evelyn Araluen, "Too Little, Too Much," in *Fire Front: First Nations Poetry and Power Today*, ed. Alison Whittaker (St Lucia: University of Queensland Press, 2020), pp. 39–45 (p. 42).

8 Scott, *That Deadman Dance*, p. 4.

9 Scott, *That Deadman Dance*, p. 5.

10 Scott, *That Deadman Dance*, p. 166.

11 Tony Hughes-d'Aeth, "For a Long Time Nothing Happened: Settler Colonialism, Deferred Action and the Scene of Colonization in Kim Scott's *That Deadman Dance*," *The Journal of Commonwealth Literature*, 51.1 (2016): pp. 22–34 (p. 28).

12 Scott, *That Deadman Dance*, p. 4.

13 Kim Scott and Hazel Brown, *Kayang & Me* (Fremantle: Fremantle Press, 2013), p. 93.

14 Neville Green, *Aborigines of the Albany Region, 1821–1898: The Bicentennial Dictionary of Western Australians, Volume VI* (Perth: University of Western Australia Press, 1989).

15 Scott, *That Deadman Dance*, p. 358.

16 Cf. Scott and Brown, *Kayang & Me*, pp. 36–37; Scott, *That Deadman Dance*, p. 368.

17 Kim Scott, "An Anomalous History and a Noongar Voice: A Literary Investigation of the 'Friendly Frontier'"(PhD thesis, University of Western Australia, 2009), p. 55. See also van Toorn, *Writing Never Arrives Naked*, pp. 186–194.

18 Matthew Flinders, *A Voyage to Terra Australia Undertaken for the Purpose of Completing the Discovery of that Vast Country and Prosecuted in the Years 1801, 1802, and 1803 in His Majesty's Ship The Investigator* (London: G. and W. Nicol, 1814), p. 67.

19 For discussion of Scott's involvement in the Wirlomin Noongar Language and Stories Project, see Natalie Quinlivan, "The Wirlomin Project and Kim Scott," in *A Companion to Kim Scott*, ed. Belinda Wheeler (Rochester, NY: Camden House, 2016), pp. 130–145; Lilly Brown, "The Wirlomin Books," in *Kim Scott: Readers, Language, Interpretation*, ed. Philip Morrisey, Ruby Lowe, and Marion Campbell (Perth: University of Western Australia Press, 2019), pp. 45–60.

20 Cf. Bill Ashcroft, Gareth Griffiths, and Helen Tiffin, *The Empire Writes Back: Theory and Practice in Post-Colonial Literatures* (London: Routledge, 2002).

21 Kim Scott, Hannah McGlade, Denise Smith-Ali, and John Henderson, "A Protocol for Laves' 1931 Noongar Field Notes," (2006) pp. 5–6: www.wirlomin.com.au/wp-content/uploads/2020/05/Language-Laves_Protocol.pdf.

22 Scott, *That Deadman Dance*, p. 2.

23 Scott, *That Deadman Dance*, p. 2.

24 Scott, *That Deadman Dance*, p. 166.

25 Scott, *That Deadman Dance*, p. 5.

26 Scott and Brown, *Kayang & Me*, p. 16.

27 Penny van Toorn, "Indigenous Texts and Narratives," in *The Cambridge Companion to Australian Literature*, ed. Elizabeth Webby (Cambridge: Cambridge University Press, 2000), pp. 19–49 (p. 23).

28 Kim Scott, *Benang: From the Heart* (Fremantle: Fremantle Arts Centre Press, 1999), p. 261.

29 Scott, *That Deadman Dance*, p. 163.

30 Mark McGurl, *The Program Era: Postwar Fiction and the Rise of Creative Writing* (Cambridge, MA: Harvard University Press, 2009), p. 22.

31 For further consideration of the MFA model, see Chad Harbach, *MFA vs NYC: The Two Cultures of American Fiction* (New York: Farrar, Straus, and Giroux, 2014) and Loren Glass, ed., *After the Program Era: The Past, Present, and Future of Creative Writing in the University* (Iowa City: Iowa University Press, 2016).

32 See David Carter, "Publishing, Patronage and Cultural Politics: Institutional Changes in the Field of Australian Literature from 1950," in *The Cambridge History of Australian Literature*, ed. Peter Pierce (Cambridge: Cambridge University Press, 2009) pp. 360–390.

33 Christina Stead Papers. MS 4967. National Library of Australia; John Kristoffel Kannemeyer, *J. M. Coetzee: A Life in Writing*, trans. Michiel Heyns (London: Scribe, 2012). Howarth also appears in Coetzee's *Youth* (London: Random House, 2003).

34 Paul Dawson, *Creative Writing and the New Humanities* (London, Routledge, 2004), pp. 121–157.

35 Dawson, *Creative Writing*, p. 154.

36 Thomas Shapcott, *The Literature Board* (St Lucia: University of Queensland Press, 1989), p. 123. For discussion of Garner's writer-in-residencies, see Joseph Steinberg, "Helen Garner's Education," *ALS: Australian Literary Studies* 36.3 (2021): pp. 1–21.

37 Nigel Krauth, "Evolution of the Exegesis: The Radical Trajectory of the Creative Writing Doctorate in Australia," *TEXT* 15.1 (2011): www.textjournal.com.au/april11/krauth.htm.

38 Graeme Harper, "Creative Writing Doctorates," in *The Handbook of Creative Writing*, ed. Steven Earnshaw (Edinburgh: Edinburgh University Press, 2007), pp. 383–390 (p. 385).

39 Michael Wilding, "And Then There Was One," *Australian*, December 19, 2007, p. 22. He is correct with the caveat that, as Dawson notes in *Creative Writing and the New Humanities*, "from 1990, [UTS] was the first to offer a higher degree in Creative Writing by name" (p. 156).

40 Brian Castro, "Blindness and Deafness in Literary Reception," *The Sydney Review of Books,* July 10, 2018: https://sydneyreviewofbooks.com/essay/blindness-and-deafness-in-literary-reception/.

41 Luke Carman, "Getting Square in a Jerking Circle," *Meanjin*, Autumn 2016: https://meanjin.com.au/essays/getting-square-in-a-jerking-circle/.

42 Tim Winton, personal correspondence, February 21, 2020.

43 Michael Mohammed Ahmad, "Bad Writer," *The Sydney Review of Books*, October 4 2016: https://sydneyreviewofbooks.com/essay/bad-writer/.

44 University of Technology Sydney, "Next Up for Miles Franklin Award Winner Melissa Lucashenko...," December 9, 2019: www.uts.edu.au/about/faculty-arts-and-social-sciences/news/next-miles-franklin-winner-melissa-lucashenko...-o.

45 Nicholas Birns, *Contemporary Australian Literature: A World Not Yet Dead* (Sydney: Sydney University Press, 2015), p. 176. For discussion of the recent emergence of mid-century historical fictions, see Nicholas Birns, "The New Historical Novel: Putting Mid-Twentieth-Century Australia into Perspective," *Commonwealth: Essays and Studies* 41.1 (2018): pp. 7–18.

46 James F. English, "Now, Not Now: Counting Time in Contemporary Fiction Studies," *Modern Language Quarterly*, 77.3, 2016, pp. 395–418 (p. 414). See also James F. English, *The Economy of Prestige: Prizes, Awards and the Circulation of Cultural Value* (Cambridge, MA: Harvard University Press, 2005)

47 See Scott, "An Anomalous History," pp. 36–37; Grenville, *Searching for the Secret River*, p. 164.

48 Scott, *That Deadman Dance*, p. 177.
49 For discussion of the racial demographics of the creative writing classroom, see Claire Grossman, Juliana Spahr, and Stephanie Young, "Literature's Vexed Democratisation," *American Literary History*, 33.2, 2021, pp. 298–319; Juliana Spahr and Stephanie Young, "The Program Era and the Mainly White Room," in Glass, ed. *After the Program Era*, pp.137–176.
50 Scott, "An Anomalous History," p. 26.
51 Scott, "An Anomalous History," p. 25.
52 Graham Huggan, *The Postcolonial Exotic: Marketing the Margins* (London: Routledge, 2001), p. 6.
53 Scott, *That Deadman Dance*, pp. 403, 399.
54 Scott, "An Anomalous History," p. 40.
55 Scott, *That Deadman Dance*, p. 164.
56 Oodgeroo Noonuccal, "Aboriginal Literature," *Identity*, 2(3), 1975, pp. 39–40 (p. 39).
57 Alexis Wright, "The Ancient Library and a Self-Governing Literature," *Sydney Review of Books*, June 28, 2019: https://sydneyreviewofbooks.com/essay/the-ancient-library-and-a-self-governing-literature/.
58 Scott, *That Deadman Dance*, p. 403.

PART III

Futures

13

LACHLAN BROWN

The Contemporary Western Sydney Novel

Arrival

In December 2013, Geordie Williamson, the chief literary critic for *The Australian* newspaper, wrote that Luke Carman's debut novel *An Elegant Young Man* arrived as "a special kind of shock."[1] Given the scale of Western Sydney, the sheer number of people who lived there, and given the waves of migration from Europe, Asia, and the Middle East that Sydney's Western Suburbs had accommodated across the postwar period, Williamson noted that "the absence of writing from and about the Western Suburbs is a gap in our national experience."[2] Carman's novel *An Elegant Young Man* (2014), which ranged across Mount Pritchard, Liverpool, and Granville, was joined in 2014 by Michael Mohammed Ahmad's *The Tribe*, largely set in Lakemba. Carman and Ahmad were named among *The Sydney Morning Herald*'s Best Young Australian Novelists in consecutive years, 2014 and 2015, and Carman was shortlisted for the Australian Literature Society Gold Medal. Alongside them, Felicity Castagna had published *The Incredible Here and Now* (2013), an innovative Young Adult novel set in and around Parramatta, which won the Prime Minister's Literary Award for Young Adult Fiction in 2014.

To many at the time, these three books appeared as the vanguard of a hungry and talented literary movement. Indeed, Matt McGuire from Western Sydney University wrote in 2015 that Western Sydney was "the new Australian literary frontier."[3] These works were followed by novels by writers including Peter Polites (*Down The Hume*, 2017; *The Pillars*, 2019), Carly Cappielli (*Listurbia*, 2019), Vivian Pham (*The Coconut Children*, 2020), Rawah Arja (*The F Team*, 2020), and Stuart Everly-Wilson (*Low Expectations*, 2021). What drove the first of these novelists was undoubtedly an instinct to map Western Sydney in a significant literary way, to make a claim for its potency as a site for remarkable and diverse stories, but also as a site inhabited by those capable of generating complex literature. As Michael Mohammed Ahmad declared in the *Guardian* in 2013, "Western

211

Sydney Deserves to be Written About."[4] Bounded by the local government areas of the Hawkesbury in the north, Wollondilly in the south, Canterbury and Bankstown in the east, and Penrith in the west (the Blue Mountains has maintained its own identity, even while technically within the governmental area of "Greater Western Sydney"), Western Sydney had grown into a diverse and multifaceted location since the end of World War II. In her examination of the novel and Australian suburbia, Brigid Rooney describes Greater Western Sydney as:

> [B]oth socio-economically and culturally diverse and geographically expansive, housing around half of Sydney's total population, and ranging from relatively affluent, so-called aspirational classes to working, underclass and welfare-dependent communities. The region's mix of new (often precarious) affluence and entrenched disadvantage has made it electorally volatile and thus politically influential. The rich heterogeneity, and the economic and political significance of Sydney's west, contrasts however with its negative cultural image, its mediatized reputation as a boring, blighted, criminal waste-land.[5]

Rooney alerts us to the complexity and scale of Sydney's west that has long existed, despite the "westie" stereotypes and its reputation for a lack of cultural clout. Indeed, Diane Powell's collection of media articles in her 1993 study *Out West* documents the relentless stigma the Western Suburbs of Sydney had received in the media and in cultural commentary.[6] This continued throughout the 1990s and into the 2000s, even as the Western Suburbs relentlessly grew through new housing tracts and suburbs opening up in the city's west, northwest, and southwest growth corridors. However, with rapid population growth (the Center for Western Sydney estimated that Greater Western Sydney's population had risen to more than 2 million by 2011) came increased recognition, and, as neoliberalism flexed its muscles, an increased market sway.[7] This manifested in political clout. For example, a highly theatrical "People's Forum" was added to the 2013 federal election, taking place at the Rooty Hill RSL, a licensed club operated under the banner of the Returned and Services League of Australia. It also led to increased budgets for the arts in local council areas, where house prices, and hence land rates, were rising.[8]

The Western Suburbs of Sydney continue to be set apart and marked out in various ways. One of the more intriguing examples of this is the demographer Bernard Salt's tongue-in-cheek "Red Rooster Line" that showed the proliferation of the fast-food restaurant in certain locations in 2016.[9] For Salt, the "Red Rooster Line" indicated a large demographic divide splitting the inner west, north shore, and eastern suburbs of Sydney from the west. Salt wrote that the suburbs beyond the line were "a different world orbiting the city like an asteroid belt at a distance of 7km to 50km from the CBD."[10] This continual and recurring impulse to carve the west from the rest is why Felicity Castagna opens *The Incredible Here and Now* with: "Some people say 'West' like it is something wrong, like ice-cream that fell into a gutter. I think West is like my brother's music."[11] Castagna's novel is a delicate series of vignettes told from the lyrical perspective of the teenage narrator Michael. These emerge as lovingly curated snapshots of Parramatta and the rituals of its inhabitants as they drive cars, hang out in the McDonald's parking lot, share charcoal chicken, and walk beside the river. After Michael's brother Dom is killed in a car accident, the novel takes on a haunted yet tender tone as various friends and family members deal with his departure. Castagna's use of brief chapters gives the entire work a sense of restraint, drawing attention to the "here and now" of a particular Western Sydney location. "This whole place," Michael observes in the final chapter, "it's just a bunch of peoples' memories bubbling up from the ground."[12] In this way, the work's title is a claim for a narrative position that navigates the temporal and spatial immediacies on the ground and close to the action. But it also enacts a broader call for a specific type of writing in and from the Western Suburbs.

Precursors

Williamson's "shock" in 2013 at seeing *An Elegant Young Man* appear *sui generis* from Sydney's Western Suburbs is echoed by the publisher's claims on the novel's cover: "For a long time Western Sydney has been the political flashpoint of the nation, but it has been absent from Australian literature."[13] Indeed, it is telling that Western Sydney was largely absent from the wave of novels that are now considered part of the Grunge Lit movement. Andrew McGahan's *Praise* (1992) is set in Brisbane, Christos Tsiolkas' *Loaded* (1995) takes readers through Melbourne. Luke Davies' *Candy* (1997) mainly maps suburbs in Melbourne, though the novel is bookended by Sydney sections that depict the city as "a *harbourside* paradise of cheap heroin and corrupt police."[14] When Sydney appears in more detail, such as in Justine Ettler's 1995 novel *The River Ophelia*, it is the grittiness of inner Sydney locations such as Kings Cross that grabs the spotlight. In fact, through the 1990s heroin trade was being conducted extensively within Cabramatta, a suburb in Western Sydney, one was more likely to see Western Sydney depicted in true crime or other nonfictional ways during that era (such as in sections of John Birmingham's 1999 book *Leviathan: The Unauthorised Biography of Sydney*, which dredged the seediest stories from Sydney's history).[15] Thus, one possible way of accounting for the rise of the Western Sydney novel post-2010, with its grittiness, violence, and overwhelming sense of energy, might be to posit the belated arrival of Grunge Lit to locations where it should have existed in the 1990s.

However, despite this sense of absence, there are earlier Western Sydney literary precursors worth mentioning. For example, Patrick White's *The Tree of Man* (1955) was written after he moved to a property near Castle Hill, which he and his partner Manoly Lascaris named "The Dogwoods." Set in what was to become, for White, a recurring location between city and bush, within an expanding suburban frontier, *The Tree of Man* concerns the lives of Stan and Amy Parker, their family, and their neighbors, within the changing landscape of Sydney. White would go on to write a series of suburban novels and plays set in locations such as the fictionally named "Sarsaparilla" and its neighboring suburb of "Barranugli" (most notably in his 1961 novel *Riders in the Chariot* and his 1962 play *The Season at Sarsaparilla*). Yet Rooney has argued that *The Tree of Man* is important because in it White "reconfigures and modernizes settler Australian social and built space as suburban."[16] Many of White's subsequent suburban novels attend to the distinction between stifling pernicious conformity that suburbia demands and the mysteries of (abject) transcendence that can be found in unlikely locations and extraordinary individuals.

White received the Nobel Prize for Literature in 1973, and three years later, David Ireland (born 1927 in Lakemba) won the Miles Franklin Award with *The Glass Canoe* (1976). Set at the Southern Cross Pub in Northmead in Western Sydney, *The Glass Canoe* is populated by a revolving cast of working-class drinkers with names such as Alky Jack, Aussie Bob, The King, and Dog Man. The novel is narrated by Lance, nicknamed "Meat Man," and opens with children "[d]own the back [...] shooting butterflies."[17] It continues with incessant violence (both accidental and deliberate), sexual brutality, and constant states of inebriation. Its fragmentary, non-plot-driven mode, with short vignettes in the style of the sketches of Henry Lawson, gives the work both a buoyancy and nightmarish insularity.

Peter Carey's *The Tax Inspector* (1989) is set in Franklin, a fictional location on the outskirts of Sydney loosely based on Campbelltown in the south west (which the Airds poet Benjamin Frater once described as "the shit camp / of / a belltown / Campbelltown').[18] Carey's Franklin, with its polluted waterways, poor urban planning, and festering intergenerational dysfunction, paints Sydney's west as ripe for the kinds of alienation that the intersecting worlds of commerce and rapid suburbanization made possible in the 1980s. It is the Catchprice family's Franklin car dealership with its prison-like cyclone fencing that holds many of the characters within its corrupt clutches, despite their desire for escape – pursued variously through religion, country music, or self-help tapes. Indeed, the disturbing nature of the novel's final scenes, set in a torture chamber under the burning car yard, assigns the trauma and monstrosity to suppressed and incestuous family histories in the outer suburb.

Jennifer Maiden's *Play with Knives* (1990) also takes the Western Suburbs (in this case the areas of Mount Druitt and Penrith) as the setting for the novel's scenes of sadistic violence. However, Maiden begins her work with the disclaimer: "*no disparaging representation of real/Western Suburbs venues or services is intended in this story.*"[19] The book concerns Clare Collins, who is released on probation after killing her siblings as a child, and is narrated by her probation officer, George Geoffries, as he traverses locations such as the Roundabout Pub in Mt Druitt, Woodstock Avenue, or the "Great Western Shopping Complex." Maiden overlays the story with various literary intertexts – such as Robert Frost's "Stopping by Woods on a Snowy Evening" (1923) and Thomas Hardy's *Tess of the d'Urbervilles* (1891) – as well as serious psychological discussion. Yet her focus on psychological depths rather than specific places makes this a different type of Western Sydney text: one that seems to hold its locations lightly.

It could be argued that these precursors do have some degree of influence. David Ireland's use of the placed-based vignette prefigures Felicity Castagna's vignettes. The startling violence of *The Glass Canoe* and its manifestations of sexual dysfunction can be seen in the random brawls of Granville that occur in Luke Carman's *An Elegant Young Man*, as well as in Everly-Wilson's depiction of misogyny and payback on Asciff Street, North Auburn, in *Low Expectations*. White's moments of inverted transcendence in the relationship between Waldo and Arthur in *The Solid Mandala* (1966) are faintly echoed when Carman's narrator Luke meets with his bullied brother Adam and they discuss religion in a café in Warwick Farm, "letting the light suggest holiness in the missed scraps of facial hair [Adam had] been unable to shave away that morning."[20] Even Maiden's attempts to bring literary texts to locations like Mt Druitt prefigure Carman's playful and ironic mode of dragging literary texts across Liverpool and its surrounds.

American Influences

For the post-2010 Western Sydney novelists, this list of precursors not only appeared slight, with a great deal of distance between novels. These earlier Australian authors also offered far less than the racial and ethnic diversity that the post-2010 writers required. I would argue that the failure of these precursors to lodge themselves in the literary imaginary as particularly salient *Western Sydney* writers meant that the vanguard of the early 2010s often turned to

American influences instead. For example, Michael Mohammed Ahmad's work consistently returns to a series of influential African American theorists and activists in a quest for examples of collective organization and resistance. Handel Wright, bell hooks (whose idea of "coming to voice" is part of the ethos of the Sweatshop literary collective), and Malcolm X (whose critical definition of "literacy" gifts Sweatshop its subtitle as "Western Sydney Literacy Movement") all figure prominently in Ahmad's writing and interviews. Carman's narrator in *An Elegant Young Man* skims a variety of American writers across the surfaces of the Western Suburbs, from Bob Dylan to Walt Whitman, F. Scott Fitzgerald to Jack Kerouac. None of them seem to take: "I don't care for Fitzgerald all that much," the narrator intones at one point. Yet the pace and bravado of the narrative is obviously influenced by American voices (Sophia Barnes labels this "Beat Poet Kool-Aid" in her review of the book).[21] Peter Polites' *Down The Hume* transplants and modifies the noir style of Raymond Chandler or James M. Cain, and yet, as Dion Kagan points out: "*Down The Hume* is interested in how literary and cinematic noir conventions might adapt to and accommodate intersectional Australian identities in neoliberal times."[22] Vivian Pham's *The Coconut Children* opens with a quote from James Baldwin that frames the protagonist Sonny's search into her family's refugee past. Baldwin's 1964 essay "Why I Stopped Hating Shakespeare" is referenced in the acknowledgment section of *The Coconut Children* and is an inspiration for parts of the novel in which one of the characters, Vince, who has returned from a juvenile prison, must learn to recite Shakespearean monologues.[23]

In attempting to find a voice or style to accommodate various locations in Western Sydney, it is telling that some novelists turned to contemporary American writers such as Junot Díaz, who stylishly and poetically deploy diasporic dialects throughout his oeuvre. Castagna's *The Incredible Here and Now* gives a subtle yet significant nod to Díaz in her description of a pool in Parramatta:

> The sign that runs the pool always has something new on it. As well as "No Diving, No Running, No Eating in the Pool," "No Lebs" has been written in and crossed out, "No Rangas" has been written in and crossed out, "No Asians" with gangsta tattoos has been written in and crossed out, until everyone has decided on the one thing they can all agree on. "No Fat Chicks."[24]

One of Díaz's most read and taught short stories is "Drown" (1996), which contains a similar scene:

> I sit near the sign that runs the pool during the day. No Horseplay, No Running, No Defecating, No Urinating, No Expectorating. At the bottom someone has scrawled in No Whites, No Fat Chiks and someone else has provided the missing c.[25]

In this playfully, intelligent calling across to the Dominican-American writer from what Sneja Gunew might call the "post-multicultural" spaces of Western Sydney, Castagna is drawing her work into the orbit of Díaz with its attention to small acts of rebellion, the racial vectors, the casual misogyny that appears as part of the fabric of diasporic youth culture.[26] In this way, Castagna "cites," in Ken Gelder's transnational sense, those things that Díaz might have stood for at the time (not least of which was a particular style).[27] The multilayered scope of US influences on Western Sydney novels seems to fill the ancestral void that these writers have often brandished as part of their identity. For example, Carman's *An Elegant Young Man* argues on its cover that Western Sydney "has been absent from Australian literature."[28] Tellingly, Carman's main character Luke has a conversation with a poet, Brent, about Australian literature: "We talked about Patrick White for a while, but we had nothing between us to say."[29] There is a clever doubling here, as the author of the phrase, "the Great Australian Emptiness" is himself presented as something like a null set.[30] This deadpan rejection of a literary heritage opens the space for the cultural muscle of US cultural influence (portrayed in the figure of Henry Rollins by Carman), even as novelists such as Polites and Ahmad call out US post-9/11 military interventionism.

Preparing the Field in Western Sydney

Any account that privileges the immaculate conception of the contemporary Western Sydney novel is also complicated by the preparation of the "field" of Western Sydney literature by various institutions and forces. In considering the literary output of Tim Winton, Robert Dixon fruitfully analyses some of the "institutions, personnel, practices and dispositions that work in combination to shape" the "possibilities and outcomes" of what Pierre Bourdieu labels "the field of cultural production."[31] This approach is also helpful when considering Western Sydney writing because, from the late 2000s and through the 2010s, a series of overlapping factors have helped shape the terms of Western Sydney's appearance in the novels mentioned above.

In particular, the convergence of literary institutions and forces is extremely significant. On the one hand, the Writing and Society Research Centre (WSRC) at Western Sydney University in 2006, allowed emerging writers from Western Sydney to inhabit the same circles as more experienced, award-winning authors, including Alexis Wright and Gail Jones. The appointment of the publisher and academic Ivor Indyk as Writing and Society's Gough Whitlam Professor of Writing also came at a time when a series of young writers from Western Sydney were undertaking studies.[32] Indyk's establishment of the Western Sydney Writing Project in the Powerhouse

Youth Theatre in Fairfield in 2007 was one of the first Western Sydney writing workshops with the backing of a tertiary institution and opportunities to read at the Sydney Writers' Festival. The group, which included writers such as Michael Mohammed Ahmad and Tamar Chnorhokian, later relocated to Bankstown Youth Development Services (BYDS), where, in Indyk's words:

> We met regularly in the upstairs common room in the old BYDS offices opposite Bankstown station, with its assortment of sunken couches, office chairs, cushions and beanbags. Mohammed ensured there was felafel, watermelon, pickled vegetables, grapes on the table. No one pulled their punches. Criticism was offered and accepted.[33]

Soon, under Indyk's mentorship and Ahmad's organization, the group had incorporated other writers such as Felicity Castagna, Peter Polites, Fiona Wright, and Luke Carman. Importantly, funding was provided by the Writing and Society Research Group, by the Australia Council, by Arts New South Wales, and by Bankstown council for various projects and publications. At the 2008 and 2009 Sydney Writers' Festivals, events were held, both at Walsh Bay (on Sydney harbor) and in Bankstown Town Hall. These were both highly performative, scripted readings, overlapping with the kinds of community and urban theatre that had traditionally been funded and practiced in the suburbs. Indeed, the Bankstown Poetry Slam rose to national prominence at this time, and became a key plot device in Rawah Arja's *The F Team*. In 2010, the group "performed" an unscripted version of the workshop itself, with a guest appearance by Alexis Wright as an interlocutor in the BYDS rehearsal space.

By 2014 a clutch of institutions – the Writing and Society Research Group, Sydney Writers' Festival, and the Information, Cultural Exchange (ICE) Parramatta – were inviting people to a reading that boldly promised festival goers "a night of storytelling, moving image and provocative discussion about Western Sydney. The centre of Sydney."[34] This sense of confidence and brio, and the attempt to recalibrate the cultural weight of the city itself, was part of a kind of paratextual display of force. It was an example of the ways in which literary scaffolding was drawn up by these writers, even as they wrote and published. In terms of the "field" of Western Sydney literature, the cultural importance and involvement of the Sydney Writers' Festival cannot be underestimated. Since 1998, the Sydney Writers' Festival had clung to the shoreline at Walsh Bay, one of the most expensive real estate locations in the state, with minor, usually library-based concessions made to the vast interior of the city. The continued involvement of Western Sydney artists allowed the definition of "Sydney" in the festival title to be molded to include the west/rest. In other festivals, including the Emerging Writers' Festival (EWF) and the National Young Writers' Festivals (NYWF), literary legislators, to take up Pascale Casanova's term, were already declaring a new order. As Sam Twyford-Moore, director of the Emerging Writers' Festival, noted in an interview in 2014: "Western Sydney is the capital of Australian Literature."[35]

This is not to say that such festivals were not considered problematic by the writers themselves, for places such as Walsh Bay were often conceptualized as cultural centers from which Western Sydney was distanced and estranged. It is interesting, for example, that Carman's *An Elegant Young Man* includes scenes where the protagonist Luke and his friend Brent travel to Walsh Bay in order to listen to Christopher Hitchens speak at a Writers' Festival event. The experience, like much of the novel, is disorienting and deflating, as Hitchens is glimpsed drinking his own hair as it falls into his soup. This double reversal, the irreverence about the "atheist gunslinger" engaging in "accidental autosarcophagy" is set into a critique of the shallowness of the festival experience – something that Carman has elsewhere explored in essays like his 2015 "Diabolus In Festum."[36]

Alongside the writing workshop, which had finished by 2011, the doctorate of creative arts (DCA) program at Western Sydney University provided an institutional context for further honing both the creative components of Western Sydney novels and their theoretical and research backgrounds. Ahmad's *The Lebs* (2018), Castagna's *No More Boats* (2017), and Carman's *An Elegant Young Man* were all completed as part of doctoral studies. These doctoral projects – Carman's "Sons of Shame: Deconstructing White Male Subjectivity in Greater Western Sydney" (2016), Ahmad's "Writing the Arab-Australian Narrative" (2016), and Castagna's "Space, Anxiety and the Politics of Belonging in Suburban Australia" (2015) – all involved an exegetical component. All three were supervised by Indyk. Carly Cappielli's experimental novella *Listurbia* (2019) was the creative component of her 2018 masters of research.

In 2016, the opening up of Packer foundation money, which Sam Twyford-Moore interrogates in *The Lifted Brow*, including $30 million for arts in Western Sydney, also shifted more arts funding west.[37] Though this success led to some tension, the money allowed various projects to grow and change. For example, Sweatshop ("a literacy movement based in Western Sydney" that grew out of BYDS) strengthened and gained further independence under the leadership of Ahmad and Winnie Dunn during this period. In Parramatta, Felicity Castagna mentored various writers, including Rawah Arja, in monthly workshops under the Studio Stories project at Parramatta Artists' Studios (later known as the Finishing School). Running in conjunction with these organizations were groups such as Westwords, with its array of activities, including teacher resource packs that channeled Western Suburbs writing into schools, and the Story Factory, a not-for-profit creative writing center for young people that helped Vivian Pham write *The Coconut Children*, later published by Penguin Random House in 2020.

The field for the contemporary Western Sydney novel was also prepared by the various publications that enfolded, promoted, and published Western Sydney writers. These include journals such as *HEAT*, *The Lifted Brow*, and *Seizure*, which championed new writing, and in particular writing from Sydney's west. Alongside this were the publications edited by Ahmad in his time at Bankstown Youth Development Service and as a director of Sweatshop (for example, *Westside* and *The Big Black Thing*). The *Sydney Review of Books*, which was established in 2013 as an initiative of the Writing and Society Research Group at Western Sydney University, was particularly notable for its long-form yet accessible, non-paywalled criticism, placing the works of writers such as Ahmad, Carman, Castagna, and Polites under the kinds of sustained scrutiny that helped to richly explain them for a wider audience, and commissioning these writers to contribute essays of their own. This criticism was shareable via social media channels, such as Facebook and Twitter, which dominated the internet at the time. The journal's commitment to revisiting and re-examining traditional "canonical" Australian works under various guises also injected these new Western Sydney voices into the broader national literary conversation. Giramondo Publishing, at the time housed in offices at Western Sydney University, was the starting point for many of these writers. In 2021, it published a book of essays on Western Sydney titled *Second City* edited by Luke Carman and Catriona Menzies-Pike, the editor of the *Sydney Review of Books*.

The nexus of shifting relations is, of course, impossible to map exhaustively. Yet what we see in this outline is that the 2013 vanguard of Western Sydney novels arose at precisely the time that a constellation of community organizations, university structures, writers' festivals, publications, and even private donations were providing momentum for writing in the Western suburbs. There was concentration at Western Sydney University at a time when cultural capital was being built, and then dispersal from 2016 as different groups, organizations, and writers came to the fore. This is not to take away from the singularity and extraordinary range of the writing itself, of course. But it is to say that the Western Sydney novel arises just as new points of literary connection are being established, and ways of assigning and building value are shifting, aligning, and realigning across the Australian literary scene.

A Poetic Field Test

One way of tracing the development of this "field" is to consider how various Western Sydney novels handle poetry. For many of the first wave of

Western Sydney writers, poetry becomes a shining example of artistic failure – that or the poetic vocation was depicted as almost impossible in the hardened soil of the Western Suburbs. As Carman wrote in an essay for *Southerly* in 2015, "as everyone knows, poetry is just born to lose."[38] The character of Bani in Ahmad's *The Lebs* has grand ideals that involve poetry ("I will bring poetry to Punchbowl Boys!").[39] But his attempt to wear a beret is met with immediate ridicule and bullying: "Punchbowl Boys is not ready for poetry."[40] Carman's *An Elegant Young Man* is richly informed by poetry, but the poetry often seems ill-suited to the landscapes his characters inhabit. For example, Carman introduces a character named "Brent the Poet" who burns a Peter Altenberg poem into the Werrington hillside in view of the Great Western Highway.[41] When a policeman arrives to investigate the scene, he argues about the interpretation of the poem and castigates Brent: "fuck your ideas about poetry mate. All you need is a job."[42] Brent's resulting "deep despair" causes him to move to Newtown in Sydney's inner west, a bohemian neighborhood where poetry and creativity ostensibly should be valued. But in Carman's novel, the parties, readings, and writers' festival events become just another kind of phony posturing. "People say poetry is dead," intones the narrator at one point, "Only I don't think it's ever been alive in this country."[43] In *The Pillars* (2019), Peter Polites casts his protagonist Pano as a commercially unsuccessful poet, who has published a single book of prose poems with a small press, selling only 300 copies.[44] Pano takes a commission to ghostwrite the life story of an emerging developer, Basil, and this is just one of a series of artistic and moral compromises that he makes in the rapidly changing landscape of Sydney with its fast money, brand names, and real estate deals. Nicholas Birns has written about Australian literature in the wake of the "winners and losers" generated by neoliberalism's reach.[45] So it is interesting that both Carman's and Polites' novels posit the poet as existing outside the world of jobs and the world where a book is a marketable commodity. In theory, this should free the poet artistically, and yet it actually renders them an inert and ineffectual figure, and still just as compromised by the tendrils of neoliberalism in other guises.

By way of contrast, the second wave of contemporary Western Sydney novels depicts poetry in a much more positive light. In Pham's *The Coconut Children*, for example, the romantic hidden center of its wayward heart-throb Vince is a poem he wrote and recited in high school. Because Vince had been accused of plagiarism and had never written again, the poem "I will be" becomes a symbol of his hidden tenderness, his sense of self. In Pham's epilogue, the poem miraculously reappears as the culmination of the lyrically redemptive arc that runs through the book.[46] Like Pham, Arwa sees a positive, empowering role for poetry within the Western Suburbs.

In many ways, Arwa's novel is an attempt to shed light humorously on the functional successes of the very institutions that earlier Western Sydney novelists would have likely diagnosed in scathing terms (e.g. the public education system, organized sport, the media, the family, community arts programs). To this end, Arwa deploys Bankstown's Poetry Slam as part of the account of the rich opportunities that are presented to her young male protagonist, Tariq. Indeed, the successful poetry slam performance by Tariq and his football teammates consists of a positive description of Punchbowl Boys High School.[47] In this way, Arwa's slam depicts the ways that systems can symbiotically cohere to achieve change. Contra Ahmad's *The Lebs*, in Arwa's *The F Team* Punchbowl Boys *is* ready for poetry.

Ironically, it could be argued that this generational change in attitudes to poetry as a symbol of artistic practice can only come about because of the 2013 vanguard and the very programs that they established and in which they continue to be involved, including Sweatshop, Westwords, The Finishing School Collective, and The Writing Zone. Yet the literature of that first generation is itself extremely skeptical of the ways that artistic fields can be constructed, noting their racialized shapes, their pretensions, and their inextricable links with capital. In this manner, therefore, attitudes to poetry become a marker in the sand, indicating some of the ways that the field of literature in Western Sydney has changed and developed.

Conclusion: Times and Places, Lines and Centers

What of the future? Contemporary Western Sydney novelists have demonstrated that various times and locations are ripe for literary excavation. Pham's *The Coconut Children* examines a teenage love story against the background of a Cabramatta in the grip of the heroin trade in 1998. Stuart Everly-Wilson's *Low Expectations* (2021) recuperates an entire suburb, North Auburn, in 1975 from the perspective of a teenage boy with cerebral palsy. Felicity Castagna's *No More Boats* delves into the year 2001 as it unfolds in the family life and consciousness of a post-World War II migrant. The novel charts the course of the Italian migrant Antonio Martone, and his descent into xenophobia in the wake of the Australian political obsession with refugees and boats. One backdrop is the *Tampa* affair, in which a Norwegian captain rescued 433 asylum seekers north of Christmas Island but was denied harbor in Australia due to the government's strict border policing. Castagna works and reworks various notions of flooding and inundation, as the home-builder Antonio increasingly absorbs the metaphor of Australia as a house, while political and familial complexities threaten the stability of his own psychological and social boundaries. Of course, for

Western Sydney novelists, there are many other eras and areas that could be addressed, and voices from backgrounds that have summarily been ignored by the literary establishment. However, viewing such times and spaces as novelistic opportunities may be indicative of a problematic colonial mind-set. Despite the indebtedness of the first generation to writers such as Alexis Wright, Indigenous voices have been largely absent from the Western Sydney novel. Given the fierce advocacy and commitment to decolonization within movements such as Sweatshop, one might expect this to change in the near future.

Yet the emergence of the contemporary Western Sydney novel has also come with a series of overlapping incidents and concerns. Some of these are responses to specific historical events. For example, both Ahmad's *The Lebs* and Carman's *An Elegant Young Man* depict Western Sydney school-yards the day after 9/11.[48] Castagna's *The Incredible Here and Now* sees a character named Joe posing like a gangster for a journalist in what ends up as a front-page article for the *Daily Telegraph* titled "In Lakemba, guns more available than Pizza."[49] In Ahmad's *The Lebs* an arts worker named Jo shows Bani a similar article "with six Lebs in the picture, [where] the pull quote reads, 'Gang says it's easier than buying pizza'."[50] There are even hints at a loose "Western Sydney Novelistic Universe" in which a character such as Bucky, the artistic savior of Bani Adam in Ahmad's *The Lebs* is very similar to Buck, the protagonist of Polites' *Down The Hume*. Cappielli's *Listurbia* takes this to metafictively playful levels, including Polites and Carman in a list of "Twelve New Australian Writers You Need to Know About" (and including an apocryphal novel for Polites titled *Public Spaces: Mind Street Virus*).[51] This sense of the enmeshed and overlaid literary universe of Western Sydney offers its own opportunities for writing across and back to the worlds generated by the first generation of novelists. As Castagna herself notes: "Bad writing has always been about having the last word and leaving others in silence. Good writing opens up a conversation about who we are that may never end."[52]

Another possible future for the Western Sydney novel comes via Aravind Adiga's *Amnesty* (2020). Adiga attended James Ruse Selective Agricultural High School in Sydney's northwest before going to study at Columbia University in New York and the University of Oxford. In the same way that Adiga's 2008 work *The White Tiger* satirizes the Indian caste system in the globalized Asian century, *Amnesty* excoriates the entirety of "small-hearted" Sydney, and by extension, contemporary Australian culture more broadly.[53] Where Bernard Salt popularized "the Red Rooster line," divid-ing the Western Suburbs from the rest of Sydney, Adiga sees an almost infinite array of brutal lines, striating the city at every point, starting at the "seven exits" that lead out of Central Station but radiating outwards to the city's edges and beyond.[54] These are the borders that the country is known for policing so fiercely, which cut across every space and every body, with claims about legal and illegal status. These are also the lines of inequality that separate those with wealth from those without, even as both groups inhabit parallel locations.

Adiga's protagonist Dhananjaya Rajaratnam ("Danny") has escaped torture at the hands of the Sri Lankan police force, arriving in Australia as an international student, but rendered "illegal" after he drops his sham course. Exploited by a Greek convenience store owner, Danny traverses Sydney as a cleaner, and is caught up in the knowledge of a murder after an Indian woman's body is dumped in Toongabbie Creek in Sydney's west. The dilemma of whether to speak out and hence expose his own status as "illegal" is drawn out by Adiga in the fashion of a nineteenth-century novel, with ideas about the law placed alongside personal notions of morality and duty. But twenty-first-century Sydney, with its thrum of grammatically incorrect signs and constant threat of surveillance, proves to be no place for this older form of novelistic moral reflection.

Importantly, within this depiction of Sydney as utterly divided and divisive, the Western Suburbs are themselves implicated in the vast system of inequality that fuels global capitalism. At one point, Danny notes "the amiable glances of the Western Suburbs Indians, smug in their jobs and Toyota Camrys."[55] On another occasion, he recalls being summoned to an odd job in Campbelltown, which involved the removal of Texas cacti from the garden of someone who used to be an illegal immigrant in the US. The Parramatta River is a location for walking with his girlfriend, or with his eccentric gambling-addicted clients. For Danny, suburbs aren't divided into the west and the rest, rather he sees them as *thick bum*, where the working classes lived, ate badly, and cleaned for themselves; and *thin bum*, where the fit and young people ate salads and jogged a lot but almost never cleaned their own homes."[56] At the climax of the novel, Danny feels a loose pavement square under his feet in Parramatta and feels its prophetic shudder: "as it trembled, he felt all of Sydney from Richmond to Manly, with Parramatta in between, tremble with it. 'I'm here', Danny told all of those people. 'And I'm *never* going back'."[57] In this novel, the Western Suburbs are themselves folded back into the city's corruption. Parramatta itself becomes the loose capstone of the entire system. It is a sobering take on Parramatta as the "center" for which earlier Western Sydney writers had made ambitious claims. This is not to say that those claims were naïve. For example, Polites in both *Down The Hume* and *The Pillars* gives his own sense of neoliberal saturation as he casts his eye across the gentrifying and developing Western suburbs with their sheen of contradictions. "Neo Belmore, streets paved in gold. Junkies who wore Air Max could slip on the twenty-four-carat pavement," observes the protagonist Bucky in *Down The Hume*.[58] But Adiga's clear indictment of Sydney indicates the possibility that Western Sydney has already been subsumed into the rigged system of global inequality. Perhaps it has been all along. This means that the rise of the contemporary Western Sydney novel is concomitant with, and maybe even dependent upon, certain modes of neoliberal exploitation that render it an already compromised artistic form.

Notes

1 Geordie Williamson, "Life Flares in Suburban Void," *The Weekend Australian*, December 14–15, 2013, p. 23.
2 Williamson, "Life Flares in Suburban Void," p. 23.
3 Matt McGuire, "The New Australian Literary Frontier: Writing Western Sydney," *The Conversation*, February 17, 2015: https://theconversation.com/the-new-australian-literary-frontier-writing-western-sydney-37284.
4 Michael Mohammed Ahmad, "Western Sydney Deserves to be Written About," the *Guardian*, July 18, 2013: www.theguardian.com/commentisfree/2013/jul/18/western-sydney-representation-community.
5 Brigid Rooney, *Suburban Space, the Novel and Australian Modernity* (London: Anthem Press, 2018), p. 143.
6 Diane Powell, *Out West* (Sydney: Allen & Unwin, 1993).
7 "Western Sydney (LGA)', idcommunity demographic resources: https://profile.id.com.au/cws/populations.
8 Oliver Laughland, "Rooty Hill People's Forum: They Came, They Saw, They're Still Undecided," the *Guardian*, August 28, 2013: www.theguardian.com/world/2013/aug/28/rooty-hill-forum-voters-undecided.
9 Bernard Salt, "Why Did the Chicken Cross the Divide? It Didn't; not While Hipsters Have Avocados to Smash," *The Weekend Australian*, February 25, 2016, p. 28.
10 Salt, "Why Did the Chicken Cross the Divide?," p. 28.
11 Felicity Castagna, *The Incredible Here and Now* (Sydney: Giramondo, 2013), p. 1.
12 Castagna, *The Incredible Here and Now*, pp. 185–186.
13 Luke Carman, *An Elegant Young Man* (Sydney: Giramondo, 2013).
14 Luke Davies, *Candy: A Novel of Love and Addiction* (London: Vintage, 1998), p. 33. Emphasis added.
15 John Birmingham, *Leviathan: The Unauthorised Biography of Sydney* (London: Vintage, 2000). Remarkably, it took until 2020 for Vivian Pham's novelistic depiction of Cabramatta during the 1998 heroin epidemic to be published. See Vivian Pham, *The Coconut Children* (Sydney: Vintage, 2020).
16 Rooney, *Suburban Space, the Novel and Australian Modernity*, p. 18.
17 David Ireland, *The Glass Canoe* (South Melbourne: Macmillan, 1976), p. 1.
18 Benjamin Frater, "Ourizen," *6am in the Universe: Selected Poems by Benjamin Frater* (Wollongong: Grand Parade Poets, 2011), p. 87.

19 Jennifer Maiden, *Play with Knives* (Crows Nest: Allen & Unwin, 1990).

20 Carman, *An Elegant Young Man*, p. 179.

21 Carman, *An Elegant Young Man*, p. 13; Sophia Barnes, "Beat Poet Kool-Aide," *Sydney Review of Books*, March 28, 2014: https://sydneyreviewofbooks.com/review/beat-poet-kool-aid/.

22 Dion Kagan, "Nursing Grievances: Neoliberal Noir in Peter Polites' *Down The Hume*," *Sydney Review of Books*, May 11, 2018: https://sydneyreviewofbooks.com/review/peter-polites-down-the-hume/.

23 Pham, *The Coconut Children*, p. 282.

24 Felicity Castagna, *The Incredible Here and Now* (Atarmon: Giramondo, 2013), pp. 59–60.

25 Junot Díaz, "Drown," in *Drown* (London: Faber & Faber, 2008; 1996), pp. 71–86 (p. 73).

26 Sneja Gunew, *Post-Multicultural Writers as Neo-Cosmopolitan Mediators* (London: Anthem Press, 2017).

27 Ken Gelder, "Proximate Reading: Australian Literature in Transnational Reading Frameworks," *JASAL: Journal of the Association for the Study of Australian Literature* (2010): pp. 1–12 (pp. 5–9).

28 Carman, *An Elegant Young Man*.

29 Carman, *An Elegant Young Man*, p. 121.

30 Patrick White, "The Prodigal Son," in *Macquarie PEN Anthology of Australian Literature*, eds. Kerryn Goldsworthy, Anita Heiss, Nicholas Jose, David McCooey, Peter Minter, Nicole Moore, and Elizabeth Webby (Crows Nest: Allen & Unwin, 2009), p. 558.

31 Robert Dixon, "Tim Winton, Cloudstreet and the Field of Australian Literature," *Westerly* 50 (2005): pp. 240–260 (p. 245).

32 The former Prime Minister Gough Whitlam (1916–2014) is a talismanic figure in Western Sydney for various reasons, including the fact that he initiated the National Sewerage Program that connected tens of thousands of Western Sydney residences to sewer lines between 1973 and 1975. See "Cities and Suburbs," Whitlam Institute: https://www.whitlam.org/whitlam-legacy-cities-and-suburbs.

33 Ivor Indyk, "Writing Western Sydney," in *Retro: Twenty Years of Community Arts in Bankstown*, eds. Michael Mohammed Ahmad, Roslyn Oades, Felicity Castagna, Samantha Hogg, Mariam Chehab, Caitlin Doyle-Markwick, and Filip Stempien, (Bankstown: BYDS, 2013), pp. 28–34 (p. 31).

34 "The Centre of Sydney: Promotional Video," Information and Cultural Exchange, Parramatta, May 12, 2014: www.youtube.com/watch?v=UBjfpOElY_c.

35 Simon Farley, "Digital Writers Festival Co-Director Sam Twyford-Moore," *Everguide*, February 10, 2014: https://web.archive.org/web/20150316110248/http://everguide.com.au/arts-and-culture/literary/interview/digital-writers-festival-director-sam-twyfordmoore.aspx.

36 Carman, *An Elegant Young Man*, p. 125; Luke Carman, "Diabolus in Festum," *Sydney Review of Books*, October 2, 2015: https://sydneyreviewofbooks.com/2-october-2015-diabolus-in-festum/.

37 Sam Twyford-Moore, "Capital Week: 'My Bad: How a Book and an Essay about Bad Writing Made Good on my Social Democratic Ideals'," *The Lifted Brow*, December 8, 2016: www.theliftedbrow.com/liftedbrow/capital-week-my-bad-how-a-book-and-an-essay.

38 Luke Carman, "Revelators, Visionaries, Poets and Fools: The Palimpsest of Sydney's Western Suburbia," *Southerly*, May 7, 2015: https://southerlylitmag .com.au/revelators-visionaries-poets-and-fools-the-palimpsest-of-sydneys-western-suburbia/.

39 Michael Mohammed Ahmad, *The Lebs* (Sydney: Hachette, 2018), p. 23.

40 Ahmad, *The Lebs*, p. 23.

41 Carman, *An Elegant Young Man*, pp. 116ff.

42 Carman, *An Elegant Young Man*, p. 118.

43 Carman, *An Elegant Young Man*, p. 149.

44 Peter Polites, *The Pillars* (Sydney: Hachette, 2019), p. 22.

45 Nicholas Birns, *Contemporary Australian Literature: A World Not Yet Dead* (Sydney: Sydney University Press, 2015), pp. 3–24.

46 Pham, *The Coconut Children*, p. 282.

47 Rawah Arja, *The F Team* (Atarmon: Giramondo, 2020), pp. 323–325.

48 Ahmad, *The Lebs*, pp. 49ff.; Carman, *An Elegant Young Man*, pp. 139ff.

49 Castagna, *The Incredible Here and Now*, pp. 153–154.

50 Ahmad, *The Lebs*, p. 181.

51 Carly Cappielli, *Listurbia* (Sydney: Brio Books, 2019), p. 38.

52 Felicity Castagna, "Hopefully the Future is Dark," Sydney Review of Books, April 17, 2019: https://sydneyreviewofbooks.com/essay/hopefully-the-future-is-dark/.

53 Aravind Adiga, *Amnesty*, (London: Picador, 2020), p. 222.

54 Adiga, *Amnesty*, p. 46.

55 Adiga, *Amnesty*, p. 49.

56 Adiga, *Amnesty*, p. 11.

57 Adiga, *Amnesty*, p. 251.

58 Peter Polites, *Down The Hume* (Sydney: Hachette, 2017), p. 136.

14

DECLAN FRY

First Nations Transnationalism

In a continent where the issue of nationhood and First Nations sovereignty remains unresolved – coexistent? mutually exclusive? one or the other simply nonexistent? – it feels both radical and impertinent to ask about the connections between First Nations in Australia and overseas, as well as how First Nations writings have traveled globally. The nation-state framework tends to lead to familiar dichotomies of Black/white, or occasionally Black/White/Asian, in Australia, and in such a way that "Black" and "Asian" become minor or additional parts of an Anglo-Celtic/European survey. Ouyang Yu, in his poem "Fuck You, Australia," writes one of the more succinct couplets directed to this experience: "you thought I had wanted to learn your english that called me nimes / that fucked whenever you could anybody especially us."[1]

Nonetheless, a sense of attention to the local within the global, embodied in perhaps the most meaningful slogan of the twenty-first century – think global, act local – has been one of the guiding impetuses for First Nations writers seeking to cultivate or simply become part of a global network of literatures. In describing the process of writing her celebrated 2006 novel *Carpentaria*, Alexis Wright invokes the presence of a number of writers around the world, even if none happen to be First Nations.[2] Her invocation speaks, however, to the regionality of international influence. Mexican author Carlos Fuentes is referenced several times by Wright as a touchstone for how she wrote her story of the Gulf community and their lives on Waanyi country. Regional specificity here births an act of linguistic and cultural preservation, with Wright trying to channel an authentic voice that Capable of maintaining fidelity to the way people in her community spoke, respecting the integrity both of the background she wanted to write into fiction and the integrity of those fictions that informed it, and all of the global communities and backgrounds that they form part of in turn.

This has become a common narrative of the new century. Countries have had to deal with the condition of postcoloniality or ongoing coloniality in considering how land rights, linguistic hegemony and sovereignty, and cultural independence can occur both after and during the complex process of invasion/discovery, appropriation, and the denial of Indigenous rights that have particularities unique to the Australian context, as well as aspects shared with other countries across the globe.[3] This new transnationalism is also spurred by an impatience with national narratives that depend on a view of the globe that was racist and ecocidal, and maintained through violence and exclusion. That this impatience is occurring at the same time as colonization continues in the form of globalization's socioeconomic imperatives and evolving forms of state power stands as both a cruel joke and, moreover, proof of the need for ongoing radical action to match our actions to our awareness, at the risk of having the short-sightedness of history repeat and render our own present as equally fraught and historically contentious. Attention to the specific local creates avenues for connection between First Nations, not least because part of the political impulse underlying First Nations writing is a questioning of the nation-state and an attentiveness to the specificity and diversity of the many First Nations communities who predate the nation-state and who have continued despite, or in conjunction with, its overlay.

It is also necessary to state at the outset that part of examining the connections between First Nations in Australia and elsewhere requires attention to locations disavowed by White supremacy. Asia is a pertinent example here. It is a region that has often featured in Australia's racial imaginary and received renewed political and academic attention during the 1990s under Paul Keating's Labor government, but which has mostly been viewed through a lens in which its nation-states, and their relative importance, are assessed on the basis of cultural and economic proximity to white Australia. The result tends to forego the question of how First Nations live in both the Asian region and in the consciousness of migrants from the region. In some cases, this is embodied in the identity of the writer themselves. Eugenia Flynn, for example, has spoken of her identity as an Aboriginal (Larrakia and Tiwi), Chinese Malaysian and Muslim woman.[4] Chinese-Australian journalist Monica Tan, in *Stranger Country* (2019), has reflected on her own lack of awareness of First Nations in Australia and the long history of First Nations and Asian interaction on the continent.[5] The value of this recognition lies in how it would help undo the Black/white reference point, reminding us that there is also a consideration of relationships between First Nations and Asia available, as well as First Nations in Asia. Paul Giles' masterful survey of the literary relationships between America and Australasia, for example, relates all of its literary references to Indigenous writing by way of white and Black American authors.[6] Admittedly, this is because written collaboration and intertextual reference between First Nations in Australia and First Nations outside of Australia is relatively recent (even if it were not, the dynamic of this relationship in terms of awareness of the "transnational" could only have occurred in recent decades, given the terms of reference and their foundation in a postwar global order). The Black American poet Yusef Komunyakaa is interesting in this regard, as a non-First Nations writer from overseas who, nonetheless, in his poetry links First Nations, in what he calls a "deep and complex relationship," between Native Americans and African Americans.[7] In his 2000 book *Blue Notes*, Komunyakaa describes encountering an Aboriginal singer performing Leadbelly in Sydney's Kings Cross, of which he remarks, viewing it as an example of "complexities and contradictions": "I think he could interpret the feelings."[8]

It also ties into the anxiety of history and canon-building in a country where all modes of communication exist vis-à-vis Indigenous writings, whether transliterated, written on the body, on sand, on rocks or bark or other materials, or written in English or other languages. Hence, as Hodge and Mishra argue:

> Aboriginal writers must use (white) literary genres as a political weapon with which to challenge white hegemony. They must redefine genres, explode discourses, delegitimate standard English, subvert expectations, challenge assumptions while maintaining their rage and their centrality in an Australia which, after all, ultimately and preeminently belongs to them.[9]

When the Latin alphabet was taken on by First Nations post-invasion, its accoutrements – signification, inscription, and speech – were "not what they were made to be by Europeans but what they have become" for First Nations.[10] The institutionalization of this language led to what Fogarty poetically described as "caused us to be collaborator."[11] This resonant phrase and its complexities suggest multiple readings, one of which might be, as Penny van Toorn writes, how "[w]ith regard to writing, colonial governance was thus not only repressive, it was also malignantly productive. It required Aboriginal people to produce written texts and to exercise individual agency."[12]

The centrality of strategic translation is also one that Kim Scott talks about in relation to sovereignty. Although "sovereignty" is not a Noongar concept, Scott writes that:

> [S]overeignty is a translation – it's a metaphor and it's strategic. It's not a Noongar word. Noongars talk about *birt* or *biirt* or *bidi* in other dialects. It becomes *birdiya*. *Birdiya* comes from the root word, *birt*, which means "sinew," "path," "energy," the "life force" [...]. Birdiya, is one who's mastered that or, at least, understands it.[13]

It is thus an open question why, or indeed whether, First Nations should be seen as self-contained entities quarantined within nation-states and connecting across national borders, rather than, say, as sovereign entities whose encounter with Europeans was one of many, and not one of First Nations vis-à-vis Europe but of Europe vis-à-vis them.[14] In a continent of so many stories and languages, this positioning places First Nations storytelling as a sovereign practice that it was then up to Europeans – as it is today – to understand and work with. In other words, the European encounter with First Nations produced a literature that crossed new borders, perhaps especially for Europeans, albeit not in a way that has been widely understood by their descendants and will require time to continue being worked out. It is this lens that seems closer to the experience of invasion on January 18, 1788, when the arrival of the First Fleet in Botany Bay, who were illiterate in the language of the community they met, attempted to describe – and to transcribe – what they heard.[15] The inability to understand and come to terms with this encounter led regularly to instances of farce, as when, as Penny van Toorn remarks, the modes of transcribing Indigenous speech gave birth to a cross-cultural rendering in which "the stentorian tones of a villain of gothic romance" were applied to Bennelong.[16] In this, the failure to accurately transcribe speech leads to its own cross-cultural patois, just as the word "mob," originally known in Australia as a cockney speech-marker, has become associated today primarily with Aboriginal English.

I mention all of this background concerning the encounter between Europeans and First Nations by way of introducing the question of cross-cultural exchange and transnationalism, and to give some context as to why the field of transnational influence and collaboration between First Nations writers in different countries is only very recent and emerging.[17] First Nations have had both to attend to their own communities in the first instance, wherever they are located, and then to work against the impacts of colonization upon their language, cultures, and homelands before they might consider transnational collaboration and solidarity. The question of, and referents for, a survey of transnational Indigenous literature(s) and the connections between them is thus a vexed one. Commonalities may be formed based on solidarity and a desire to undo the hegemony of nation-states founded upon the supremacy of a colonizing language and culture. For many, the relationship between the writer and their community or communities will take precedence, as a matter of cultural protocol, even as it is intertwined with or coexists alongside questions of transnational solidarity and the desire to write across borders in ways that recognize that struggles against the colonies and the colonizing impulse haunt all literature produced in Australia, and perhaps especially that of migrant and settler writers.

At present, an attitude of denial persists at the macro level regarding Australia's self-presentation, and the question of settler legitimacy remains ambiguous and unresolved. In their important 1991 study *The Dark Side of the Dream*, Bob Hodge and Vijay Mishra diagnose the attitude that denies that a problem even exists in Australia as a type of schizophrenia.[18] They suggest that the obsession with legitimacy in settler literatures gives proof to the assertion that settler literature in Australia is not so much engaged with exile as knowledge of what possession required. The focus on this literature for much of the nineteenth and twentieth centuries has meant the repression of First Nations, and stymying of those transglobal connections that might have been fostered earlier. Compare, for example, the number of poetry and writing prizes named after White Australian authors. Few of these are named after "migrant" writers and those named after Indigenous authors tend to be for Indigenous writers. Cultural protocol and the assertion of First Nations independence in the face of colonization are undoubtedly a major factor here. But what of the relative absence of migrant authors?[19] My larger point is that we might read in the relative absence of prizes named, say, after "migrant" authors – to say nothing of those named after overseas authors, First Nations or otherwise – that the boundaries of nation-statehood and national identity, however simplified or arbitrary, remain powerful. I offer this thought experiment because the *realpolitik* of ongoing colonization means that, in the realm of politics and economics, the idea of "recognizing" First Nations is rarely given as much deference as it is in the taboos and niceties of the arts and middle-class intellectual production. Perhaps those realms (more explicitly or visibly than in a sphere that depends on language and graceful modes of communication) reveal what Philip Mead has called a "will to nation, driven more than anything by an unassuageable hunger for identity in possession of the land."[20] Apart from the priorities of First Nations, it is this – the vexed question of Australian nationhood – that represents one of the greatest difficulties in speaking of transnational connections between First Nation literatures. The prism of Australian nationhood, a nationhood that is coded white, male, and Christian (or at least agnostic) undergirds the terms of reference. "Some might," as Kim Scott puts it, "place Australian Indigenous writing within the realm of Australian Literature, but there is a wider context; that of the emergence of Australia, as a nation, at the same time as some of the stories which have grown from our land continued or were adapted, or died forever. Australian literature in such a context is a sickly stream."[21]

Anne-Marie Te Whiu and the Red Room Project

Anne-Marie Te Whiu, a Te Rarawa writer, has described beginning the Red Room Project (RR), during a meeting in Meanjin (Brisbane). The Red Room is an organization that commissions and promotes collaborations between writers. Te Whiu was present with David Stavanger, Joy Harjo (a member of the Muscogee Creek Nation), Harjo's partner Owen Sapulpa (a respected Elder of Muscogee), and Yankunytjatjara poet Ali Cobby Eckermann. The meeting resulted in "Fair Trade," which is a part of Poetry Month (August 2021), a new initiative presented by Red Room Poetry intended to increase the profile of Australian poetry, poets, and publishers. As Te Whiu relates it:

> I was back in Wellington that October attending Te Hā Kaituhi Māori – National Māori Writers' Hui. Afterwards, the return trip to Australia was like a severing. For four days I had been a part of something deeply transformative and nourishing. Workshops, panel discussions, performances, readings and everything in-between including sharing kai (food) and sleeping over marae-style on site had filled my cup. Profound connections were made with some incredible writers whom I am now lucky enough to call very dear friends. I returned to Gadigal lands (Sydney) with fire in my belly, inspired to keep connected and more so, to keep connecting – to looking at ways I could bring writers together. I was deep in the process of finalising the anthology *Solid Air: Australia and New Zealand Spoken Word* (UQP 2019) and it was a natural step to start to thinking [sic] of ways to thread writers from across many shores together. Not just any writers though. I specifically wanted to bring First Nations writers from across the globe together – to listen to their poetic harmonies and read how their voices would sing on a page together.[22]

One of the many notable examples of of these First Nations collaborations include that of Samuel Wagan Watson and Sámi writer Sigbjørn Skåden in "Postcards of Colonial Ghosting." As in work such as Christos Tsiolkas and Sasha Soldatow's 1996 book *Jump Cuts*, neither of the two writers in each poetry sequence are named, leaving the reader to either identify the writer in their style and concerns or other stylistic markers, or to simply savor the poems without attempting any attribution. In the first part of the poetry sequence, the tropes and concerns suggest the work of Watson – gothic imagery and a concern with split identities, although it must be noted that recorded videos of the poems, where available, work to upset this anonymity. In the case of this sequence, a video recording shows this section to indeed have been written by Watson:

> *"All Aborigines from Sydney onwards are to be made prisoners of war and if they resist they are to be shot and their bodies hung from trees in the most conspicuous places near where they fell, so as to strike terror into the hearts of surviving natives..."*

Governor Lachlan Macquarie...orders to troops...circa, 1816...
I will not be moved...
Long have I recognised the states of being on this country; collaborator or
captive...the drought takes too many prisoners...and those who are compliant
end up living on their knees anyway...in the heat-haze, barbed-wire fences
sing 3-bar-blues...twang, twanging twang, twang...accompanied by murders
of crow. In their black capes punctuating an endless blue horizon...red-dust
twisters smothering everything in sight...wind-swept plains of nothing are still
something...the rich ghost nation we have sewn into the fabric of our identity...this scorched earth...
I will not be moved...[23]

Such multiplaying of voices and identities marks the work also of Lionel
Fogarty and Kim Scott; one line in particular – "Long have I recognised the
states of being on this country; collaborator or captive" – directly recalls
Fogarty's "CAUSED US TO BE COLLABORATOR':

Please Oodgeroo Noonuccal and Mr Kevin Gilbert pregnant us again,
I all in dawns of the night's day's writer's futures.
Because us writers arts can do it all for all thanks and thanks again
Call us the collaborators of their books.......[24]

Scott's fiction and nonfiction, for their part, do not depict these contests as
reconciled, nor do they attempt to resolve these differences by constructing a singular national identity. Rather, Scott tends to question Australia's
postcolonial status. In his 2007 essay "Covered up With Sand," Scott points
out that in Australia the typical markers of postcolonial society do not exist
whereas the racial classification of the colonized and colonizer – as well
as the "power relationship characteristic of colonial societies" – continues,
resulting in a nation where "Indigenous communities remain at a disadvan-
tage compared to the rest of the population."[25]

Another impressive piece of First Nations collaborative writing is Ellen
van Neerven and Layli Long Soldier's "Circuit Breaker" (2021), which
begins with a parody of platitudinous liberal bureaucratese – Evelyn Araluen's
"Acknowledgment of Cuntery" mines a similar vein of humor – and moves
into a series of interrogatives and imperatives that double as affirmations:
"TRY affirming / being / beginning / preparing / mourning / living / to understand."[26] Its primary meaning becomes one of questioning the imbrication
of the self in language and playing with the language of the self, together
with the notion of solidarity as "a framework for poetic dialogue": "transforming by language / crawling in a footnote / blazing in a title / not being
defined / being a relative / being yourself."[27] The poem stages a number of
modest but arresting formal experiments, including a page without the letter

"a," resulting in the following: "I feel the cycle of trauma, abuse and pain keeps stacking on unless there is a circuit breaker. Which means Land Back, which means get our people out of jails and poverty, which means better health outcomes and autonomous lives."[28] Interestingly enough, the digital formatting of this poem requires that it be typeset in square blocks, which are invisible to the human eye reading the work on a screen, but can be seen when photographed, as if the capturing or witnessing revealed the poem as a series of bricks or a building, whether of safety or of the "prison-house of language" being open to the reader's interpretation. The motif of building recurs in the following page of the poetry sequence, which stages what appears to be a dialogue between the two poets, framed on either side of each other with the words "Note: It's okay to share anything with me. I hope I can offer more of the same" running down the middle.[29] The poet on the right-hand side writes: "It's telling when Settlers-Colonizers see buildings as more sacred than First Nations peoples."[30]

Alexis Wright in France

As often happens in the case of stories moving between between languages and national borders, the French translation of Alexis Wright is not quite the same as her English-language iteration. Two translations of Wright's work have been published in French to date, one of them being a collection of short stories, *Le Pacte du serpent arc-en-ciel* (2002), a work that has not appeared as a collection in English.[31] Indeed, at this point in her English-language career, Wright is hardly known for short stories. Most of them appeared in the 1990s, a period that also yielded some of Wright's early criticism and poetry. French publisher Actes Sud had already issued her *Les Plaines de l'espoir* (1999), followed by *Croire en l'incroyable* in 2000. The book's translator, Sylvie Kandé, has recounted finding Kerry Davies' anthology *Across Country: Stories from Aboriginal Australia* (1998), and being inspired by two of the Alexis Wright stories it contained: "The Chinky Apple Tree" and "When Devils Call."[32]

"After the Storm" first appeared in the *Sydney Morning Herald* on January 7, 1999. In the French version, a second layer is added, based upon the events of the 2000 Sydney Olympics. As Sylvie Kandé explains:

> In the second version of the story, Gibbo learns of the Olympic Games through mailbox advertising and resolves to go to Sydney as a self-appointed Indigenous spokesperson. Though his project fails for lack of institutional support, the old man's political consciousness is raised in the process. [...] The story has an ambivalent ending: the narrator, one of Gibbo's children, remarks in a sarcastic manner that in the international

limelight, his father would have looked like a primitive old man, straight out of Prehistory. Between the lines, we can read that Gibbo's exclusion from the Olympic Games, that of non-commissioned Indigenous people, moreover unconvinced by the notion of Reconciliation, enabled Australia to look more like the modern and unified imagined community a nation is supposed to be.[33]

Kandé's remarks here remind us that, as she writes, "the collection's coherence comes from Wright's clearly stated intention – to fastidiously explore the long-term effects of the trauma caused by colonization, and the ancillary loss and remapping of Aboriginal land."[34]

It is also worth remembering that, in a sense, Alexis Wright is an Aboriginal Chinese author. Ouyang Yu has described conversations in which she talked to him about her grandparents growing vegetables along the river.[35] The fact that it does not seem to make sense to speak of Wright as an "Aboriginal Chinese writer" stems both from the linguistic sources of her writing and of the degree of public connection she has established with China. From private communication, however, and glancing references in interviews – not to mention the presence of Chinese language in *The Swan Book* (2013) – it is clear that part of her public identity may depend on the binary divisions and clear borders drawn in the Australian geopolitical imagination defining who belongs where. Nam Le, too, writing about the author J. M. Coetzee, has described the ordering of hyphenated identity in Australia as constituting a rather confused, frequently white-favoring semiotics, which marginalizes some identity markers and privileges others. The discussion occurs in the context of his book *On David Malouf* (2019), which reflects on how Malouf's literary identity is premised, in part, on the disavowal of the Lebanese side of his nominally "Lebanese-Australian" literary identity:

> Coetzee is never referred to as "South African-Australian." If, like me, he was born in one place and migrated to another, why should I be the one stuck with the hyphen? What does the hyphen actually signify? "Australian" is geopolitical fact (even if its appellation may be contestable). "Vietnamese-Australian" is historical inference, compressing within it war, aftermath, the converse migration where left to right across the hyphen brings you East to West. [...].
> As for West to West: by far the greatest number of migrants to Australia are from England and New Zealand and yet you rarely come across "English-Australians" or "New Zealander-Australians." Coetzee is not "South African-Australian" – he's just somewhat less than a dinky-di, true-blue Australian. There's a clubbiness at play here, coupled with a mutual accord that if you're from the Anglosphere, your origins are never superseded, let alone renounced – they remain your enduring birthright.[36]

Ellen van Neerven, Evelyn Araluen, Billy-Ray Belcourt

I referred earlier to the ways in which writers have described their experiences of connection with First Nations transnationally, and in this section, I wish to address how this politics plays out in the work of Ellen van Neerven, Evelyn Araluen, and Billy-Ray Belcourt.

In the poem "Playing in the Pastoral," published in her debut collection *Dropbear*, Araluen paraphrases several lines from D. H. Lawrence's *Kangaroo* (1923):

> and it was dreamt: the country where men might
> live in a sort of harmless Eden
> but it was: rather like falling out of a picture and
> finding oneself on the floor, with all the gods
> and men left behind[37]

Araluen notes that the line "the space and sun and unworn-out air" are also a reference to Lawrence's novel. Lawrence and *Kangaroo* are familiar reference points when it comes to discussions of transnational appreciations of Australia, but it was some of the collection's relationships to global First Nations poetry – including First Nations poets from Taiwan, a context that is less commonly referred to in English-language literature – that struck me. Reviewing the book for the *Guardian*, I pointed out particularly how Araluen's work was part of "a broader First Nations practice": "From Leanne Betasamosake Simpson in Canada and Esther G Belin and Michael Wasson in Turtle Island to Walis Norgan and Adaw Palaf in Taiwan, it is not uncommon to see various modes and forms incorporated into the poetics of First Nations."[38] I felt it necessary to draw connections with Taiwanese First Nations poets such as Walis Norgan and Adaw Palaf because, despite being close geographical neighbors – and cultural neighbors, notwithstanding that Chinese cultures in Australia have been frequently disavowed and buried by decades of racism and the White Australia Policy – First Nations in "Asia" tend to be referenced less frequently in discussions of Indigeneity, especially in Australian First Nations writing. What we need to do now is continue this exploration and connecting.

Both *Dropbear* and Ellen van Neerven's collection *Throat* (2020) draw heavily, too, from Eve Tuck and K. Wayne Yang's influential essay "Decolonization Is Not a Metaphor" (2012).[39] For Araluen, it becomes a line in the aforementioned poem ("For: the settler move to innocence"); for van Neerven, the section "Whiteness is always approaching" comes with "a further reading list" that includes Tuck and Yang.[40] In "The Only Blak Queer in the World," van Neerven writes about witnessing how Mardi Gras transforms the Eora Nation's unceded land: "[T]he street becoming a site of multi-time, the past-present beat, the future love, and forty years of Black Queer pride spread into more than sixty thousand years of we-have-always-been-here."[41] The poem celebrates not only queer histories, but also First Nations conceptions of gender and sexuality, and is itself indebted to the Cherokee Two-Spirit and queer writer Qwo-Li Driskill. Another major transcultural reference point of Ellen van Neerven's *Throat* is its attention to gender in Australia and Canada. A prominent example of this is the poem "Silenced identity," which was written on Treaty 7 Territory in Banff, Alberta, and is dedicated to murdered and missing trans, Two-Spirit, and gender non-conforming First Nations people in Australia and Canada:

> I think about those murdered and missing
> counted, described and spoken about
> in courts and in tabloids
> without their true gender identities
> dissected, violated, robbed and autopsied
> no affirmation
> no justice
> continuing violence
> every night and in every silence
> I watch and listen out for you[42]

Online communities have helped facilitate increased awareness of First Nations in a global and supranational context. In *False Divides* (2018), Lana Lopesi writes of how "[t]his embrace of the internet by Indigenous peoples worldwide means that we are now exchanging, conversing and situating ourselves within a globalised world."[43] Ballardong Noongar writer Timmah Ball has described their own experience as a writer of having "jumped into a global Indigenous community before I knew myself as a writer, exposing vulnerabilities and layered identities" after they responded to a call for participants in an online exchange through the Iowa Writers Program with tutors Ali Cobby Eckermann and Jennifer Elise Foerster.[44] Ball has called the Internet "a non-space that blak and First Nations people occupy globally for connection, protest and some form of sovereignty, however fragile it might be."[45]

I would like to conclude this admittedly brief overview by turning our attention to Billy-Ray Belcourt, with whom I had the pleasure and privilege of being able, at length, to talk explicitly about the question of transnational First Nations writing in publishing today (the conversation originally appeared online in *Archer*). Belcourt's writing in *A History of My Brief Body* explores the idea that "NDN boys are ideas before they are bodied," how "[f]eet like ours are singed with a history that isn't done with us." Belcourt explores the idea of there being at least two types of anger: one that is imprisoning, and another which is "quieter but equally denigrating, a slow injunction on happiness and possibility." Speaking to him, he employed a lovely phrase, describing how he had to "learn how to live in a way where I didn't put an embargo on my own happiness." He described his "predilection for theorisation" as "a kind of vulnerability," because "no one runs to theory unless there's a dirt road in it":

> In terms of writing with a sense of global indigeneity in mind, I think I thought continentally, perhaps specifically across Canada and the US. Although the settler projects are quite different in these two countries, the structure operates in a similar way. In my first book there's a suite of poems called the "Oxford Journal." In one I write about how Cornel West says that there are moments in which we cannot escape the normative gaze of the white man. The normative gaze of the white man is the air you breathe; it makes a jail of your lungs. This is what it is to live in existential limbo. I really did feel like I was in some kind of existential limbo. I felt like an empty signifier, and I refuse to exist as an empty signifier for people, for white people, for British people. And that meant that I wouldn't assimilate – that I would be an outsider of sorts. [...] I thought, what if I just begin not at the beginning but right in the thick of it? And care about readers who already understand the context, [as well as] other Indigenous readers and folks who come to the conversation from a poetic and theoretical place?[46]

Belcourt's remark about context and beginning "in the thick of it" speaks strongly to the state of writing in Australia. In Australian publishing, memoirs of the marginalized – refugees, First Nations peoples – are often heavily journalistic. Yet the theorists we often read in university, or gain a curiosity for as a teenager, so often start, not with the intent of being slovenly journalistic or educational but with joy, with disturbance, with what is troubling. They seem to say to us: "If you want to read about me, go and read the paper." It is unfortunate to see publishers reiterating what can be read there, rather than starting with what we experience "in the thick of it," which is the poetry, and the joy, and the disturbance. The degree of frankness with which we were able to pose and respond to this question together leads me to conclude, finally, by quoting at length from our conversation:

> I consider my work to have a social critique element, but I think it's problematic when the framework of our literature, being seen as social work, is imposed or expected or becomes a publishing norm, while work outside of that vein is seen as too illegible or experimental. In Canada, certainly in the US as well and perhaps also in the UK from what I can tell – I'm not sure about Australia – it's clear that a relatively small cadre of people are determining what books are published. I think for a while that wasn't necessarily something that was talked about. This small cadre was, predominantly,

shockingly white and cisgender. And I think that part of the something that needs to be urgently considered going forward from all those who participate in publishing, is that we want our literature, our Indigenous literature, to be diverse and polyphonic. Both knowable and unknowable, legible and illegible. We want multiple literatures and literary traditions, and we don't want to be homogenised. And I think part of that means reclaiming some of that power as writers.[47]

Notes

1 Ouyang Yu, *Moon over Melbourne and Other Poems* (London: Shearsman Books, 2005; 1995), p. 34.
2 Alexis Wright, "On Writing Carpentaria," in *Indigenous Transnationalism: Alexis Wright's "Carpentaria,"* ed. Lynda Ng (Sydney: Giramondo, 2018), pp. 217–234.
3 Cf. John Kinsella, "Groups and Mavericks," in *The Cambridge History of Australian Literature*, ed. Peter Pierce (Cambridge: Cambridge University Press, 2009), pp. 476–477.
4 Eugenia Flynn, "Building Aboriginal-Asian Solidarity," *Peril* December 15, 2020: https://peril.com.au/topics/activism/building-aboriginal-asian-solidarity/.
5 Monica Tan, *Stranger Country* (Sydney: Allen & Unwin, 2019).
6 See Paul Giles, *Antipodean America: Australasia and the Constitution of U.S. Literature* (Oxford: Oxford University Press, 2013).
7 Yusef Komunyakaa, *Blue Notes: Essays, Interviews, and Commentaries*, ed. Radiclani Clytus (Ann Arbor: University of Michigan Press, 2000), pp. 83–84.
8 Komunyakaa, *Blue Notes*, pp. 83–84.
9 Bob Hodge and Vijay Mishra, *Dark Side of the Dream: Australian Literature and the Postcolonial Mind* (Sydney: Allen & Unwin, 1990), p. 115.
10 Nicholas Thomas, *Entangled Objects: Exchange, Material Culture, and Colonialism in the Pacific* (Cambridge, MA: Harvard University Press, 1991), p. 4.
11 Lionel G. Fogarty, "CAUSED US TO BE COLLABORATOR," in *Eelaharoo (Long Ago) Nyah (Looking) Möbö-Möbö (Future)* (Syndey: Vagabond Press, 2014), pp. 102–104.
12 Penny van Toorn, "Early Writings by Indigenous Australians," in *The Cambridge History of Australian Literature*, pp. 52–72 (p. 54).
13 Kim Scott, as quoted in A. Brewster, "Can You Anchor a Shimmering Nation State via Regional Indigenous Roots? Kim Scott talks to Anne Brewster about That Deadman Dance," *Cultural Studies Review* 18.1(2012): pp. 228–246 (p. 243).
14 There are many examples working in the opposite direction. Malpas finds in Proust and Wordsworth something like the "intrinsically perspectival" mapping of location as a "significant point of connection between place and memory" in Australian Indigenous traditions. See J. E. Malpas, *Place and Experience: A Philosophical Topography* (Cambridge: Cambridge University Press, 1999), pp. 14, 34, 41, 50.
15 See Watkin Tench, *A Narrative of the Expedition to Botany Bay* (Sydney: University of Sydney Library, 1998; 1789).

16 van Toorn, "Early Writings by Indigenous Australians," p. 58.
17 For more on the history of these encounters, see for instance Shino Konishi, *The Aboriginal Male in the Enlightenment World* (London: Routledge, 2015).
18 Hodge and Mishra, *Dark Side of the Dream*, p. 217.
19 It is interesting to speculate, too, on what sort of pressures or desires for national legitimacy might have led those who could have presented themselves otherwise, such as David Malouf, to disavow much of the non-white and non-Christian side of their identity.
20 Philip Mead, "Nation, Literature, Location," in The Cambridge History of Australian Literature, pp. 594–567 (p. 549).
21 Kim Scott, "Foreword," in Anita M. Heiss, *Dhuuluu Yala: To Talk Straight: Publishing Indigenous Literature* (Canberra: Aboriginal Studies Press, 2003), p. i.
22 Anne-Marie Te Whiu, "Fair Trade: A Way to RE/order/image/code the world," *Cordite Poetry Review*, August 1, 2021: http://cordite.org.au/essays/fair-trade/3/.
23 Sam Wagan Watson and Sibjørn Skåden, "Postcards of Colonial Ghosting," *Red Room Poetry*, August 22, 2021: https://redroompoetry.org/poets/sam-wagan-watson/postcards-of-colonial-ghosting/.
24 Fogarty, "CAUSED US TO BE COLLABORATOR," p. 104.
25 Kim Scott, "Covered up With Sand," *Meanjin* 66.2 (2007): pp. 120–124 (p. 123).
26 Ellen van Neerven and Layli Long Soldier, "Circuit Breaker," *Red Room Poetry*, August 30, 2021: https://redroompoetry.org/poets/ellen-van-neerven/circuit-breaker/.
27 van Neerven and Long Soldier, "Circuit Breaker."
28 van Neerven and Long Soldier, "Circuit Breaker."
29 van Neerven and Long Soldier, "Circuit Breaker."
30 van Neerven and Long Soldier, "Circuit Breaker."
31 Coincidentally, this title, *Le pacte du serpent arc-en-ciel*, recalls Tristan Tzara's "Chanson du Serpent," a Dada performance of a song cycle from the Loritja people of Central Australia, which appeared in the second issue of *Dada* published in Zurich in 1917.
32 Sylvie Kandé in Demelza Hall, "Translating the Stories of Alexis Wright," *JASAL: Journal of the Association for the Study of Australian Literature* 16.2 (2016): pp. 1–9 (p. 2).
33 Kandé in Hall, "Translating the Stories of Alexis Wright," pp. 6–7.
34 Kandé in Hall, "Translating the Stories of Alexis Wright," p. 5.
35 Personal correspondence with Ouyang Yu, January 2022.
36 Nam Le, *On David Malouf* (Melbourne: Black Inc., 2019) pp. 65–68.
37 Evelyn Araluen, *Dropbear* (Brisbane: University of Queensland Press, 2021), p. 19.
38 Declan Fry, "*Dropbear* by Evelyn Araluen Review – A Stunning Scalpel Wielded Through Australian Myths," the *Guardian*, March 26, 2021: www.theguardian.com/books/2021/mar/26/dropbear-by-evelyn-araluen-review-a-stunning-scalpel-wielded-through-australian-myths .
39 Eve Tuck and K. Wayne Yang, "Decolonization Is Not a Metaphor," *Decolonization: Indigeneity, Education & Society* 1.1. (2012): pp. 1–40. For a useful discussion of this essay, see Priyamvada Gopal, "On Decolonisation and the University," *Textual Practice* 35.6 (2021): pp. 873–899.
40 Araluen, Dropbear, p. 20; Ellen van Neerven, *Throat* (Brisbane: University of Queensland Press, 2020), p. 133.

41 van Neerven, *Throat*, p. 21.
42 van Neerven, *Throat*, p. 85.
43 Lana Lopesi, *False Divides* (Wellington: Bridget Williams Books, 2018), p. 72.
44 Timmah Ball, "Aboriginality in Writing: Mapping Identity Through Words," *Archer* 22 June 22, 2020: https://archermagazine.com.au/2020/06/aboriginality-in-writing-mapping-identity-through-words/.
45 Ball, "Aboriginality in Writing."
46 Billy-Ray Belcourt in Declan Fry, "Archer Asks: Billy-Ray Belcourt," *Archer*, June 29, 2021: https://archermagazine.com.au/2021/06/archer-asks-billy-ray-belcourt/.
47 Belcourt in Fry, "Archer Asks."

15

MICHELLE CAHILL

Beyond the Cosmopolitan

Small Dangerous Fragments

Body Language

For a migrant, the labor of writing is intensive and suffered in the body. Because we are required to excavate a space where there is absence, and then to graft ourselves there. The pushbacks from gatekeepers are retraumatizing. They can shatter your life. Recent years have been particularly difficult for me. The bones and muscles in my neck cramp from hyperflexion as I sit at my desk, stooped, my eyes are strained and fatigued. Ping by ping, drip-fed by a constant trickle of emails. As a mixed-ancestry Indian Australian writer, I have broken the rules and theorized modes of resistance. White supremacists wanted to make an example of me. They wanted me punished for my work on interceptionality. Who knows why the Murdoch and Fairfax news media reviews of my prize-winning short story collection, *Letter to Pessoa*, have vanished? Search engine optimization is the official explanation, but for those who doubt this can happen in a democratic literary culture, a Google search will punctually reveal erasures. When I self-censure, however, these same reviews sometimes reappear, fleetingly, online and I sense my cooperation is being courted. The algorithm watches over each of us and manages those who resist.

Through my work as a journal editor, I became transplanted into a body of literary criticism. I became the brown eyes of a national industry, that curates and manages cultural difference with the complicity and cooperation of its discursive border police. It's tough out there in the real world for people of color. In the pursuit of creative vision, some of my cohorts have died: Candy Royalle, Ramon Loyola. Others, such as Behrouz Boochani, have been incarcerated, in Boochani's case in the Australian-run detention center on Manus Island. From different quarters, there is expectation, adverse exchange, manipulation of social media, and surveillance. Through rivalries, bylines and chatlines, my critical voice has faltered, and this essay is so overdue, it ceases to amuse.

Where to begin? What say I begin with the provisional, with belonging-and-not-belonging, with what Stuart Hall describes as "an unstable identity, psychically, culturally, and politically" but which is also "a narrative, a story, a history."[1] Let's consider the erasures that are felt as a pummeling sweep, surge after surge after surge, from all directions, to crush the footnotes from where, as one among many minority voices, I speak. Let's acknowledge the white supremacist agenda behind the media that consolidate power over the nation-state and its national story. How much time do you have? Take a seat, why don't you, as Max Porter intones in *The Death of Francis Bacon* (2021).[2] And kindly pay attention to the body language. There are powerful stakes in the industry, toxic egos with a good dose of heady colonial, misogynist thinking. Oh dear, I can feel an introductory assault coming on shortly ... presently, ... So let me begin about eighteen months ago with the abstract and notes that I wrote for Nicholas Birns and Louis Klee in the body of an email:

White Capital

The Australian novel is embedded in capitalist and colonial assumptions that are regulated by critics, by industry, and by institutional readings. Selective parameters of taste and literary merit formulate the boundaries of the canon, restricting membership particularly to the literary novel. Determining and underpinning the genre of the novel is the exclusionary logic of the colonial apparatus, modeling for readers its representation of nation. Avoiding many uncomfortable truths, Australian fiction continues to transcendentalize the precept of *terra nullius* on which white invasion and settlement was premised, while Aboriginal sovereignty was unceded. Aileen Moreton-Robinson writes that a "non-Indigenous sense of belonging is inextricably tied to this original theft: through the fiction of *terra nullius* the [British] migrant has been able to claim the right to live in our land."[3] Fiction's complicity with coloniality cannot be underestimated.

How does this impact the experience of readers? Consider how many acclaimed novels are written as if invasion never happened, as if Aboriginal people never existed. Where Aboriginal people do appear, they are often assimilated passive characters and/or reductive stereotypes. How many novels overlook how the racist White Australian policy sanctioned social and cultural exclusion of Asians for almost seventy years, and how it continues to operate politically and culturally to restrict citizenship and manage non-citizens? Consider the cumulative erasure of these imbricated dynamics and contexts in celebrated canonical novels that ultimately occupy spaces of whiteness as property in bookshops, libraries, curriculums, and on shelves while concurrently being reviewed, endorsed, and disseminated through print and electronic media?

The Australian novel invariably explores settler colonial identity and otherness in terms of space and place, whether that be urban or remote, center or periphery. Quest, voyage, haunting, love, grief, violence, and climate are often imagined through a topographical lens that assumes and endorses a single chronology tied to dispossession, shackled to assimilation and to racial hierarchy. While the organizing rubric of Australian literary studies engages with novels of transposition and transit, with crossing cultures and geographical borders, it also confers national identity. Yet the kind of monolithic, seamless, representational performativity in writing risks essentializing cultural specificity, language idioms, and unspeakable histories – which are in their materiality fragmented – in order to represent and to reproduce conventional values of permanence, identity, and stability. Moreover, realism, the novel's dominant methodology, relies on causality, character, summation, and style to conceal the structured scaffolding through which story and history entwine. But this reconciled logic of whiteness fails to align with those who are provisional, nor with the experience of Australia's hybrid and heterogeneous subjects. This essay explores the politics of experimentation, focusing on short fiction by Asian Australian writers as well as white settlers' provocations of nationalism in literary fiction.

Letter to Pessoa

How does fiction conduct elements of rebellion, contingency, fragmentation, incomplete histories, the experience of disorientation, amnesia, the retrograde, or looping time – conditions that are ubiquitously the real, lived experience of minorities, half-castes, migrants? This is something I learned in writing my collection of short fiction, *Letter to Pessoa* (2016), which had humble beginnings as an unpublished novel manuscript, *Riding Without Krishna*.[4] *Letter to Pessoa* assembles epistolary stories addressed to authors I have admired, because of how they mediate, sometimes provoke, complex personas, perspectives and genders in writing (such as Pessoa, Coetzee, Woolf, Genet, Borges, Derrida). Australian authors such as Gail Jones and J. M. Coetzee (who naturalized in 2006) have also written metafictional novels, while Ceridwen Dovey's *Only the Animals* (2014) achieves this element from non-human perspectives. Writers of color, by contrast, are often burdened by the expectation that they will write on "migrant" or ethnic topics. Mirandi Riwoe's *The Fish Girl* (2017) is a notable exception to the genre of metafiction. Her novella subverts "the Malay trollope" in Somerset Maugham's 1928 short story, "The Four Dutchmen," inverting the white colonial gaze.

Some stories in *Letter to Pessoa* were adapted from select chapters of *Riding Without Krishna* (its nuanced, hybrid characters challenged marketing categories, as does my Christian name). A novel chapter is quite different from a short story, so the process was lengthy, if instructive. As a writer, one is always learning. Who is going to teach the exile, the foreigner, how to speak and articulate their story in stable and commercial prose forms? I gradually, palpably discerned how the migrant refugee voice inhabits a disrupted time because of contingencies, transitions between countries, languages, histories, and cultures. This, of course, is my own experience and not an appropriation. Intuitively, I resisted polemic tropes and identity-wrapped binaries where migrant anger about racism in the new home oscillates with nostalgia for the "country of origin."

The short forms exempted me from pressure to assimilate, to reconcile differences absorbed in the homogenized cultural and linguistic codes that are readily absorbed by publishing and marketing brands. My stories are often rhizomic, and whilst being transnational, they are distinct from mainstream liberal cosmopolitanism, located as they are in offbeat suburbs and districts: Dee Why in Sydney, Lalitpur in Nepal, Seville in Spain, George in South Africa, and Hull in the UK, for example. The protagonists, while biracial, are Anglophone, educated global citizens. Yet they move in informal and marginal spaces, encountering barriers but finding solidarity with those whose struggles are unfairly positioned in the global cosmopolitics. This discrepant cosmopolitanism is one of opposites, where refuge and varied forms of conflict coexist. In "Finding the Buddha," the Australian tourist, Jo, whilst staying in a monastery, is confronted by the distress of a Rohingya orphan, Azima, as well as the grief of the widow Noi, whose German husband has died.

In "A Wall of Water," Sarita's story is the lived experience of recurring trauma, loss, and migrant departure. It begins on the day the SIEV-11 (the name Australian authorities gave to an Indonesian fishing boat, abbreviating "Suspected Illegal Entry Vessel") crashes off the coast of Christmas Island, and fifty Iraqi and Iranian refugees drowned. On this day of mourning Sarita's flashbacks flood her mind with other traumas she has witnessed or read about: a Tibetan freedom fighter in Dharamsala, a young Sikh man who is viciously stabbed, her own leave-takings. In the story "To Show a Little Hustle," set in Hong Kong, Nabina learns that Nathan's Filipino maid, Juliette, has been financially exploited by a surrogacy gynecologist after she miscarries. Despite her privilege, how can she help Juliette? This story exposes how the ethics of cosmopolitics are distorted by desire, race, and commerce. The vulnerability of minorities is repurposed by resisting the official neoliberal narrative, blending fiction with reportage. As James Halford explains:

In Cahill's writing, the former imperial outposts have begun to communicate among themselves, bypassing the empire. Secondly, the postcolonial nation state is far less central to Cahill's practice than it was to postcolonial writers of an earlier period. Neoliberal globalisation is the dominant context for Cahill's short stories, not decolonisation (though the two are, of course, related). Her stories unfold in a world where the consolidation of the global market means North and South now infuse one another, "distributing inequalities and barriers along multiple and fractured lines." Thus, her displaced characters cross indiscriminately between metropolis and periphery, encountering similar inequities of race, gender and class wherever they go.[5]

While the short story may function as a compressed version of the novel, or the essay for that matter, short fiction can be innovative, permitting structural variations and experimentations that might be harder to sustain in a full-length novel. "The Flower Thief" in *Letter to Pessoa* was an experiment in writing about flowers as a motif for queer desire, and *jouissance* in writing as creative process. Incidents and accidents bloom in the ruffles and surfaces of the language. I wanted the baroque, dreamlike descriptions to contour the narrator's actions and perceptions as she drifts along the dystopian nocturnal streetscape of Birchgrove or Glebe Island Bridge with the woman she takes home, who alters her life, and with characters associated with flowers suffusing her thoughts: Sally Seton from *Mrs Dalloway* (1925), for instance, and the Mexican artist Frida Kahlo. I wanted to see how language gathers meaning in the trembling shadows, how richly voice could carry the reader into the interstices and into the void, the silences that swallow so many faceless and nameless personas in the republic of letters.

Smart Ovens and *Look Who's Morphing*

(1) *Note-to-self*: I'm sorry, I am not your compliant and obedient contributor who will be corralled into homilies that theoretically reproduce and venerate the white-centered canon. (2) *Note-to-self*: when I wrote the abstract for this essay, I was thinking of Tom Cho's *Look Who's Morphing* (2009), with its satirical, inventive embodiment of iconic identities.[6] Stories such as "The Sound of Music," "I, Robot," and "Dirty Dancing" blur mainstream film and television celebrities with queer Asian identities, using unforced satire, sprightly language, and a restrained pace. For Cho, there are no declarations to expose or demand from the legacy of white heteronormative literary culture, no origins to claim. The mock instruction manual tone of "Chinese Whispers" invites readers into these light-hearted transgressions, while the play of accents, and use of neologisms critiques English-language dominance. This is clever, sculptural prose with rapid flights of association that shift in subject from the popular

party game, Chinese whispers, the object of which is to observe change, to Chinese burns, "a form of playground punishment or torture" then via martial arts to a PlayStation game of the same title, thereafter to Elvis Presley, who liked martial arts, then to Nagasaki, a song, and to the atomic bomb dropped on the city which caused "real burns." Serious themes emerge: Asians appropriating Elvis is a clever subplot that reverses the axis of racial and cultural dominance. Cho does not pander to the mainstream nor mind in the slightest whether the reader is impressed or not. *Look Who's Morphing* is surely one of the most inventive collections of short fiction published in recent years.

Another short-fiction writer whose work exemplifies the flexibility of the form to repurpose the surreal is Elizabeth Tan, whose collection *Smart Ovens for Lonely People* (2020) received the 2021 Readings Prize. Tan fuses the human, consumption, and the digital (such as the mobile-phone cat game Neko Atsume) in a darkly satirical way that meditates on capitalism, excess, and vulnerability. In an interview for the Melbourne Writers Festival, Tan acknowledges that the writing process is decentered, and arises from language rather than plot:

> Sometimes I think of a phrase that would make a good title – because it has a beautiful sound, or it makes me go "hehehe" – and then I write a story that fits that title. I used to be embarrassed about this – I was worried it meant I was a shallow writer – but I've kind of embraced it now. A story exists on the page where there wasn't one before – what does it matter how it began.[7]

As a migrant of three countries, I am at home in language. Language is the vehicle and the journey; I appreciate Cho's imaginative leaps and I marvel at Tan's speculative combinations that might begin simply with a beautiful sound, and the pursuit of illusory reasoning.

Bapo

The short stories in Nicholas Jose's *Bapo* (2014) are not structurally experimental but, in conceptual terms, they contest conformity, whiteness, and nationalism. Their essayistic logic probes into love, China, art, erotics, with an animated subversive dialectic, that becomes its own unique wisdom on fortune and destiny. *Bapo* is named after an avant-garde collage style of Chinese art that assembled calligraphies, epigraphs, rubbings, seals, and burned letters, composite forms of riddling that are often suffused with gentle irony. It surfaced in the nineteenth-century after the Opium Wars, when China was dominated by the West and many of its cultural treasures plundered under the currencies of cosmopolitan trade. Jose writes: "The *bapo* aesthetic appreciates incompleteness.

Questions of origin and authorship recede into enigma. The fragment, the shard, can be known only in part."[8]

As cultural counsellor at the Australian embassy in Beijing from 1987 to 1990, Jose played an important role in Australian-Chinese cultural exchange. Drawing on this, he mostly writes from the third-person omniscient point of view; his subjects are educated and privileged yet there are radical undercurrents that expose social conventions as vulnerable. In "Marriage Bonds" and "A Game of Go," relationships of control and humiliation convey an emotional savagery that is matched by adroit shifts of tone that actively engage the reader. There is an acting out of domestic violence, almost a howl against asphyxiating binary and heteronormative gender roles. Jose strikes a fine balance between the erotic humor of seduction, cuckolding, and duplicity, and a relentless, absolving candor. "Does it matter which instance of cruelty I recount for you since all of them incarnate the same pattern? The masochist finds the sadist every time."[9] The blurring of pleasure and suffering, art and confession, abandonment and confinement haunts Arthur, the protagonist lover of Robert and husband of Martha in "Marriage Bonds." Beyond mere frustration with convention, there's a deeper sense of futility with social order or family bonds, as well as inherited legacies to which characters are tied. China is not exoticized or stereotyped: Jose's characters fart and pick their nose; they are anchored by cultural and political relations that are not commensurable with the West. He is also not afraid to take aim at socialist art, education, and propaganda in "Ha – Ha – Ha!" Through the artist character who refuses to "glorify the national soul," "[d]eflecting envy and slander" Jose adopts a humanist stance that is nonetheless able to critique the role of all cultures in naturalizing the national interest.

In *Bapo*, China functions not as an inferior but as a neutral space nullifying the presumed superiority of Western culture that is encompassed by Anglophone literature and its readers. In "Diamond Dog," Lanlan, a young Chinese girl growing up on a southern island off Australia, befriends Luke, an orphan fostered by an old couple. The story is almost an allegory of hope between the respective countries. "He saw no barrier between himself and the girl. She was Universe, Infinity too, in the form of a place called China, far down the road."[10] In a juvenile frolic of cross-dressing, they swap clothes. Luke morphs into a Manchu princess, while Lanlan cuts off her plait for an androgynous hairstyle, wears a cricket suit, and leather gloves. Lanlan, the more resolute of the two children, beats a python with a stick after it has almost swallowed her dog, earning her a rightful place in the island's legends. Her father, the artist in the story, will record that "visual history."

Jose has ancestral ties to curators and colonials who formed networks of trade and travel between Australia and Asia. China and India both suffered from turbulent and exploitative dynamics based on race. It is important to remember that discriminatory strategies operated from within Australia through the Immigration Restriction Act 1902, which marginalized the Chinese Australian community. China was ravaged by colonial invasions by the British and French, leading in 1911 to the overthrow of the imperial dynasty, and subsequent wars with Japan. The characters and stories in *Bapo* evoke a post-Mao Zedong cultural rapport that is inclusive, if not always in harmony, supporting a cosmopolitics that questions these persisting hegemonies. Before COVID-19, China's expansions in the region were considered a threat to peace and security. With the rise of aggressive Anglo-US-Australian nationalisms the strategic partnership has soured between China and Australia since *Bapo* was published. Yet these fictions are timely reminders, whole fragments of complex encounters, a revitalizing dialogue. Informed by intergenerational responsibility, they manifest as the settler quest for forging decolonizing and reformative cultural bonds.

Sixty Lights

Both China and India suffered colonial crimes and brutal discrimination under the White Australia Policy. The focus on ethnicity in Indian Australian writing is susceptible to quarantining caste and class differences, suppressing the complex demographics that exceed institutional readings of Indian-Australian citizenship. Within the macro hyphenations, there are micro divisions. Exclusionary filters and dynamics are inflected from the legacies of caste oppression, colonial violence, and its compradors. How is India handled by white authors in Australian fiction?

Recently, I came across a copy of Gail Jones' novel *Sixty Lights* (2004), a finely crafted lyrical portrait of the sensitive and intense Lucy Strange, a young Victorian woman and student of early photography who travels the imperial circuit, traveling to London then India, before she dies of tuberculosis at the age of twenty-two. The sixty chapters (and sixty thousand words) reflect on modernism and ephemerality, performing also as exquisite short fictions. *Sixty Lights* has been described as "a post-modern use of the bildungsroman form for a study of modernism."[11] The novel begins after Lucy's mother dies. She and her brother Thomas are adopted by their uncle Neville, and journey to live with him in London, where cultural and class tensions emerge. At sixteen, Lucy is shown by her uncle a daguerreotype of an elderly colleague, Isaac Newton, and she is sent to India to be his spouse, though she falls pregnant to an exploitative man on the journey. Lucy extends her quest for light and her study of photography in India, where she is visually stimulated and alert to cultural differences. While traveling with her servant Bashanti, Lucy wants to immerse herself in the heady exoticism of India; she visits the temples and markets and tries chewing *paan*. She recognizes her romanticism and her preference for the mystical, the aesthetic over the abject and scatological. "She was ashamed at the vulgarity of her wish to beautify."[12] On returning to London, Lucy is nostalgic for India and suffers cultural disorientation. She is appalled by her brother's magic lantern show, themed on the Indian Mutiny, an imperialist propaganda that depicts Indians as "snarling barbarians [...] and the British a noble race."[13] Colonial violence is critiqued by a mode of appreciation of difference. *Sixty Lights* opens with a prolepsis, and what for Jones is a characteristically painterly scene. Lucy awakes from sleep, remembering an accident she has seen. An Indian man wearing a white dhoti and an orange turban, climbs a scaffolding holding a mirror, loses his step and falls. The "utter shattering" of the mirror, which spears him in the chest and severs an artery, causing him to bleed to death, also casts a spray of minute reflections of the unfortunate glazier's world, represented as "pieces of sliced India."

Most of the reviews of *Sixty Lights* explore Jones' thematic layering and her photographic intelligence, light, the past and present, and her interest in visual and linguistic codes. Other criticism focuses on modernism, cosmopolitanism, and the Victorian woman in global migrations as a refiguration of narrative. Through Lucy, the novel affirms attitudes of cultural respect towards India, yet there is little or no interest among Australian critics in how this novel contributes to the discourses of racism or multiculturalism. Lucy describes herself as being triangulated, yet the complex threads of race and colonialism that forged exploitative trade and fraught legal and immigration frameworks between Britain, India, and Australia are oversimplified in *Sixty Lights*. Indeed, it is possible that some readers may be haunted by and even aggrieved at the specter of the Indian tradesman who is violently sacrificed for the purpose of aesthetics, particularly as the scene is revisited at a later stage in the novel. The narrator suggests he dies absurdly, betrayed by his credulity: he "could not release the mirror, but clutched it as though it was a magic carpet."[14] Shouldn't the ethics of this description be accountable since the narrator-protagonist focalization lessens the Indian man? The reader is required to be complicit in witnessing a devaluation in words, in "small dangerous fragments," of an entire nation.[15] After all, this was an era when India was under British subjugation and shackled economically, at great cost to India's people, Indian lives. The narrator's indifference reads as a form of "caucasity," to use a social media term for white audacity, and it needs to be said that Blak and Brown Australian readers may well find this insensitive and tone deaf:

There were many deaths in India – everyone knew this – but death by mirror seemed to her particularly meaningless, the counter-logic to finding one's own face, there, alive, as one dressed, or admired oneself, or leaned forward critically or vainly to examine a feature.[16]

And furthermore, Jones evokes the magic carpet tropes of Orientalist discourse, and misappropriates them in her creation of an Indian subject. Nevertheless, the precise imagery, the reductive figure of the Indian man seduces us: "The mirror and the blood were an irresistible combination."[17] Even Lucy is disturbed by her fascination. She turns to meditate on art and death, a hallowed theme, she drinks tea and eats cardamom-flavored sweets with Bashanti, her servant companion, but even with this superior harmony, this "glorious" perfume, the disproportionate value given to representing India in the blood-spattered fractured shards is deeply disturbing, and problematic. This is particularly so because the accident is no more than an illusion, created by the design, the intent of the author. The opening of *Sixty Lights* is mesmeric, arresting, harnessing mystery and authority from this single dramatic incident, revisited in Chapter 39.

Yet *Sixty Lights* is also a novel of cosmopolitan sensibility and complexity, with luminous prose. A clue to the dissonance that may explain how India is represented can be found in the history of Australia's racist and colonial relations with India, which were never based on equality. Kama Maclean has researched the white imaginary evidenced in reductive discourse about hawkers, the non-white labor legislation and citizenship laws that severely restricted Indians' capacity to work in Australia, or to vote: "India was more imagined than experienced in Australia, with the vast majority of transnational connections heavily mediated through the white mechanisms of the British Raj."[18] India is violently abstracted to exsanguinate the Indian body in *Sixty Lights*. Certainly, the White Australia Policy has been dismantled, though we continue to observe racist inequalities in sport, from our politicians, and in our courts. We need only think of the recent travel ban and five-year jail sentence facing travelers returning from India during the outbreak of the Delta strain of coronavirus.

Australia Day

With popular nationalisms on the rise, diasporic Asian Australian writers, or those who integrate or advocate for diversity, are at times considered to be elite or privileged. Partly, this has resulted from systems of meritocracy in which globalism and transnationalism flatten out differences and result in homogeneity and assimilation. Yet we witness fracture lines: increased violence imposed on the bodies of immigrants, whether they be north or south Asians, irrespective of whether they hail from besieged countries (Sri Lanka, Myanmar, Palestine, or Afghanistan), whether this is caused by structural racism or by targeted attacks, or whether it follows the callous state-sanctioned treatment of refugees since 9/11, since Australia's Anti-Terrorism Act 2005 and the ascendancy of right-wing border politics under John Howard (prime minister of Australia, 1996–2007) and subsequent leaders. We see everywhere the pervasiveness of borders; their heterogeneity and evasiveness exceed the single purpose of territorial demarcation. Borders encompass social practice, dividing, resettling, and hindering people, differentiating citizens from non-citizens. Étienne Balibar writes that "borders are no longer the shores of the political but have indeed become [...] things within the space of the political itself."[19]

Melanie Cheng's award-winning collection of stories, *Australia Day* (2017), embraces this heterogeneity while turning its ethical intelligence to addressing social cohesion. Yen-Ron Wong describes it as a "holistic snapshot of Australian life" simultaneously "cynical and hopeful."[20] The stories question what it means to be Australian, presenting the different facades of citizens who range from professional doctors, which Cheng is herself, to public servants, international students, and new migrants. Cheng's medical themes and terminology are organic to her stories, rather than being obtrusive. A Melbourne doctor and writer of a medical column for *The Saturday Paper*, her knowledge of illness and trauma subtly informs her fiction. She has a knack for taking us into the heart of people's lives, to their dinner tables, and private conversations. Her language effortlessly blends compassion and wit, developing complex layers of memory, discordance, even conflict in her characters. The prose is unerring in its registers of everyday speech.

In "Fracture," an Indian doctor, Deepak, working at a hospital, becomes the subject of a complaint by a disgruntled patient. Tony, who has been made redundant, suffers a fracture after falling from a ladder. He develops a chronically painful limb as a complication but blames Deepak, blowing up his photograph from the hospital website to print posters that shame him with the words FUCKWIT. Cheng takes us into the characters' lives by turns. Deepak's family have attempted to matchmake him to a suitable Indian bride, whereas his girlfriend Simone is a blonde-haired, successful and assured orthopedic surgeon. Simone withdraws her support for him when the complaint is escalated. Unlike Deepak, who suffers from a stutter, and who failed medical exams in the past, Simone hails from an ultra-privileged world that creates a barrier between them. These characters feel real: a strand of Simone's blonde hair is the fine image that marks their difference, and Deepak winds it around his finger "watched his fingertip swell with blood. Here was the hair spun of gold he had read about, as a child, in fairytales."[21] Cheng's sentient and erotic images are lightly brushed; she sculpts Simone's white privilege into hard copy: "Her perfect breasts jiggled and bounced."[22]

"Fracture" is breathtaking for the way in which the intersectional complexity of racism, cultural difference, intolerance, and violence are presented in clear everyday storytelling, mediated by the hierarchies of class, even within the healthcare system. It becomes crucial to Australia's future as a nation to question these structural systems of discrimination and to bring attention to more truly "cosmopolitan" representations of difference. The character of Deepak is beautifully observed, refreshingly presented, not as a Brahmin Hindu, but as a secular subject. Cheng's humor in describing the prearranged date between Deepak and Priya creates an urban, relatable mood. Yet everything remains ever so subtly troubled, until the climax when Tony's belligerent, ice-smoking grandson Luca encounters Deepak in the hospital grounds and stabs him. Cheng gives Deepak a complex psychological and physical life in fiction, even though it culminates in sacrifice: "the pool of blood" at Deepak's feet, "the flickering red emergency sign."[23] The spilled blood of Cheng's prose makes us viscerally feel Deepak's heartbeat. We are shaken, interrogated as a community to disavow racial assault and the violence of white settlership on the stolen, colonized lands we inhabit, but equally on the page.

Fine

Fine (2016) is the debut short-story collection by Michelle Wright, a Melbourne novelist with Sri Lankan ancestry who has lived in Paris. Wright's stories have won several awards and are striking for the way they capture memory and ephemerality in themes of personal trauma, grief, family relations, and catastrophes. Several of the stories are intentionally fragmentary in an effort to address the 2004 tsunami that devastated Sri Lanka. "Water Hours" uses the poetic image of a "coconut shell pierced through with a tiny hole" filling up until "it would silently slip below the surface" to describe the experience of children drowning.[24] In this ancient Sinhalese system for measuring time, a coconut shell would fill in twenty-four minutes, marking out a water hour, and there were sixty water hours in a day. Written in the third person and from the point of view of an un-named young girl who is waiting with her niece at the bus stop when the tsunami waves rise, the story is dreamlike, the language and tone almost comforting. The girl watches the steady beat of a clock face, a little girl swept under the beam of the bus shelter holding on to a plastic washing tub as it fills and sinks. Wright keeps the story submerged in sensory dissociation, as if conscious thought is muted and overwhelmed by the noise and asphyxiation of drowning. The girl is paradoxically numbed by horror and panic, "humming something soft in her mind" and remembering the water hours.

This exquisite tenderness inhabits another story "Blur," which describes the tsunami's aftermath. A young boy, Saminder, and his uncle take the road to Galle, from Balapitiya to Hikkaduwa to his parent's house in search of them. A train from Colombo has derailed and thousands of people have drowned. Even in this loss, Wright's poetic intensity reminds us of rich detail. Saminda and his uncle follow the risen sea, the smell of debris and bodies souring "like a pot of buffalo curd left out too long in the sun" or like "overripe wood apple pulp."[25] They are meanwhile listening to a test match between Sri Lanka and Australia broadcast over the radio. On arriving, they discover the house engulfed in black sludge, the silence daunting. In all her stories, Wright's prose superbly centers the physical body, which is mutable, permeable, and vulnerable. Simultaneously the body is the site of both personal and collective suffering. She takes the reader into the boy's physical identity: "His arms hang heavy by his sides with dread, and his tongue is swollen in his mouth."[26] "Keeping Tabs" is perhaps the most poignant story, about a servant girl, Silent Night, who is so dark she cannot be seen and who cannot speak the language of the masters. Told from the perspective of a cosmopolitan Australian writer, it entirely authenticates the fractional and segregated bond created by coloniality, race, and privilege. The gaps and silences are even more enrichening because of Wright's wise and unassuming voice.

Coda

Australian writing is entering a phase of greater freedom in which genres blur and writing may increasingly apply poetical dimensions, historical elements or autofictional processes as suited to its task. Short stories can shift shape, weaving threads from surreal elements, exploring the ambulatory possibilities of words, finding personal and even political refuge in their images, rhythms, and textures. The short story can potentially look outwards beyond the borders of the nation, to challenge the ubiquity of borders and border thinking. Minorities are vulnerable to state-determined frameworks of rights and governance, but the short story's cosmopolitan outlook is discrepant and opposite, inclusive of migrant workers, refugees, tourists, and other mobile communities. In a variation from conventional fictional practice, the position or role of the omniscient worldly traveler is contested – neither peacemaker nor innocent bystander. Such a national imaginary can also look to Asia from the perspective of white settlers' responsibility, with historical awareness of the work that needs doing to decolonize Australian literary paradigms. We see this in the work of authors such as Nicholas Jose and Gail Jones. Shorter forms can arguably free subjectivity from singular, oppressive linearities that are structurally requisite to the novel. Short fiction can jump-cut, unhinge, subvert, and complicate narrative time, allowing poetical, metafictional, speculative, and surreal elements to embody marginal and hybrid characters, all of whom are equally Australian.

Notes

1 Stuart Hall, "Minimal Selves," in *Black British Cultural Studies: A Reader*, eds. Houston A. Baker, Jr, Manthia Diawwara, and Ruth H. Lindeborg (Chicago: University of Chicago Press, 1996), pp. 114–119 (p. 116).
2 Max Porter, "One," in *The Death of Francis Bacon* (London: Faber & Faber, 2021).
3 Aileen Moreton-Robinson, "'Our Story Is in the Land': Why the Indigenous Sense of Belonging Unsettles White Australia," *ABC Religion & Ethics*, November 9, 2020: www.abc.net.au/religion/our-story-is-in-the-land-indigenous-sense-of-belonging/11159992.
4 See Michelle Cahill, *Letter to Pessoa* (Sydney: Giramondo, 2016).
5 James Halford, "Reading the South Through Northern Eyes: Jorge Luis Borges's Australian Reception, 1962–2016," *Australian Literary Studies* 33.2 (2018): www.australianliterarystudies.com.au/articles/reading-the-south-through-northern-eyes-jorge-luis-borgess-australian-reception-19622016.
6 Tom Cho, *Look Who's Morphing* (Sydney: Giramondo, 2009).
7 Elizabeth Tan, "Meet Elizabeth Tan," Melbourne Writers Festival, July 29, 2020: https://mwf.com.au/blog/meet-elizabeth-tan/ (website since deleted).
8 Nicholas Jose, *Bapo* (Sydney: Giramondo, 2014), p. 3.
9 Jose, *Bapo*, p. 145.
10 Jose, *Bapo*, p. 215.
11 John Ryan, "Memory: The Theatre of the Past," *Coolabah* 13 (2014): pp. 156–163 (p. 156).
12 Gail Jones, *Sixty Lights* (London: Random House, 2013), p. 147.
13 Jones, *Sixty Lights*, p. 185.
14 Jones, *Sixty Lights*, pp. 3–4.
15 Jones, *Sixty Lights*, p. 157.
16 Jones, *Sixty Lights*, pp. 156–157.
17 Jones, *Sixty Lights*, p. 156.
18 Kama Maclean, *British India, White Australia: Overseas Indians, Intercolonial Relations and the Empire* (Sydney: University of New South Wales Press, 2020), p. 55.
19 Étienne Balibar, *Politics and the Other Scene*, trans. Christine Jones, James Swenson, and Chris Turner. (London: Verso, 2002), p. 8.
20 Yen-Rong Wong, "Will We Be Right?: Melanie Cheng's *Australia Day*," *Kill Your Darlings* August 24, 2017: www.killyourdarlings.com.au/2017/08/will-we-be-right-melanie-chengs-australia-day/.

21 Melanie Cheng, *Australia Day* (Melbourne: Text Publishing, 2017), p. 92.
22 Cheng, *Australia Day*, p. 93.
23 Cheng, *Australia Day*, p. 122.
24 Michelle Wright, *Fine* (Sydney: Allen & Unwin, 2016), p. 7.
25 Wright, *Fine*, p. 52.
26 Wright, *Fine*, p. 52.

16

NICHOLAS BIRNS

Craft and Truth

The Australian Verse Novel

The Origins of the Australian Verse Novel

If Australian fiction is worth examination as a discrete subject, its delineation will have to be not just national identity but form. If we ask what the characteristic forms of Australian literature are, one of the most evident might be the verse novel. This was especially so in the 1980s and 1990s, when a series of Australian verse novels by writers of very different backgrounds and ideologies gained extensive notice. By 2013, Sarah Holland-Batt could remark confidently that nowhere "was the verse novel more popular than in Australia."[1] The Australian verse novel was vital in the internationalization and diversification of Australian fiction. It enabled Australian writers to gain more world attention. Equally, the verse novel has extended the definition of Australian literature in racial, ethnic, gender, and conceptual terms.

The verse novel can be traced to Lord Byron's *Don Juan* (1819–1824) and Alexander Pushkin's *Eugene Onegin* (1833), both of which adapted past comic epics to modern life while retaining rhyme and meter. As Linda Weste has pointed out, the verse novel must possess both "poeticity' and "narrativity."[2] It has similarities to the poetics sequence or the long poem as such, and the genre boundary between these forms cannot be definitively policed. But in practical terms, one can say that the verse novel is directed much more towards telling a story and operates as a typical novel might in all circumstances other than being in verse rather than prose. The verse novel has always epitomized a chance for poetry to gain a wide audience and, in general, for what Mike Cadden calls "blends and crossovers" to occur between verse and prose.[3] As Stefanie Markovits has commented, even in the Victorian era, verse novels engaged in "genre-mixing" as a road to concocting their own "hybrid creations."[4] David McCooey concurs that Australian verse fiction, also, is generically heterodox.[5] Yet then and now, a form that achieves acclaim in the public sphere does not necessarily stimulate widespread emulation. In a country where many prominent novelists – David Malouf, Roger McDonald, Thomas Shapcott, to name only a few – started out as poets, the verse novel has been a way to pull a reverse, for writers identifying mainly as poets to reach a more story-driven audience. But the verse novel is also an in-between genre that has spoken to a certain Australian sense of being in-between: neither a developing country nor a great power, a developed country but not a metropolitan one. This certainly emerges in the case of Les Murray, the Australian verse novelist most devoted to exploring the concept of the nation. But it is also there in the four other cases we will consider at extended length in this chapter: the 1980s trio of John A. Scott, Alan Wearne, and Laurie Duggan; the bestselling crime-verse-novelist Dorothy Porter; the Indigenous writer Ali Cobby Eckermann; and the Filipina-Australian Ivy Alvarez, whose *Disturbance* (2013) brings together many of the traits canvassed in the earlier writers. Holland-Batt has theorized that "perhaps it is a remnant of the relatively strong historical tradition of narrative poetry and balladry" in Australia.[6] On the other hand, though, Australian verse fiction is laden with conscious craftsmanship and very rarely tells a story simply for the story's own sake. Catherine Addison has pointed out that verse novels such as the Polish poet Adam Mickiewicz's national epic poem *Pan Tadeusz* (1834) were strongly linked to national self-assertion of peripheral or marginalized peoples.[7] The presence of *Eugene Onegin* (a precursor to which Dorothy Porter paid tribute) and, for instance, the Danish poet Frederik Paludan-Müller's *Adam Homo* (1842–1849) at the beginning of their language's emergence into the world literary arena might be analogous to Australian writers taking up the form in the past seventy years.

Verse novels carry with them a formal emphasis that counters the content-oriented bias of Australian literature promulgated by both nationalism and the framing of the publishing industry. Australian verse fiction is formally conscious not because it uses traditional verse forms or comments on itself in an overtly metafictive way, but because, when they succeed, Australian verse novels exist more in their language and style than a denotative relation to their subject. Although Australian verse novels vary both in terms of poetic style and the viewpoint of their poetic personae, they share common traits, such as a colloquial and unmannered style. Anthony Lawrence's *The Welfare of My Enemy* (2011), Paul Hetherington's *Blood and Old Belief* (2003), and Geoff Page's verse novels, such as *Lawrie & Shirley: The Final Cadenza* (2006), are Australian verse fiction in which formal rhyme is used to good effect. But the dominant tradition has been less strictly formalist. Wearne's *The Nightmarkets* (1986) ingeniously uses rhyme, but its meter is irregular. Even Murray's first sequence, which uses a loosened version of the traditional sonnet form, is more characterized by narrative propulsion than formal closure.

The verse novel must be at once more referential and less sententious and oracular than lyric poetry. Any deployment of forms must adapt to these discursive necessities, which are generic traits that readers of novels expect.

Australian verse novels generally unfolded in poetry that is imagistic, suggestive, and, despite their social concern, not molded to fit an agenda. Verse can be more gossamer than prose. But it can also be more apothegmatic. By speaking to the ontology of feeling, verse can resemble nonfiction in a way not directly possible for realistic fiction. Because the verse novel does not have the deep history of the prose novel in English, verse novelists are less bound by scheme or precedent. They are thus free to unfold a truth to which, in ontological terms, the lyric core of poetry always lays claim. Sometimes, in the terms of Johann Wolfgang von Goethe, the issue is not the opposition between *Dichtung* and *Wahrheit*, poetry and truth, but the problems caused by their proximity.

Les Murray

In the mid-twentieth century, prominent Australian poets such as Douglas Stewart and Rex Ingamells wrote verse novels. But the form did not achieve international impact until Les Murray's two verse novels, *The Boys Who Stole the Funeral* and *Fredy Neptune*, were published twenty years apart, in 1979 and 1999 respectively. *The Boys Who Stole The Funeral* (1979) is a verse novel comprised of 140 sonnets. Kevin Forbutt and Cameron Reeby are intent on removing the corpse of Kevin's uncle, the military veteran Clarence Dunn, and burying him, as Clarence had wished, in his rural homeland. Both a critique of the sophisticated urban elite and a knowing attempt to engineer an Australian rural mythology, *The Boys Who Stole The Funeral* is laden with themes of renewal and regeneration. Brigid Rooney points out that the poem's lampooning of trendy liberalism can be read as "a critique of the sixties generation."[8] Yet these lines near the closing have an air of healing, of catharsis, and the poem is less offering a solution to urban malaise than an idiosyncratic rendition of hope. The villain of the poem, the militant feminist Noeline Kampff, portrayed as an angry, resentful fury, is also acknowledged in her humanity:

> She sweeps from the table a bucket of watery beef-blood
> And with a dancing attach uplifts and discharges
> It fabulously down, a halo, a robe of smashed scarlet[9]

The strong inflection of "fabulous," recalling that now-trivial word's roots in fable and the fabled (from the Latin *fabulosus*), the spiritual aura of the halo, and the incarnadine vigor of the poured blood all belie picturing

Kampff as a monotonal harridan. Even the reader sympathetic to feminism can bracket Murray's immediate polemics and focus on the ideals of the homed, the humble, and the vernacular that Murray is affirming.

Murray's second verse novel, *Fredy Neptune* (1998), centers on Fredy Boettcher, a German Australian who lacks the ability to feel. Fredy goes through a series of adventures amid twentieth-century European tumult, bewildered but necessarily stoic amid the tough times in which he is projected. These adventures culminate in this highly problematic catharsis:

> You have to pray with a whole heart, says my inner man to me,
> and you haven't got one. Can I get one?
> Forgive the Aborigines. What have I got to forgive?
> They never hurt me! For being on our conscience.[10]

In his lyric poetry, Murray addressed the need for religion and imagination to coinhabit and cohere in order to make experience whole. Murray, like many white Australian writers, sees acknowledging First Nations people as part of this quest for wholeness. The unexpected idea of a white man forgiving the Aborigines (and, a few lines later of a gentile German forgiving the Jews) is Murray's critique of the way white guilt sometimes gets in its own way by caring more about its own remorse with respect to racial injustice than the injustice itself. Fredy's inability to feel operates highly effectively as an operational tactic. It enables Murray to depict atrocities such as the Armenian Genocide without being voyeuristic or exploitative and to give vivid descriptions, such as that of wartime Jerusalem, "its towers husked and unhusked on the cob / in its high stone box."[11] It also renders episodes such as the German navy in the Black Sea disguising itself as the Turkish navy without being too bound to the historical record. But Fredy's emotional induration also means that his response to experience is at one remove, in the realm of opinion rather than knowledge. Though partisan and opinionated, *The Boys Who Stole The Funeral* is pitch-perfect (within its presumptions). *Fredy Neptune* seems, at times, and despite its many inspired and valuable passages, to have a tin ear. But its portrait of a life lived amid the violence and trauma of war is nonetheless moving.

The *Scripsi* Triumvirate: Wearne, Duggan, and Scott

In the US and UK, the most successful and widely acclaimed verse novel of the late twentieth century was Vikram Seth's *The Golden Gate* (1986). This work, notwithstanding the Indian origin of his author, was set in a rather stylized version of then-contemporary California and using a rhymed stanza borrowed from *Eugene Onegin* as translated by Charles Johnston.

In contrast, few of the Australian verse novels after Stewart rhymed or used conventional meter. This is even true of Murray, who is widely perceived (and tended to style himself) as a more traditional poet. The UK writer Bernardine Evaristo's verse novels *Lara* (1997) and *The Emperor's Babe* (2001) had the flow and readability of prose fiction and, as is demonstrated by the inclusion of Evaristo along with several Australian verse novelists in Linda Weste's 2020 book of interviews of global practitioners of the genre, are close formally to the mode that prevailed in Australia.

Wearne, Duggan, and Scott were three verse novelists who all went to Monash University in the 1970s. The three emerged under the aegis of the short-lived but influential *Scripsi* magazine in the 1980s. Edited by Peter Craven and Michael Heyward, *Scripsi* was at once markedly rooted in the State of Victoria and staunchly cosmopolitan. At the peak of its influence in 1987, *Scripsi* published excerpts from, and reviews of, important verse novels such as Duggan's *The Ash Range* (1987), Scott's *St Clair* (1986), and Wearne's *The Nightmarkets*. All three had prominent publishers (Picador, UQP, and Penguin) and this moment marked the point at which Australian verse fiction became not just interesting but *au courant*. All were tacitly on the political left, and Wearne and Scott's works contained early soundings of or criticisms with respect to what came to be called neoliberalism. Yet their angle on political economy is oblique.

Duggan's *The Ash Range* focuses on the region of Gippsland, which he defined as roughly the eastern third of the state of Victoria. It is a documentary poem consisting of excerpts from letters and newspaper articles (real and feigned), prose remembrances, and verse that gives an interpretive frame to recollection and memory:

> A small group
> Surrounded at Lady Bay
> > > Managed to escape
> They crossed the Mitchell, Nicholson, and Tambo Rivers,
> Eventually tracked down by the "boys"
> Offering little resistance to bullets,
> At Butchers Creek,
> Bancroft Bay.[12]

This passage showcases two of the salient elements in the poem: the thick deployment of Gippsland referents (the reader who does not know everything about Omeo and the Tambo River at poem's end is an inattentive reader) and the sense of social protest by the underclass against the injustice of constituted authority. The name of Butchers Creek, bluntly and without fanfare, conveys both of these. *The Ash Range* immerses the reader in the dense texture of contemporary Australia by focusing on a specific patch of the territory, insisting on the importance of the minor. There is a soft-footed spiritual affirmation in the poem's final quatrain:

> There is a message at the bottom of every glass.
> Dust blows off the road outside,
> And the stars, Crux, Bunjil, look down
> On a telephone booth in the middle of the bush.[13]

Humanity and nature, landscape and technology interfuse in an palpable way that is hardly innocent.

John A. Scott's *St Clair: Three Narratives* is composed of three parts, oriented towards the past, present, and future. The first, "Preface," is narrated by a compositor who plays no direct "part within the narrative."[14] It concerns two lovers, Carl Brouwer and the mysterious Julia, in a stylized Paris of the early 1980s, poised between the avant-gardism of the past and the multiculturalism of the future. The connivances of the sinister Gus, half-*artiste*, half-sex criminal, and Julia's disappearance lend a minatory air. This is continued in the middle, title poem, "St Clair," set in an Australian mental asylum. Carl appears as a minor character confided in by the wife of the main character, Warren, who is incarcerated in the St Clair asylum. Both in "St Clair" and the third part, "Run In the Stocking" reference is made to a "South" – roughly Melbourne – that is contrasted to the "North" – roughly Sydney – in a postapocalyptic antithesis, where, after an unspecified catastrophe, the South has become a zone of devastation and the north one of traumatized retrenchment. The third part concerns a man named Dover Andersson, who realizes that he is the same person as Terry Rutherford, a prominent dissident against an oppressive future dictatorship who has been reconditioned to have no memories of his earlier self. When Dover/Terry confronts his old flame and nemesis, Judith Anders, aka Ingrid, she tells him, "where you remembered suburbs, there's only desert."[15] Like Carl, who asks if we are "to be condemned by histories / In which we took no apart," Dover/Terry is not sure whether he is perpetrator or victim.[16]

Though the three poems of *St Clair* seem separate, references to Carl and the South in the second part stitch them together. Furthermore, all three share common themes of crime, dark fantasy, and erotic obsession. A dystopian thrust coexists with a splayed temporality. Dover/Terry does not realize that it is in fact fifteen years later than he thinks. Carl is questing for the ghost of the Parisian past as much as for Julia. This takes the narrative out of realism, but into a sphere that is more fantastic than metafictive. *St Clair*, with its science-fictional overtones, began what has been a very fruitful engagement of the Australian verse novel with genre fiction. It also shares in its North-South division, themes of regionalism with *The Ash Range*, and very obviously a topos of nightmarish politics and a sense of the poetic world as an arena for the quest for justice with *The Nightmarkets*.

Wearne's *Nightmarkets* is the most ambitious and complicated of the three poems. Wearne's story of political intrigue and personal disillusionment revolves around six points-of-view: those of Sue Dobson, and Ian Metcalfe, who are ex-lovers; Ian's brother Robert Metcalfe, who runs for Parliament; Terese "Terri" Lockhart, a high-class prostitute who becomes Ian's love interest; John McTaggart, scion of a Liberal Party grandee who decides to form a new party in the uncertainty after the forced departure of Gough Whitlam's government in 1975; and Elise McTaggart, his mother. Wearne's poem was conceived as a protest against Whitlam's replacement by Fraser and the rightward social shift it represented. Yet it took take eight years to write and be published, By then, in an ironic, recursive turn, Labor was back in power – but had adapted itself under the policies of Paul Keating, as treasurer, to economic rationalism and neoliberalism.

The *Nightmarkets* succeeds, though, not just in its conception but in its granular iteration. The novel's language is at once colloquial, specific, and conceptually challenging:

> Max calls me The Suburban Guetrilla
> And Frank, El Presidente. She's known as the Grim Reaper
> With, "Oooh, that Max, he delights to recoil in fright,
> Thinks it mock fright (My kids keep chanting, scaredy cat/from Ballarat[17]

The jauntiness and thickness of local reference are at once ingratiating and somewhat overwhelming. Indeed, the poem, for all its arsenal of self-conscious language and its electric responsiveness to the right-wing political turn, both of which would have resonated through the Anglophone world, is delightfully unexportable, and for all its worldly sophistication brandishes its own locality as an effect. In an era when Australian fiction was flourishing worldwide and was only indirectly political, *The Nightmarkets*, in its display of convincing dialogue, compelling characterization, and psychological depth, shows that the Australian verse novel can present a version of Australia full-bore, teeming with authenticating detail, and not have to streamline it for marketing purposes. As Martin Duwell points out, a particular triumph here is the portrait of Elise McTaggart, widow of one iconic politician, mother of his would-be Baby Boomer successor.[18] Wearne, as a young man of the Whitlam generation, furious at the Liberal Party (Australia's major center-right political party) for undermining Whitlam's progressive rule, represents the anthesis of all that Elise is. Yet his portrait of her country villa at Koornung, her vexatious friendship with the Liberal power broker Molly Crawford, and her half-realized, half-disappointed dynastic hopes in her son (who bolts from the Liberals to found a new progressive party) reveal her as a human being. Her son John is also portrayed complexly, fascinated by women but aware that to succeed in politics he will have to engage with men in a way that is almost sexual, where after "most rallies" a "pissed admirer" will want to "touch me."[19] John would love to be the Australian John F. Kennedy. But it is too late in the day, both in terms of the waning of white male supremacy and the corruption of Australian politics to really hope for this. Whereas so many Australian novels are content to depict toxic masculine villains as stereotypical "ockers" – Australian slang for men who behave badly – Wearne shows how, in the late twentieth century, toxic masculinity was monetized and financialized. This is why Terri's section is the key to the book, and her monologue one in which rhyme, as a trope both subversive and suturing, is deployed to superb effect:

> But if Ken made me very annoyed for years,
> He wasn't an utter failure, just not a success. Barracked for Collingwood,
>   Get the picture?
> Doesn't it sound like Ross? Anyway, do I want some big-noting success?
> When we met, selling or buying over the counter, who'd've thought I'd
> End up being kissed, caressed.
> And kinda loved by this walrus?[20]

The "success / caressed" end-rhyme, bolstered by the earlier mention of "success" and the assonance of "kissed" – and for that matter "Ross" and "walrus" – gives the lines an ingenious, in-joke, a knowing flow even as it delineates the interaction of status, gender, and power in Terri's world. (The reference to the sporting canonicity of the Collingwood football club is also characteristically Wearne.) Sue and Ian's relationship is very different from Terri's dealing with men. It is the heart of the book, its beginning and ending. In how Sue and Ian handle their breakup and their tentative rapprochement – at the end of the book, Sue and Ian are still "yet to cohabit" – there is maturity and generosity. This quality questions hierarchies not just of gender but of politics, and for all the novel's sense of dystopia promises a hidden utopia of re-envisioned interpersonality.[21] Wearne's later, longer verse novel, *The Lovemakers* (2001), continued this emphasis, which was in a different way carried on again by twenty-first-century verse novels that bordered on autofiction: Heather Sladdin's *Patterns of Being* (2015), Beth Spencer's *Vagabondage* (2014), and Christine Evans' *Cloudless* (2015). These works used the verse novel form to solicit intimate, interpersonal space, and to elucidate what might be called the sociality of the interior.

The Popular Verse Fiction of Dorothy Porter

Dorothy Porter was the foremost Australian writer to be known mainly for their verse novels. Most verse novelists are known more as poets than prose writers, though Brian Castro, whose *Blindness and Rage* appeared in 2017 had already developed a significant reputation as an experimental novelist. Porter's *The Monkey's Mask* (1994) was an internationally successful book, published in the UK and US (with a remarkable glossary of Australian English that reveals to overseas readers such details as "chook" meaning "chicken") and adapted into a movie directed by Samantha Lang and starring Kelly McGillis in 2000. In the novel, Jill Fitzpatrick is a detective hired by a wealthy family to find their missing daughter, Mickey. Though Jill is a lesbian herself, she is nonetheless surprised when Mickey's older lover turns out not to be the charismatic male poet she had suspected, but her female former professor, Diana Maitland. By the time she realizes this, Jill, having interviewed Diana in the context of finding background about the missing Mickey, has fallen in love with Diana and begun a torrid affair with her. Diana is seemingly omnisexual, being married to an urbane, politically progressive man named Nick, "scourge of the fascist courts," as well as carrying on with other female lovers.[22] Jill is at once enthralled by Diana and uneasy at Diana's protean affect as well as her class privilege – Jill is a working-class woman who lives in the Blue Mountains as it is more convenient to her Western Sydney clients. She lives in the mountains, though, not the suburbs themselves "because Blacktown / or Penrith / would kill me."[23] Working-class, an "ex-cop," Jill is estranged from one world by her social status, just as her sexuality makes her different in another way.[24] That Diana is herself a poet allows the poem to be conscious of its own form, with poetry as not just the medium but the partial subject of the narrative, and yet still have the narrative flow forward without obtruding or interfering in the readers' immersion in the story. Far from being overawed by the poetry world, Jill realizes it is a grubby, competitive, and "grotty" world with "not much to go around."[25] Indeed, one of the provocative narrative stratagems in *The Monkey's Mask* is that the implied reader of the book knows more about poetry than Jill, the protagonist. As another sort of referential braiding, Mickey's poems are included in the book: "Your smell fills the room like flowers / but your eyes fill my heart like thorns."[26] We wince, with Jill, at the lines' jejune fervor. But we also acknowledged the voice of the victim, whom malice (and even the structure of the book), has silenced. Jill is an outsider to the poetry world. Indeed, most readers will know more about poetry than Jill ever will. Just as there is this structural dramatic irony in literary terms, what might be called the presumed reader suspects that Diana is Mickey's lover when one of

Mickey's poems calls her lover a "mysterious goddesss."[27] Jill fails in uncovering the truth for Mickey's parents. In a detective novel, this would signal a metaphysical open-endedness. But in Porter's detective verse novel, it yields a more delicate pathos closely wound in with the fabric of the novel's own construction. Porter's portrait of Bill McDonald, one of Mickey's poet-crushes, is not exactly a dead ringer for Les Murray. This is so even though both are Christian and equipped with a facile touch as relates to getting Arts Council grants. Yet there are enough Murrayesque aspects to him to make his character a sort of intertextual rejoinder to Murray's caricature of Noeline Kampff in *The Boys That Stole the Funeral*. Thus Porter presents a recursive verse-novel-genre autocorrection. What Penny Jones calls the "large number of Australianisms" in the text, and the unmistakably local reference to Toorak, Penrith, and Blacktown, also have some of the rebarbatively Australian quality of Murray.[28] As Jones points out, *The Monkey's Mask* succeeded worldwide despite being anchored in an Australian locale featuring a cast of mostly lesbian characters. Received in the 1990s as a lesbian text, today *The Monkey's Mask* seems even more a broadly queer or LGBTQI+ work, with the title of "AZT and Sympathy" referring to the AIDS crisis.[29] There is also the possible transgender identity of Diana's husband, an "effeminate man" (with a "sweet smell").[30] Provocative at the time in terms of voice, gender, and representation, *The Monkey's Mask* has only gained in connotation in the ensuing decades. It shows the capacity of the verse novel to raise primary questions about literary expression while extending literary language to reach a broad and curious public. Peter Kirkpatrick has discerned a "falling off of critical interest" in Porter.[31] But as evidenced by Amanda Leigh's *Crimson Mind* (2014), also a lesbian-centered crime-oriented verse novel, Porter's experiments with identity and genre have fostered a tradition that is informed by but not limited to her own work.

The Verse Novel and the Problem of a Subject

Despite the verse novel's curious proximity to nonfiction, too much of a manifest subject matter can weigh it down. Just as Murray burdened *Fredy* with a determinate subject that weighted it down more than the more buoyant *The Boys*, so *The Monkey's Mask* was a kind of gossamer concoction that was kept afloat by its sheer ingenuity, while its predecessor, *Akhenaten* (1992), was burdened by the constraints of its formulated content. The very treatment of Akhenaten must take on determinate questions. The most troublesome of these is, do we see the Egyptian pharaoh's monotheism as a phenomenon in itself, or do we link it to Moses and Judaism? The cleaner solution is to treat Akhenaten in terms of his own beliefs, but that risks making him a mere historical footnote. Porter's making Akhenaten a cuddly, misunderstood megalomaniac raises questions. Is Akhenaten part of a dead past available to be sourced by Westerners? Or can contemporary Egyptians and other people of color claim their own relation to the material? Porter's *Akhenaten* hypothesizes its period as one of bacchanalian romps. Yet the period's main documentary source, the Amarna Letters, provides little warrant for a milieu "clear and erotic and sexy."[32] This is not to say that verse novels cannot take on historical subjects. Lesley Lebkowicz's *The Petrov Poems* (2013) dramatized a well-known 1950s Cold War spy episode with brio and flair. But Lebkowicz at once pays attention to the truth of the events and has fun with them. This is congruent with how truth is theorized within the poem, as ASIO, the Australian intelligence agency, "*falsifies – amends, adjusts, even corrects*" the documents it pilfers.[33]

Colder Lessons: Porter's *Wild Surmise*

Porter's 2002 verse novel, the astronomical *Wild Surmise*, is a feast of ingenuity and imagination. With its title taken from Keats' image of an astronomer gazing upon a newly discovered planet, the novel concerns an astronomer, Alex, who is looking for life on "Jupiter's smoothest moon," what she calls the "melanoma spot" of Europa. Europa is a "new world" where Alex seeks to learn "colder lessons than nothing."[34] The Jovian satellite may not have creatures resembling "our fish, our squid, our whales."[35] Alex loves her husband Daniel, whose yen for poetry from Dante to Rilke provides a humanistic counterweight to the scientific preoccupation of much of the poem's imagery. Yet Alex is haunted by a fling she had with a fellow astronomer, Phoebe, on Hawaii. When Phoebe announces that she is coming to Melbourne on a fellowship, Alex discerns that their old passion will resurge. The alien fascination of the astronomical object, life "as she doesn't know it" is compared, in its distance and inscrutability, to Daniel, while Phoebe promises a more earthy and fruitful liaison.[36] But the poem has two surprises in store for the reader. Daniel speaks of the astronomical analogies of the problems of dependence and significance in a relationship: "My wife is no one's moon. I am no one's sun."[37] One is the sudden illness and tragic death of Daniel, which leaves Alex bereft. The other is that Alex finds that though Phoebe is her Europa, a "mystery / I wanted to conquer / and crack."[38] Daniel, always "ardently present" is her true love, that the strange and distant is her erotic truth.[39] This is a potential surprise to the reader who has assumed from *The Monkey's Mask* that Porter will privilege queer over heterosexual attachments. An added element is the presence of another astronomer, the asexual Rachel, who is looking for life on Mars, rather than Europa, and perhaps actually finds it. *Wild Surmise* searches for life in the solar system, but is bursting with life on its own ground:

> This morning,
> behind the lace-work
> of foggy gum-trees,
> a currawong is calling
> Alex awake calling
> Like a sun-pinging creek.[40]

Porter's two other verse novels, *What A Piece of Work* (1999), concerning a Sydney mental hospital in the late 1960s, and *El Dorado* (2007), about a Melbourne serial killer, continue the critique of social institutions and double-sided insight into rogue individuals that were her oeuvre's hallmark. Porter's legacy was to take the verse novel as a form out of the realm of literary cachet where the *Scripsi* era had at once elevated and kept it, and onto a more accessible plane. On this plane, the form could find inflection by science fiction and fantasy-tinctured practitioners such as Lisa Jacobson in *The Sunlit Zone* (2012). It also achieved considerable popularity among writers for young adults such as Steven Herrick (*Love, Ghosts & Nose Hair* [1996], *Pookie Aleera is Not My Boyfriend* [2012]), Tim Sinclair (*Run* [2013]) and Margaret Wild (*Jinx* [2001] and *One Night* [2003]). In the hands of these authors, the verse novel became a fluid form that registers adventure, conflict, and aspiration for younger readers, while also introducing them to the indelibly, if here not obtrusively, formal aspects of verse.

The Impact of Colonization: Ali Cobby Eckermann's *ruby moonlight*

The Yankunytjatjara/Kokatha woman Ali Cobby Eckermann's *ruby moonlight* is the most acclaimed verse novel so far by an Indigenous Australian writer. Published by the Indigenous-run firm Magabala Books in 2012, it is set in "mid-north South Australia" (the unwieldy geographical term perhaps being an index of settler misnaming of Ngadjuri country) just as settler nationalism is gaining steam. The novel measures "the impact of colonisation."[41] Ruby Moonlight is a young Indigenous woman who meets an Irish migrant trapper named Jack. Furtively, they discover each other's eating habits; their romantic rapprochement is also a cultural encounter. Jack hides his relationship with Ruby from his genocidal white supremacist-peers, while Ruby knows she is not doing what the Elders of her people would wish. Jack's "simple life" offers Ruby "safety" against the "powerful" master of dance.[42] Ruby is a woman of "few needs" who actually cherishes the "remoteness" offered by Jack.[43] Ruby and Jack's relationship not only transgresses ingrained social expectations and the colonial gaze but also seizes its own moment of affect, and does not demand an intuitive comprehension by the two lovers of all that is in themselves. That Jack is a man of few words, and that neither speak the other's language, renders the poem an attempt to navigate linguistic incommensurability, something also instanced by the appearance of Indigenous words in the poem. Eckermann took words from the Pitjantjatjara/Yankunytjatjara language, since the Ngadjuri language that would have been present in the region in the time of the characters is no longer spoken in the twenty-first century.[44]

The most winning aspect of Jack's love for Ruby is his realization that, as a colonial, he can never truly understand her:

> Jack sits with reality.
> Ruby will always be a gem.
> Jack will always be a miner![45]

The exclamation point after "miner" brings across Jack's shock at his own inherent distance from the woman he loves. Jack is a sympathetic character as opposed to the lecherous old Indigenous man who tries to inveigle Ruby into a sexual relationship. Eckermann avoids stereotyping either race. She also frustrates any attempt of white guilt to fetishize a morally melodramatic landscape for its own gratification. Jack has weaknesses, such as the lure of gold and drink. But he is contrasted to the dehumanized "music-less man," who perpetrates the massacre of the Indigenous people.[46] As the danger increases, Ruby comes more into contact with her Kuman, or guardian spirit, who functions in structural contrast with the all-too-human white priest who condoned the massacre. Although *ruby moonlight* appears to be a historical verse novel, the last lines inventory the continuing colonialism of the present:

In this country / there is sadness
In this sunset / a ruby moonlight.[47]

No longer the proper name of the lead character but an elegiacally conveyed natural sensation, "ruby moonlight" (and note that the title of the book itself is not capitalized) as a sensation escapes the personal and is folded into the scene. This scene is conveyed in the present, not the past, tense. Ruby's survival of the massacre affirms the ongoing sustenance of Indigenous relation to Country. As in the other successful Australian verse novels, Eckermann, although setting the tale in a context, lets the story have its own verbal pulse, its own affective magic.

I Ask My Questions: Ivy Alvarez's *Disturbance*

The Filipinx-Australian writer Ivy Alvarez, in her 2013 verse novel *Disturbance* (published by the Wales-based publishing house Seren) portrays a middle-aged man's domestic abuse of his wife, and his eventual murder of his wife and his daughter. Aside from the final poem, most of the sections in the book are short, and the writing style is direct and transparent, though at times also pointed and acerbic. Alvarez uses the crime to give cameo portraits of everybody intimately and peripherally affective; these include family members of the perpetrators who, given the nature of the crime are also family members of the victims; detectives; the journalist covering the crime; and the priest officiating at the victim's funeral. The journalist's poems are inversely genre-justifying, showing how the poet can provide a perspective on the story that journalism, for all its attentiveness and accuracy, cannot.

> I ask my questions
> Extract details
> Take these flesh gobbets
> To feed the hounds
> Condense doubt from the air[48]

Although everyone's perspective is honored equally, creating a sort of democratic kaleidoscope, the poem is anchored by a visceral abhorrence of domestic violence and the mechanisms by which society sweeps the effects of toxic masculinity under the rug. The family friend is there for:

> A white lie at the hospital
> To blame the door
> The stairs
> Or clumsiness[49]

Jane, the wife, and Hannah, the murdered daughter, are victims of the "distorted face" of the perpetrator, Tony.[50] Jane knows she is living on borrowed time, that her life is "interstitial," but that what should be a developed framework of social institutions can do nothing about it.[51] Though Alvarez paints a terrifying portrait of Tony, she is not out to illustrate an individual's pathology but to show that his violence is somehow inculcated and made normative by the collective frameworks that should be fighting against it. In this way, *Disturbance* is as dystopian as *The Nightmarkets* or *St Clair*.

The final perspective in *Disturbance* is that of the surviving daughter. She delivers an angry, multipage peroration about how society assumes any family is an organic unit when the place "called home" was somewhere she "never wanted to be" and that the family was a "ramshackle / arrangement people thrown together / by accident / an imitation of happiness."[52]

Disturbance is not just an account of a crime and an exposé of society's indifference towards violence against women. It is a poem of radical protest calling for a reconceptualization of the terms under which we live. Alvarez fulfills the dual mandate of the Australian verse novel: to make us conscious about the craft of our own utterance, and to insist upon truth.

Notes

1 Sarah Holland-Batt, "Verse Novels in Review," *Southerly* 72.3 (2013): pp. 41–46 (p. 41).
2 Linda Weste, *The Verse Novel: Writers on Writing* (Sydney: Australian Scholarly Publishing, 2020), p. xi.
3 Mike Cadden, "The Verse Novel and the Question of Genre," *The ALAN Review* (2011): pp. 21–27 (p. 21).
4 Stefanie Markovits, *The Victorian Verse Novel: Aspiring to Life* (Oxford: Oxford University Press, 2017), p. 20.
5 David McCooey, "The City and the Contemporary Australian Long Poem," in *Australian Writing and the City*, eds. Frances de Groen and Ken Stewart (Sydney: Association for the Study of Australian Literature, 2000), p. 122.
6 Holland-Batt, "Verse Novels in Review," p. 41.
7 Catherine Addison, *A Genealogy of the Verse Novel* (Newcastle: Cambridge Scholars, 2017), p. 81.
8 Brigid Rooney, *Literary Activists: Writer-Intellectuals and Australian Public Life* (St Lucia: University of Queensland Press, 2007), p. 107.
9 Les Murray, *The Boys Who Stole The Funeral* (Sydney: Angus & Robertson, 1980), p. 108.
10 Les Murray, *Fredy Neptune* (Melbourne: Black Inc, 2007), p. 264.
11 Murray, *Fredy Neptune*, p. 24.
12 Laurie Duggan, *The Ash Range* (Sydney: Pan Books, 1987), p. 164.
13 Duggan, *The Ash Range*, p. 237.
14 John A. Scott, *St Clair* (St Lucia: University of Queensland Press, 1986), p. 6.
15 Scott, *St Clair*, p. 129.
16 Scott, *St Clair*, p. 79.
17 Alan Wearne, *The Nightmarkets* (Ringwood: Penguin, 1987), p. 126.
18 Martin Duwell, "Review of Wearne, *These Things Are Real*," *Australian Poetry Review*, September 1, 2017: www.australianpoetryreview.com.au/2017/09/alan-wearne-these-things-are-real-and-ed-with-the-youngsters/.
19 Wearne, *The Nightmarkets*, p. 147.
20 Wearne, *The Nightmarkets*, p. 186.
21 Wearne, *The Nightmarkets*, p. 291.
22 Dorothy Porter, *The Monkey's Mask* (London: Serpent's Tail, 1997), p. 221.
23 Porter, *The Monkey's Mask*, p. 11.
24 Porter, *The Monkey's Mask*, p. 34.
25 Porter, *The Monkey's Mask*, p. 152.
26 Porter, *The Monkey's Mask*, p. 108.
27 Porter, *The Monkey's Mask*, p. 123.

28 Penny Jones, "A Pint-sized Cliff Hardy: Dorothy Parker and the Niche Marketing of Australia," *Antipodes* 18.2 (2004): pp. 105–112 (p. 107).
29 Porter, *The Monkey's Mask*, p. 229.
30 Porter, *The Monkey's Mask*, p. 242.
31 Peter Kirkpatrick, "'Trouble, on the Rocks': On Getting Down and Dirty in Dorothy Porter's Verse Novels," *JASAL: Journal of the Study of Australian Literature* 20.1 (2020): pp. 1–16 (p. 13).
32 Jones, "A Pint-sized Cliff Hardy," p. 109.
33 Lesley Lebkowicz, "Bones," in *The Petrov Poems* (Sydney: Pitt Street Poetry, 2013).
34 Dorothy Porter, *Wild Surmise* (Sydney: Picador, 2002), p. 21.
35 Porter, *Wild Surmise*, p. 28.
36 Porter, *Wild Surmise*, p. 12.
37 Porter, *Wild Surmise*, p. 23.
38 Porter, *Wild Surmise*, p. 223.
39 Porter, *Wild Surmise*, p. 223.
40 Porter, *Wild Surmise*, p. 226.
41 Ali Cobby Eckermann, *ruby moonlight* (Broome: Magabala: 2012), p. 3.
42 Eckermann, *ruby moonlight*, p. 50.
43 Eckermann, *ruby moonlight*, p. 37.
44 Eckermann, personal correspondence, August 11, 2020.
45 Eckermann, *ruby moonlight*, p. 52.
46 Eckermann, *ruby moonlight*, p. 52.
47 Eckermann, *ruby moonlight*, p. 90.
48 Ivy Alvarez, *Disturbance* (Bridgend: Seren, 2013), p. 20.
49 Alvarez, *Disturbance*, p. 39.
50 Alvarez, *Disturbance*, p. 41.
51 Alvarez, *Disturbance*, p. 49.
52 Alvarez, *Disturbance*, p. 79.

17

LESLEY HAWKES AND MARK PICCINI

Queering Mateship

David Malouf and Christos Tsiolkas

This chapter examines the queer critique of masculinity and mateship in the works of David Malouf and Christos Tsiolkas. "Mateship," in the Australian context, is something like "friendship, but bloke-ier."[1] First recorded in its Australian sense in 1864, the term carries complex connotations that are not just cultural, political, military, but also *literary* in origin.[2] In this chapter, we explore how Malouf's novels subvert conventional notions of mateship through his original, lyrical, and disruptive language. Malouf's writing exposes erotic desires, alternative masculinities, and the dismantling of notions of nationality but does so through a regionalism in which South East Queensland becomes the scene of subversion. Twenty years later, same-sex desire is one of the libidinal investments disrupting the backyard barbeques, drug-fueled house parties, and porn theatres of Tsiolkas' suburban Melbourne. Across his work, these desires disrupt cultural, geopolitical, and temporal borders. We seek to show how these two writers foreground the inseparability of mateship and heteronormativity from a queer masculinity and homosociality.

Queer theory is today one of the dominant frameworks for reading Malouf and Tsiolkas – one that encompasses, but is not limited to, their novels.[3] In this context, "queer" is no longer a term of homophobic abuse. Rather, as Annamarie Jagose writes in *Queer Theory: An Introduction* (1997), it has come "to be used differently, sometimes as an umbrella term for a coalition of culturally marginal sexual self-identifications and at other times to describe a nascent theoretical model which has developed out of more traditional lesbian and gay studies."[4] For Jagose, queer theory's "debunking of stable sexes, genders and sexualities develop out of a specifically lesbian and gay reworking of the post-structuralist figuring of identity as a constellation of multiple and unstable positions."[5] In the case of Malouf and Tsiolkas, queerness emerges chiefly from the way neither writer conforms to the mainstream expectations surrounding their gayness, and by the way neither represents Australianness, especially Australian masculinity, as stable, separate, or ideal. In other words, their novels are not queer because these authors are gay, but because they resist and subvert the dominant perspectives on identity and nationhood in their writing. For all their differences, Malouf's and Tsiolkas' writing defies categorization and pushes the boundaries of normality. For Malouf, this is achieved through a ludic approach to language, while for Tsiolkas, physicality and violence are dominant modes of exploration.

From the heat and humidity of the city of Brisbane and wider South East Queensland to the mud and desolation of the Western Front during World War I, Malouf's characters are grounded in lived reality. But their eyes are upturned in pursuit of the sublime. Between these poles, Malouf's celebrated experimental prose stretches language, pushing it to see how far it can go beyond the bounds of acceptability. Though queer approaches to Malouf's work have focused on the many instances where characters move through same-sex desire in their poetic pursuit, these characters do not settle into committed same-sex relationships. Malouf's unsettled characters call Australian identity into question.

Of course, Malouf isn't the first novelist to have written characters who question the construction of identity and mateship. Frank Moorhouse's edited book on Henry Lawson, *The Drover's Wife: A Celebration of a Great Australian Love Affair* (2017), demonstrates how nonconformity to the dominant masculine culture has always existed in Australia. Moorhouse notes that any hint of "effeminacy" tends to be left out of discussions of Henry Lawson, even though Lawson himself often used the word "feminine" to describe his own personality.[6] Alternative masculinities are still obscured in contemporary Australian culture. It is in Malouf's characters' in-betweenness, their vacillation and unease, and their experiences with language, that we locate the queerness of his narratives.

Whether Tsiolkas' characters are tethered to the suburban peripheries of Melbourne by mainstream Anglo-Celtic Australian attitudes towards their ethnicity or have left ethnic enclaves for bourgeois comforts and backyard barbeques, their stories are mired in physical excess. Tsiolkas' prose could be described as a kind of "visceral realism," to borrow a term from Roberto Bolaño (to whom Tsiolkas is often compared). Andrew McCann, for instance, declares that both Tsolkias and Bolaño displace "metropolitan norms of taste and judgement."[7] While Malouf attempts to transcend reality, Tsiolkas interrupts its social construction with atavistic violence by way of magical realism and horror in his novel *Dead Europe* (2004), for example, or with the sudden, corporal punishment of a child for which his phenomenally successful novel *The Slap* (2008) is titled. As society descends into chaos under Tsiolkas' pen, sexual desire is reduced to the fulfillment of appetites, collapsing heterosexual and homosexual identities, and turning sexual partners into victims of a generalized violence against the Other. Where this violence threatens the often carefully constructed boundaries between insiders and outsiders, self and Other, and us versus them, we locate Tsiolkas' queerness.

The unsettled sexual identities of characters in Malouf's work parallel the author's own reticence to reveal his homosexuality to the public. Dean Kiley describes Malouf's coming out in 1996 as "sending a generation of OzLit students scrambling back to all those coy critical circumlocutions about mateship, adolescent crushes, emotional intensity and tawny thighs."[8] Until Malouf "moved officially and gracefully from his glass closet," his sexuality played a small part, if any, in critical discourse, which focused on questions of national and cultural identity.[9] Indeed, Malouf's queerness, as we understand it, resides in the contradictions inherent in the framing of our chapter, which designates him as a gay Australian novelist. Malouf and his characters avoid self-identifying as gay as they search language for more poetic alternatives to express their desires. Second, Malouf's Lebanese and Jewish ancestry unsettles narrow constructions of white Australian masculinity and identity. Finally, Malouf moves beyond the novel format in his writing, from plays to poetry to librettos.

Tsiolkas and his characters also reject cultural constructions of gayness, Australianness, and literariness. In *Arena Magazine*, Tsiolkas writes: "I am a man who fucks other men. I am a man who also lets other men fuck me."[10] In a similar vein, Ari, the protagonist of Tsiolkas' debut novel *Loaded* (1995), throws the constructedness of sexual and cultural identity into sharp relief: "Faggot I don't mind. I like the word. I like queer, I like the Greek word pousti. I hate the word gay. Hate the word homosexual. I like the word wog, can't stand dago, ethnic or Greek-Australian."[11] *Loaded* typified the 1990s Australian grunge lit genre, but since then, Tsiolkas has transcended regionalism and courted critical acclaim with *Dead Europe*, revisited the classical era with *Damascus* (2019) in a trajectory that mirrors Malouf's, and, most recently, made a foray into an autofiction with *71/2* (2021), which declares upfront: "I don't want it to be about politics; I don't want it to be about sexuality; I don't want it to be about race; I don't want it to be about gender. [...] All of those matters [...] now bore me."[12] Tsiolkas has also written for theatre and produced screenplays. He is a public intellectual, contributing often controversial opinions and social commentary to publications ranging from the *Guardian* to *The Australian*, and serving as *The Saturday Paper*'s film critic. Like Malouf, Tsiolkas has exceeded the novel format in his ambitions.

In this chapter, we focus on Malouf and Tsiolkas' novels. In this longer form, we most keenly observe the playful and exceedingly heart-breaking explorations of limitations and categorization. Tsiolkas' novels bring the uncomfortable violence of everyday life to the forefront: there is no hiding behind elaborate writing strategies or lyrical descriptions of landscapes.

Malouf's novels continually struggle between lyrical beauty and the horror of injustices. Malouf searches for the answer to these injustices in metaphysical language, but each time the reality of lived experience shakes the illusion of perfection. For Malouf, landscapes, characters, and language struggle for harmony. Both write novels that create hopeful alternatives, not illusionary utopias. Their novels open spaces for different lives to be lived and accepted.

Both Malouf and Tsiolkas keep their readers not only engaged but unsettled. Malouf's readers are enticed by his lyrical style and beautiful language, but beneath this beauty is the violence of the everyday – not an essential violence that cannot be changed but rather a violence perpetrated by the dominant structures against those who have less agency and power. Language, in Malouf's works, appears on the surface, to side with the oppressors. However, Malouf offers alternatives and possibilities – you just must have the courage to see them. What if language and the beauty it creates belonged to everyone? Malouf's characters seek stability, but they are constantly given change. Some stumble beneath the weight of these changes while others accept these changes with open arms and, in doing so, force change upon the world around them. They reveal what language is capable of if it is freed from constraints and boundaries, when realities that are already lived can finally be celebrated.

Tsiolkas' readers are confronted by an assault on the senses: The body looms large. The physicality of bodies moving through space and the violence that these bodies can inflict on other bodies is felt on every page. Tsiolkas' novels are a stark reminder of the lasting damage that injustice can cause. Revenge does not work but it is the go-to default setting for a society that finds it easier to repress than discuss. It is easier to search for scapegoats than it is to face the reality of the inherent violence within mainstream society. Both Tsiolkas and Malouf expose the consequences of these limitations. The queerness of these two authors' works is in the way they expose alternatives and possibilities, not only to be a more inclusive society but as a recognition that if these alternatives are not given the same standing, then the violence that surfaces and hides under the label of normality will continue.

David Malouf

When David Malouf is discussed in literary terms, it is usually as a much awarded and celebrated Australian writer of lyrical literary fiction. He is the author of nine novels and novellas, five short-story collections, nine poetry collections, one play, and four opera libretti. He is held up as an Australian author who has made it on to Australia's canonical list of great writers. Malouf has gained insider status in the sense that his work is much awarded and respected by the literary and public communities. In 2016, he received the Australia Council Award for Lifetime Achievement in Literature. His works are studied at high schools and universities, where they are chiefly read as treatments of the tensions surrounding Australian identity and senses of place. He is also seen as a regional writer of South East Queensland who writes of his city of Brisbane with minute detail and an insider's knowledge. Brisbane and the South East is the backdrop against which Malouf explores notions of growth, masculinity, and maturity. In his work the masculine, rough, unpolished exteriority of the city of Brisbane, or the regions of Harrisville, Beaudesert, and the Gold Coast, are home to young men who long for poetry, love, culture, and tenderness. Malouf's work interweaves the physical, the philosophical, and the imaginary and each work reveals the tensions inherent when these huge overarching structures collide. Malouf's novels include *Johnno* (1975), *An Imaginary Life* (1978), *Fly Away Peter* (1982), *Child's Play* (1981), *Harland's Half Acre* (1984), *The Great World* (1990), *Remembering Babylon* (1993), *The Conversations at Curlow Creek* (1996), and *Ransom* (2009). His choices of historical periods for his stories are flexible: His selection of time can hark back to classical periods of early Europe or just as readily be set in contemporary Australia. His stories are beyond or without time restrictions. His settings and places range from Queensland to Italy and in time from BCE to the present.

Malouf's novels draw eclectically from a wide range of popular and intellectual sources. His narratives can incorporate Greek myths into the same story as descriptions of Brisbane's local streets. His writing has always sought to bring binaries together – to reveal their coexistence. In *Harland's Half Acre*, Malouf writes of this paradox: "S' funny how a place you hate can be a place you miss."[13] Young men and women who spend hours discussing the nuances of poetic language yell obscenities in the next breath. *Johnno* is filled with instances of these lived contradictions. Johnno and Dante can be deep in conversation about language structure when suddenly Johnno will act out and abuse a passer-by, causing both men to run frantically down alleys and streets. This is one of Malouf's strengths: his ability to reveal the contradictions at the heart of his characters and the places in which they reside. Critics have long identified concerns with history, geography, myth, and identity in Malouf's work. They have also recognized the central preoccupation with language, which unifies and energizes all his works. For Malouf, language creates and defines boundaries, but it also struggles to eliminate them. His characters either have a great love of words (Dante, Ovid) or a mistrust of the dangers and limitations of words (Gemmy from *Remembering Babylon*, Jenny from *The Great World*). Each character, through their love of or distrust of language, is striving to find a sense of acceptance and home.

Malouf's sexuality was seldom remarked upon in early critical work. If it was mentioned, it was as an aside, quickly skipped over, and linked to larger questions of national identity. When queer theory came to be applied to past Australian works and Australian authors, Malouf's novels began to be included in this project. With this inclusion came a revisionist application of queer theory to his work. Yet when sexuality was examined in Malouf's novels, it was generally reductive, emphasizing a repressed form of gay fiction: male characters longing for other gay characters, but hiding their desire. Andrew Taylor, for example, offers a Freudian reading of Malouf's work, which explores each novel in terms of the return of the repressed.[14] Such readings emphasize how sexual desire is hidden among symbols and metaphors. As rewarding as these hermeneutic strategies might be, Malouf's writing cannot be reduced to symbolism. Queer readings of his works can move beyond this, as is evidenced by Stephen Kirby's groundbreaking 1987 article in *Meanjin*. Malouf's novels, Kirby contends, are queer, rather than gay.[15]

From today's perspective, it is hard to read Malouf's novels and not feel the sense of longing and desire some of the male characters exhibit for each other. In fact, it is hard to believe that there were times in the recent past when male desire in Malouf's novels was not noticed or, if noticed, glossed over. Even though Malouf's work was not analysed in terms of sexuality, it has always been read as a place where an "outsider" can fight against notions of heteronormative power and reveal the negativities that come with being forced to fit into preassigned boundaries and definitions. In *Johnno*, for instance, the character of Johnno is "forced to suicide because this heteronormative discourse allows no space for the existence of his queer identity."[16] Perhaps surprisingly, Johnno is the most "masculine" figure in the story. He is the archetypal Australian bloke: hard-living, hard-drinking, playing practical jokes, and good at sports. Malouf obscures Johnno's sexual desires and identity with familiar stories of larrikinism. As Peter Pierce observes: "Malouf richly imagines key moments of Australian history, both obscure and familiar, from which national mythologies are forged."[17] Yet Johnno's identity fits only partly within the parameters of national myth-making stories. By having Johnno reveal his real desire but also by having Dante not recognize it, Malouf shakes the foundations of masculinity. Dante has searched his entire life for perfection through poetry and language and yet, when the physical manifestation of this perfection reveals itself in Johnno, Dante cannot see it. Dante is like the early readers of Malouf: confronted with same-sex desire and sexual possibilities, he remains curiously unseeing.

Malouf has always been interested in language and the absolute to which literary language can aspire. However, he combines this absolute with grounded experience. It is this constant struggle between metaphysical ideals and lived realities that creates tensions within his works and gives his stories their distinctive homely but unsettling feeling. Malouf's novels struggle with the disjunction of achieving a sense of belonging in the places that are meant to be home. His characters can never settle, either by choice or by force. For example, Jim in *Fly Away Peter* is forced by war to relocate to the muddy fields of war-torn France, while Dante travels Europe to find "home." Neither of these characters ever feel at home. On this point, Abblitt argues that "the relationship of queer identity to space cannot be one of stasis but has to be one of movement."[18] Malouf's characters are always moving, even if they desire stability.

The physical relationships in Malouf's novels are always insecure; they are always over quickly. The actual relationships between the male characters may last for decades, but the sex itself is always hurried. Early in *Johnno*, Dante recounts Johnno's homoerotic experiences at Cadet Camp where he "organizes 'sessions' in the showers at which he wins over three pounds by being able to come faster and further and more often than any other boy in his platoon."[19] The physical act is here equated to financial gain. The quicker Johnno can ejaculate, the more money he can make. In *Hart Crane's Queer Modernist Aesthetic* (2015), Niall Munro states that "the queer body is oppressed by the world around it."[20] This seems apt for Johnno, who conceals desire and longing from ejaculation by transforming it into something financial. Dante doesn't pick up on any of these queer subtexts or social cues. So locked into what society expects of him, he doesn't see the other possibilities being lived out before his eyes. Amanda Nettelbeck reminds us that one "of the most striking features of Malouf's writing, in fact, is its accommodation of different perspectives."[21] Dante doesn't see these different perspectives until much later in the narrative, after Johnno has died.

Damien Barlow has written on the limitations of labeling texts "queer." "[S]hould," as he puts it, "the criterion for inclusion be the non-normative sexuality of the author, or is the actual content of the literary work in question more pertinent?"[22] Barlow reminds us that queer literature is far more complex than merely looking at the sexuality of the author. More important, for instance, is the way that Malouf questions dominant power structures, and plays with ideas of reality and fantasy. Malouf questions notions of reality and truth. Australian fiction has a long history of realist writing, and queer fiction can enter these realist spaces and bring new awakenings and possibilities. These voices and lives were often rejected and cast aside from mainstream, realist narratives. Malouf's novels rebel against an outdated version of dominant, Australian heteromasculinity, and instead offer ideas of differences and acceptance. Malouf is thus not only a great writer of identity – of the searching for a sense of belonging and spatial understanding – but also, importantly, a writer of possibilities. One might say that he writes "myths" for Australia because "myths" can be of the future as well as the past. In Abblitt's words: "[w]riting and existing in both the heteronormative and queer discourses, [Malouf] stumbles into the space in between, filled with gender-revolutionary possibilities, from which he can begin the quest for that queer utopia."[23] Malouf knows that utopias are impossible, and yet alternative realities must be possible. We would stress that Malouf's search for wholeness is not mere idealism: It is not a utopian dream. Rather, it is a recognition that society will always be lacking until it stops oppressing differences.

There is an interesting image that Malouf reuses in his novels: the tightrope walker or acrobat. This repeated image suggests that the characters are always aware they are treading a very fine line and could fall off at any moment. In *An Imaginary Life*, the image is presented in negative terms, but in later novels, Malouf recuperates the tightrope walker as an image of the wonderful implicit in the ordinary. This feeling of wonder is only available to those with an openness to flexibility and imagination: "But I am here, and all this, all of it, is far behind me. How foolish it now seems, my irony, my little impieties, my dancing on the tightrope over the abyss."[24] While it is here a negative image of flirting with danger and escaping mundane existence, in later writings Malouf has a different take.

In *Harland's Half Acre*, Clem recounts the beauty of witnessing a girl among horses in a paddock: "'Right in among the horses and sort of rolling over their backs like an acrobat. She was naked of course'. He swallowed. His adam's apple went up and down and his eyes were wide above the tanned cheeks." Eager to get a better look, Clem climbs a tree, but his vision is lost: "'Only the moment I took my eyes off of 'er she was gone.'"[25] Like the acrobatic woman from *Harland's Half Acre*, a tightrope walker appears in *Remembering Babylon*: "'Oh, and thing Ah saw once, a tightrope walker –' she felt no oddness in the transition. 'He had a rope fae wan side o' the street t' the ither, and he walked on it, in baggy troosers, wi' a bar in his han'.'"[26] Meanwhile, in *The Conversations at Curlow Creek*, a discussion between a man and woman about transcending reality is framed by a troupe of brightly dressed acrobats speaking a foreign language: "They turned off into a clearing, strung a rope between two trees, and went walking up and down on it carrying parasols which they opened, tossed in the air, and caught twirling on a fingertip." When the woman's colorful recollection challenges the man's "firm and unblinking" notion of truth, he refuses "to do what she was doing, to take flight from dusty reality and make their dull world yield up wonders"[27]

In *An Imaginary Life*, Ovid sees tightrope walkers or acrobats as an expression of his foolishness. Malouf's later novels present them in more positive tones. They are celebrated and embraced: The characters delight in the differences of life. We might consider these later tightrope walkers as an image of possibility in terms set out by queer theory. José Esteban Muñoz argues that "queerness is essentially about the rejection of a here and now and an insistence on potentiality or concrete possibility for another world," while, for Barlow, "Malouf's fiction can be read as arguing for and desiring a radical openness, a potentiality which is constantly deferred, unlimited and unhindered: a type of queer futurity that reaches towards and as far as infinity."[28] It could be a coincidence, of course, that the tightrope walker reappears across novels, but in the hands of an author as meticulous and stylistically precise as Malouf it is unlikely. The tightrope walker connotes magic, fear, and thrill but it also stirs feelings of hope and possibility.

Malouf's 2009 novella *Ransom* tells of the desire and love that Achilles has for Patroclus. Malouf writes: "Patroclus was to be his adoptive brother, and the world, for Achilles, reassembled itself around a new centre. His true spirit leapt forth and declared itself. It was as if he had all along needed this other before he could become fully himself."[29] When Patroclus is killed by Hector, Achilles' grief is insurmountable: "His runner spirit has deserted him. It is the earth-heaviness in him of all his organs beginning with his heart, that he must throw off if he is to be himself again."[30] Achilles is searching for a way to heal but both words and violent revenge fail. He still feels a lack. Nikki Sullivan argues that queer theories "aim to make strange, to frustrate, to counteract, to delegitimise, to camp up – heteronormative knowledges and institutions."[31] Malouf has often written about his aim to defamiliarize everyday life – to make it strange – much as Patrick White remarked in "The Prodigal Son" (1958): "I wanted to discover the extraordinary behind the ordinary, the mystery and the poetry which alone could make [life] bearable."[32] Similarly, in *12 Edmondstone Street* (1985), Malouf writes about his father's not recognizing a burglar: "my father had seen him and found him ordinary. Which means only, perhaps, that he has no eye for things, or no powers of description. What does ordinary mean?"[33] Malouf's novels suggest that meaning comes not from an absolute but from an energized interplay of the complex relationships of all things.

Christos Tsiolkas

Unlike Malouf, Tsiolkas is often discussed in terms of sexuality. *Loaded*, his first novel, follows nineteen-year-old gay, Greek-Australian protagonist Ari as he navigates the suburbs of Melbourne, as well as his performance of hypermasculinity, the deprivations of capitalism, and the threats to his nihilism posed by his peers' class or cultural consciousness. "The autobiographical dimension" here, as Andrew McCann writes, "is not terribly hard to trace."[34] Critics were quick to draw the kinds of correlations between Ari's and Tsiolkas' homosexuality that they were much slower to draw between Malouf and characters such as Dante in *Johnno*. While McCann suggests that "counter-hegemonic identities are central to [Tsiolkas'] thinking and writing," existing constructions of sexual identity never sufficiently satisfy the unsettled social and political aims of either Tsiolkas or his protagonists.[35] Indeed, the displacement of dominant ideological forms is "the horizon against which Tsiolkas' often bitter explorations of alienation take place," and the protagonists of Tsiolkas' early work embody "a range of emotional and corporeal responses (arousal, anger, hatred, shame) that register their distance from this admittedly hypothetical horizon."[36] Tsiolkas' characters often fail to contain themselves, expressing desire where disgust should be or slapping a child when they should know better. They cause offense but also exceed dominant ideological forms. In this way, Tsioklas' characters obverse, we maintain, counter-hegemonic identities.

Tsiolkas' novels include *Loaded* (1995), *The Jesus Man* (1999), *Dead Europe* (2004), *The Slap* (2008), *Barracuda* (2013) and *Damascus* (2019). Like Malouf, he is not bound by time or space in his writing. In *Loaded*, Ari is unable to leave Melbourne, save for the escapism of sex, drugs, and rock 'n' roll. Meanwhile, *Dead Europe*'s protagonist Isaac Raftis, a thirty-six-year-old Greek-Australian photographer, travels through Europe, like the eponymous Johnno of Malouf's novel. Moreover, the novel's subplot is set in a village near the town of Karpenissi in central Greece during and after World War II and tells the story of Isaac's grandmother Lucia Panagis. *Dead Europe* collapses differences between the Old World and the New, disrupting Australian narratives of innocence and isolation. While *The Slap* and *Barracuda* return readers to contemporary suburban Melbourne, *Damascus* takes readers to the ancient Roman Empire in telling the story of the conversion of Saint Paul the Apostle. Tsiolkas and Malouf are similarly eclectic creative writers. Tsiolkas' writing aligns with postmodern irreverence in its collapsing of high and low culture, the corporeal and the sublime or spiritual – preferencing, always, the libidinal. In *Loaded*, Ari lists some records that "everybody has," from Fleetwood Mac's *Tusk* to Public Enemy's *Yo! Bum Rush the Show*. He concludes: "I can't recite you a poem, any poem, but my mind is an automatic memory teller of pop music."[37] Meanwhile, the epigraph of *Dead Europe* is taken from "A Poem for the End of the Century" by Czesław Miłosz, and the sections of the novel – "Ante-Genesis," "Apocrypha," and "The Book of Lilith" – allude to aspects of the Jewish tradition.

Critics frequently identify the way Tsiolkas' novels are split between early, experimental writing that explores and exacerbates the instabilities of identity – particularly Tsiolkas' own identity – and the social realism of later novels such as *The Slap* and *Barracuda*. The book-length critical works on Tsiolkas that have been published to date – Andrew McCann's *Christos*

Tsiolkas and the Fiction of Critique (2015) and Jessica Gildersleeve's *Christos Tsiolkas: The Utopian Vision* (2017) – thoroughly examine the author's trajectory. Crucially, both books understand queerness as just one of Tsiolkas' concerns. As McCann puts it: "Every time Tsiolkas' work seems to settle into an affective, gestural or political groove, it also threatens to explode the very space it has carved out for itself."[38] But perhaps this is what makes his works queer: the constant dismantling of meaning.

Crucially, it is the libidinal that short-circuits the connection between individual bodies and the cultural, political, and historical contexts in Tsiolkas' early writing, signaled by its "compulsive gravitation towards the obscene."[39] For example, Ari declares: "The Polytechnic is history. Vietnam is history. Auschwitz is history. Punks are history. God is history. Hollywood is history. The Soviet Union is history," and offers a libidinal solution to our seemingly depoliticized, ahistorical (and thus thoroughly ideological) present: "Take more drugs."[40] According to McCann, Tsiolkas' first three novels "explore the impossibility of extricating the libidinal from its integration into the forms of life defined by the atomized, hedonistic subjectivity of consumer capital."[41] Indeed, by the end of *Dead Europe*, Isaac is fully invested in the libidinal economy. In London, where Isaac's ill-fated tour of Europe ends, lust becomes bloodlust. Isaac kills and partly consumes two men, cementing the text's designation as a vampire novel.

Gildersleeve writes that the shift from the chaotic tone of *Dead Europe* to the controlled voice of *The Slap* "has more to do with Tsiolkas' attempt to create something more like a 'readerly' text, as opposed to what might be seen as the 'writerly' tendencies of High Modernism."[42] Whether it is the modernist experimentation of *Loaded* or *Dead Europe*, or the social realism of *The Slap* or *Barracuda*, Gildersleeve writes: "Together [Tsiolkas' works] can be taken as a call on the reader to consider their own affective body, their own ethical relation, their own responses and responsibilities in the world."[43] At the heart of Tsioklas' project – one which identifies the networks of social, cultural, and economic exploitation responsible for the mistreatment of the marginal – is the subject of desire. Tsiolkas wants to know how our life depends on the subjugation and exploitation of Others, of and from whom violence is expected.

To return to queerness, though, McCann notes that identifying queerness in the author's work is a limited critical approach "that stems in part from the fact that other media can circulate these forms of difference and identity much more rapidly and much more broadly than academic criticism."[44] While literary critics and queer theorists returned to what Kiley calls Malouf's "coy critical circumlocutions about mateship, adolescent crushes, emotional intensity and tawny thighs" with a fervor, homosexuality has been writ large in Tsiolkas' work from the outset.[45] Not only is queerness but one of many subordinated identities that Tsiolkas' characters embody, queerness is only one piece of a bigger puzzle that confronts critics of his work. Indeed, the repetition of violence subsuming identities and the stability of communal structures, even those grounded in opposition and antagonism between ethnicities, ideologies, and sexualities, is the animating force of Tsiolkas' work. It is borne out in recurrent images of corporal punishment, scapegoating, and atavism throughout his novels.

The moment when Henry, one of eight characters whose perspectives are given in *The Slap*, hits the precocious three- or four-year-old Hugo at a backyard barbecue is a central image – almost like the primal scene of Tsiolkas' novels. It serves to elicit generally negative reactions from the community of characters in the novel and to expose their hypocrisies and invite their culpability. Simultaneously, this "slap" itself could be thought of as a metafictional event, one that radically expanded Tsiolkas' audience and solicited similar consideration, condemnation, and self-scrutiny from a global audience. McCann calls *The Slap* "a watershed publication in Tsiolkas' career," but writes that it "embodies a departure from the sort of fiction Tsiolkas had hitherto been writing."[46] Across Tsiolkas' work, abhorrent acts of retributive violence at once reveal the frustrated desires of the agents of violence and close the distance between these victimizers and the well-intentioned, cosmopolitan characters (and readers) who are quick to condemn them.

If *The Slap* departs from the more directly visible, visceral violence of novels such as *Dead Europe*, the title story of Tsiolkas' 2014 short story collection *Merciless Gods* bridges this gap and provides a succinct key to the way that violence operates in Tsiolkas' work. Ivan Cañadas, for instance, has noted how *Merciless Gods* "recaptures [Tsiolkas'] novels' immediacy, vividness and insight into sociopolitical and cultural conflict," and that the collection's "force and resonance" is "most striking of all in the collection's title story."[47] "Merciless Gods" centers on a group of nine old university friends at a dinner party in Melbourne who take turns telling their best stories about revenge. It culminates in one of them, Vince, describing a trip to Kurdistan and bragging about having beaten a boy who attempted to rob him there, severing the boy's hand with a hatchet as punishment. According to Cañadas: "Vince leaves his friends shaking with outrage, revulsion, even a sense of traumatic personal insecurity, when he – one of *them*, after all – claims to have committed an unpardonably brutal crime, implicitly incorporating xenophobic impulses or motivation, while in a remote, foreign land."[48] This is how Tsiolkas uses violence: to confuse his readers' comfortable distinctions between good and bad, us and them, villain and victim. This is the same trope Tsiolkas uses in *The Slap*, confusing his readers, and forcing them to make ethical decisions.

Details Vince shares about his childhood, during which he was looked down upon by the Greek community for having a single mother and bullied for being Greek in a predominantly Turkish school, complicate readers' judgments. For Cañadas, Vince's is "a story of disproportionate vengeance upon a scapegoat."[49] Through the tenuous libidinal logic that is typical of Tsiolkas' work, the Kurdish child becomes the cause of Vince's childhood ills and the source of his vengeance.

Dead Europe evokes the same logic against the apocalyptic backdrop of World War II. The first part of *Dead Europe* tells the story of Lucia Panagis, a Greek villager. Lucia and her husband agree to shelter a Jewish child from the Nazis. Lucia later falls pregnant to the boy. Desperate to conceal her pregnancy from the anti-Semitic, superstitious villagers and her husband, Lucia convinces her husband to kill the Jewish boy. This murder unleashes the curse of anti-Semitism that in turn crosses every border in *Dead Europe*, besmirching her grandson Isaac Raftis, whose descent into violence and vampirism is the subject of the second part of the novel.

But Lucia, like Vince, is herself a victim of the kind of stigmatization and superstition that operates in anti-Semitism and was reified in Nazi ideology. Lucia is designated "the most beautiful woman in all of Europe" by the residents of her village.[50] Her reputation spreads "from village to village, from village to town, from town to city, until carried in whispers through the roaming of commerce and war, it became a legend that began to cross even borders."[51] In Tsiolkas' words: "By the time of her thirteenth birthday Lucia's myth had spread so wide that travellers would go miles out of their way [...] in hope of glimpsing the radiant girl."[52] At home, Lucia is subject to ambivalence: "Between the twin sentries of her father's ravenous desire and her mother's fearful jealousy, Lucia spent most of her days cloistered in silence."[53] Her father's desire takes him from "thrashing her" and "exhausting himself with his brutality" to "kissing her feet, pleading for, demanding apologies, licking clean her bloodied hands or brow or back."[54] At one point, Lucia's father forces her to masturbate him while she is imprisoned in a cellar beneath the family house. Unrepentant, Lucia's father declares: "You are the most beautiful woman who has ever lived. Satan take you. [...] Don't forget I am with the saints, Lucia. I am a saint for not raping you."[55] Here, as elsewhere in Tsiolkas' work, sexuality and aggression merge, as do love and hate. Violence is at once extreme, as in the specter of the Shoah, and intimate, threatening to escape confinement to the domestic sphere or the dark past of a dead Europe.

Certainly, Tsiolkas' work concerns the identities subject to discrimination and violence as well as the identities of those who discriminate against them. However, none of these identities is stable. This in-betweenness is embodied by the character Colin in *Dead Europe*. Colin is Isaac's boyfriend and something of a moral compass for him during his travels. However, Colin refuses to get rid of the swastika tattooed on his right arm – "Faded to a watery blue" – because, as he tells Isaac: "This is my history and this is my shame."[56] In Tsiolkas' work, everyone is capable of good and bad, and innocence is an impossible, and probably unethical, position to maintain.

Notes

1 See Na'ama Carlin, Benjamin T. Jones, and Amanda Laugesen, "'Friendship, but Bloke-ier': Can Mateship Be Reimagined as an Inclusive Civic Ideal in Australia?," *Journal of Australian Studies* (2021): pp. 1–15.

2 See Bruce Moore, *Speaking our Language* (Melbourne: Oxford University Press, 2008), p. 104.

3 Damien Barlow, "'As If My Bones Had Been Changed into Clouds': Queer Epiphanies in David Malouf's Fiction," *JASAL: Journal of the Association for the Study of Australian Literature* 14.2 (2014): pp. 1–9; Stephen Abblitt, "Journeys and Outings: A Case Study in David Malouf's Closet," *Australian. Geographer* 39.3 (2008): pp. 293–302; Jean-François Vernay, "Only Disconnect – Canonizing Homonormative Values: Representation and Paradox of Gayness in Christos Tsiolkas's *Loaded*," *Antipodes* 20.1 (2006): pp. 41–45.

4 Annamarie Jagose, *Queer Theory: An Introduction* (New York: New York University Press, 1996), p. 1.

5 Jagose, *Queer Theory*, p. 3.

6 Frank Moorhouse, *The Drover's Wife: A Celebration of a Great Australian Love Affair* (North Sydney: Knopf, 2017), p. 1.

7 Andrew McCann, "Discrepant Cosmopolitanism and the Contemporary Novel: Reading the Inhuman in Christos Tsiolkas's *Dead Europe* and Roberto Bolaño's *2666*," *Antipodes* 24.2 (2010): pp. 135–41 (p. 136).

8 Dean Kiley, "Un-Queer Anti-Theory," *Australian Humanities Review* 9, February 1998: http://australianhumanitiesreview.org/1998/02/01/un-queer-anti-theory/.

9 Kiley, "Un-Queer Anti-Theory."

10 Christos Tsiolkas, "Raining on Your Parade," *Arena* (1995): pp. 14–15 (p. 14).

11 Christos Tsiolkas, *Loaded* (Sydney: Vintage, 1995), pp. 114–115.

12 Christos Tsiolkas, *7½* (Sydney: Allen & Unwin, 2021), pp. 2–3.

13 David Malouf, *Harland's Half Acre* (London: Chatto and Windus, 1984), p. 107.

14 See Andrew Taylor, "The Great World, History, and Two or One Other Things," in *Provisional Maps: Critical Essays on David Malouf*, ed. Amanda Nettelbeck (Nedlands: Centre for Studies in Australian Literature, 1994), pp. 35–51.

15 Stephen Kirby, "Homosocial Desire and Homosexual Panic in the Fiction of David Malouf and Frank Moorhouse," *Meanjin* 46.3 (1987): pp. 385–393.

16 Abblitt, "Journeys and Outings," p. 297.

17 Peter Pierce, "Problematic History, Problems of Form: David Malouf's Remembering Babylon," in *Provisional Maps*, pp. 183–196 (p. 183).

18 Abblitt, "Journeys and Outings," p. 295.

19 David Malouf, *Johnno* (St. Lucia: University of Queensland Press, 1975), p. 15.

20 Niall Munro, *Hart Crane's Queer Modernist Aesthetic* (London: Palgrave Macmillan, 2015), p. 177.
21 Amanda Nettelback, "Introduction," in *Provisional Maps*, pp. i–ix (iii).
22 Barlow, "'As If My Bones Had Been Changed into Clouds'," p. 2.
23 Abblitt, "Journeys and Outings," p. 294.
24 David Malouf, *An Imaginary Life* (London: Chatto and Windus, 1978), p. 27.
25 Malouf, *Harland's Half Acre*, p. 5.
26 David Malouf, *Remembering Babylon* (Sydney: Chatto and Windus, 1993), p. 112.
27 David Malouf, *The Conversations at Curlow Creek* (London: Chatto and Windus, 1996), p. 67.
28 José Esteban Muñoz, *Cruising Utopia: The Then and There of Queer Futurity* (New York: New York University Press, 2009), p. 1; Barlow, "'As If My Bones Had Been Changed into Clouds'," p. 8.
29 David Malouf, *Ransom* (London: Chatto and Windus, 2009), p. 14.
30 Malouf, *Ransom*, p. 35.
31 Nikki Sullivan, *A Critical Introduction to Queer Theory* (Edinburgh: Edinburgh University Press, 2003), p. vi.
32 Patrick White, "The Prodigal Son," in *Patrick White Speaks* (London: Penguin, 1990), pp. 13–17 (p. 15).
33 David Malouf, *12 Edmondstone Street* (London: Chatto & Windus, 1985), p. 29.
34 Andrew McCann, *Christos Tsiolkas and the Fiction of Critique: Politics, Obscenity, Celebrity* (London: Anthem Press, 2015), p. 1.
35 McCann, *Christos Tsiolkas*, p. 15.
36 McCann, *Christos Tsiolkas*, pp. 6–7.
37 Christos Tsiolkas, *Loaded* (London: Vintage, 2011; 1995), p. 122.
38 McCann, *Christos Tsiolkas*, p. 17.
39 McCann, *Christos Tsiolkas*, p. 7.
40 Tsiolkas, *Loaded*, p. 87.
41 McCann, *Christos Tsiolkas*, p. 13.
42 Jessica Gildersleeve, *Christos Tsiolkas: The Utopian Vision* (Amherst: Cambria, 2017), p. 9.
43 Gildersleeve, *Christos Tsiolkas*, p. 19.
44 McCann, *Christos Tsiolkas*, p. 16.
45 Kiley, "Un-Queer Anti-Theory."
46 McCann, *Christos Tsiolkas*, p. 85.
47 Ivan Cañadas, "Abjection and Sacrifice in Christos Tsiolkas' *Merciless Gods*," *English Language and Literature* 65.3 (2019): 441–453 (p. 441).
48 Cañadas, "Abjection and Sacrifice," p. 442.
49 Cañadas, "Abjection and Sacrifice," pp. 447–448.
50 Christos Tsiolkas, *Dead Europe* (Melbourne: Vintage. 2005), p. 15.
51 Tsiolkas, *Dead Europe*, p. 5.
52 Tsiolkas, *Dead Europe*, p. 15.
53 Tsiolkas, *Dead Europe*, p. 15.
54 Tsiolkas, *Dead Europe*, p. 16.
55 Tsiolkas, *Dead Europe*, p. 19.
56 Tsiolkas, *Dead Europe*, p. 10.

18

TONY HUGHES-D'AETH

Australian Fiction in the Anthropocene

The Anthropocene announces that the human species has affected the living and dynamic systems of the planet in numerous and profound ways. This chapter attempts to trace the effect that the Anthropocene has had on Australian literature. In this respect, the focus is on contemporary fictional texts that either thematize the effects (and causes) of the Anthropocene, or formally manifest the moment of recognition that the Anthropocene designates. In terms of literary criticism and literary history, the Anthropocene induces a critique of the kind of methodological nationalism that underpins, or at least unites, the study of Australian literature. There is thus something of a performative tension between the concept of Australian literature, on the one hand, and the intrusion of the planetary dimension signaled by the conceptual emergence of the Anthropocene, on the other. The English ecocritic Timothy Clark, following the work of Dipesh Chakrabarty, Bruno Latour, and Timothy Morton, has suggested that the Anthropocene has created a radical problem of scale, in which planetary time and space become dynamic rather than stable. The planetary dimensions of the Anthropocene pose challenges to the human imagination, upending the usual historical and geopolitical coordinates that situate us as people in the world. As Amitav Ghosh suggests in *The Great Derangement: Climate Change and the Unthinkable* (2016), creative writers have struggled to *write* the Anthropocene, as if coming up against some fundamental unrepresentability.[1] This same argument, that the Anthropocene presents as a problem of representation, has been advanced by Emily Potter with respect to Australian fiction.[2] But, for Clark, it is also difficult to *read* the Anthropocene: "No real precedents exist for reading at the scale required by the Anthropocene."[3]

To some extent, the term Anthropocene has, in the current moment, superseded words like environment and ecology. At the very least, it belongs in that sequence of terms. But in this chapter, I would like to hold on to the specificity of the term Anthropocene, and in particular its *evental* quality, which signals the advent of something whose qualities may exceed the limits of intelligibility. There are two dimensions that intersect in the term Anthropocene. One is that change is actually taking place whether we name it or not – the planet is warming, the polar ice sheets are vanishing, ocean levels are rising, species are disappearing, fire seasons are lengthening, storm frequencies and intensities are increasing, and so on. The other dimension is that we *know* it and that we know we are causing it. Knowing that once-stable planetary systems are being altered by us changes the way we think and exist, not just in material ways, but in terms of the basic fantasies that hold us as speaking subjects. Thus, while the term Anthropocene formally denotes a proposed geological epoch, its effect is to instigate a particular moment in consciousness in which humans are now considered actors in what Dipesh Chakrabarty calls the "parametric conditions of life."[4] For Chakrabarty, the Anthropocene marks a collapse of the constitutive split between human and natural history that inaugurated the humanist revolution in Western modernity. In this respect, we see that the Anthropocene's primary effect is a temporal one, and while it has resulted in an upsurge in dystopian fiction, it is perhaps better conceived in terms of "dyschronia," in which time is thrown out of joint.[5] In fact, the Anthropocene marks a distinct limit to the spatial turn that was one of the hallmarks of postmodernism, concomitant with what Fredric Jameson famously termed the "waning of historicity."[6] The Anthropocene, insofar as it marks a paradigm shift in deep time, places temporality back into question. Moreover, because it names "the break in consciousness and understanding" that human-induced planetary effects have produced, Timothy Clark considers the Anthropocene a "threshold concept."[7] It changes our being-in-the-world, forcing us to reckon with the fact that we live, not just in cities or countries, but inside atmospheric, oceanic, and biotic systems that we had previously taken for granted.

So, how has this changed the way that writers write and readers read in Australia? The most overt literary response to climate change has been a species of speculative fiction known as climate fiction or "cli-fi." Cli-fi mainly takes the form of dystopian fiction, where the effects of global warming (such as sea-level rise) have produced a catastrophic reorganization of human society. In George Turner's *The Sea and Summer* (1987; published in the US as *The Drowned Towers*), Australia lays claim to one of the seminal texts in this genre.[8] Deborah Jordan has produced an instructive study, *Climate Change Narratives in Australian Fiction* (2014), detailing cli-fi as a literary phenomenon in Australia. While there are earlier examples, cli-fi really takes off in Australia in the 2010s, and is broadly in line with global patterns in this regard.[9] Within literary fiction, there have also been works responding to Australia's increasingly catastrophic fire seasons, such as Amanda Lohrey's *Vertigo* (2009),[10] Eliza Henry-Jones *Ache* (2017), and Alice Bishop's *A Constant Hum* (2019). Jane Harper's celebrated detective novel *The Dry* (2016), adapted into a film, refracts a murder mystery in a country town through the realities of a drying climate. A secondary effect of Anthropocene consciousness has been to trigger a form of revisionism that reexamines the terms by which the nonhuman world was encountered and rendered in earlier literary texts. As Clark notes, "shifting the scalar context produces ironies of retrospect in the way in which the present-day or future readers may consider a past literary text."[11] The acerbic portraits of inland New South Wales by Henry Lawson now present as an "ecophobic misreading [of] the outback."[12] Given that concepts like the bush, the outback, and landscape formed such an overwhelming part of the national literary tradition in the nineteenth and twentieth centuries, it is not difficult to imagine that many classical Australian literary texts would be susceptible to Anthropocenic rereading. Even contemporary writers have taken on a new visage in light of the Anthropocene. Carrie Tiffany's *Everyman's Rules for Scientific Living* (2005) becomes a fable of the Anthropocene, John Kinsella's poetry becomes exemplary of the "Anthropocene lyric," and Chloe Hooper's *A Child's Book of True Crime* (2002) becomes an example of what Deborah Bird Rose has dubbed "Anthropocene Noir."[13] But in this chapter, I will largely eschew the revisionist task and concentrate instead on the effects within Australian fiction of the Anthropocene as a reflexive moment. Instead of attempting to review the field, which is burgeoning and currently emergent, in its entirety, I have selected features in the literature that seem instructive of the distinct shifts in the cultural imaginary caused by the Anthropocene as an ontological event.[14]

Glitch

In the Australian television series *Glitch* (2015–2019), a detective in a small town is suddenly confronted with a bizarre phenomenon in which dead residents begin emerging from the grave. Rather than decayed and ghoulish, the "Risen" appear untouched by their interment, even though some had died many decades ago.[15] While they appear perfectly healthy, they have no recollection of who they had been during their lives. This situation, in which the outward surface of small-town life is imperceptibly altered by elements that are not so much out of place as out of time, or dyschronic, is quite distinctive of the Anthropocene. The eeriness is caused by the fact that planetary collapse seems utterly incompatible with the sheen of late capitalism. How does one reconcile the disappearance of thousands of species with the appearance of the latest iPhone and the advent of self-driving cars? It is in this context that dystopian novels, films, and television programs have emerged to give a dramatic shape to something that in daily life is noticed mainly in the form of the glitch or the inconsistency.

Richard Flanagan's novel *The Living Sea of Waking Dreams* (2020) tellingly figures this aspect of the Anthropocene by transcribing it onto the human body.[16] In the novel, three adult children are dealing with the illness and eventual death of their beloved mother in their family home in Tasmania. The novel is mainly focalized through the daughter, Anna, a successful architect now living in Sydney. She initially puts the concern for her mother down to her flaky younger brother's tendency to exaggerate. When she visits, however, she notices something inexplicable, and seemingly unrelated to anything else going on in the novel. One of Anna's own fingers is missing. She looks upon the space where her finger used to be with a mixture of horror and shame. There is no scar, no bleeding wound, just nothing where there used to be something. As the novel unfolds, Anna loses other parts in the same manner. One morning she awakes to discover her knee has disappeared, then a breast, then an eye. Others, too, start to lose body parts. These "vanishings," as they come to be known, are entirely painless and seem to go almost unnoticed. It is as if, we are told, they have simply been Photoshopped away. The uncanny part is not the loss of the limb or other body part, but the fact that the phenomenon is going unremarked. Everyone seems to intuit that it is best not to talk about it, that there is something unseemly in this hideous eventuality. The polite thing is to keep going on as if nothing is actually happening, even though it is patently obvious that people are missing body parts left, right, and center.

The fact that *The Living Sea of Waking Dreams* uses the device of the vanishing limbs seems at one level to cast it irrevocably beyond the dimensions of realism that would make its world contiguous with ours. But isn't this what extinctions feel like to those of us living in cities and who only know about species because we have seen them on television or the internet? Something is gone that was once there. We are briefly confused, but then we reassemble the picture and push on. Extinctions are invisible, after all, as Jane Rawson has noted.[17] The psychoanalytic name for this reaction, in which one "knows" that something is going on but goes about one's life as if it isn't is *fetishistic disavowal*. Because liberal democracies pride themselves on speaking openly about matters of concern, Slavoj Žižek has suggested that fetishistic disavowal has replaced the more overt forms of repression within late capitalism.[18] For Freud, the fetishist finds the truth of sexuality, its assignations and basic mechanisms, unbearable. The fetish object – the shoe, the nape of the neck, a particular material or substance – is unconsciously selected to neutralize the unbearable demands of sex but retain its erotic charge. As a social mechanism, fetishistic disavowal helps explain global inaction on climate change. The truth is not concealed (i.e. repressed), it is just rendered inert, unable to trigger the call to action that that would seem necessary if it were really true. The paradox of fetishistic disavowal is that outward acquiescence masks a more fundamental denial. In this sense, the very words "climate change" can mask the acceptance of its fact. Bruno Latour makes a similar point when articulating the logic of inaction: "[W]e receive all this news [of environmental collapse] with astonishing calm, even with an admirable form of stoicism. If a radical mutation were really at issue, we would all have already modified the bases of our existence from top to bottom. We would have begun to change our food, our habitats, our means of transportation, our cultural technologies, in short, our mode of production [...] In any case, we would already have acted."[19] Yet, because the world is not acting, then there must not be a problem.

In Flanagan's novel, as we watch the dying of the mother play out with the domestic pathos of deaths everywhere, there are intrusions from the outside world via the increasingly intimate screens that articulate social reality. Anna scrolls past mass extinctions, coral bleachings, fires that will not end – the whole continuous telemetry of the Anthropocene. These dispatches, which are by turns apocalyptic and quotidian, take place in a kind of virtual space that Lacan calls the *extimate*, in this case, the intimate exteriority of the personal device. Textually, the background of planetary collapse sits somewhere between the slippage of free indirect discourse that is the hallmark of the modern novel, and the dramatic irony of stage pantomime: *It's behind you! The Anthropocene is right there! Behind you!* Is Anna aware of these things? They are happening on her phone after all. Does it matter? What does it mean to know the Anthropocene? This is the kind of fundamental ambiguity that fetishistic disavowal introduces to the question of knowledge. Interestingly, it is only the dying mother who can arrest the free scrolling of meaningless juxtaposition in the novel. The mother's dying in the novel is not to be denied, despite Anna's attempt to do this by batting away the facts. Anna's attempts at denial, though, are not finally a sign of her callousness, but a symptom of the fact that her mother's mortality was fundamentally unbearable. Here, we can see the alignment of the mother's death with the fetishistic response to sexuality, and then to the psychic structure of the Anthropocene. Put simply, it is happening, but it *can't* be happening, so it isn't happening.

Dyschronia

While dystopian fiction has been the dominant modality of cli-fi (particularly as genre and young adult fiction), as noted the Anthropocene's most signal effect has been dyschronia. Jennifer Mills' novel *Dyschronia* (2018) deserves special mention for apprehending this aspect of the Anthropocene. In some ways, the novel is conventional and modest in its basic terms. It follows the lives of people living in the small coastal town of Clapstone in South

Australia. In Australian terms, the *mise-en-scène* bears a resemblance to Randolph Stow's *Tourmaline* (1963).[20] Like Stow's town, Clapstone is dying and the inhabitants are waiting plaintively for messianic deliverance. The asphalt plant, the town's main employer, is closing down. Before the asphalt boom had come to give the town a new lick of paint and seal its straggling roads, the town had been the center of a struggling farming region. Over the years, the soils, always poor, were wrecked by the machinery and chemicals applied vigorously but in vain. Likewise, the rain, fickle at the best of times, had declined further: "Clapstone was a shell crumbling at the edge of a dry plain. It hadn't taken long."[21] The protagonist, Samandra, is a woman we meet in early adulthood, but the novel moves back and forth across moments of her childhood and upbringing. From her early childhood, Sam had been afflicted by powerful migraines that were accompanied by strange and frightening dreams. It gradually becomes clear that these waking dreams were visions of the future in which the natural cycles had radically altered.

The decisive event in the novel is intriguing because it is a reversal of the usual inundation narratives, which reference the rising of sea levels under global warming. In the novel, instead of an oceanic incursion, there is a sudden and drastic retreat of the ocean away from this once coastal town. In terms of a tropology of the Anthropocene, the interface of land and water (the "coast line") constitutes the horizon of meaning. Thus, while inundation removes the horizon of meaning so, too, does the retreat of the ocean. In the first case, the subject (or community) is enveloped and overwhelmed by an ocean that has escaped its boundaries. In the second case, the subject is *abandoned*. Stranded, to use Jean Baudrillard's famous phrase, in the "desert of the real."[22] The disappearance of the ocean deprives the members of this coastal community of their basic coordinates, indeed strips away the living edge of their universe. But in the novel, the ocean does not leave without first signaling its intentions. The living signifier it offers up on the shores of this town's meaning is the cuttlefish. As James Bradley points out: "The alien otherness of the cuttlefish glides through the fabric of *Dyschronia*, echoing not just the strangeness of Sam's condition, but [...] something deeper."[23] When the ocean retreats, thousands and thousands of migrating cuttlefish are stranded where the water had been. In another key moment in the novel, a gargantuan cuttlefish appears in the town, its dying body an object of horror and pathos.

Terra Nullius

But what if we are already there? What if the end of the world were not imminent, but right here around us, hiding in plain sight? For Indigenous people, the catastrophe is not lurking just beyond the future's horizon, but has broken fiercely across the world, destroying every dimension of life and belief. Various Indigenous intellectuals have made this point, including Tony Birch is in his essay "It's Been, It's Here" (2018). While those living in the developed world need speculative fictions set in the future to figure out the horrific dimensions of the end of the known world, Indigenous people need do nothing more than remember. As Birch writes: "For Indigenous people, the impact of climate change is not a future event. It has occurred in the past, and is occurring now."[24] Like Žižek, Birch apprehends a fetishistic quality to dystopian ecofiction: "Are these narratives of impending apocalypse something of a Western fetish? And do these stories lull people into thinking that a fictional *future* ravaged by climate change (by each of *us*, actually) is nothing more than a disaster narrative produced for our entertainment?"[25] What Birch and other Indigenous intellectuals have noted is the close relationship between the Anthropocene and colonization. In the first instance, the modern Australian nation is a product of the Anthropocene, just as much as it is now one of its producers.[26] The rapid (and ongoing) colonization and exploitation of a continent were made possible by the mechanisms of industrialization. At the same time, though, for Indigenous people, the colonization of Australia was the end of the world. It was an end every bit as terrifying and total as the ends imagined in dystopian fiction. They find themselves trying to articulate the situation of being between two endings, the one that has happened (colonization) and the one that is to come (planetary ecological catastrophe), yet at the same time feeling as if both are still, and already, happening.

The apparent symmetry between the colonization that took place across Australia and much of the world at the hands of European powers, and the apocalyptic scenarios of dystopian fiction, is captured in Claire G. Coleman's Indigenous futurist novel, *Terra Nullius* (2017).[27] Set in the South Coast hinterland of Western Australia, in the traditional country of her ancestors, the Wirlomin Noongar, Coleman's book seems at first a rather schematic retelling of the colonial history of the nineteenth and twentieth centuries. The setting is familiar from the plays of Jack Davis, from Doris Pilkington Garimara's *Follow the Rabbit-Proof Fence* (1996), and Kim Scott's novels. All the key elements are rehearsed: the land grabs by rapacious settlers, the devastating introduced diseases, the loss of food and water resources, the semi-enslavement of Natives, the emergence of the protection system and the stealing of children, the pernicious but ambivalent role played by missions and humanitarians. There is even a puffed-up Native Administrator called Neville and known as "Devil" by his Native subjects.[28] The twist, when it arrives, is that the settlers are not the British after all but amphibian-humanoid invaders from a distant planet, and the Natives are not just Noongar people, but all human beings. The aliens have colonized the planet just as the Europeans did, almost as if they were following the same handbook. The plot resembles Ursula K. Le Guin's *The Word for World is Forest* (1972) and, of course, H. G. Wells' *The War of the Worlds* (1897). In Wells' novel, humanity is saved by a virus that kills the aliens, but in Coleman's novel the pathogenic balance was with the invaders. Far from being saved by one of Earth's viruses, the Earth and its biological systems faced the same exact kind of devastation as Indigenous people when they were invaded. Introduced plants and animals proliferate, and begin to rapidly change the ecosystems of earth.

When we shift from speculative fiction to literary fiction, or "Aboriginal realism" to borrow Ellen van Neerven's phrase, the same basic equivalence between the Anthropocene and Australian settler colonialism persists.[29] Tara June Winch's novel *The Yield* (2019) is set in a lightly fictionalized version of the Wiradjuri lands of her father in Western New South Wales, near the junction of the Murrumbidgee and Murray rivers. The setting of the novel is a stylization of the essential *dispositif* of agrarian settler colonialism. The town of Massacre Plains, whose name belies the seemingly benign expanse of farmland, has a mixed population of Indigenous and nonIndigenous inhabitants. In the historical background is a mission that has mediated Indigenous life for several generations and intruding into the present is a fracking company offering up the latest scheme to pillage the land and release yet more greenhouse gases into the atmosphere. In the present of the novel, August Gondiwindi, an Aboriginal woman in her thirties, returns from several years in Europe to attend the funeral of her grandfather, Albert Gondiwindi. On the plane, she is given a newspaper to read: "Printed in the newspaper was a small photograph of a rhino. Above the picture it read in big ink block letters: GONE FOREVER – BLACK RHINO EXTINCT. An animal zip! Gone!"[30] The situation echoes the casual encounters that Anna has with extinction while scrolling through her phone in Flanagan's novel. Like Anna, August is thrust into the reality of extinction, and out of its virtualized pseudo-existence in the media-sphere, by the death of a beloved:

> The rhino in the news reminded August that she'd never been to the zoo, never seen a rhino in real life – it might as well have been a dinosaur. The paper listed other recent extinctions. And just like that she thought, zip! Gone! Poppy: Albert Gondiwindi was extinct. No more Albert Gondiwindi roamed the earth, and no more black rhino either.[31]

In this moment, we can underline a key difference in the Indigenous and nonIndigenous responses to the Anthropocene, in the direct identification with the concept of extinction. For August, her cherished grandfather Albert, the patriarch of the family and keeper of cultural knowledge, is not just dead – but extinct. It is true that the novel is about regeneration, and offers in the end, a hopeful narrative of cultural courage and resilience. But it is the fact that the novel is organized around the implacable fact of extinction that makes it distinctive of fiction in the Anthropocene. The novel thus draws a direct correspondence between Anthropogenic ecocide and Indigenous genocide, which is the exemplary Indigenous literary response to radical planetary ecological change.

It is also from within Indigenous writing that the single most significant literary response to the Anthropocene to date has emerged: Alexis Wright's *The Swan Book* (2013). The novel has generated a rich critical literature both in Australia and internationally. After the success of Wright's *Carpentaria* (2006), which along with Kim Scott's *Benang* (1999) dominated Australian literary scholarship in the 2000s and early 2010s, there was huge expectation around her next novel, particularly as it was going to directly address a climate-altered world. Yet this was no set-piece response that would unite the causes of Indigenous sovereignty and climate action, and the novel was written in a mode that had no ready analogs. Even the basic story could only be distilled with effort and patience. The narrative follows the life of Oblivia Ethyl(ene), a traumatized Aboriginal girl who is rescued from her magical encasement in a tree hollow by a European climate refugee, Bella Donna. From there, she finds herself married off to the nation's first ever Indigenous prime minister, Warren Finch. But beyond these basic narrative facts, the novel strenuously resists paraphrase. Indeed, critics wrestled with the basic form. Was it magical realism?[32] Or, was its elliptical lyricism best understood as a form of Indigenous modernism or postmodernism?[33] Or again, was it best thought of as centered in the patterns of oral storytelling of the Waanyi people, as Wright herself has stated? It is fair to say that the novel has defied formal categorization, even as it was immediately hailed as one of the great works of climate fiction.

What is most interesting and enigmatic in the novel, however, is that it does not follow the patterns of either cli-fi (as a dystopian genre) or the broadly liberal redemptions of social realism. In fact, in *The Swan Book* climatic inversion is neither an end nor a beginning. In this sense, it is fundamentally dyschronic, or as Daniel Fisher puts it: "*The Swan Book* is a grand play with time itself, drawing together syntactic, narrative, and poetic features in a chronotope of temporal indeterminacy."[34] This is not to suggest that the novel greets the collapsing ecosystems of the Anthropocene with a relativist shrug of its shoulders. Rather, the book *enters the collapse*. The collapse is not an event that has happened and whose symptoms are enumerated in the form of a litany, as happens in James Bradley's *Clade*, but a moment of radical, terrible possibility. In this respect, the novel seems to typify the imagination of disaster in the modern age, which Eva Horn has termed "catastrophe without event."[35] While *The Swan Book* often sits at the level of a satire, it keeps bending into myth, a mode Susan Sheridan connects with feminist fabulation.[36] The world in *The Swan Book* is recognizable but only in glimpses, as if we are within the epistemology of a primal scene, or indeed a kind of "Dreaming," in which the world is being destroyed and remade in real time.

Uncanny Objects

While climate has tended to dominate the discourse of the Anthropocene, extinction has provided the moment with its existential gravity. Indeed, the Anthropocene is largely coterminous and often synonymous with the sixth mass extinction, or Holocene extinction. Thus, while it is tempting to situate Turner's *The Sea and Summer* as the novel that signals the Anthropocene turn in Australian fiction, in many respects it is Julia Leigh's *The Hunter* (1999) that decisively ushers in a new sensibility.[37] In Leigh's novel, and in keeping with popular legend, the thylacine ("Tasmanian tiger") was not made extinct in the 1930s but survived in the remote alpine wilderness of western Tasmania. The existence of the thylacine is discovered by an unnamed biotech company and they secretly send an agent, known in the novel as "M," to hunt and capture the thylacine. In the climax of the novel, the female thylacine is captured and killed by M. Her ovaries are removed so that the genetic information can be harvested. It is a moment that evokes the Anthropocene as a crossing of parametric limits. If the iconic animal had simply been killed and stuffed as a trophy, this would have been devastating but it would have resulted in a mournable event and a certain degree of cathartic circumspection. Of course, that may seem a paltry, indeed indecent, compensation for the brute removal of a life-form. But the novel does not terminate in death. M is not a trophy hunter, but a functionary, an agent of a system that demands the transmutation of life into information. In other words, the thylacine does not quite die, but lives on in a place that is no longer the domain of life, its ova sequenced into genetic code.

Perhaps it is not surprising in a nation that leads the world in extinctions, that extinction is a pronounced feature of Australian fiction in the Anthropocene. An example (though it is largely set in the United States) is the Australian novelist Chris Flynn's comic novel *Mammoth* (2020).[38] The book is narrated by a 13,000-year-old Mammoth, still sentient even after its death, whose bones are being auctioned in New York City in 2007. The wry observations of the events that have led this animal from his home on the frozen steppes of Central Asia to a warehouse in New York offer a particular account of the Anthropocene from the imagined vantage point of the nonhuman other. In this respect the novel resembles, and occasionally matches, the comic brilliance of Kurt Vonnegut's *Galápagos* (1985).[39] A recent twist in the thematization of extinction has been the appearance of novels of *de-extinction*, most notably James Bradley's *Ghost Species* (2020) and Donna Mazza's *Fauna* (2020).[40] Both novels share the same premise: scientists working on de-extinction (the revival of extinct species through genetic material in preserved cell tissue) have found a way to resurrect the Neanderthal species of human primate. While Mazza's book focuses on the human dimensions of raising a child that is ineluctably different, Bradley's book explicitly places this eventuality within the context of the Anthropocene. In Bradley's novel, the Neanderthal child emerges from a science experiment and, like the Frankenstein story that provides the enduring archetype for all such narratives, the experiment in *Ghost Species* exceeds its parameters.[41] The paradox in this Promethean archetype is that the excess of the experiment is always the human stain. In other words, insofar as science proceeds on the basis of excluding the human subjective component from the experiment, this dimension is fated to reappear in the results of the experiment as an excess. The novel's heroine Kate, a scientist employed by the company, focalizes this effect:

> But even a superficial glance is enough to reveal she is not normal. Beneath the thick red-brown hair plastered against her scalp her head is larger, the face more simian, the rounded cheeks and jaw reminiscent of those of a chimpanzee, her subtly shorter forehead emphasising the unusual largeness of her eyes.[42]

As is evident, the experiment in trying to produce a creature that is *less* human results somehow in a creature that is *more* human, in producing humanness as an excess, rather than a lack:

> Yet it is not these differences that strike Kate most forcefully, but her fragility, the wonder of her. She is them but not them, human but not human, extinct yet somehow here, in the world. But most of all she seems to embody a new kind of possibility, something both dizzying and terrifying to contemplate, her presence in the world changing everything. And nothing.[43]

This is an Anthropocene moment *par excellence*. Everything changes and nothing changes. And the fact of extinction is marked not by an absence, but by uncanny presence.

One of the key features of Australian Anthropocene fiction is the manifestation of these strange objects, indeed what Hannah Stark, Katrina Schlunke, and Penny Edmonds have called the "uncanny objects" of the Anthropocene.[44] For Stark, Schlunke, and Edmonds, because "the Anthropocene has rendered the familiar strange and the strange familiar," it has changed our basic object relations: "The unpeeling anthropocenic object not only occupies multiple times, but also diverse and contradictory

discourses."[45] In some respects, these objects might be understood as revenants of the sixth mass extinction – as "ghost species," or at least their emis-
saries. But as well as being relictual, these objects are also announcements
of a radical newness. Indeed, the very ambiguity between their archaic and
unprecedented qualities seems to be the defining feature of such objects.
Noticing this allows us to put together the uncanny objects (creatures) that
recur in *Dyschronia* (cuttlefish), *The Swan Book* (swans), and Bradley's and
Mazza's novels (Neanderthal infants).

Another example that conforms clearly to the scheme of uncanny objects
are the "plantpeople" that appear in Ellen van Neerven's novella "Water"
from her short-story collection *Heat and Light* (2014). In van Neerven's
story, a future Australia has undertaken to aggregate the sand islands of
Moreton Bay to form a new landmass known as Australia2. The plantpeople appear as a direct symptom of this geoengineering mega-project, as the
narrator Kaden tells us:

> These creatures, beings, I'm not yet comfortable on how to place them, were
> formed when they started experimenting here, mining the sea in preparation
> for the islandising. It was a young botanist [...] who first discovered them: he
> distinguished their green human-like heads lined up on the banks of Russell
> Island. A lot doesn't make much sense to me yet. I have a feeling the docu-
> ments don't say everything.[46]

Kaden has been employed as Cultural Liaison Officer, a "mediator" as she
puts it, to work with the plantpeople. The plantpeople also elicit the distinctive quality of uncanny fascination. As Kaden tells us: "Seeing them for
the first time, I am struck both by how startlingly human-like they are, and
how alarmingly unhuman they are. Green, like something you would see in
a comic strip, but they are real."[47]

What marks out the Anthropocene as a moment in consciousness is a particular conjunction between radical interconnection (symbiosis, biosystems, atmospheric and oceanic systems) and final annihilation (cascading collapses of these
very same systems). The recognition is signaled in these Anthropocene fictions
by strange disappearances, like the vanishing limbs in Flanagan's novel, but
also by strange appearances, and in particular by the appearance of uncanny
objects.[48] In either case, it should be noted, it is the quality of strangeness that
attaches to the process of something appearing or disappearing. Despite the
uncanny nature of these new objects – living creatures defined equally by their
irreducible otherness and their eerie familiarity – we should resist the temptation to mystify them. Perhaps the best way to characterize them is in terms of
the emergence of a new signifier. In the case of *The Swan Book*, it is the swan
that heralds the advent of speech in the constitutively mute Oblivia. In van

Neerven's novella, which transpires as a love story between Kaden and the plantperson Larapinta, the creatures themselves are learning to speak and also teaching humans a new language. In the final image of the story, the plantpeople do indeed present as a new (but at the same time ancient) script:

> In the clear water behind the ferry I can see them. They are everywhere. Stretching out as far as my vision reaches. And then I know there are as many behind them. The brown reeds of their hair are all that is showing. They move in formations, in shapes similar to the last letter of the alphabet. Larapinta is one of them. There must be thousands.[49]

Australian Anthropocene fiction, particularly in its most recent iterations, has been punctuated by a particular kind of uncanny object, which this chapter has sought to map. There has been, certainly, a turn to objects with recent critical theory – notably in the intersecting philosophical schools known as new materialism and object-oriented ontology (OOO). Within the context of ecophilosophy, Timothy Morton has characterized climate change as a "hyperobject," a term they use to describe entities that have a dimension of singularity but escape every attempt to objectify them within localizable limits.[50] In this respect, we can see that punctuating the uncanny objects of Anthropocene fiction as avatars of the broader hyperobject of the Anthropocene. In much the same way, Stark, Schlunke, and Edmonds have noted that "icebergs have taken on a new repertoire of meaning, metonymically representing unstable icesheets, shrinking glaciers and rising seas."[51] The meaning of the Anthropocene, over and beyond the slew of its observable data, is something that humanity must now determine. Tracing its patterns through Australian literature, and indeed its more general symptomatology within culture, remains an ongoing challenge.

Notes

1 Amitav Ghosh, *The Great Derangement: Climate Change and the Unthinkable* (Chicago: University of Chicago Press, 2016).
2 See Emily Potter, "Ecological Crisis and Australian Literary Representation," *Australian Humanities Review* 37 (2005): pp. 1–8; Emily Potter, "Climate Change and the Problem of Representation," *Australian Humanities Review* 46 (2009): pp. 69–79.
3 Timothy Clark, *Ecocriticism on the Edge: The Anthropocene as a Threshold Concept* (London: Bloomsbury Academic, 2015), p. 123.
4 Dipesh Chakrabarty, "The Climate of History: Four Theses," *Critical Inquiry* 35.2 (2009): pp. 197–222.
5 See Emily Zong, "Anachronism in the Anthropocene: Plural Temporalities and the Art of Noticing in Ruth Ozeki's *A Tale for the Time Being,*" *Lit: Literature Interpretation Theory* 32.4 (2021): pp. 305–321.

6 Fredric Jameson, *Postmodernism, or the Cultural Logic of Late Capitalism* (Durham, NC: Duke University Press, 1991), p.21.

7 Clark, *Ecocriticism on the Edge*, p. 115.

8 See Lucy Sussex, "An Anthropocene Tale and its Writer: *The Sea and Summer*," *Sydney Review of Books*, June 6, 2017: https://sydneyreviewofbooks.com/review/anthropocene-tale-writer-sea-summer/.

9 Adam Trexler, *Anthropocene Fictions: The Novel in a Time of Climate Change* (Charlottesville: University of Virginia Press, 2015); Adeline Johns-Putra, *Climate Change and the Contemporary Novel* (Cambridge: Cambridge University Press, 2019); Andrew Milner and J. R. Burgmann, "Climate Fiction: A World-Systems Approach," *Cultural Sociology* 12.1 (2018): pp. 22–36.

10 See Julieanne Lamond, "Reading Crisis: The Politics of Fire in Amanda Lohrey's *The Reading Group* and *Vertigo*," *Westerly* 65.1 (2020): pp. 156–170.

11 Clark, *Ecocriticism on the Edge*, p. 123.

12 Clark, *Ecocriticism on the Edge*, p. 118.

13 Jack Kirne, "Agricultural Catastrophes: Revising Settler Belonging and the Farming Novel in *Everyman's Rules for Scientific Living*," *JASAL: Journal of the Association for the Study of Australian Literature* 20.1 (2020): pp. 1–12; Tom Bristow, *The Anthropocene Lyric: An Affective Geography of Poetry, Person, Place* (Basingstoke: Palgrave Macmillan, 2015); David Farrier, "Animal Detectives and 'Anthropocene Noir' in Chloe Hooper's *A Child's Book of True Crime*," *Textual Practice* 32.5 (2018): pp. 875–893.

14 During this chapter, there will be some inevitable slippage between the Anthropocene as an event in the fundamental fabric of reality and the Anthropocene as a moment in consciousness, but in most cases when I use the term, I wish to designate the latter.

15 In this respect, the show's premise matches that of the French film *Les Revenants* (2004), which was adapted into a television series of the same name (2012–2013), and which in turn was remade in the United States as *The Returned* (2015).

16 Richard Flanagan, *The Living Sea of Waking Dreams* (Sydney: Knopf, 2020).

17 Jane Rawson, "The Invisible Extinctions," *Meanjin*, Spring 2018: https://meanjin.com.au/essays/the-invisible-extinctions/.

18 Slavoj Žižek, *Event: Philosophy in Transit* (London: Penguin, 2014).

19 Bruno Latour, *Facing Gaia: Eight Lectures on the New Climatic Regime*, trans. Catherine Porter (Cambridge: Polity Press, 2017), p. 8.

20 See Randolph Stow, *Tourmaline* (London: Macdonald, 1963).

21 Jennifer Mills, *Dyschronia* (Sydney: Picador, 2018), p. 3.

22 Jean Baudrillard, "Simulcra and Simulations," in *Selected Writings*, ed. Mark Poster (Stanford: Stanford University Press, 1988), pp. 166–184 (p.166).

23 James Bradley, "*Dyschronia* by Jennifer Mills," *Australian Book Review* 399 (2018): www.australianbookreview.com.au/abr-online/archive/2018/217-march-2018-no-399/4647-james-bradley-reviews-dyschronia-by-jennifer-mills.

24 Tony Birch, "It's Been, It's Here: Tony Birch on Climate Change's Present and Past," *The Wheeler Centre*, March 24, 2015: www.wheelercentre.com/notes/it-s-been-it-s-here-tony-birch-on-climate-change-s-past-and-present.

25 Birch, "It's Been, It's Here."

26 See also Alexis Wright, "We All Smell the Smoke, We All Feel the Heat: This Environmental Catastrophe is Global," the *Guardian*, May 18, 2019:

www.theguardian.com/environment/2019/may/18/we-all-smell-the-smoke-we-all-feel-the-heat-this-environmental-catastrophe-is-global; Ambelin Kwaymullina, *Living on Stolen Land* (Broome: Magabala, 2020).

27 One can also see a similar transmutation of the scene of (Australian) colonization into the moment of the Anthropocene in the novelistic trajectories of nonIndigenous writers such as James Bradley (from *Wrack* to *Clade*), Rohan Wilson (*The Roving Party* to *Daughter of Bad Times*), and Andrew McGahan (*The White Earth* to *The Rich Man's House*). "Indigenous futurism" is a term coined by Grace Dillon in relation to North American writing, but Australian exponents include Ambelin Kwaymullina's *The Interrogation of Ashala Wolf* (2012) and Ellen van Neerven's *Heat and Light* (2014).

28 The reference is to Western Australia's notorious Chief Protector of Aborigines A. O. Neville (1875–1954).

29 Ellen van Neerven, "*The Yield* by Tara June Winch," *Australian Book Review* 412 (2019): www.australianbookreview.com.au/abr-online/archive/2019/371-august-2019-no-413/5676-ellen-van-neerven-reviews-the-yield-by-tara-june-winch.

30 Tara June Winch, *The Yield* (Sydney: Hamish Hamilton, 2019), p. 6.

31 Winch, *The Yield*, p. 8.

32 Maria Takolander, "Theorising Irony and Trauma in Magical Realism: Junot Díaz's *The Brief Wonderous Life of Oscar Wao* and Alexis Wright's *The Swan Book*," ariel: *A Review of International English Literature* 47.3 (2016): pp. 95–122; Ben Holgate, "Unsettling Narratives: Re-evaluating Magical Realism as Postcolonial Discourse through Wright's *Carpentaria* and *The Swan Book*," *Journal of Postcolonial Writing* 51.6 (2015): pp. 634–647; Jamie Derkenne, "Richard Flanagan's and Alexis Wright's Magic Nihilism," *Antipodes* 31.2 (2017): pp. 276–290.

33 Honni van Rijswijk, "Encountering Law's Harm through Literary Critique: An Anti-Elegy of Land and Sovereignty," *Law and literature* 27.2 (2015): pp. 237–252.

34 Daniel Fisher, "Untidy Times: Alexis Wright, Extinction, and the Politics of Apprehension," *Cultural Anthropology* 33.33 (2018): pp. 180–188 (p. 182).

35 Eva Horn, *The Future of Catastrophe: Imagining Disaster in the Modern Age* (New York: Columbia University Press, 2018), p. 55.

36 Susan Sheridan, "Feminist Fables and Alexis Wright's Art of the Fabulous in *The Swan Book*' *Hecate* 43.1–2 (2017): pp. 197–214 (p. 201).

37 Julia Leigh, *The Hunter* (Ringwood: Penguin, 1999).

38 Chris Flynn, *Mammoth* (St. Lucia: University of Queensland Press, 2020).

39 In Vonnegut's novel, a group of tourists to the Galápagos survive a global nuclear apocalypse and gradually de-evolve back into non-speaking animals, losing the "big brain" that was so ingenious it had invented the atomic bomb. See Kurt Vonnegut, *Galápagos* (New York: Delacorte, 1985).

40 See James Bradley, *Ghost Species* (Sydney: Hamish Hamilton, 2020); Donna Mazza, *Fauna* (Crows Nest: Allen & Unwin, 2020).

41 In Mazza's book, the Neanderthal baby is a solution offered by a company specializing in fertility treatment, and the novel is, as much as anything else, a story about motherhood.

42 Bradley, *Ghost Species*, p. 58.

43 Bradley, *Ghost Species*, p. 59.

44 Hannah Stark, Katrina Schlunke, and Penny Edmonds, "Introduction: Uncanny Objects in the Anthropocene," *Australian Humanities Review* 63 (2018): pp. 22–30.

45 Stark, Schlunke, and Edmonds, "Introduction," p. 22, p. 28.

46 Ellen van Neerven, "Water," in *Heat and Light* (St Lucia: University of Queensland Press, 2014), pp. 67–124 (p. 76).

47 van Neerven, "Water," p. 78.

48 Mark Fisher draws on the Lacanian distinction between the experience of *nothing where there should be something* (as in, for instance, the missing limbs in Flanagan's novel, or the disappearing ocean in *Dyschronia*) and *something when there should be nothing*. The Anthropocene seems to oscillate between these two modalities. Mark Fisher, *The Weird and the Eerie* (London: Repeater Books, 2016).

49 van Neerven, "Water," pp. 122–123.

50 See Timothy Morton, *Hyperobjects: Philosophy and Ecology after the End of the World* (Minneapolis: University of Minnesota Press, 2013).

51 Stark, Schlunke, and Edmonds, "Introduction," p. 28.

19

KEYVAN ALLAHYARI

What is the (Australian) Refugee Novel?

Against Liquid Borders

The refugee novel is something of an awkward neologism – more so when we add "Australian" to it. All three terms – "Australian," "refugee," and "novel" – carry political and formal contentions, each with its own limits, which only become more elusive when combined. To start with, putting a national cap on refugee writing causes its own issues, for refugees as a demographic category stand in a degree of distance to the Australian land: Refugees arrive (or not); they drown in Australian waters; they are in detention; they fit in; they make Australia home, and so forth. Robert Dixon has reminded us that the questions of "social construction of space and scale into a national literature" unsettle the correspondence between Australian letters and human geography that constitutes the nation.[1] "This is," he writes, "to throw open almost everything we might normally ask about an Australian text."[2] It is indeed important to contour "refugee novel" as a literary category that resists the demands of nation-building that the Australian literary field has carried around since its inception, to avoid the reproduction of the binary distinction between Australian literature proper and its subgenres according to their ethnic or migratory authorship, which so often defines the *modus operandi* of Australian literary studies.[3] When does a refugee novel become Australian? Can we imagine a refugee authorship that is "ours" against "theirs," Australian as opposed to French, and so on? What is Australian about the Australian refugee novel? What circumstances of production and circulation should a refugee novel have to enter the territory of national or transnational literature? Now a refugee in Aotearoa New Zealand, Behrouz Boochani, the Kurdish-Iranian author of the award-winning *No Friend but the Mountains* (2018), has never set foot in Australia, but he has been welcomed by many prominent members of the Australian literary community, including Richard Flanagan, who called him "a great Australian writer."[4] *No Friend but the Mountains* was translated by the Iranian-Australian academic, Omid Tofighian, and published by Picador Australia to remarkable commercial and cultural traction. Boochani is rarely, if at all, referred to as a novelist in the Australian media or by other Australian writers, despite his insistence that he is one. Does all this make him an Australian refugee novelist?

The bracketed (Australian) in the title of this chapter evokes two of its fundamental tenets: first, it affirms the priority of refugee experiences in relation to the liquidity of Australia's borders over the presumed solidity and sovereignty of its land. The contemporary (Australian) refugee novel can be best understood as a product of the country's unique borderscape, which stands in historical continuity with the ways that its settler colonial project has dispossessed First Nations People and denied Aboriginal Sovereignty over the land.[5] Post-settlement Australia as one block is indeed a direct result of colonization's utter disregard for the preexisting national borders of Indigenous peoples.[6] Instead of framing the discussion as being about the literature of a nation state, we might focus instead on the state*less* condition of the refugee and the complex ways in which the geographies of water can be just as important as those of land. By taking into consideration Australia's liquid borders, we can start appreciating how profoundly its position as an island nation has shaped its literary imaginary.[7] Second, it points to the mercurial correlation of regional and global literary imaginaries and systems of cultural circulation. In English-speaking countries, the "refugee novel" tries to encompass too much. It becomes the futile attempt to capture the movement of more than 1 percent of the world's population (according to the UNHCR's latest report, more than 1 per cent of the world's population are currently forcefully deracinated).[8] The sheer volume of forced migration goes hand in hand with the persistence of military interventionism, the civil conflicts in the Middle East and South East Asia, increasing internal displacement of people in Africa and the Middle East due to climate change and disastrous environmental management, economic collapse in Central and Latin America, as well as the consistency of asylum-deterring policies in the Global North, such as Trump's travel "ban" and Australia's offshore detention system.

The dimming possibility of asylum can only occur in the attempt to cross these cruel borders. To configure refugees in contemporary fiction in any national context, therefore, is to imagine them exposed to the militarized logic and language that jettisons refugees from the category of the civilian and reframes them as threats to national security. Agnes Woolley observes that contemporary refugee fiction presents an "alternative to the liminality of the 'ban'; a space of permanence that is hospitable to the heterogeneous experiences that constitute forced migration [...] [against] the intricate functioning of national decision-making on asylum."[9] Often these fictional accounts make no attempt at subtlety about their subject matter right on the level of the title. Famous examples of this trend are Viet Thanh Nguyen's *The Refugees* (2017), Mohsin Hamid's *Exit West* (2017), Sharon Bala's *The Boat People* (2018). In many other contemporary instances, the refugee has become a steady character either in the center or on the peripheries of the fictional world of novels. For example, no refugees appear in Michelle de Kretser's *The Life to Come* (2017), but they are constantly evoked to parody the performative solidarity of the aspirational, progressive class. The main character, Pipa, an up-and-coming Australian novelist, situates herself online and in her writing at a safe distance from refugees, so that she can have a claim on them, but not close enough to have anything to do with them in real life.

As de Kretser shows, in an ironic register, the contingencies between the proliferation of the displaced person and the *fictional refugee charac- ter* usher in concomitant ethics of representation and consumption. The challenge of the refugee character for the contemporary novel lies in the inseparability of what Lyndsay Stonebridge calls "political morality from *realpolitik*," beyond the reification of the refugee "crisis."[10] There are risks associated with this common misrecognition. First, we may curtail refugee subjectivity to fit the prevalent humanitarian imaginary, by coming to know the immiserated refugees as first and foremost in need of humanitarian aid. In *The Cultural Politics of Emotion* (2004), Sara Ahmed warns against the problematic "transformation of the wound into an identity" for the subal- tern subject and the fetishistic attachment to this level of abject visibility of cultural markets in the Global North.[11] Second, the current trend for refugee fiction occasions the ideological overlaps of interventionist strategies and the humanitarian appeal of refugee writing. Gillian Whitlock argues that the depiction of refugees "contained within the framework of humanitarian concern [...] organizes the commodification of subaltern lives as appropri- ate subjects for compassion."[12]

Novelistic representations of asylum unfold in the tension between this experiential hyperimmediacy and the progressive-libertarian agenda, where the reader gets to hear a story about refugee characters, or of non-refugee characters who come in contact with refugees. The elephant-in-the-room of the refugee novel, then, becomes the acute coexistence of Western capitalist expansionism, which continues to deracinate larger groups of people from the Global South, and what Lilie Chouliaraki terms the "ironic solidarity" of the activist-spectator. This mode of engagement "explicitly situates the pleasures of the self at the heart of moral action, thereby rendering solidar- ity a contingent ethic that no longer aspires to a reflexive engagement with the political conditions of human vulnerability."[13] This feels like a more obvious conundrum when we consider that most of the refugee fiction is written by white writers. In Australia, writing about refugees by refugees remains almost exclusively autobiographical, apart from such high-profile works such as Boochani's *No Friend but the Mountains* and Nam Le's collection of short stories, *The Boat* (2008). It is also important that the political status of authors as refugees does not automatically grant classification of their works as refugee literature, as exemplified by Shokoofeh Azar's *The Enlightenment of the Greengage Tree* (2017), shortlisted for the International Booker Prize. While Azar settled in Australia as a political refugee in 2011, there is nothing explicit about refugees or the travails of asylum-seeking in her novel.

Once we configure refugee literature in relation to the international waters that surround Australia and the grievability of the lives of refugees, we come to face a different set of assumptions and questions. As Suvendrini Perera shows in *Australia and the Insular Imagination* (2009), no category renders the porous and arbitrary borders, so frequently subjected to fluid regimes of refoulment and excision, than refugee border-crossing. In this context, Bill Ashcroft argues for the conceptual relevance of the term "transnation" in the context of the increasingly punitive border politics as a space "migrating *outside* of the state that begins *within* the nation." He writes:

> The transnation is a way of talking about subjects in their ordinary lives, subjects who live in-between the categories by which subjectivity is normally constituted. If we think of the transnation extending both within and beyond the geographical, cultural, religious, and imaginative boundaries of the state, we discover it as a space in which those boundaries are disrupted, in which national and cultural affiliations are superseded, in which binaries of centre and periphery, national self and other, are dissolved.[14]

Transnation is a useful concept insofar as it can loosen the attachment to the nation/world dichotomy, often prefaced by an emphasis on a state of twoness and receptivity of the national in the international – for instance, in David Damrosch's *What is World Literature?* (2003) – or on the refraction of unequal power relations in the struggles between emerging and dominant literary nations that constitute the global "republic of letters," as Pascale Casanova formulated in *The World Republic of Letters* (1999).[15] In these formulations, the fluid movement of the literary work stands in relation to the relative stability of belonging to a certain cultural geography. The perpetual informality and illegality of refugee movement can thus easily slip through the cracks of comparativist and world literature paradigms of refugee literature. This owes above all to these disciplines' exuberant emphasis on the transactional logic that underpins the literature's circulation. While refugee writing can easily travel beyond borders with the click of an online book buyer anywhere in the world, refugee authors may simply be unable to do so. Writers, such as the Iraqi Hassan Blassim and Behrouz Boochani reside in their host countries of Finland and Aotearoa New Zealand, but still face restrictions in crossing borders.

The remainder of this chapter gives an overview of the different ways that the refugee *figures* in the contemporary Australian novel, across two of its dominant themes of detention fiction and boat narratives. I discuss some recent novels to illustrate these themes. My examples are representative rather than exhaustive of each genre. In conclusion, I hazard a few conjectures about the future of the Australian refugee novel.

Detention Fiction

Detention centers have become a synecdoche for the brutality of neoliberal military-industrial governance, where the stateless and the impoverished are incarcerated in substandard structures, built by multinational corporate construction firms and run by private security companies. The logic of outsourcing security goes hand in hand with the steady move to the right in global politics in the past few decades. A simple chronology of parliamentary decisions in Australia tells a story of criminalizing asylum and legalizing the indefinite detention of asylum seekers and refugees. Since 1992, when the Labor government introduced mandatory detention for people arriving without a valid visa, every Australian government has managed to escalate the system to higher levels of savagery. Following the *Tampa* affair in 2001, John Howard's unironically named "Pacific Solution" transferred boat arrivals to Christmas Island, and then to the Pacific Island nations of Nauru and Papua New Guinea. The Kevin Rudd government introduced the existing iteration of Australia's border rules under the Regional Resettlement Arrangement (RRA) between Australia and Papua New Guinea in 2013. This deal mandated that the asylum seekers would be held indefinitely on Nauru and Manus Island in Papua New Guinea, with resettlement in the latter country as their only option. In 2015, under the government of prime minister Tony Abbott, the Australian Border Force Act mandated that detention contractors could face up to two years of imprisonment for whistleblowing. In 2019, Scott Morrison's government repealed the "medevac bill' to disallow relocating critically ill refugees to the mainland. In May 2021, the Migration Amendment Act was passed, with support from both Liberal and Labor parties, to authorize the indefinite detention of refugees – in obvious violation of international law.

In the face of Australian government secrecy, most of what we know of the cruelty of Australian processing centers is from the detention "literature." This body of writing includes archives of oral testimony and correspondence by detainees (for example, see Julian Burnside and Kate Durham Papers and Elaine Smith Papers at the Fryer Library of the University of Queensland), autobiographical accounts such as *The Escape from Manus: The Untold True Story* (2021) by the former detainee Jaivet Ealom, and detention novels. There is also the spin-off genre of memoirs by people who have come into direct or indirect contact with incarcerated refugees and have experienced some political awakening. Vanessa Russell's thinly disguised memoir, *The World Is Not Big Enough* (2021), for instance, rides on the author's implicit movement from innocence to experience through revisiting her reluctant correspondence with an Afghan refugee in Port Hedland Immigration Reception and Processing Centre in Western Australia in the early 2000s. The author informs us that the subject of her study was murdered in 2009 by a fellow refugee. Most chapters begin with one of the refugee's letters – poorly reproduced for an aura of aged authenticity – that laments the agony of indefinite anticipation and the sheer frequency of suicidal impulses.

The fictional accounts of the experience of the detention center are emerging in this narratorial context not so much as a corrective but a space of imaginative possibility, with the potential to reflect an element of vicious play in the dystopian logic of detention. Indeed, one of the most disturbing aspects of the offshore detention regime is that, at its heart, it has always been an experimental exercise with no clear objective in sight other than vying for political support from xenophobic portions of the Australian voting public. Daniel Wilsher has shown a range of "bureaucratic instrumental" objectives ensured by the symbolic role of detention against the alleged alien threat for the sovereign nation: for one, detention facilities sanction the "liberal state's capacity for extraordinary measures against 'outsiders' to protect 'insiders'."[16] Detention centers share a political DNA with the military-industrial complex. Linda Briskman, Susie Latham, and Chris Goddard have noted that Australia's offshore detention centers were modeled on the Guantánamo Bay detention camp.[17] Notorious for the torture of its detainees, Guantánamo is also where the US processed thousands of Haitian boat arrivals in the mid-1990s.[18] The gamelike banality of this race between the two major Australian political Parties, Labor and the Coalition, has begotten little than utter failure across a spectrum of operational and humanitarian domains. It is no accident that the rise of technobureaucrats in governments globally is synchronous with the proliferation and evolution of the prison-industrial complex in the hands of multinational security companies such as the now-defunct ACM (Australian Correctional Management),

Wilson, and Serco. The reports from detention centers in Australia and off-shore remain steadily harrowing: women who hang themselves, men who sew their lips together, children's suicide attempts.

Clare Atkins' Young Adult novel, *Between Us* (2018), brings together the Vietnamese boat arrivals in Darwin and Wickham Point Detention Centre in the Northern Territory.[19] Ana, a teen Iranian asylum seeker from the detention center, meets Jono, the son of a Vietnamese refugee who works at the detention center, during the hours that she spends in the community to attend school. Short chapters alternate between the voices of the teen characters – Anna's in prose and Jono's in verse. The teenagers' new association soon provokes local suspicion, amid a sense that refugees have an unwholesome influence on the community. *Between Us* touches on the disillusionment of impoverished remote communities in the new "industry." Despite government promises of local employment, many of these remote communities find that that services have already been outsourced and most newly created jobs filled by fly-in, fly-out workers. As a global phenomenon, offshore detention centers are by default neocolonial projects. Manus offshore detention center, for instance, was declared unconstitutional by Papua New Guinea's High Court in 2017. The notoriously underresourced and overcrowded Christmas Island Immigration Detention Centre was built on a defunct phosphate mining area, already exploited to depletion by economic powers. Similarly, Nauru's Regional Processing Centre is the small island nation's largest source of income in the aftermath of the environmental disaster caused by phosphate mining carried out by firms from Australia, Aotearoa New Zealand, and Britain.[20] Furthermore, Australia has its share of "exporting" the detention industry. Australia funds detention centers in other countries, including, for example, Indonesia, where reports indicate unlawful treatment and incarceration of detainees. Backed by Australian money, Indonesian officials are more prone to detain asylum seekers and punish those who attempt escape.[21]

The complex interaction of bureaucratic-technological elements at play in the detention industry creates two competing realities: one with a deep interest in illegalizing asylum and prolonging time in detention facilities, and one that longs for detention to end desperately. Detention fiction deals primarily with a problem of temporality, of mingling two different times together: the agonizing time of waiting and the time for action. As Judith Butler recently noted: "Indefinite detention, [...] the protracted condition of unknowingness and uncertainty," opens up "a problem of narrative time" that is cognate with the world of fiction.[22] In Tristan Bancks' *Detention* (2019), a teenage Iranian girl, Sima, escapes an onshore detention center, only to be found by a local teenager called Dan. In this instance, refugee fiction poses the question of the aftermath of the involuntary release of young refugees into the Australian community. In this way, the appeal of detention fiction lies, in part, in the fascination with the other, and in part pokes at the boundaries of acceptance and the xenophobia of the Australian public. Refugee characters, after all, have to be met and named. As long as they live inside detention centers, they are only a number within the detention system.

Boat Narratives

Matthew J. Gibney shows (2004) that Australia's current responses to boat refugees continue an increasingly punitive development since the first arrival of Vietnamese asylum seekers on the shores of the Northern Territory in 1977.[23] The Fraser government (1975–1983) led the discussions at the United Nations for what came to be known as the "orderly departure" of Vietnamese refugees after the capture of Saigon by the North Vietnamese army in 1975. The arrival of Vietnamese refugees on Australian shores triggered the reformulation of the principles of the postwar migration consensus. Since then, Australia has instituted such strict regimes of deterrence and refoulment to make it "arguably the most unwelcoming country towards asylum seekers in the Western world."[24] The War in Afghanistan (2001–2021) and the US-led Iraq War (2003–2011) exacerbated the refugee crises globally. The arguments around deciding who crosses Australia's borders "and the circumstances in which they come" gained greater political traction during John Howard's term as prime minister (1996–2007).[25] Australian governments have proclaimed themselves the border police for the liberal democratic world and become trend-makers in intercepting the already perilous asylum routes in the past two decades. Gillian Whitlock argues that "stop the boats" – a slogan associated with militant efforts to halt asylum seekers established in 2013 and known as Operation Sovereign Borders (OSB) – transforms the boat into a political tool, while denying the lived experience of asylum seekers. The boat, as Whitlock puts it, becomes: "sign of invasion and contamination. This metonymically displaces the presence of the people who claim sanctuary to focus on the vessels that carry them into the Australian migration zone."[26]

The boat in Australian fiction refers back to the human story, so frequently occluded by contemporary political rhetoric. Wenche Ommundsen demonstrates the persistence and the valence of boat narratives across the history of Australian literature. Boat stories, she argues, are integral to Australian history as they interweave various personal and political temporalities. Boat stories, in Ommundsen's words: "highlight questions of identity (personal, national, cultural) in the evolving narrative around continuity and change which characterizes the nation's brief history."[27] Felicity Castagna's *No More Boats* (2017) narrates the coincidence of the "existential crisis" in the life a former boat arrival, Antonio Martone, from southern Italy and that of the entire nation, obsessed with boats, and now triggered in the face of the *Tampa* affair. Francis' life unfolds between the assumed legitimacy of three boat narratives after World War II, and the racialized hierarchy that defines the discourse around boat people. Italians were boat people, too; even Vietnamese could be tolerated, but Muslims do certainly push the nerve buttons of many. Castagna sets her novel in the multicultural suburb of Parramatta in western Sydney between the *Tampa* affair and 9/11. In August 2001, the Norwegian container ship MV *Tampa* responded to a request from the Australia Coast Guard. There was a wooden fishing vessel sinking in international waters, which contained 433 refugees, many of them Hazara from Afghanistan. The MV *Tampa* rescued the asylum seekers and took them into Australian territorial waters. However, the Howard government refused them permission to land, and ordered members of the Special Air Services Regiment to board the vessel. Within a few days, the Australian government introduced the Border Protection (Validation and Enforcement Powers) Act 2001 into the House of Representatives. The aftermath of the *Tampa* affair was the Pacific Solution: asylum seekers were now taken to Nauru where their refugee status was considered, rather than Christmas Island.

Conjectures for the Future of Refugee Writing

There seems to be no end in sight for the criminalizing of asylum under the populist rhetoric of security in Australian politics. There is, however, a growing interest worldwide in bolder, more complex ways of writing about the broader questions of asylum, both among general readers of fiction and in literary circles that lend their cultural legitimacy to it. The spectacle of a militarized border alongside the proliferation of detention camps, and growing environmental inhospitality, creating more and more climate refugees (especially in the Global South), will mean that the refugee as character and trope will occupy a more pronounced place in Australian and global fiction. There is indeed an emerging trend in the contemporary global novel that engages with the imaginary of the border in the face of the increasing possibility of forced migration for humanitarian and environmental reasons. These novels signal the ways that militarized borders project the contemporary subject's deepest anxieties about the effects of large-scale displacement for both refugees and their host societies.

The high-profile reception of novels, such as Jenny Erpenbeck's *Gehen, ging, gegangen* [*Go, Went, Gone*] (2015) and John Lanchester's *The Wall*

(2019), indicates public interest in literary representations that better appreciate the consequences of refugee intake, especially in countries such as Germany and Sweden in the aftermath of the "summer of migration" in 2015, as well as the militarization of border regimes in Australia, the US, and Eastern Europe. In less favorable cases, like Jeanine Cummins' *American Dirt* (2018), the publishing hype can turn into literary controversies for appropriation or misrepresentation of refugee experience.[28] The contested engagement with the radicalized border in novels plays to the refugee's amplified position in the political discourse. While the refugee marks an irreversible anxiety about the constitution and imaginary of nation-states in the Global North, the contemporary novel registers the rapid evolution of "technologies of power," such as the camp, offshore detention centers, and travel bans in the "production of bare life."[29]

Both well-known and newly acclaimed authors from around the world are concerning themselves with the border imaginary in various ways; they include Abdulrazak Gurnah (Tanzania-UK), Viet Thanh Nguyen (Vietnam-US), Edwidge Danticat (Haiti-US), Hassan Blasim (Iraq-Finland), John Lanchester (UK), Alexis Wright (Waayni), Pajtim Statovci (Kosovo-Finland), and Jenny Erpenbeck (Germany). One common element among these authors is that they have enjoyed a remarkable critical and commercial success in the wake of the refugee crisis. For instance, Gurnah and Thanh Nguyen, themselves refugees, were awarded respectively the 2021 Nobel Prize in Literature and the 2019 Pulitzer Prize. This new species of contemporary global novel is remarkable, not only as thematic or narrative depiction of the abject asylum seeker, but as a genre whose urgency is in tapping deeply into the trepidations of the twenty-first-century political subject, abandoned to the structural incompetence of liberal, capitalist systems. Some of these novels point to how the logic of control and surveillance that governs draconian border technologies, such as the camp or indefinite detention, also appears in host societies on the other side of the border. In Alexis Wright's ecoapocalyptic *The Swan Book* (2013), Australia's third centenary has turned a military-fenced swamp into "the world's most unknown detention camp" for First Nation people. Wright seems to be asking questions of a planetary magnitude: What will become of us in a world in which a greater number of people will have to seek refuge? Who will be next?

Notes

1 Robert Dixon, "National Literatures, Scale and the Problem of the World," *JASAL: Journal of the Association for the Study of Australian Literature* 15.3 (2015): pp. 1–10 (p. 2).

2 Dixon, "National Literatures, Scale and the Problem of the World," p. 2.

3 Daniel Hourigan, "Australian Seekers and Refugees in Australian Literature," *The Routledge Companion to Australian Literature*, ed. Jessica Gildersleeve (New York and London: Routledge, 2021), p. 258.

4 Behrouz Boochani, *No Friend but the Mountains*, trans. Omid Tofighian (Sydney: Picador Australia, 2018), p. x.

5 Brigitta Olubas, ""Where We Are Is Too Hard": Refugee Writing and the Australian Border as Literary Interface," *JASAL: Journal of the Association for the Study of Australian Literature* 15.3 (2015): pp. 1–15.

6 Sarah Maddison, "Indigenous Peoples and Colonial Borders," in *Border Politics Social Movements, Collective Identities, and Globalization*, ed. Nancy A. Naples and Jennifer Bickham Mendez (New York: New York University Press), pp. 153–157 (p. 158).

7 Elizabeth McMahon, *Islands, Identity and the Literary Imagination* (London: Anthem Press, 2016), p. 4.

8 "UNHCR Global Trends: Forced Displacement in 2020," UNHCR: The UN Refugee Agency: www.unhcr.org/flagship-reports/globaltrends.

9 Agnes Woolley, *Contemporary Asylum Narratives: Representing Refugees in the Twenty-First Century* (Basingstoke: Palgrave Macmillan, 2014), p. 9.

10 Lyndsay Stonebridge, *Writing and Righting: Literature in the Age of Human Rights* (Oxford: Oxford University Press. 2021), p. 3.

11 Sara Ahmed, *The Cultural Politics of Emotion* (Edinburgh: Edinburgh University Press, 2004), p. 32.

12 Gillian Whitlock, *Soft Weapons: Autobiography in Transit* (Chicago: University of Chicago Press, 2007), p. 71.

13 Lilie Chouliaraki. "Solidarity and Spectatorship," *questions de communication* 30 (2015): pp. 359–372, p. 361.

14 David Damrosch, *What is World Literature?* (Princeton: Princeton University Press, 2003); Bill Ashcroft, "Borders, Bordering, and the Transnation," *English Academy Review* 36.1 (2019): pp. 5–19 (p. 11).

15 Pascale Casanova, *The World Republic of Letters*, trans. M. B. DeBevoise (Cambridge, MA: Harvard University Press, 2004).

16 Daniel Wilsher, *Immigration Detention: Law, History, Politics* (Cambridge: Cambridge University Press, 2012).

17 Linda Briskman, Susie Latham, and Chris Goddard, *Human Rights Overboard: Seeking Asylum in Australia* (Melbourne: Scribe Publications, 2008).

18 Briskman, Latham, and Goddard, *Human Rights Overboard*, p. 48.

19 Clare Atkin, *Between Us* (Carlton: Black Inc, 2018).

20 For an excellent study of phosphate mining in the Pacific, focusing on Banaba, see Katerina Martina Teaiwa, *Consuming Ocean Island: Stories of People and Phosphate from Banaba* (Bloomington and Indianapolis: Indiana University Press, 2015).

21 Amy Nethery, Brynna Rafferty-Brown, and Savitri Taylor, "Exporting Detention: Australia-funded Immigration Detention in Indonesia," *Journal of Refugee Studies* 26.1 (2013): pp. 88–109 (p. 89).

22 Judith Butler, "Indefinite Detention," *Qui Parle*. 29.1 (2020): pp. 15–24 (p. 17).

23 Matthew J. Gibney, *The Ethics and Politics of Asylum: Liberal Democracy and the Response to Refugees* (Cambridge: Cambridge University Press, 2004).

24 Gibney, *The Ethics and Politics of Asylum*, p. 167.

25 John Howard, "Election Speech," *Australian Federal Election Speeches: The Museum of Australian Democracy at Old Parliament House*, October 28, 2001: https://electionspeeches.moadoph.gov.au/speeches/2001-john-howard.

26 Gillian Whitlock, "The Hospitality of Cyberspace: Mobilizing Asylum Seeker Testimony Online," *Biography* 38.2 (2015): pp. 245–266 (p. 252).

27 Wenche Ommundsen, "'This Story Does Not Begin on a Boat': What is Australian about Asian Australian Writing?" *Continuum* 25.4 (2011): pp. 503–513 (p. 507).

28 Sujatha Fernandes, "The Great White Social Justice Novel, *Sydney Review of Books* May 25, 2020: https://sydneyreviewofbooks.com/review/cummins-american-dirt-krien-act-of-grace/.

29 Sonja Buckel and Jens Wissel, "State Project Europe: The Transformation of the European Border Regime and the Production of Bare Life," *International Political Sociology* 4.1 (2010): pp. 33–49 (p. 45).

FURTHER READING

COMPILED BY JOSEPH STEINBERG

Archibald, Jo-ann, Jenny Lee-Morgan, and Jason De Santolo (eds.), *Decolonizing Research: Indigenous Storywork as Methodology* (London: Zed Books, 2019)

Banivanua Mar, Tracey, and Penelope Edmonds (eds.), *Making Settler Colonial Space: Perspectives on Race, Place and Identity* (London: Palgrave Macmillan, 2010)

Benterrak, Krim, Stephen Muecke, and Paddy Roe, with Ray Keogh, Butcher Joe Nangan, and E. M. Lohe, *Reading the Country: Introduction to Nomadology* (Fremantle: Fremantle Arts Centre Press, 1984)

Bird Rose, Deborah, *Reports from a Wild Country: Ethics for Decolonisation* (Sydney: University of New South Wales Press, 2004)

Birns, Nicholas, *Contemporary Australian Literature: A World Not Yet Dead* (Sydney: Sydney University Press, 2015)

Birns, Nicholas, and Rebecca McNeer (eds.), *A Companion to Australian Literature Since 1900* (Rochester: Camden House, 2007)

Birns, Nicholas, Nicole Moore, and Sarah Shieff (eds.), *Teaching Australian and New Zealand Literature* (New York: Modern Language Association, 2017)

Bode, Katherine, *Reading by Numbers: Recalibrating the Literary Field* (London and New York: Anthem, 2012)

Boyd, Robin, *The Australian Ugliness* (Melbourne: F. W. Cheshire, 1960)

Brewster, Anne, *Reading Aboriginal Women's Life Stories* (Sydney: Sydney University Press, 2015)

Callahan, David, *Contemporary Issues in Australian Literature* (London: Routledge, 2001)

Carman, Luke, and Catriona Menzies-Pike (eds.), *Second City: Essays from Western Sydney* (Sydney: Sydney Review of Books, 2021)

Carter, David, *Always Almost Modern: Australian Print Cultures and Modernity* (Melbourne: Australian Scholarly Publishing, 2013)

Carter, David, and Roger Osborne, *Australian Books and Authors in the American Marketplace, 1840s–1940s* (Sydney: Sydney University Press, 2018)

Carter, Paul, *Living in a New Country: History, Travelling, Writing* (London: Faber & Faber, 1992)

  The Lie of the Land (London: Faber & Faber, 1996)

  The Road to Botany Bay: An Essay in Spatial History (London: Faber & Faber, 1987)

Clendinnen, Inga, *Dancing with Strangers* (Melbourne: Text Publishing, 2003)

Coombs, Anne, *Sex and Anarchy: Life and Death of the Sydney Push* (Ringwood: Viking, 1996)

Comyn, Sarah, and Porscha Fermanis (eds.), *Worlding the South: Nineteenth-Century Literary Culture and the Southern Settler Colonies* (Manchester: Manchester University Press, 2021)

Connell, Raewyn, *Southern Theory: The Global Dynamics of Knowledge in Social Science* (Cambridge: Polity Press, 2007)

Dale, Leigh, *The Enchantment of English: Professing English Literatures in Australian Universities* (Sydney: Sydney University Press, 2012)

Dalziell, Tanya and Paul Genoni (eds.), *Telling Stories: Australian Life and Literature 1935–2012* (Melbourne: Monash University Publishing, 2013)

Daniel, Helen, *Liars: Australian New Novelists* (Ringwood: Penguin, 1988)

Dixon, Robert, and Brigid Rooney (eds.), *Scenes of Reading: Is Australian Literature a World Literature?* (North Melbourne: Australian Scholarly Publishing, 2013)

Dixon, Robert, Brigid Rooney, and Peter Kirkpatrick (eds.) *Republics of Letters: Literary Communities in Australia* (Sydney: Sydney University Press, 2012)

Dixon, Robert, Brigid Rooney and Veronica Kelly (eds.), *The Impact of the Modern: Vernacular Modernities in Australia 1870s–1960s* (Sydney: Sydney University Press, 2008)

Docker, John, *Australian Cultural Elites: Intellectual Traditions in Sydney and Melbourne* (Sydney: Angus & Robertson, 1974)

Eldershaw, M. Barnard, *Essays in Australian Fiction* (Melbourne: Melbourne University Press, 1938)

Farrell, Michael, *Writing Australian Unsettlement: Modes of Poetic Invention 1796–1945* (Basingstoke: Palgrave MacMillan, 2015)

Franklin, Miles, *Laughter, Not for a Cage: Notes on Australian Writing* (Sydney: Angus & Robertson, 1956)

Gelder, Ken and Paul Salzman, *After the Celebration: Australian Fiction 1989–2007* (Melbourne: Melbourne University Press, 2009)

  The New Diversity: Australian Fiction, 1970–88 (Melbourne: McPhee Gribble, 1989)

Gelder, Ken, Paul Salzman, and Jane Margaret Jacobs, *Uncanny Australia: Sacredness and Identity in a Postcolonial Nation* (Melbourne: Melbourne University Press, 1994)

Gelder, Ken, Paul Salzman, and Rachael Weaver, *Colonial Australian Fiction: Character Types, Social Formations and the Colonial Economy* (Sydney: Sydney University Press, 2017)

Gilbert, Kevin, *Because A White Man'll Never Do It* (Sydney: Angus & Robertson, 1973)

Gildersleeve, Jessica (ed.), *The Routledge Companion to Australian Literature* (London: Routledge, 2020)

Giles, Paul, *Antipodean America: Australasia, Colonialism, and the Constitution of U.S. Literature* (Oxford: Oxford University Press, 2013)

  The Planetary Clock: Antipodean Time and Spherical Postmodern Fictions (Oxford: Oxford University Press, 2021)

Green, H. M., *A History of Australian Literature, Pure and Applied* (Sydney: Angus & Robertson, 1961)

Griffiths, Michael, *The Distribution of Settlement: Appropriation and Refusal in Australian Literature and Culture* (Perth University of Western Australia Press, 2018)

Gunew, Sneja, *Framing Marginality: Multicultural Literary Studies* (Carlton: Melbourne University Press, 1994)
  Haunted Nations: The Colonial Dimensions of Multiculturalisms (London: Routledge, 2004)
Hage, Ghassan, *White Nation: Fantasies of White Supremacy in a Multicultural Society* (New York and London: Routledge, 2000)
Harrison, Martin, *Who Wants to Create Australia? Essays on Poetry and Ideas in Contemporary Australia* (Sydney: Halstead Press, 2004)
Heiss, Anita, *Dhuulu-Yalaq, To Talk Straight: Publishing Indigenous Literature* (Canberra: Aboriginal Studies Press, 2003)
Heiss, Anita, and Peter Minter (eds.), *Macquarie PEN Anthology of Aboriginal Literature* (Crows Nest: Allen & Unwin, 2008)
Hergenhan, Laurie (ed.), *The Penguin New Literary History of Australia* (Ringwood: Penguin Australia, 1988)
Hodge, Bob, and Vijay Mishra, *Dark Side of the Dream: Australia Literature and the Postcolonial Mind* (Sydney: Allen & Unwin, 1991)
Huggan, Graham, *Australian Literature: Racism, Postcolonialism, Transnationalism* (Oxford: Oxford University Press, 2007)
Huwells, Coral Ann, Paul Sharrad and Gerry Turcotte (eds.), *The Oxford History of the Novel in English Volume 12: The Novel in Australia, Canada, New Zealand, and the South Pacific Since 1950* (Oxford: Oxford University Press, 2017)
Johnson, A. [Amanda] Frances, *Australian Fiction as Archival Salvage: Making and Unmaking the Postcolonial Novel* (Amsterdam: Rodopi, 2016)
Jose, Nicholas, and Benjamin Madden (eds.), *Antipodean China: Reflections on Literary Exchange* (Sydney: Giramondo, 2021)
Keneally, Thomas, *Australians: A Short History* (Sydney: Allen & Unwin, 2016)
Kerwin, Dale, *Aboriginal Dreaming Paths and Trading Routes* (Eastbourne: Sussex Academic Press, 2010)
Konishi, Shino, *The Aboriginal Male in the Enlightenment World* (London and New York: Routledge, 2016; 2012)
Kramer, Leonie (ed.), *The Oxford History of Australian Literature* (Oxford: Oxford University Press, 1981)
Kwaymullina, Ambelin, *Living on Stolen Land* (Broome: Magabala, 2020)
Land, Clare, *Decolonizing Solidarity: Dilemmas and Directions for Supporters of Indigenous Struggles* (London: Zed Books, 2015)
Langton, Marcia, "*Well, I Heard It on the Radio and I Saw It on the Television ...*": *An Essay for the Australian Film Commission on the Politics and Aesthetics of Filmmaking by and about Aboriginal People and Things* (Sydney: Australian Film Commission, 1993)
Ley, James, and Catriona Menzies-Pike (eds.), *The Australian Face: Essays from the Sydney Review of Books* (Sydney: Sydney Review of Books, 2017)
Macintyre, Stuart, *A Concise History of Australia* (Cambridge: Cambridge University Press, 2020)
Macintyre, Stuart, and Anna Clark, *The History Wars* (Melbourne: Melbourne University Press, 2003)
Marr, David, *Patrick White: A Life* (Sydney: Random House, 1991)
Mead, Philip, *Networked Language: Culture and History in Australian Poetry* (Melbourne: Australian Scholarly Publishing, 2008)

McKernan, Susan, *A Question of Commitment: Australian Literature in the Twenty Years after the War* (Sydney: Allen & Unwin, 1989)

McMahon, Elizabeth, *Islands, Identity and the Literary Imagination* (London: Anthem Press, 2016)

Moreton-Robinson, Aileen, *The White Possessive: Property, Power, and Indigenous Sovereignty* (Minneapolis: University of Minnesota Press, 2015)

Morgan, Peter (ed.), *Text, Translation, Transnationalism: World Literature in 21st Century Australia* (Melbourne: Australian Scholarly Publishing, 2016)

Mudrooroo, Narogin. *Writing from the Fringe: A Study of Modern Aboriginal Literature* (Melbourne: Hyland House, 1990)

Muecke, Stephen, *Textual Spaces: Aboriginality and Cultural Studies* (Sydney: New South Wales University Press, 1992)

Neidjie, Bill, *Story About Feeling*, ed. Keith Taylor (Broome: Magabala Books, 1989)

Ng, Lynda (ed.), *Indigenous Transnationalism: Alexis Wright's "Carpentaria"* (Sydney: Giramondo, 2018)

Nicolacopoulos, Toula, and George Vassilacopoulos, *Indigenous Sovereignty and the Being of the Occupier: Manifesto for a White Australian Philosophy of Origins* (Melbourne: re.press, 2014)

Palmer, Nettie, *Her Private Journal "Fourteen Years," Poems, Reviews and Literary Essays*, ed. Vivian Smith (St Lucia: University of Queensland Press, 1998)

Pascoe, Bruce, *Dark Emu: Black Seeds: Agriculture or Accident?* (Broome: Magabala Books, 2014)

Pavlide, Eleni, *Un-Australian Fictions: Nation, Multiculture(alism) and Globalisation, 1988–2008* (Cambridge: Cambridge Scholars Publishing, 2008)

Phillips, A. A., *On the Cultural Cringe* (Melbourne: Melbourne University Publishing, 2005)

Povinelli, Elizabeth, *The Cunning of Recognition: Indigenous Alterities and the Making of Australian Multiculturalism* (Durham, NC: Duke, 2002)

Ravenscroft, Alison, *The Postcolonial Eye: White Australian Desire and the Visual Field of Race* (London and New York: Routledge, 2012)

Rodoreda, Geoff, *The Mabo Turn in Australian Fiction* (Oxford: Peter Lang, 2018)

Rodoreda, Geoff, and Eva Bischoff (eds.), *Mabo's Cultural Legacy: History, Literature, Film and Cultural Practice in Contemporary Australia* (London: Anthem, 2021)

Rooney, Brigid, *Literary Activists: Writer-Intellectuals and Australian Public Life* (St Lucia: University of Queensland Press, 2009)

Suburban Space, the Novel and Australian Modernity (London: Anthem Press, 2018)

Russell, Lynette, *Roving Mariners: Australian Aboriginal Whalers and Sealers in the Southern Oceans, 1970–1870* (Albany: State University of New York Press, 2013)

Shaikh, Fariha, *Nineteenth-Century Settler Emigration in British Literature and Art* (Edinburgh: Edinburgh University Press, 2018)

Shellam, Tiffany, *Meeting the Waylo: Aboriginal Encounters in the Archipelago* (Perth: University of Western Australia Press, 2020)

Sheridan, Susan, *Nine Lives: Postwar Women Writers Making their Mark* (St Lucia: University of Queensland Press, 2011)

Shoemaker, Adam, *Black Words White Page: Aboriginal Literature 1929–88* (Canberra: Australian National University Press, 1989)

Smith, Linda Tuhiwai, *Decolonizing Methodologies: Research and Indigenous Peoples* (London: Bloomsbury Publishing, 2021; 1999)

Standfield, Rachel (ed.), *Indigenous Mobilities: Across and Beyond the Antipodes* (Canberra: Australian National University Press, 2018)

Steer, Philip, *Settler Colonialism in Victorian Literature: Economics and Political Identity in the Networks of Empire* (Cambridge: Cambridge University Press, 2020)

Stephen, Ann, Andrew McNamara and Philip Goad, *Modernism and Australia: Documents on Art, Design and Architecture 1917–1967* (Melbourne: Miegunyah Press, 2007)

Stewart-Harawira, Makaere, *The New Imperial Order: Indigenous Responses to Globalisation* (London: Zed Books, 2005)

Te Punga Somerville, Alice, *Once Were Pacific: Māori Connections to Oceania* (Minneapolis: University of Minnesota Press, 2012)

  Two Hundred and Fifty Ways to Start an Essay about Captain Cook (Wellington: Bridget Williams Books, 2020)

Turner, Henry Gyles, and Alexander Sutherland, *The Development of Australian Literature* (Melbourne: G. Robertson, 1898)

van Toorn, Penny, *Writing Never Arrives Naked: Early Aboriginal Cultures of Writing in Australia* (Canberra: Aboriginal Studies Press, 2006)

Veracini, Lorenzo, *Settler Colonialism: A Theoretical Overview* (London: Palgrave Macmillan, 2010)

Vernay, Jean-François, *A Brief Take on the Australian Novel*, trans. Marie Ramsland (Adelaide: Wakefield Press, 2016)

Wallace-Crabbe, Chris, *Melbourne or the Bush: Essays on Australian Literature and Society* (Sydney: Angus & Robertson, 1974)

Weaver-Hightower, Rebecca, *Frontier Fictions: Settler Sagas and Postcolonial Guilt* (London: Palgrave Macmillan, 2018)

Webby, Elizabeth (ed.), *The Cambridge Companion to Australian Literature* (Cambridge: Cambridge University Press, 2000)

Wheeler, Belinda (ed.), *A Companion to Australian Aboriginal Literature* (Rochester: Camden House, 2013)

Wilde, William H., Joy Hooton and Barry Andrews (eds.) *The Oxford Companion to Australian Literature* (Oxford: Oxford University Press, 1995)

Williamson, Geordie, *The Burning Library: Our Great Novelists Lost and Found* (Melbourne: Text Publishing, 2012)

Wilson, Janet and Chandani Lokuge (eds.), *Mediating Literary Borders: Asian Australian Writing* (London: Routledge, 2018)

Wolfe, Patrick, *Settler Colonialism and the Transformation of Anthropology: The Politics and Poetics of an Ethnographic Event* (London and New York: Cassell, 1999)

Zavaglia, Liliana, *White Apology and Apologia: Australian Novels of Reconciliation* (Amherst: Cambria, 2016)

INDEX

Cambridge Companions To ...

AUTHORS